CAMBRIDGE SOUTH ASIAN STUDIES

AGRARIAN BENGAL

AGRARIAN BENGAL

*Economy, social structure
and politics, 1919–1947*

SUGATA BOSE

*Department of History,
Tufts University*

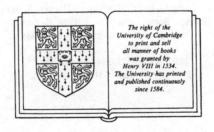

The right of the
University of Cambridge
to print and sell
all manner of books
was granted by
Henry VIII in 1534.
The University has printed
and published continuously
since 1584.

CAMBRIDGE UNIVERSITY PRESS

CAMBRIDGE

LONDON   NEW YORK   NEW ROCHELLE

MELBOURNE   SYDNEY

CAMBRIDGE UNIVERSITY PRESS
Cambridge, New York, Melbourne, Madrid, Cape Town, Singapore, São Paulo

Cambridge University Press
The Edinburgh Building, Cambridge CB2 8RU, UK

Published in the United States of America by Cambridge University Press, New York

www.cambridge.org
Information on this title: www.cambridge.org/9780521304481

First published 1986
This digitally printed version 2008

A catalogue record for this publication is available from the British Library

Library of Congress Cataloguing in Publication data
Bose, Sugata.
Agrarian Bengal: economy, social structure, and politics, 1919–1947.
(Cambridge South Asian studies)
Originally presented as the author's thesis
(doctoral – University of Cambridge, 1982)
Bibliography
Includes index.
1. Peasantry – India – Bengal – History. 2. Peasantry –
India – Bengal – Political activity – History. 3. Bengal
(India) – Social conditions. I. Title. II. Series.
HD875. B67 1985   305.5'63   85 14989

ISBN 978-0-521-30448-1 hardback
ISBN 978-0-521-05362-4 paperback

CAMBRIDGE SOUTH ASIAN STUDIES

These monographs are published by the Syndics of Cambridge University Press in association with the Cambridge Centre for South Asian Studies. The following books have been published in this series:

To

CHARU CHANDRA CHOWDHURI

and

CHHAYA DEVI CHOWDHURANI

CONTENTS

MAPS

PREFACE

This book would not have been possible without help from many people and institutions. It first took shape as a doctoral dissertation submitted to the University of Cambridge in December 1982. I am grateful to the Master and Fellows of St Catharine's College, Cambridge, for electing me into a Research Fellowship in 1981 and for making generous contributions towards the costs of research. I would like to thank the Government of West Bengal, India, for awarding me a State Scholarship in 1978 which supported the first three years of my studies on the subject. The Smuts Memorial Fund at Cambridge provided a grant for research and field-work in India and Bangladesh in 1979-80. The government of Bangladesh graciously gave permission to consult sources in the Bangladesh Secretariat Record Room and district record offices. Dr Sirajul Islam introduced me to these archives. It was a great pleasure to be a visitor at the Department of History, University of Dacca, where I received warm hospitality from everyone. The Home Department of the West Bengal government allowed me to use a large collection of Confidential Political files. Mr Debabrata Bandyopadhyay, Mr A.B.M.G. Kibria, Mr R.N. Sengupta and especially Mr S.P. Mallik helped make research in the subcontinent a success. A grant from the Nuffield Foundation enabled me to return to India in 1983 to look at new material which had become available.

Librarians, archivists and staff of various institutions met voracious demands for source material: the India Office Records and Library, London; University Library, Cambridge; South Asian Studies Centre Archives and Library, Cambridge; West Bengal State Archives, Calcutta; National Library, Calcutta; Secretariat Library, Calcutta; Board of Revenue, Calcutta; Land Records Directorate, Calcutta; Bangladesh Secretariat Record Room, Dacca; Bangla

ix

Academy, Dacca; University Library, Dacca; and the district
collectorate record rooms and registration offices of Dacca,
Mymensingh, Midnapur, Burdwan and West Dinajpur. I
owe a special word of thanks to Mr B.H. Farmer, formerly
Director, and Dr Lionel Carter, Librarian, of the South
Asian Studies Centre, Cambridge; to Mr Asoke Sen who has
the records of the West Bengal State Archives at his finger
tips; and to Mr Ashis Gupta who supplied me with material
at the Home Department. Many friends including Suman
and Kasturi Chattopadhyay rendered much assistance
during research in Calcutta. Kamal in Bangladesh and
Atanu in West Bengal helped transcribe masses of data. Mrs
Shirley French in Cambridge typed various drafts of the
manuscript with patience and skill.

My intellectual debts are as great as those of the Bengal
peasant and can hardly be listed. However, I would specially
like to mention Professor Amartya Sen who took the time to
read the first part of this book with great care and gave
detailed comments, criticism and encouragement. Paul
Greenough invited me to spend a semester at the University
of Iowa in spring 1984; his searching comments on various
aspects of substance and style in an earlier draft and his
many useful suggestions were a great help to me in the final
revision of the manuscript. In Cambridge, Shapan Adnan's
sharp theoretical insights have always been stimulating. I
have also learnt from discussions with and comments by
Christopher Baker, Raj Chandavarkar, Professor Binay
Bhushan Chaudhuri, Charu Chandra Chowdhuri, Gordon
Johnson, Rajat Ray, Tapan Raychaudhuri and Anil Seal. I
profited from discussions at two seminars in the United
States: one at the University of California, Berkeley, and
the other at the University of Wisconsin, Madison.

My deepest debts are to the late Professor Eric Stokes and
to Dr C.A. Bayly who were my research supervisors. Eric
Stokes was a great source of inspiration. I can only hope that
I have been able to do some justice to the faith he placed in
the early fragments of this work. He is remembered with
much affection. Chris Bayly has known this work closely
from its very inception and has given invaluable criticism,
guidance and friendship. My parents, Sisir Kumar Bose and

Krishna Bose, my sister Sarmila and my brother Sumantra were always there. Ayesha Jalal gave unflagging support and understanding over the years and did much in the final stages to improve the quality of this text and sustain morale.

St Catharine's College   SUGATA BOSE
Cambridge
August 1984

ABBREVIATIONS

Addl	Additional
Agr.	Agriculture (Department)
Br.	Branch
BSRR	Bangladesh Secretariat Record Room
CCRI	Cooperative Credit and Rural Indebtedness (Department)
Cms.	Commission
Cmsner	Commissioner
Cmt.	Committee
Conf.	Confidential (File)
DG	District Gazeteer
DM	District Magistrate
Dt	District
Dn	Division
Dy	Deputy
EPW	*Economic and Political Weekly*
FR	Fortnightly Report
GB	Government of Bengal
IESHR	*Indian Economic and Social History Review*
IOR	India Office Records and Library
ISI	Indian Statistical Institute
LR	Land Revenue (Branch)
MAS	*Modern Asian Studies*
MLA	Member of the Legislative Assembly
Poll Conf.	Political Confidential (Files)
Progs.	Proceedings
RCA	Royal Commission on Agriculture
Rev.	Revenue (Department)
SASC	South Asian Studies Centre, Cambridge (Archive)
Secy	Secretary
SR	Settlement Report
WBSA	West Bengal State Archives
SDO	Subdivisional Officer

PART I

AGRARIAN ECONOMY AND SOCIETY
STRUCTURE AND TRENDS

1

Introduction: A typology of agrarian social structure in early twentieth-century Bengal

The close intermeshing of revenue-collection structures with land tenures in the pre-colonial agrarian order brought the British face to face with the question of the basic tenure of land during their efforts to set up effective land revenue systems in India. The answer to this question, they reckoned, would help determine the point on the tenurial scale at which a private property right should be lodged. This 'modern' form of proprietary right was to be attached not to the land itself but to its revenues; the existence of a distinct customary right of physical dominion over the soil was never denied. An implicit, though not perfectly clear intention of British revenue law was, if possible, 'to weld the novel property attaching to the revenue-collecting right to this primary right of dominion'.[1] The Permanent Settlement of the land revenue in 1793 with the zamindars of Bengal accorded the property right to a class of people whose role in rural society as territorial magnates and tax-farmers had been to collect revenue and remit it to government, not to hold or exploit land as such. The discrepancy between colonial revenue law infused with its particular concept of property and the manner in which land was actually held and operated in Bengal ensured from the very outset that the legal classification of agrarian society was far removed from its working structure.[2]

Yet 'the zamindari system' in its deceptive legal mould has continued to provide a basic framework for the study of

1 Eric Stokes, *The Peasant and the Raj* (Cambridge, 1978), p.2.
2 One historian has described the Permanent Settlement with the zamindars as 'a case of mistaken identity'. Ratnalekha Ray, *Change in Bengal Agrarian Society*

3

Bengal's rural economy and society. Beyond clarifying ideological strands in the formulation of colonial revenue policy and cataloguing the fortunes of the few who occupied the top rungs of the revenue-collecting ladder,[3] such an approach could only mislead. The circulation of revenue rights has often been misinterpreted as a revolution in land. As late as 1980 it has been seriously claimed that as a result of the Permanent Settlement 'the peasant was dispossessed of the land which now became the "property" of the zamindar. . . The land*lord* became land*owner*. Land was now "bourgeois landed property". . .'.[4]

Even those who are aware of the problems of making too easy an equation between ownership of the revenue right and actual possession of land have nevertheless seen Bengal's agrarian structure primarily in the context of the colonial land-revenue administration. A recent essay on pre-1947 Bengal opens with the statement: 'We must begin with a consideration of the conditions imposed on Bengal's agrarian economy by the fact of colonialism. The primary and abiding interest of the colonial government in the agriculture of Bengal, or for that matter anywhere else in India, was the extraction of a part of the surplus in the form of land revenue.'[5] The arrangement by which a class of persons designated 'proprietors' were assigned the property in revenue collection in 1793 together with late nineteenth-century amendments 'to protect as far as possible the predominant organizational form of agricultural production, *viz.* small-peasant farming'[6] is still the main context within which the evolution of Bengal's agrarian structure in the late nineteenth and early twentieth centuries is analysed. The resulting

1760–1850 (Delhi, 1980), p. 73. The compulsory saleability of the new property right meant, of course, that there would have been nothing to prevent the revenue-collecting right and the primary right of dominion, even if initially strung together, from parting ways in course of time.

3 Excellent monographs on these aspects of Bengal's rural history are Ranajit Guha, *A Rule of Property for Bengal* (Paris, 1963), and Sirajul Islam, *The Permanent Settlement in Bengal: A Study of Its Operation 1790–1819*, (Dacca, 1979).

4 Hamza Alavi, 'India: Transition from Feudalism to Colonial Capitalism', *Journal of Contemporary Asia*, 10, 4 (1980), p. 371.

5 Partha Chatterjee, 'Agrarian Structure in Pre-Partition Bengal' in A. Sen *et al.*, *Perspectives in Social Sciences 2* (Delhi, 1982), pp.113–14.

6 *Ibid.*, p.114.

emphasis is on revenue history and rent relations, forma landlordism and tenancy.[7] Yet land revenue and rental demands, important as they were during the nineteenth century, became after 1860 a less significant aspect of the colonial context than the capitalist world economy and the financial policies of the colonial government, and steadily diminished in importance from the late nineteenth century onwards. By the early twentieth century, the agrarian economy of Bengal rested on an extensive subsistence base while at the same time participating in a growing international trade. The history of a subsistence-oriented peasantry engaged in petty commodity production for a well-integrated world market has to be set in the context of the demographic constraint on resources as well as the international and regional dimensions of the colonial political economy.[8] A study of the network of agrarian credit relationships is more relevant in the late colonial period than a focus on ties of revenue and rent. It not only provides the critical linkage along which fluctuations in the world economy were transmitted to the region's agrarian economy, but also forms the most important element in the complex of agrarian relations within the region. This shift of perspective is, therefore, necessary for a better understanding of the connection between changes in the agrarian structure and the nature and course of peasant politics in the final decades of colonial rule.

Trends in the wider economic system were transmitted to the regional economy through the refracting prism of the agrarian class structure and affected various social classes in significantly different ways. The first analytical task is to define the nature of agrarian social structure in early twentieth-century Bengal. Here the dominant 'jotedar' thesis requires serious amendment. The 1970s saw major advances in historical research on agrarian Bengal: the facade of legal tenures was penetrated to offer a glimpse of the economic and social structure. Rajat and Ratna Ray pointed out the important distinction between two structures of land tenure

7 Asok Sen, 'Agrarian Structure and Tenancy Laws in Bengal 1850–1900' and Partha Chatterjee, 'Agrarian Structure in Pre-Partition Bengal' in A. Sen *et al.*, *Perspectives in Social Sciences 2*, pp.1–224.
8 This is attempted in chapter 2 below.

in Bengal – the revenue-collecting structure over the village
and the landholding structure within the village. British
policy-makers, both proponents and opponents of the
Permanent Settlement, often failed to take account of the
latter.[9] In consequence of this oversight, the framers of the
Permanent Settlement had conferred proprietary rights on a
class of zamindars who did not have land in their actual
possession. Its critics denied altogether the existence of
proprietors of land. But according to the 'jotedar' thesis 'there
existed in Bengal, as tenants of the revenue-collecting
zamindars and talukdars, a class of men known as jotedars
who owned sizeable portions of village lands and cultivated
their broad acres with the help of sharecroppers, tenants-at-
will and hired labourers'.[10] The holdings of these men were
believed to run from 50 to 6000 acres. Combining these
substantial landholdings with the social authority of village
headship and the economic authority of moneylending and
grain-dealing, these jotedars exercised supreme control over
the labour of the poor peasantry.

The 'jotedar' thesis, which with minor variations became
the ruling orthodoxy, has had important implications for the
interpretation of social conflict and political upheaval in the
Bengal countryside over the last two centuries. The relative
quiescence of the first half of the nineteenth century has been
attributed to a working alliance between zamindars and
jotedars. The agrarian disturbances of the later nineteenth
century are explained in terms of a breakdown in this
collaborative relationship when the zamindars, attempting to
enhance rents in a period of rising prices, could no longer
afford special privileges to the favoured jotedars. The colonial
government, on this view, now backed tenancy legislation
favouring 'the village landlords against the superior
landlords'.[11] For the analysis of twentieth-century political
developments, the zamindar–jotedar thesis appeared to
correspond closely to the revenue-collecting landlord and the
village-controlling dominant-peasant pattern of northern

9 See Rajat and Ratna Ray, 'Zamindars and Jotedars: A Study of Rural Politics in
   Bengal', MAS, 9, 1 (1975), pp. 81–102.
10 *Ibid.*, p. 82.
11 Ratnalekha Ray, *Change in Bengal Agrarian Society*, p. 294.

India and was quickly assimilated into a broader 'dominant-peasant' thesis. This views the nationalist movement simply as a competition between the British government and the Indian National Congress for the allegiance of these dominant elements in the countryside.[12] It is argued that in Bengal, the nationalist movements were most successful where the jotedars provided the driving force but zamindar–jotedar conflict was patched up by common caste identity, as in the case of the Mahishyas of Midnapur. The origins of the Krishak Praja movement, Muslim 'separatism' and even the partition of Bengal are seen to lie in the conflict between the Hindu zamindar and Muslim jotedar of east Bengal. 'In each area of Bengal', it is asserted, 'the strength or weakness of the nationalist and separatist movements bore a close relationship to the local relationship of zamindar and jotedar'.[13] The tebhaga movement of the sharecroppers on the eve of independence adds another dimension to the 'jotedar' thesis. The 'jotedari system' is once again regarded as central to the agrarian structure but the focus here is on the conflict between the jotedars, 'a new category of large land-owners', and the adhiars or sharecroppers employed by them.[14] In short, by virtue of his crucial position in the rent-collecting hierarchy and more importantly, by his place at the head of the village landholding and credit structure, the 'jotedar' is widely seen to have held the key to the social and political destiny of rural Bengal.

The radical exhortation of the Maoist communists of Bengal in the late 1960s and early 1970s to 'bury the jotedar, the reactionary kulak', had scarcely died away when

12 D.A. Low, 'Introduction' in D.A. Low (ed.), *Congress and the Raj* (London, 1977), pp. 1-45.

13 Rajat and Ratna Ray, 'Zamindars and Jotedars', p. 101; see also Sumit Sarkar, *The Swadeshi Movement in Bengal, 1903-08* (Calcutta, 1974), pp. 463-4. John Gallagher referred to the 'vitality of agriculture' in east Bengal which spurred the Muslim 'jotedars' to raise their demands against Hindu zamindars; in parts of west Bengal, Gallagher believed the role of Mahishya 'jotedars' to have been crucial: 'it was their domination which gave the resistance the flavour of a mass movement in those areas'. See John Gallagher, 'Congress in Decline: Bengal 1930 to 1939' in J. Gallagher *et al.* (eds.), *Locality, Province and Nation* (Cambridge, 1973), pp. 269-325; also Hitesranjan Sanyal, 'Congress Movements in the Villages of Eastern Midnapore, 1921-1931', in Marc Gaborieau and Alice Thorner (eds.), *Asie du Sud: Traditions et Changements* (Paris, 1979), pp. 169-78.

14 Sunil Sen, *Agrarian Struggle in Bengal 1937-47* (Calcutta, 1972), pp. 1-15.

he was resurrected in the historiography of agrarian Bengal. After distinguishing between the revenue and rent structure on the one hand, and the landholding structure on the other, a particular characterisation was offered of the latter in which the ubiquitous 'jotedar' loomed large. Quite apart from the difficulty that 'jotedar' was variously defined as village landlord, rich farmer and dominant peasant, there are two problems with this view. Firstly, a rather rigid and literal distinction between landlords and lords of the land has obscured the role rent-collectors played, at least in some regions, in the village landholding and credit structures. Secondly, and this is more important, the 'jotedar' thesis generalises for Bengal as a whole an atypical form of agrarian organisation that prevailed in the main in north Bengal, but which happened to be graphically portrayed in Buchanan-Hamilton's surveys of Rangpur and Dinajpur and later settlement reports of those districts. Indeed, it may be said that 'jotedars' in the sense of *de facto* village landlords or village-controlling dominant peasants had no existence in Bengal except in unusual frontier regions. It is necessary to find a more adequate representation of the agrarian social structure in Bengal than the one turning entirely on the role of the big 'jotedar', thrusting for advantage against the declining zamindar while simultaneously holding down the poor peasantry in debt bondage and by extra-economic coercion in a 'semi-feudal' situation.[15] Using the 'jotedar' thesis as a point of departure, this chapter seeks to outline a basic typology of the agrarian social structure in early twentieth-century Bengal. The answer to the over-simplifications and distortions of the jotedar thesis is not a retreat into localism which a haphazard wandering through the Bengal districts inevitably entails.[16] The aim here is to extract from the enormous complexity of agrarian Bengal a few broad, general patterns displaying certain enduring characteristics. Without these there can be no meaningful analysis either of the

15 The theoretical underpinning to much of the historical literature on jotedars has been provided by Amit Bhaduri's important article 'A Study in Agricultural Backwardness under Semi-feudalism', *Economic Journal*, 83 (1973), pp. 120–37.
16 For the infinite variety of local agrarian structures, see, for instance, Abu Abdullah, 'Landlord and Rich Peasant under the Permanent Settlement', *Calcutta Historical Journal*, 5, 1 (1980), pp. 89–108.

region's agrarian economy and society or its response to trends in the wider economic system. A fuller elucidation of the relations of production and surplus-appropriation and the interlocking conditions of reproduction that held the structure together, as well as the stresses and strains to which it was subjected between the First World War and the end of colonial rule, will form the subject matter of subsequent chapters.

A typology of agrarian social structure in early twentieth-century Bengal

J.C. Jack and · F.O. Bell, two of the more perceptive of settlement officers of Bengal districts, presented totally contrasting representations of socio-economic hierarchy among the cultivating classes of Bengal. Jack wrote of the east Bengal district of Faridpur:

the cultivators are a homogeneous class. . . It is clear that the agricultural wealth of the district is divided with considerable fairness in such a way that the great majority of the cultivators have a reasonable share. This is no country of capitalist farmers with bloated farms and an army of parasitic and penurious labourers.[17]

Bell, on the other hand, wrote of the north Bengal district of Dinajpur:

The most significant feature of Dinajpur rural life is the inequality in social status and standards of living of different rustic families. Almost every village will reveal some large family of substantial cultivators. . . As elsewhere in North Bengal, this jotedar class is socially supreme in the countryside. The jotedar families may hold several hundreds or even thousands of acres of land in their own possession. . . All these men are of a class which may be described as practising large-scale farming, though it is farming not with any large capital sunk in machinery, but through the traditional methods, employing either labourers or adhiars (sharecroppers).[18]

The contrasting observations of Jack and Bell reveal in a striking manner two different types of agrarian social structure in Bengal. In east Bengal a predominantly peasant

17 J.C. Jack, *Economic Life of a Bengal District* (Oxford, 1916), pp. 81–2.
18 *Dinajpur SR*, 1934–40, pp. 16–17.

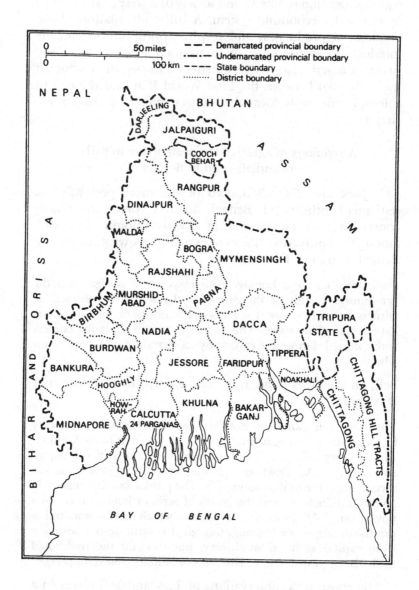

Map 1: Bengal districts

smallholding structure was over-laid by various rentier and creditor groups. In north Bengal (and the southern fringe) rich, enterprising farmers who had helped clear the scrub and jungle during the nineteenth century were still the dominant elements in a highly polarised agrarian structure. There were further layers of variation and complexity. The most important of these was the existence of considerable personal demesne of the landlords (revenue-collectors) in west and central Bengal casting a shadow on the lands operated by (tenant) peasant smallholders; the demesne lands were cultivated by attaching a locally available reserve of landless labour. Each of these different types could be tied to the wider economic system in one of two ways: either directly through an agricultural exporting sector which produced commercial crops for the world market or indirectly through the network of credit even where the world market was less significant for the crops produced and rural elites shielded the primary producers from direct exposure to internal market forces. The capitalist plantation would form a distinct type in a broader typology of colonial agrarian societies. It existed only on the northern fringe of early twentieth-century Bengal in the Himalayan foothills where European capitalists had established tea plantations. Its very special features have kept it beyond the scope of this work. In the discussion below, three major types of agrarian social structure will be analysed: the village landlord/rich farmer–sharecropper system which predominated in north Bengal, the peasant smallholding system which prevailed in east Bengal (and became the principal agricultural exporting sector), and the peasant smallholding–demesne labour complex which was the most common pattern in west and central Bengal.

The village landlord/rich farmer–sharecropper system in the frontier regions

The jotedari–adhiari system of north Bengal grew out of conditions wholly atypical of the older settled regions of west Bengal and east Bengal. Vast areas in this region were uncultivated jungle and settled for reclamation with enterprising tenant-farmers called jotedars. This process was started by the big zamindars prior to the Permanent Settlement and continued in the post-1793 period. Ecological factors had an important bearing on this particular form of agrarian organisation. Large tracts of land were assigned to substantial men of capital at low fixed rents and with permanent and transferable rights to facilitate organisation of large-scale reclamation from jungle. The reserves of labour provided by the semi-tribal Koches and Paliyas – the Rajbansis of later years – and by the immigrant Santal tribes were utilised to conquer the inhospitable wasteland. Once the work of reclamation was completed, they remained as sharecroppers with no right of continued occupancy of the land they tilled and often only in permissive possession of a little homestead on a fragment of the wasteland they themselves had cleared.

During the nineteenth century, the jotedar–adhiar pattern became the dominant feature of the agrarian structure in much of north Bengal. In parts of Rangpur, Jalpaiguri and the Siliguri subdivision of Darjeeling (which were wrested from Cooch Behar and Bhutan and came under British sway about the middle of the nineteenth century), the practice of leasing out tracts of wasteland to men with capital to organise reclamation had already been resorted to by the Cooch Behar Raj. These leases were recognised by the British and most of the zamindaris included within the permanently settled area. As the District Gazetteer of Jalpaiguri states: 'The tenants in these estates are divided into tenants-in-chief (jotedars), subtenants (chukanidars, darchukanidars and daradarchuka-nidars) and holders under the metayer system (adhiars). The jotedars are tenants holding immediately under the zamindars; a large number of their rank as tenureholders and others as raiyats under the provisions of the Bengal Tenancy Act'.[19] In Dinajpur where in the aftermath of 1793 the territory of the old Raj was auctioned off in 'lots', the big jotedars held their lands under the new zamindars known as 'lotdars'.[20] The existence of considerable waste in north Bengal usually placed the jotedars in a powerful bargaining position *vis-a-vis* the absentee zamindars and from the later nineteenth century they

19 *Jalpaiguri DG* 1911, pp. 83–4.
20 *Dinajpur SR*, p. 69.

were also armed with formidable legal rights. Their jotes, either as permanent tenures or as raiyati holdings, became protected interests while they remained free to rack-rent their under-tenants and exact a lion's share of the produce from dependent adhiars.

In north Bengal, big jotedars were the dominant elements in the agrarian structure. But there were also a fair number of small jotedars. It would appear that small and scattered parcels of zamindars' lands were let out to peasants, whereas lands concentrated in large units, usually vast tracts of jungle, were leased *en bloc* to substantial tenant-farmers. The Bengali word, jote, from its Sanskrit original yotra, simply means cultivation or cultivable land. A local officer of Jalpaiguri noted in 1909: 'The term *jote* is applied to any holding, large or small, held direct from a proprietor or from a holder of a recognized tenure, such as a *patni*. I find in Mr. Glazier's book on Rangpur mention of a *jote* paying a rent of Rs. 50 000, while the same word is used to describe the peasant's holding of a few *bighas*. . .'[21] The Gazetteers of all the north Bengal districts of the early twentieth century also refer to the enormous variation in the size of jotes. But where the jote right had not passed to non-agriculturalist moneylenders the jotedar was 'generally a substantial farmer representing the original reclaimer of the soil'.[22]

F.O. Bell in his Dinajpur Settlement Report presents the best profile of the various grades of jotedars and their multifarious moneylending and grain-dealing activities. First, there were the giant jotedars who held several hundreds or even thousands of acres of land in jote or raiyati right and may even have bought into superior proprietary rights in some estates. At the same time, they financed the smaller cultivators and controlled the marketing of the exportable surplus. The famous Chaudhuries of the village of Porsha received 60 000 maunds of paddy each year in their 'golas'. Such men let out some land on cash rents but were more keen on the grain they received from adhiars. Then, there were the

---

21 F.J. Monahan to P.C. Lyon, Jalpaiguri, 21 June 1909, Note on the Extension of Survey and Settlement Proceedings under the Tenancy Act to the districts of this (Rajshahi) Division, Progs. of the Conference of Cmsners at Shillong, Oct. 1909, Govt of Eastern Bengal and Assam (WBSA).
22 *Darjeeling DG* (1907), pp. 47–8.

jotedars who held some 100 acres and worked on similar methods as the giants but on a smaller scale. 'This well-to-do jotedar class', Bell points out, reminding us of Buchanan-Hamilton's 30–100 acre farmers, 'is no new feature of the district, and no creation of the Permanent Settlement, or the Bengal Tenancy Act'. Finally, in the gradation of jotedars came 'the men who possess a raiyati holding which can provide subsistence for the family, and these men who have a few acres add to their produce by working as an adhiar'.[23]

The adhiars, it was found in the 1930s, were, as in the early nineteenth century, usually men with ploughs and cattle and a little land in raiyati right. Yet they were regarded 'more as the servant of the jotedar, or landlord, than as independent landholders. They are mostly the poorer villagers, and the jotedars now finance them through the difficult months. *The jotedar also decides what crop is grown*, and it is frequently divided at the khamar, or other place appointed by the jotedar, a sign of the master and servant relationship.'[24] It is important to note that the jotedar of north Bengal exercised actual possessory dominion over the soil and took the major production decisions. An enquiry into the position of adhiars in Jalpaiguri in 1909 is also quite categorical on this point: 'The giri (i.e. the adhiar's employer) selects the crop which is to be cultivated each year. The adhiar cultivates the crop in the best manner possible, but is bound to comply with instructions issued by the giri.'[25] The degree of dependence of the adhiar on the jotedar, of course, tended to vary. It was observed at the time of the tebhaga struggle:

As there are Jotedars of various types there are also adhiars of various kinds. . . There are adhiars whose Jotedars have to pay even for the midwife in case of birth and coffin in case of death in adhiars' family [*sic*]. . . In such cases Jotedars apparently give half of the produce to the adhiars but indirectly take back almost the entire[*sic*]on account of advances, interest etc. The process is repeated annually. Let us consider the question of another type of adhiar. They are those who have land of their own and have their own plough and cattle. Their

23 *Dinajpur SR*, pp. 16–17.
24 *Ibid.*, p. 22 (emphasis added).
25 Beatson Bell's Note on the Position of Adhiars in Jalpaiguri, 21 Feb. 1909, Progs. of the Conference of Cmsners at Shillong, Oct. 1909, Govt of Eastern Bengal and Assam (WBSA).

own land being not sufficient for their ploughs they take a few bighas of land from some other neighbouring jotedars. Such adhiars do not much depend upon their Jotedars. . .[26]

In Rangpur the adhiars did not generally form a distinct class but were drawn from the poorer under-tenants who 'quit the land after reaping the harvest'; in the north-western part of the district, however, many adhiars were completely landless and even lived in homesteads belonging to the landlords on their adhi lands.[27] It was in the case of the tied adhiar of parts of Rangpur and Jalpaiguri that conditions approached near-serfdom. The custom of 'hauli' – adhiars having to put in unpaid labour on the jotedars' home farm – was fairly common in Jalpaiguri.

To summarise then, the bulk of the land in north Bengal was held in large parcels by substantial jotedars, the rest in small quantities by small jotedars. The big jotedars monopolised the product market and extracted a large proportion of the adhiars' produce in the form of share rent and loan interest; yet within the type of agrarian structure that had evolved in north Bengal, they played a vital role in the process of reproduction by redistributing part of the surplus both in the form of capital for basic inputs and as grain advances to keep the workers on the soil alive. They sometimes sublet their lands to inferior grades of chukanidars and darchukanidars but it was normal for them to retain large areas as khas (personal demesne) which they cultivated through numerous sharecroppers and labourers. Since the jotedars were also the principal source of credit, they effectively controlled the labour of the poorer cultivators. It was this dual role of landholder-cum-creditor which made the big jotedar of north Bengal a power to be reckoned with.

The only other region which closely approximated the agrarian structure of north Bengal was the abadi (reclaimed) area of the 24-Parganas and western Khulna. The men of substance who had leased government 'lots' in the Sunderbans for reclamation were somewhat similar to the big jotedars of the north. The 'lots' were large blocks of land held at easy rents progressively enhanced as reclamation proceeded, and subject

26 Dy Cmsner Jalpaiguri to Addl Secy Bd of Rev., 11 Mar. 1947, Rev. Dept LR Br., B. Progs. 15–107, Dec. 1948, File 6M-38/47 (WBSA).
27 *Rangpur SR* (1931-8), p. 65.

to forfeiture if clearance conditions were not fulfilled. Often speculators and land-jobbers obtained these leases and sublet to smaller lessees for cash payments with the result that the work of reclamation was actually carried out by small peasant cultivators paying rack-rents.[28] The process of dispossession of what was initially a relatively free peasantry and their conversion into near-serfs paid with a share of the crop began in these areas much later than in north Bengal and gathered pace during the first half of the twentieth century. Similar to the government-controlled 'lots' were the 'chaks' in the 24-Parganas and the south-east of Midnapur leased out to chakdars for reclamation in the zamindari estates in the Sunderbans. A chak, the 24-Parganas Gazetteer reported 'may be of any size and and sometimes in the Sunderbans consists of thousands of bighas of land'.[29] In these areas, the chakdar-bhagchashi (sharecropper) sector became dominant in the agrarian structure.

Further east along the Sunderbans in eastern Khulna and Bakarganj, the situation was already slightly different. The hawaladars and ganthidars in these parts are usually considered to be similar to the big jotedar of the north. There were, however, significant differences. The haola (literally, a charge) was 'very largely a small lease for the reclamation of forest granted to a man who was prepared to make his home in the grant and personally supervise its reclamation'.[30] The ganthis were similar in origin but probably earlier assignments. The recipients of these grants were not of the scale of the giant jotedars of north Bengal; they were 'men whose capital was ordinarily small' and who lived in the

28 The 'lots' were held under the Waste Land Rules of 1853 (99-year grants), the Large Capitalist Rules of 1879 (40-year grants), the Saugor Island Rules of 1847 (40-year grants), talukdari and malguzari leases (in Khulna) and a few under lease to 'small capitalists' and haoladars. GB Rev. Dept LR Br., B. Progs. 39–45, Sept. 1940, File 41–7 (BSRR). Note the difference with the 'lotdars' of Dinajpur who were zamindars.

29 *24-Parganas DG* (1914), p.177. In Midnapur, it was reported, that the chaks 'are large, ranging from 800 to 5300 bighas, practically none of which is now cultivated by the Chakdars'. *Midnapur SR* (1910–18), p. 45. There was considerable controversy as to whether the chakdar or the bhagchashi should be given the raiyati right. 'Status of Chakdars and Bhagchasis in Pargana Majnamutha and other Khas Mahals in Midnapore', GB Rev. Dept LR Br., Progs. 17–23, Aug. 1915, File 16-S-22 of 1915 (WBSA).

30 *Bakarganj DG* (1918), p. 87.

district of Dacca from where the revenue arrangements of Bakarganj were conducted when the British revenue system was first introduced.[31] More importantly, the physical configuration of this densely forested region, which was cut up into numerous petty blocks by streams and rivers, did not render feasible the supervision of reclamation and farming in large personal demesne. This led to an extraordinary degree of subinfeudation of tenurial rights. In marked contrast to the north Bengal situation, Jack reported in 1908 that there was 'no class of landless labourers in the (Bakarganj) district'.[32] Bargadari (sharecropping) and dhankarari (fixed produce rent) were confined to 5% of the total raiyati area and were resorted to mainly in the area where the Hindu bhadralok gentry had tended to congregate. Operational holdings in these regions were fragmented. While the jotedars of north Bengal had physical dominion over large tracts, the lands held in lease by the hawaladars and ganthidars were possessed, as it were, several times over by numerous degrees of subinfeudatory tenants. Though the tenurial scale spanned a wide range of inequality, the difference between each grade was minute and the dichotomy between classes blurred.

Among the frontier regions of Bengal, the Jungle Mahals on the western periphery and the role of the mandals or clan leaders, often equated with 'jotedars', remains to be considered. The social organisation of the reclaimers and cultivators of the land in these areas exhibited tribal forms. Leaders of tribal communities known as mandals had negotiated the conditions of settlement of an uncultivated tract with the zamindars and undertaken to collect and pay the rent on behalf of the community as a whole. By the early twentieth century, however, the 'mandali system' had virtually disintegrated. Jameson observed in the Midnapur Settlement Report of 1919: 'Mandals exist only in those areas where the aboriginal and semi-aboriginal tribes of Santals, Bhumijs, Mahatos, etc., are, or were until recently, the bulk of the population, and among these tribes the patriarchal village

---

31 *Ibid.* On the complexity of tenurial patterns in Bakarganj, see Tapan Raychaudhuri, 'Permanent Settlement in Operation: Bakarganj District, East Bengal' in R.E. Frykenberg (ed.), *Land Control and Social Structure in Indian History* (Madison, Wisconsin, 1969), pp. 163-74.
32 *Bakarganj SR* (1900-8), p. 73.

community is the regime under which they lived when the mandali system was evolved, though it has now broken down to a large extent'.[33] The decay of the mandali system was attributed by the settlement officer of Bankura to the introduction of the dikku or foreigner into the Jungle Mahals.[34] These dikkus, Bengalis from the east and Utkal Brahmins from Orissa in the west, who arrived as traders, resorted to the profitable business of moneylending, and eventually obtained a hold on the land. The mahajan first dislodged the mandal and usurped the position of tenure-holder of a village and then went on to encroach upon the best lands of the individual tenants. A special enquiry in 1909 into the conditions of the Santals revealed the alarming rate at which they were losing the most valuable rights in the land.[35] The dispossessed tenant was usually resettled at a very high produce rent or a mixed cash and produce rent. Large-scale dispossession began about the time of the great famine of 1865–66 and proceeded at a rapid pace until an amendment to the Bengal Tenancy Act in 1918 prohibited the transfer of land from aboriginals to non-aboriginals without the collector's permission. The legislation, however, came too late as the superior rights in the rice lands in the jungle area had already passed from the hands of the tribal people into those of the mahajans. It would seem appropriate to treat the tribal settlements in the western fringe as an extreme form of a demesne labour–peasant smallholding complex which is analysed below.

The peasant smallholding system in east Bengal and the peasant smallholding–demesne labour complex in west and central Bengal

In most parts of Bengal, village-controlling rich farmers even remotely approaching the scale of the big jotedars of north Bengal are scarcely to be encountered. 'Jotedars', as such, were to be found both in east and west Bengal but they were very different from their namesakes in the north. The pattern of

33 *Midnapur SR*, p. 41.
34 *Bankura SR* (1917–24), p. 59.
35 McAlpin's 1909 Report quoted in Bengal Board of Economic Enquiry, *Bulletin District Bankura* (Alipur, 1935) pp. 3–4.

settlement often left central villages inhabited by the bhadralok, an elite consisting of the upper Hindu castes as well as aristocratic and learned Muslims who shirked manual labour, surrounded by villages held by the chashis or peasants. The upper-caste gentry in east Bengal did not as a rule enter directly into cultivation as did some of their counterparts in northern India. For the most part, they were simply residential, relying on their profits as petty rent-collectors and increasingly also as moneylenders.[36] For east Bengal, the bhadralok–chashi dichotomy is important and as a broad distinction probably sufficient. The bulk of the Muslim and Namasudra cultivators may be seen to have chashi or peasant status. They held jotes – cultivable lands – owned the implements of cultivation and had solid titles to their homesteads, describing themselves as grihasthi. In west Bengal, it was not unusual for some of the landlords to direct farming on land which they held as khas or personal demesne. In addition to the chashis of the agriculturist castes, such as the Mahishyas, Sadgops and Aguris, there was in west Bengal at the very bottom of the agrarian hierarchy, a distinct layer of landless agricultural labourers drawn from among the low-caste Bagdis and Bauris and the aboriginal tribes, such as the Santals. In east Bengal, with the intensification of demographic pressure, the ranks of a land-poor peasantry swelled after 1920;[37] yet the peasantry here may be seen to merge into the landless category. In west Bengal, a certain discontinuity is apparent; the peasant and the rural proletarian there must be regarded as distinct elements in a pre-existing agrarian social structure.

The typical agricultural work-unit in Bengal was the small peasant family farm. East Bengal was not in as advanced a stage of cultivation at the time of the Permanent Settlement as west Bengal. There was an abundance of fallow land but not the same obstacles in the path of reclamation as in the case of north Bengal. During the latter half of the nineteenth century and the early part of the twentieth, a steady expansion of cultivation took place under the stimulus of a secular rise in population, mainly in the form of a proliferation of atomistic

36 On the talukdars' role as moneylenders, see chapter 4 below.
37 See chapter 2 below.

small peasant farms. The relative homogeneity of the chashis of east Bengal, and to a lesser extent in west Bengal as well, in marked contrast to the wide economic differentiation in north Bengal, is striking. Land described in northern India as sir or primary zamindari and cultivated – usually through family and tied labour – by a dominant peasant or a cultivating proprietor, who also has the right to collect tribute, sink wells, plant trees on ryoti or subordinate-cultivator-held land,[38] is virtually non-existent in east Bengal. West Bengal provides a sort of transition zone between the upper India and the east Bengal situations. Here, landlords with considerable khas khamar and a segment of rich peasantry with surplus lands which had emerged during the nineteenth century possessed some of the economic power and political clout of the sirdars of northern India. In northern India, the lords of the land derived their position not only from rent-collection and residence but also from the active direction of cultivation. Bengal in most parts did not possess the same nucleated village structure and clan cohesion. It was only in exceptional circumstances (such as the colonisation of new char lands or of pockets of jungle) that Muslim and Namasudra cultivators in east Bengal threw up a form of clan organisation with leaders ready and able to assume the role of dominant peasant. The period of the zamindari rent offensive in the first half of the nineteenth century saw the rise of a sort of seigneurial sergeant class, village leaders known variously as dewanias, mathbars, mandals and pramaniks, who colluded with the zamindars to fleece the peasantry and were allowed to hold land at favourable rates. However, their position had more to do with their ability to manipulate the administrative structure of rent-collection than with the production process itself. With the waning of the rent offensive in the later nineteenth century and the virtual end of the era of high landlordism marked by the Tenancy Act of 1885, their role became less and less relevant. In early twentieth-century rural Bengal there was a mass of peasant smallholders living under broadly similar but splintered conditions of economic existence below a superimposed network of rent-receivers who were proprietors of the land in only legal terms.

38 See Stokes, *The Peasant and the Raj*, pp. 46–62, 205–27.

In east Bengal, the landlords under the Permanent Settlement consisted of a few big zamindars and numerous petty talukdars. Most of them belonged to the upper Hindu castes but there were also a handful of Muslims. The same social groups filled the ranks of tenure-holders known also as talukdars who were intermediaries in the rent-collecting structure between the superior zamindars and the raiyats. There was not much subinfeudation of rent-collecting rights compared with districts such as Bakarganj and Khulna, and tenures rarely went below two or three degrees. In west Bengal, the dominant tenurial pattern below the level of the zamindars was that of the patni and its derivatives. The patnis had originated after 1793 in the estate of the Maharaja of Burdwan. The revenue assessment of the estate was high and in order to ensure easy and punctual realisation of rent, a number of leases to be held in perpetuity at fixed rents were given to a large number of middlemen. After the Patni Regulation of 1819 legalised and systematised the patni tenure, it gained very wide currency in west Bengal. Patni rights were often held over a whole village or small groups of villages. A considerable number of patnidars sublet part of their interests to darpatnidars, and a few repeated the process with sepatnidars. These interests were mostly in the hands of the upper-caste gentry but it was not unusual for a few members of the agricultural and intermediate trading castes to make their way into these ranks.

Apart from the so-called raiyati land, held and operated by the peasantry, it was a long-established practice of the landed gentry to keep a proportion of khamar land in their personal possession and cultivate it through sharecroppers or hired labourers. In east Bengal, landlords' khas khamar was, generally speaking, minimal. In west and central Bengal, it was considerable. In the 1910s, in the east Bengal districts of Dacca, Faridpur and Tippera, 85%, 86% and 87% of the land area respectively was held by raiyats, a great majority of whom were cultivating peasants. At the other end of the scale, in the west Bengal district of Bankura, 23% of the total area was in the direct possession of proprietors and tenure-holders, 46% in the hands of raiyats and under-raiyats, while the rest was waste and jungle over which the landlords held the primary rights.[39] Consequently, the proportion of labourers and share-croppers without any rights was much higher among the agricultural population in west and central Bengal than in east Bengal.

In early twentieth-century Bengal agricultural production was predominantly in the hands of peasant smallholders who had recorded rights of occupation. The predominance of the peasant smallholding sector over the demesne labour or khamar sector was much more pronounced in east Bengal than in west and central Bengal. In the words of the Dacca settlement officer, the settled raiyat paying his rent in cash still formed 'the backbone of the agricultural population'.[40] In the battle fought in the late nineteenth century over occupancy right and rent enhancement, it was the raiyats who had scored and won. The Bengal Tenancy Act modified the Settlement of 1793 in important ways. It gave a large body of cultivators a measure of tenurial security on moderate rents.[41] Jack, as we have seen, had the impression that the cultivators of the east Bengal district of Faridpur were a 'homogeneous class'. Bengal was not a land of bloated jotedars. But it would be misleading to suggest that the peasantry was a wholly undifferentiated mass. In east Bengal the scale of inequalities did not produce a class dichotomy within the peasantry; differences in wealth and landholding sizes were fluid within what was basically a peasant smallholding structure. In west Bengal high grain prices during the late nineteenth century had initiated a process of differentiation which had led to the emergence of a small segment of rich peasants. These rich peasants operated in the product and credit markets as partners of the

39 *Dacca SR* (1910–17), p. 70; *Faridpur SR* (1904–14), p. 29; *Bankura SR* pp. 66–9 and Appendix.

40 *Dacca SR*, p. 71.

41 The Tenancy Act was the government's response to the wave of agrarian agitation that swept east Bengal in the 1870s and the early 1880s. It provided for a right of occupancy to a tenant who had cultivated any plot of land in a village for the previous 12 years and rent could be enhanced only once in 15 years on clearly defined conditions and by not more than 12.5% of the existing rent.

Many of the protected raiyats could, of course, sublet and become landlords themselves, and there was nothing to prevent non-cultivators from buying into raiyati rights. The extent of subletting until the second and third decades of the twentieth century, when some of the major districts were surveyed, was not very great. The proportion of raiyati area sublet to under-raiyats was in Faridpur 9.1%, Tippera 2.8%, Dacca 1.3%, Mymensingh 4.1%, Midnapur 3.4%, Bankura 4% and Burdwan 2.3%. *Faridpur SR*, p. 33: *Dacca SR*, pp. 70–1; *Mymensingh SR* (1908–19), p. 44; *Burdwan SR* (1927–34), p. 34.

moneylending and grain-dealing landlords. The question of a socio-economic hierarchy within the peasantry does not lend itself very easily to a quantitative analysis. Legal categories do not fit real social categories. Nonetheless, the available statistics have to be considered before moving on to a discussion of the qualitative evidence.

It was only in 1938–40 that an attempt was made to establish the number of families in different acreage classes for Bengal as a whole. This was done at the instance of the Land Revenue Commission. Table 1.1 shows that in the districts of east Bengal, roughly 84% of agriculturist families held less than 5 acres, 11% between 5 and 10 acres and a mere 5% over 10 acres. In the districts of west Bengal, some 72% of the families held less than 5 acres, 19% between 5 and 10 acres and 9% over 10 acres. The figures in table 1.2 are taken from settlement reports of some west Bengal districts. The reports on Birbhum, Murshidabad, Howrah and Hooghly provide the additional and more significant information about the proportion of the total area covered by different acreage classes of holdings. Howrah and Hooghly appear to show a predominance of small tenancies, while in Birbhum and Murshidabad, rather larger holdings of over 15 acres are of some importance.

More revealing than statistics built around imperfect legal categories are the insights into the relations between real social categories. Differentiation within the peasantry of east Bengal around 1919 appears to be one of subtle and delicate gradation, the scale of inequalities being relatively small. The differences in landholding size were not considerable and did not at any rate allow scope for the development of exploitative class relations through the control of large amounts of surplus lands. Village-controlling landholders so common in north Bengal were conspicuously absent. What then was the position of the 'jotedars' of these regions if they were not rich farmers of the north Bengal type? As Jack discovered in the course of settlement operations in Faridpur, 'The name jot exists throughout the district as a generic name for every tenancy'.[42] In Mymensingh, apart from a few unusual tenancies, all others were 'almost universally described as jotes'.[43] Anyone in east Bengal with a

42 *Faridpur SR*, p. 27.
43 *Mymensingh SR*, p. 43.

Table 1.1 *Distribution of areas held by a family*

District	Number of families enquired into	Average area per family in acres	Proportions (%) of land held by families of different acreage categories					
			Less than 2 acres	2-3 acres	3-4 acres	4-5 acres	5-10 acres	Above 10 acres
East Bengal districts								
Bakarganj	804	2.17	61.8	13.1	9.1	3.9	10.9	1.2
Bogra	464	4.28	34.5	14.2	13.6	12.7	17.9	7.1
Chittagong	690	2.45	60.3	10.1	8.8	5.8	10.7	4.3
Dacca	508	2.13	62.4	11.6	6.1	6.1	5.1	3.5
Faridpur	1104	1.63	81.5	7.6	3.4	1.8	2.6	0.6
Khulna	356	4.78	55.6	7.8	9.0	6.1	13.9	7.6
Mymensingh	931	3.86	34.1	13.9	11.9	10.5	16.9	6.5
Noakhali	502	2.41	65.3	12.1	7.8	3.4	4.2	2.8
Pabna	701	2.39	64.1	9.2	5.8	4.1	7.1	2.4
Rajshahi	1018	5.52	31.8	9.3	9.7	9.1	25.5	14.6
Tippera	950	2.22	63.9	13.7	8.6	4.3	6.6	2.9
East Bengal	8028	3.07	55.9	11.1	8.5	6.1	11.0	4.9
West and central Bengal districts								
Bankura	670	8.17	53.7	8.9	7.8	4.5	14.8	10.3
Birbhum	727	4.64	15.1	10.1	7.4	8.5	19.2	8.2
Burdwan	803	5.63	28.6	10.9	8.9	10.8	26.6	12.8
Hooghly	595	3.74	32.4	13.1	13.0	10.9	18.8	10.2
Howrah	336	3.53	53.2	14.3	5.1	4.5	17.5	5.4
Jessore	1073	4.78	28.5	10.3	9.6	9.8	27.1	13.6
Malda	332	3.34	54.2	7.8	8.4	6.9	15.9	6.8
Midnapur	1110	4.23	38.2	16.1	10.9	10.5	17.6	6.7
Murshidabad	1178	4.30	38.3	10.1	9.3	7.5	16.9	7.7
Nadia	830	4.83	16.8	9.6	10.8	10.1	20.3	11.8
24-Parganas	1174	4.33	56.5	10.7	8.6	4.7	10.9	7.2
West and central Bengal	8828	4.7	37.8	11.0	9.0	8.0	18.7	9.2

Source: Report of the Land Revenue Commission, Bengal, Vol. 2 (1940), pp. 114–15.

Table 1.2 Acreage classes of holdings in some west and central Bengal districts

District	0-1	1-2	2-3	3-4	4-5	5-15	15-25	Over 25	Total average
1. Midnapur (1911-17)									
Percentage of holdings to total holdings		Under 5 acres:		93.2		4.8	0.7	1.3	100
2. Birbhum (1924-32)									
Percentage of holdings to total holdings	66.8	14.9	7.2	3.7	2.4	4.6	0.3	0.1	100
Percentage of area under holdings to total area	15.2	16.6	13.5	10.0	8.1	26.9	4.8	4.9	100
Average area of each holding	0.29	1.44	2.43	3.46	4.48	7.59	18.52	44.98	1.29
3. Murshidabad (1924-32)									
Percentage of holdings to total holdings	68.9	15.7	6.4	3.2	1.8	3.5	0.3	0.2	100
Percentage of area under holdings to total area	18.6	18.0	12.7	9.0	6.6	21.8	4.6	8.7	100
Average area of each holding	0.33	1.42	2.44	3.46	4.44	7.71	18.73	60.38	1.23
4. Malda (1928-35)									
Percentage of holdings to total holdings	44.0	24.0	2-5 acres:		22.0	5 acres and above:		10	100
5. Hooghly (1930-37)									
Percentage of holdings to total holdings	73.2	15.2	2-5 acres:		9.7	5 acres and above:		1.9	100
Percentage of area under holdings to total area	29.0	23.8	2-5 acres:		31.7	5 acres and above:		15.5	100
Average area of each holding	0.35	1.39	2-5 acres:		2.93	5 acres and above:		7.21	0.89
5. Howrah (1934-39)									
Percentage of holdings to total holdings	79.1	13.1	4.1	1.7	0.8	1.1	0.1	0.0	100
Percentage of area under holdings to total area	34.8	24.6	13.3	7.9	4.8	11.0	1.4	2.2	100
Average area of each holding	0.33	1.40	2.41	3.42	4.45	7.42	18.56	48.09	0.74

Source: District Settlement Reports.

long-term cultivating right in a piece of land subject to payment of rent was a jotedar. He was more often than not a smallholding peasant. In west Bengal, the term jotedar came to mean sharecropper, almost the opposite of what it usually denoted in north Bengal. The holding of a sharecropper was designated a bhag (share) jote and its holder was a bhagjotedar or simply a jotedar. This local usage was found by sociologists to persist as late as the 1960s even though by that time – in the political dictionary of Bengal – jotedar referred exclusively to the poor peasant's and sharecropper's class enemy.[44]

The terminological question is less important than the substantive issue it deals with. It is not just that the meanings of these indigenous terms varied over time and space or that the features of the agrarian structure remained unchanged. Instead of the 'master–servant relationship' between jotedar and adhiar in Dinajpur, in the Bengal heartland the roles of jotedar and bargadar overlapped and were even interchangeable. The existence of the sharecropping arrangement is too readily seen to indicate relations of dependency bordering on semi-feudalism. No doubt sharecropping and sharecroppers existed all over Bengal. But they did so in a variety of contexts. Dependency in the new areas of reclamation has already been mapped. In east Bengal the sharecropping arrangements both on khamar and raiyati land were to a great extent incidental to the predominating peasant smallholding system. It was a time-worn practice for raiyats to cultivate the khamar lands of zamindars and talukdars on a share basis, to add to their income from inadequate raiyati land or even to find full employment for their labour resources. This system survived in the Manikganj subdivision of Dacca. In 1911 it was described by the settlement officer in the following terms:

It cannot be said on the whole that the bargadars constitute a separate class: in some places especially in the more sparsely

44 André Beteille, *Studies in Agrarian Social Structure* (Delhi, 1974), pp. 129–30; A.K. and D.G. Danda, *Development and Change in Basudha* (Hyderabad, 1971), p.44. O'Malley wrote of the bhag jotedar of Bankura in 1908: 'In such a holding (a bhag jote) the tenant has the use of the land for a year or a season, and pays as rent a certain share of the produce of the land. Ordinarily one half of the produce is so paid, the jotedar cultivating the land with his own plough and cattle, and also finding seed and manure. Occasionally the superior tenant who engages the bhagjotedar finds the manure, in return for which he receives the straw in addition to his half-share of produce.' *Bankura DG* p. 102.

populated area around Mahadebpur they consist largely of landless labourers, but in the area as a whole it is the ordinary raiyat who adds to his profits by the cultivation of khamar land... I doubt whether in a single instance any family gains from its barga lands more grain than is sufficient to support itself; only in a few instances where jute is grown on barga lands is there any monetary gain and for that an extra share is given to the bargadar either in money or in kind'.[45]

Similarly, the settlement officer of Mymensingh states quite plainly that nearly all bargadars had jote lands of their own. The bargadars, he wrote, 'do not form a class by themselves... The bargadar is usually a settled ryot of the village, renting his homestead and one or two plots of arable land from the same landlord on a cash rent'.[46] In a peasant society with inequalities but no sharp differentiation or bi-polar class divisions, the sharecropping relation on a small percentage of peasants' land could in the short term adjust disparate land-labour ratios within the peasant smallholding system.[47]

The dominance of the peasant smallholding system in early twentieth-century east Bengal is undeniable. But there were disquieting reports from some areas of the *de facto* increase of khamar at the expense of raiyati land. *De facto*, because the method often employed by non-peasant rentiers as well as moneylenders and traders was to buy into raiyati rights. The Dacca settlement officer who observed this phenomenon with concern, especially in the regions of new development on the fringes of the Madhupur jungle, made clear the distinction between old barga lands as an adjunct to small peasant cultivation and new barga lands under moneylender-landords at the expense of peasant smallholding.[48] The extent to which non-peasant moneylenders were able to displace small cultivating raiyats and how far the processes of internal differentiation allowed a peasant elite to emerge will be themes we shall return to when we shift from the somewhat static analysis adopted in this chapter to a study of the

45 *Dacca SR* App. XI, xxvii–xxviii.
46 *Mymensingh SR* p. 45.
47 In Noakhali, where the bulk of the land was held and cultivated by small peasants on money rents, holdings on produce rents were 'only created as a temporary convenience, as for instance when the father of a family dies and a neighbour takes over the cultivation of the land while the children are growing up'. *Noakhali SR* (1914–19), pp. 91–2.
48 *Dacca SR*, pp. 75–7 and App. XI.

dynamic processes of the peasants' involvement in the product
and credit markets and their impact on the structure of
peasants' holdings.

Finally, the role of wage labour in the agrarian economy has
to be set into context. This will clarify the differences between
the agrarian structures of east and west Bengal. 'The landless
labourer,' Jack wrote in 1916, 'is unknown in Faridpur and
very rare anywhere in Eastern Bengal.'[49] A large number of
cultivators, of course, worked for hire at harvest time, but the
composition of these hired labourers underlined the relative
homogeneity of the peasantry. As a detailed socio-economic
survey of Faridpur showed:

The proportion of agricultural labourers amongst the poorer
families was naturally much greater than amongst the richer, but not
by any means to the extent which might have been expected. Of
cultivators in comfort 22%, of those below comfort 31%, of those
above want 36% and of the indigent 37% were enumerated as engaged
in agricultural labour. It is probable that amongst all these there
were none who were exclusively agricultural labourers. . . . All had
their land, some perhaps very inadequate in amount, but others only
inadequate because the family contained at the time an undue
proportion of young children. . . The proportion of the indigent
supported by agricultural labour is not larger mainly because this
class consists of old men who are unfit for the work or of families
whose bread-winner has died before his time.[50]

There was some interdistrict movement of agricultural labour
in east Bengal as a consequence of the uneven levels of wealth
and the slightly uneven crop cycles. Smallholders from
Faridpur, Jessore and Tippera would cut paddy in Bakarganj
and strip jute in Mymensingh. Dacca and Tippera display a
well-established and elaborate system of labour exchange
known as gnata. Labour pools of half a dozen or more
smallholders were formed at the time of harvest.[51] In Noakhali
as well no clear distinction could be made between the peasant
and the landless labourer.[52]

49 Jack, *Economic Life of a Bengal District*, p. 84.
50 *Ibid.*
51 *Dacca SR*, pp. 20, 52. S.V. Ayyar and A.K.A. Khan, 'The Economics of a Bengal
   Village', *Indian Journal of Economics*, 6 (1926), pp. 200–15.
52 As the settlement officer wrote: 'when the economy of the agricultural classes as
   a body is considered, it is unnecessary to consider the price of labour. The labour
   is entirely supplied by the same body. No outside labour is employed and to

The situation in west Bengal, on the other hand, was entirely different. It was only in the Contai and Tamluk subdivisions of Midnapur that there were no large reserves of landless agricultural labour. Here, as the Midnapur Settlement Report records, the work of cultivation was performed for the most part by the peasant himself using family labour. Owing to the small size of an average holding, this was generally sufficient. If more labour was required it was obtained by 'a system of exchange between neighbours'.[53] Elsewhere in west Bengal, a land of old settlement, high rents, uncertain harvests and a demographic arrest (owing to malaria epidemics from the mid-nineteenth century until about 1920), the Bagdis, Bauris, and tribal people supplied much of the labour on the agricultural lands, invisible to settlement statistics, as bhagdars (sharecroppers without occupancy rights), krishans (tied labourers paid with a third of the produce), munishes (day labourers) and mahindars (farm servants). These men might perhaps own a garden patch or even a share in rice fields, yet essentially they constituted a distinct landless element. Robertson, settlement officer of Bankura, described how this large pool of landless labour was put to use:

In the poorer districts of Western Bengal there is a tendency for much of the land to fall into the hands of the tenure-holders. In these districts the crop is uncertain and the people are poor and thriftless. The tenure-holders themselves are the principal moneylenders, and when a tenant has once borrowed money it is only a matter of time before his holding comes to sale. It is then bought in by the tenure-holder, who perhaps retains the more valuable lands for himself settling the less valuable lands with the tenant afresh. In a very poor district such as Bankura there is no lack of hired labourers. Indeed the Bauris as a class are usually landless men who work for others. The tenure-holders, therefore, if they retain lands in their own possession, find no difficulty in hiring labourers to cultivate them.[54]

make an entry on the debit side of the balance sheet of the whole body would merely involve the necessity of including the same figure as an asset of the body on the credit side'. *Noakhali SR*, p. 48. The accounting is dubious, but the passage does suggest the absence of a distinct landless labour class in Noakhali.
53 *Midnapur SR*, p. 30. This was an area of rising population and expanding cultivation since the withdrawal of the salt monopoly in the mid-nineteenth century.
54 *Bankura SR*, p. 67.

In 1914, Kaibarta or Mahishya families who formed the bulk
of the raiyats in Hooghly district employed Bagdi, Bauri and
Santal sharecroppers and labourers.[55] In the wake of the
malaria epidemics, the number of working members of raiyat
families were often few and far between. The two classes,
peasants and agricultural labourers, were consequently
brought together in a necessary though unequal collaboration
in order to sustain agricultural production. It was not unusual
for caste peasants to lease land from the gentry on bhag and
employ labourers who were supplied with the necessary
plough-team and seeds. For west and central Bengal, the
vision of self-cultivation by peasant smallholders has to be
modified to take account of the fairly widespread use of tied
and hired labour not only on the landlords' and rich peasants'
considerable khas lands but also on peasant smallholdings.
Table 1.3 is intended to give a general impression of the much
higher proportion of labourers (including sharecroppers
without tenancy rights) to the total agricultural population in
west and central Bengal than in east Bengal where the great
majority of cultivators had some sort of recorded right to the
soil.

This chapter has focused on certain basic distinctions in the
agrarian social structure in Bengal. A more complete
elucidation of the relations of production and surplus
appropriation in the Bengal countryside will become clearer
when we study the peasantry's involvement in the credit and
product markets.[56] The impact of these markets on the
smallholding peasantry may, however, be sketched here in
skeletal form and will be elaborated and developed later. From
the later nineteenth century onwards, zamindari rent as a
mode of surplus appropriation became less significant, even
though in west Bengal districts it continued to rule relatively
high. In these parts, the zamindars and patnidars had
extensive usurious interests. After the removal of the indigo
planters from the agrarian scene by the 1860s, they were clearly
the principal source of credit for the cultivating classes. These
groups controlled the credit and that critical proportion of

55 *Hooghly SR*, (1904–13), p. 37.
56 See chapter 4 below.

Table 1.3 *Proportions of agricultural population: 'Landlord',*
'Tenant', 'Labourer' (%)

	Landlords	Tenants	Labourers
East Bengal districts			
Bakarganj	4.26	87.75	7.99
Bogra	1.99	89.24	8.77
Chittagong	9.55	72.53	17.92
Dacca	5.08	89.24	5.68
Faridpur	6.61	88.84	4.55
Khulna	5.73	85.68	8.59
Mymensingh	2.49	92.12	5.39
Noakhali	3.36	82.50	14.14
Pabna	4.12	88.28	7.60
Rajshahi	4.60	84.18	11.22
Tippera	1.93	93.87	4.20
East Bengal	4.52	86.75	8.73
West and central Bengal districts			
Bankura	4.18	68.39	27.43
Birbhum	2.00	62.38	35.62
Burdwan	4.19	68.42	27.39
Hooghly	4.87	68.57	26.56
Howrah	8.89	61.06	30.05
Jessore	6.94	85.34	7.72
Malda	2.12	75.99	21.89
Midnapur	2.37	80.45	17.18
Murshidabad	4.15	68.99	26.86
Nadia	7.85	70.05	22.10
24-Parganas	4.39	76.19	19.42
West and central Bengal	4.72	71.44	23.84

Source: Census of India 1921, Vol,5 Bengal, Pt 2, Tables 2,3,4 and 5.

surplus lands which enabled the smallholding and landless economies to go on reproducing themselves. It was they who were the chief beneficiaries of the expanding market in grain, and while a shrewder and richer minority of the peasants were able to cash in and become patrons themselves, many peasant smallholders fell into debt and could only carry on by borrowing seed and grain from year to year; in course of time, some were reduced to a position close to that of the landless workers.

The attempt at colonial extraction through capitalist transformation of traditional production regimes ended in Bengal (the Darjeeling tea-plantations excepted) with the demise of the indigo plantations by the 1860s. However, from

the late nineteenth century and more emphatically in the early
twentieth, the small peasant economy of east Bengal was
drawn into the web of an export-oriented colonial economy.
Small peasant producers raised jute for the world market on
their minuscule holdings. The market and the credit system,
which kept the peasant family alive and helped to reproduce
the small peasant economy, became more important than rent
as the channels of the drain on the east Bengal peasant. The
control of the zamindars and talukdars over land was distant
and weak. Indeed, the rent charge over which their
proprietorship really extended was becoming increasingly
difficult to collect. Some were eliminated. Others found a firm
niche in the surplus-appropriating mechanism by resorting to
lagni karbar (the moneylending business). In addition to the
trader-moneylenders, there emerged in the early twentieth
century an important section of bhuswami mahajans
(landlords who were also moneylenders).[57]

In attempting to raise the value of his product on a
diminishing holding, the east Bengal peasant made himself
vulnerable to violent and often long-term fluctuations in the
world market. Jute was an expensive crop to cultivate,
especially since its labour costs were much higher. This in
turn enlarged the credit needs of the peasantry. The dispersed
nature of peasant production meant that the grower had little
bargaining power over prices *vis-a-vis* the highly organised
trading sector. An elaborate marketing mechanism involving
a long chain of middlemen took away a fair amount of the
peasants' due. More importantly, the peasant's lack of holding
power compelled him to sell immediately after harvest when
prices were at their lowest. Not only did he not have facilities
of storage and transport, but he required cash at harvest time
to make his exorbitant interest payments to the moneylender
and deliver rent to the landlord. Often he would have received
a dadan (advance) from a trader-moneylender and had little
choice except to sell his produce to the dadan karbari at a price
much below the prevailing market rate.[58] In the context of
increasing population pressure and diminishing holdings,
colonial extraction through the market interacted with and
reinforced the credit mechanism. This served to hold the

57 For a detailed discussion of moneylenders and moneylending, see chapter 4 below.
58 See chapter 3 below.

peasant in their pincer grip and perpetuated and impoverished the small peasant economy of Bengal.

Clearly then, possession of the chief means of production – land – did not mean that the peasant smallholders were independent agents in the process of production and reproduction in agrarian Bengal. Yet the lack of freedom of the small peasant weighed down by scarcity of land and the inequities of highly unfavourable market and credit relations bore no resemblance to the sharecroppers' dependence on the village landlord rich farmer-cum-creditor.

In east Bengal there was no strict equality among the peasantry. But it is still possible to speak of a predominating peasant-smallholding structure with imperceptible gradations from a dwarfholder-cum-bargadar to an owner-tenant-cultivator with a small surplus. While there were no serious class divisions within peasant society, the peasantry in east Bengal found themselves involved in similar sets of tenurial, credit and market relations. In west Bengal, the cleavage between the peasant and the rural proletarian was more obvious. The latter might possess a meagre patch, but he earned his livelihood primarily by hiring out his labour. Here the moneylending landlords and tenure-holders exercised a much greater direct control over the land than in east Bengal. In the dominant structural type of the peripheral regions newly reclaimed from wasteland, the refinement of delicate, graded complexities was of little importance: at the peak of the pyramid stood the giant jotedar flanked perhaps by a few chukanidars and down below were the mass of dependent adhiars.

'For historians, a structure certainly means something that holds together or something that is architectural'.[59] This chapter has identified the major architectural styles in rural Bengal and has given an impression of their contours. We must now examine how the structure held together, the pressures to which it was exposed, the faults that developed within it and the lines along which the edifice of Bengali rural society crumbled.

59 F. Braudel, 'History and the Social Sciences' in P. Burke (ed.), *Economy and Society in Early Modern Europe* (London, 1972), pp. 17–18. Beyond that, in Braudel's definition, a structure 'means a reality which can distort the effect of time, changing its scope and speed'.

2

Subsistence and the market I

Rural Bengal in the first half of the twentieth century poses
all the conceptual problems and complexities of an agrarian
society with an extensive subsistence base which at the same
time was tied firmly to a far-flung market. In such
circumstances, does the peasantry constitute a distinctive
moral and political economy largely retaining its 'non-
maximising subsistence ethic', or can it be seen as a body of
'rational economic decision-makers' responding to 'market
opportunity'? Recent historiography of the peasantry in
contemporary South-East Asia has predictably produced
antithetical views on a question posed in such antithetical
terms. The concept of a hard-headed 'political economy' has
been set against that of a more benign 'moral economy' of the
peasant; 'subsistence ethic' finds its contrast in 'investment
logic' as the true motivation behind peasant economic
behaviour, and explanations of peasant political protest
oscillate between the polarities of 'moral outrage' and
'personal gain'.[1] From a different angle, the relative strength
of the impact of demographic and market forces on agrarian
economy and society is a question that continues to divide
historians of pre-industrial Europe. Even those who treat the
evolution of pre-industrial peasant societies within the
framework of a demographic model in terms of homeostatic
ecosystems are far from agreed on the issue of the peasant
response to the market and the efficacy of market forces in
bringing about structural change.[2] Of late, a political

1 See James C. Scott, *The Moral Economy of the Peasant* (Yale, 1976) and Samuel
   L. Popkin, *The Rational Peasant* (Berkeley, 1979).
2 M.M. Postan allows a far more dynamic role to market forces in introducing
   structural change than E. Le Roy Ladurie, who tends to stress the precedence of
   the demographic factor in any causal sequence. See E. Le Roy Ladurie, *The*

34

Marxist critique has called into question all the variants of the demographically determined model and asserted the centrality of pre-existing agrarian class structures in shaping the nature of social and economic change.[3] Yet all these conflicting interpretations are not mutually exclusive, but rather stem from differences of emphasis and the choice of alternative frameworks for the analysis of interrelated themes.

In the realm of Indian historiography, in spite of a longstanding debate centering on the price responsiveness of agriculture, the aspects of demographic change and production for the market have been generally weakly integrated. Historical demography, a neglected area of research, and the study of commercialisation of agriculture have tended to run on almost parallel lines.[4] Yet positive statistical correlations between price and acreage tell us little about the motivations of the peasantry when presented in a demographic void. Powerful arguments about forced commercialisation reveal only a part of the picture without reference to natural-demographic constraints on the availability pattern of land and resources which may limit peasant options. It is necessary to address the peasantry's subsistence-basis/market-orientation dilemma in interaction to be able to understand its actual operation in any particular historical conjuncture.

From the later nineteenth century onwards, the Bengal countryside, in common with other parts of India, was subjected to two sets of pressures: the scarcity of land and other natural resources as a function of population growth on the one hand and the depredations and uncertainties of the capitalist world economy on the other. The latter operated in India within the context of a colonial political

Peasants of Languedoc (Urbana, Illinois, 1974) and 'A Reply to Professor Brenner', *Past and Present*, 79 (May 1978), pp. 55-9; M.M. Postan and John Hatcher, 'Population and Class Relations in Feudal Society', *Past and Present*, 78 (Feb. 1978), pp. 23-37, especially pp. 27-31.

3 Robert Brenner, 'Agrarian Class Structure and Economic Development in Pre-Industrial Europe', *Past and Present*, 70 (Feb. 1976), pp. 30-75. Another Marxist view would like to see the mode of production rather than the political superstructure at the centre of analysis. See Guy Bois, 'Against the Neo-Malthusian Orthodoxy', *Past and Present*, 79 (1978), pp. 60-9.

4 One notable exception is Kessinger's study of a village over a period of 100 years which lends some support to the Chayanovian notion of peasant farms even in

order whose financial policies served to compound at critical times the adverse effects of world market fluctuations. In seeking to set the agrarian economy of Bengal firmly in its demographic context and the context of the market economy, it is not intended to deny the role of the agrarian class structure in moulding its character. Indeed, over-arching trends in the world market and the consequences of a deteriorating land–man ratio were transmitted to the regional economy through the refracting prism of the local agrarian structure, and affected various social classes in significantly different ways. The aim in this chapter is to elucidate the nature of the demographic and market pressures in the first half of the twentieth century with which agrarian Bengal had to cope.

The demographic and market pressures intersected most obviously at a microcosmic level on the tiny jute-growing plot of the east Bengal peasant. Faced with a rapidly diminishing holding that could not sustain a family with subsistence crops, the peasant smallholder switched to the cultivation of a high-value and labour-intensive cash crop, exposing himself in the process to the volatility of international price movements. Rendered subservient to the forces of the world capitalist economy, the peasant family economy was perpetuated and impoverished through the operation of merchant and usury capital. The credit network served as the crucial link between the export sector and the more self-contained sectors of the agrarian economy, making insulation from the shock waves of the international economy exceedingly difficult.

At a macrocosmic level, the subsistence and market difficulties may also be seen to converge. While demographic movements showed marked divergences in different parts of Bengal, it is reasonably clear that from about 1920 in the region as a whole, population growth began to outstrip agricultural production. Between 1920 and 1946, Bengal agriculture had reached 'an equilibrium at a low level of production' shown by 'the near-constancy of cultivated area and a near-zero trend in yield per acre'[5] Over the same period,

an advanced agricultural region of the Punjab having strong market connections. See Tom Kessinger, *Vilyatpur 1848–1968* (Berkeley, 1974).
5 M.M. Islam, *Bengal Agriculture 1920–1946: A Quantitative Study* (Cambridge,

population increased at the annual average rate of 0.8%. The gap between both food production and availability on the one hand and population growth on the other opened up around 1920 and continued to widen.[6] A gathering Malthusian strain can therefore be seen to have provided a very general background to the major subsistence crisis of the 1940s. Bengal's agrarian economy was at the same time twisted to an export orientation, producing commercial crops, notably jute, for the world market under the aegis of European capital. If cracks were developing in the subsistence foundation of Bengal agriculture under the weight of demographic pressure, during the same period the region's economy also suffered some of its worst convulsions as a result of fluctuations in the world market. This was particularly marked during the 1930s slump and the unhealthy boom of the 1940s. It is only through the study of the twin strands of demographic pressures and market uncertainties, conditioned by the agrarian class situation as they bore down on the countryside, that the unfolding of the agrarian crisis of Bengal can be understood.

The demographic background

The demographic history of west and east Bengal from the later nineteenth century to the 1920s followed different courses. From the seventeeth century, the river system of the region had begun to swing to the east. This shift gathered momentum in the nineteenth century as a result of human interference in drainage facilities. The silting up of the rivers, coupled with high mortality due to malaria epidemics, brought about a demographic arrest from the mid-nineteenth century to the 1920s with a corresponding reduction in the extent of cultivation in west Bengal. Conversely, the east witnessed a rapid expansion of cultivation until 1920 under the

1979), p. 203. See also G. Blyn, *Agricultural Trends in India 1890–1947* (Philadelphia, 1966). Islam's attempt to revise demonstrably wrong official figures of acreage (generally underestimates) for the whole period 1920–46 on the basis of figures in the Ishaque Report for the single year 1944–5 is a somewhat doubtful exercise. It is possible, however, to accept his broad conclusions regarding the *trends* in acreage and yields. For a critique of Islam, see C.J. Baker's review in *MAS*, 14,3 (1980), pp. 513–18.
6 See M.M. Islam, *Bengal Agriculture*, pp. 54–5.

stimulus of a secular rise in population. About 1920, this expansion in east Bengal reached its extensive margins. Continued demographic growth resulted in migration further east and rapid fractionalisation of landholdings. In west Bengal, amelioration of malaria mortality meant that from the 1920s, the population graph began to move upwards. Towards the end of our period, it was apparent that Bengal, once famous as the granary of the East, was finding the strain of an enormous agricultural population difficult to bear both in the decaying west and in the fertile lands of the active delta in the east.

It has been usual for contemporary geographers to divide early twentieth-century Bengal into three ecological zones. The whole of Bengal was an alluvial plain, but it could be classified according to the extent of enrichment of the soil by river silt into (1) the old delta including west Bengal and central Bengal; (2) the new delta comprising east Bengal; and (3) the Ganges–Brahmaputra Doab corresponding to north Bengal.[7] West Bengal contained a portion of laterite formation on its western fringes but for the most part it was a semi-aquatic rice plain. One of the oldest regions of agricultural settlement in India which had seen eras of great prosperity, it had now, with the silting up of the rivers and the falling of the subsoil water level, turned into a land of agricultural decline where malaria was rampant. North Bengal, south of the Himalayan foothills, also had a belt of 'old alluvium' towards the west covering the districts of Dinajpur, Malda and parts of Rajshahi and Bogra, which could support only one crop – winter (aman) rice. It was consequently vulnerable to the vagaries of rainfall and carried a relatively low density of population. The population in north Bengal had tended to concentrate on the banks of the Jamuna, which bounded this region on the east, for the Jamuna was a new and active river through which the main stream of the Brahmaputra had flowed since the early nineteenth century. The lands served by this river in

7 L.S.S. O'Malley, *Bengal, Bihar and Orissa, Sikkim* (Provincial Geographies of India, Cambridge, 1917), pp. 3–16. Radhakamal Mukherji, *The Changing Face of Bengal* (Culcutta, 1938), pp. 110–13. The following discussion of the ecological zones of Bengal draws extensively from these two works, especially O'Malley, Chapter 1 and Mukherji, chapters 3–6.

Rangpur and Pabna acquired much of the character of the deltaic tracts lower down in east Bengal. The bulk of east Bengal was the land of the relatively 'new alluvium', though the movements of the rivers inevitably left some small decaying pockets of the 'old'. It was a semi-aquatic plain made by the active deltas of the Ganges and the Brahmaputra, which flooded their banks every year during the monsoons and left a fertile layer of silt. The new delta had two subregions – the upper part consisting of the districts of Dacca, Mymensingh, Faridpur and Tippera, and the lower part comprising Bakarganj, Noakhali, Khulna and Chittagong, the latter being an area of tidal waters distributed by an intricate network of streams. The lower delta, newly colonised from forest, was a productive region, and Bakarganj, in particular, together with Dinajpur in north Bengal, became the two major rice-supplying districts of the province. It was the rich alluvial tract of the upper Ganges–Brahmaputra delta in Dacca, Mymensingh, Faridpur and Tippera, along with the Jamuna catchment area in Rangpur, Pabna and a part of Rajshahi further north that proved to be especially suitable for multiple cropping and emerged as the principal jute-growing districts of Bengal.

The ecological contrast of the new alluvium in the active delta in the east and the old alluvium mainly in central and west Bengal was reflected by contrasts in the cropping pattern. The crops of the old alluvium were paddy (more of aus, the poorer autumn variety, than of aman, the winter variety), jute (to a very small extent), as well as sugarcane, maize, jowar and other millets, pulses and oil-seeds, wheat and barley. The new alluvium grew paddy (largely aman) and jute, sugarcane and pulses, oil-seeds such as linseed, mustard, castor-seed and til, cereals such as wheat, barley and oats, and tobacco.[8] The dry crops, however, accounted for an insignificant proportion of the cultivated acreage.[9] Two wet crops, paddy and jute, claimed between them in the

---

8 Radhakamal Mukherji, *ibid.*, p. 43.
9 The distinction between 'wet' and 'dry' cultivation, so crucial to ecological classification in other parts of India, is not relevant for the agriculture of Bengal. As one proceeds down the Ganges valley, dry crops such as wheat, barley, millet and maize become less and less important, and wet-zone crops predominate.

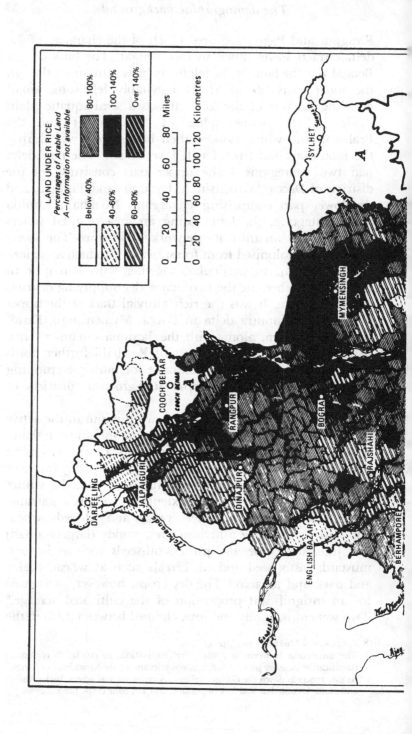

LAND UNDER RICE
Percentages of Arable Land
A – Information not available

Below 40%	80-100%
40-60%	100-140%
60-80%	Over 140%

Map 2: Land under rice
Source: S.P. Chatterji, *Bengal in Maps* (Calcutta, 1949).

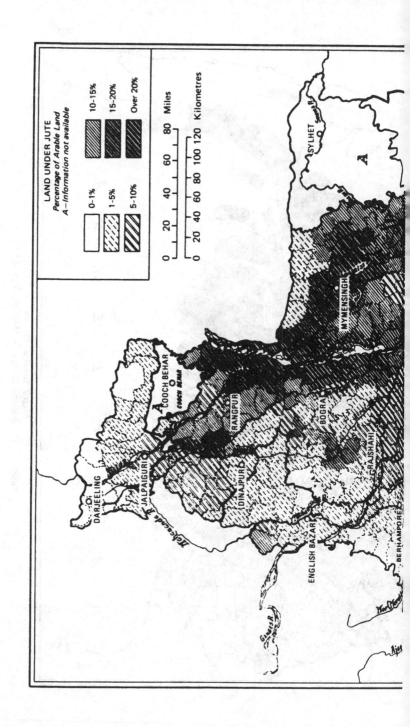

LAND UNDER JUTE
Percentage of Arable Land
A–Information not available

0-1%
1-5%
5-10%
10-15%
15-20%
Over 20%

Miles
0   20   40   60   80
0   20   40   60   80   100   120   Kilometres

DARJEELING
JALPAIGURI
COOCH BEHAR
COOCH BEHAR
A
RANGPUR
DINAJPUR
BOGRA
RAJSHAHI
MYMENSINGH
SYLHET
A
ENGLISH BAZAR
BERHAMPORE
Ganges R.
Mahananda

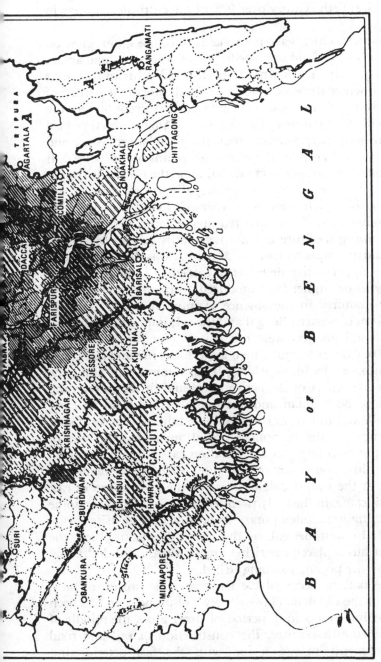

Map 3: Land under jute
Source: S.P. Chatterji, *Bengal in Maps* (Calcutta, 1949).

early twentieth century over 90% of the cultivated acreage in Bengal.

Aus rice, which gave poor yields of coarse grain, grew on relatively high land and needed much less water than aman. Consequently, it dominated in the old alluvium of west Bengal where there were no fresh floods due to the senility of the river system, and was especially susceptible to the unpredictable nature of the monsoons. Aman, which yielded the finest quality of grain, required abundant moisture and was the ideal crop for the inundated plains of east Bengal. It depended not so much on rainfall as on the rise of the river at the right time. Jute was principally of two varieties – *capsularis*, which grew on low, flooded land, and *olitorius*, on higher land. *Capsularis* required a depth of soil capable of retaining moisture but not necessarily an excessively wet soil and atmosphere. Its natural habitat was the alluvial tract of the upper active delta, as it tended to exhaust the soil. *Olitorius* on higher land produced a superior fibre, but had to be manured in the absence of inundation silt. The old alluvium of western Bengal and the salt impregnated soils of the coastal districts were not suitable for jute. The fertile lands of eastern Bengal which grew aman rice and jute could also support the high-yielding boro, summer rice, along the banks and chars of the active rivers and in the intervening marshes. Both aman and aus rice benefited from an early rainfall, and jute from early and late rain, but the key factor in Bengal in the preponderance of aman over aus and of multiple cropping was the flooding capability of the delta. The cultivation of aman and jute, often supplemented by boro, in the robust deltaic tracts of the great rivers of east Bengal came, in the early twentieth century, to support some of the highest contemporary records of rural density in the world. In west Bengal, as the river system atrophied, the poorer aus replaced the richer aman; disease and decline set in, and the population languished.

The natural decay of the rivers and the raising of most parts of the old delta above the level of inundation had been proceeding over a long period of time. From the middle of the nineteenth century, the construction of rail and road embankments played havoc with the fast deteriorating drainage system of the region.[10] The loss of the silt-laden red water resulted in a switch to inferior crops and a drastic fall in yields.[11] The stagnant waters provided an excellent breeding ground for the mosquito, and throughout the later nineteenth century, a series of malaria epidemics swept across Jessore, Hooghly, 24-Parganas, Nadia, Burdwan, Birbhum and Howrah, affecting also parts of the 'old alluvium' of north Bengal.[12] The extensive rural depopulation and the debilitating effect on the survivors that these left in their trail led to a reduction in the area under cultivation. In an attempt to escape the scourge, wholesale desertions of villages often took place. Between 1891 and 1931, the cultivated area contracted by something like 50% in Burdwan, 60% in Hooghly, 30% in Jessore and 20% in Nadia and Murshidabad.[13] As the Kaibartta, Sadgop and Aguri caste peasants retreated in the face of successive attacks of the epidemics, aboriginal labour provided by the Bauris and immigrant tribal people became crucial for the continuance of agriculture on the fallow land being encroached upon by new jungle. It was in these conditions of labour scarcity that the necessary, though unequal, collaboration between the smallholding caste peasant and the low-caste agricultural labourer was forged in west Bengal.

The agricultural expansion of the late nineteenth and early twentieth centuries in the 'old alluvium' in the Barind, the western fringe of north Bengal, after the setbacks caused by malaria, was owed entirely to the large influx of Santals, Mundas and Oraons, who cleared the shrub and jungle but failed to acquire any firm occupancy rights in the land they reclaimed. Another instance of expansion in west and central Bengal was the advance of the Pod in the coastal areas of the 24-Parganas and Khulna, which had not entirely been deprived of river spill. The most spectacular growth in a context of demographic and agricultural decadence all around

10 B.B. Chaudhuri, *'Agrarian Economy and Agrarian Relations in Bengal 1859–1885'* (Oxford, D. Phil. dissertation, 1968), pp. 1–5.
11 Radhakamal Mukherji, *Changing Face of Bengal*, pp. 83–4.
12 B.B. Chaudhuri, 'Agrarian Economy and Agrarian Relations', pp. 6–11. See also, Ira Klein, 'Malaria and Mortality in Bengal 1840–1921', *IESHR*, 9, 2 (1972), pp. 132–60. W.W. Hunter, *A Statistical Account of Bengal*, vol. 2, (London, 1875–77).
13 Radhakamal Mukherji, *Changing Face of Bengal*, p. 275; cf. B.B. Chaudhuri,

took place in the Contai and Tamluk subdivisions of Midnapur district. The availability of the jalpai lands for cultivation with the ending of the government's salt monopoly in the 1860s provided a new haven for peasants driven from their homes by malaria, and soon these areas in Midnapur emerged as the most thriving agricultural settlement of the Mahishyas. Between 1872 and 1901, the population grew by 26% in Contai and 23% in Tamluk.[14] By the second decade of the twentieth century, however, the tightness of the man–land ratio began to be felt. It was discovered in the settlement of 1911-17 that the size of an average raiyati holding was only 1.16 acres in Tamluk and 1.09 acres in Contai. As each family of five held on average three khatiyans (settlement documents), the average size of a family's holding was just a little over three acres.[15] By about 1920, the Mahishyas' new frontier of opportunity appeared to be receding.

While the ancient centres of agricultural settlement in west Bengal declined, in east Bengal not only did the old centres such as Bikrampur in Dacca and Muradnagar in Tippera retain their high density, but the region as a whole witnessed phenomenal expansion as the Muslim and Namasudra cultivators fanned out on a mission of atomistic settlement in the spill basins of the Ganga, Brahmaputra and Meghna. They then assaulted the concentrations of jungle, the Sunderbans in the south and the less attractive elevated tract of the Madhupur jungle on the border of Dacca and Mymensingh.[16] Exceptionally high rural densities were reached along the great rivers in Dacca, Mymensingh, Faridpur and Tippera where aman rice and jute flourished.[17]

'Agrarian Economy and Agrarian Relations', pp. 16-19.
14 B.B. Chaudhuri, 'Agrarian Economy and Agrarian Relations', pp. 37-40.
15 *Midnapur SR* (1911-17), p. 49.
16 Jack testifies to the expansion of cultivation in east Bengal in *Faridpur SR* (1904-14), p. 5; in Bakarganj, between 1860 and 1905 the 'unoccupied waste' shrank from 526 sq. miles to 184 sq. miles, 180 sq. miles of new alluvial land having come into existence and cultivation having registered a 23% increase on the 'occupied area', *Bakarganj SR* (1900-8), pp. 10-11; in Mymensingh, from 1872 until about 1910, the cultivated area increased from 3562 sq. miles to 4292 sq. miles, of which land reclaimed from the Madhpur jungle was about 470 sq. miles, *Mymensingh DG* (1917), p. 48. See also B. Ganguli, *Trends of Agriculture and Population in the Ganges Valley* (London, 1938), pp. 233-42.
17 The increase of population in east Bengal was due, as the Dacca Settlement

Table 2.1 *Growth and decline in east and west Bengal 1901-31*

East Bengal districts	Percentage variation in cultivated area	Percentage variation of population
Dacca	+57	+28.9
Mymensingh	+19	+28.5
Faridpur	+13	+21.8
Tippera	+11	+37.7
Noakhali	+152	+42.9
Bakarganj	+21	+27.1
West Bengal districts		
Burdwan	-40	+3.7
Hooghly	-45	+6.2
Nadia	-7	-8.1
Murshidabad	-14	+22.9
Jessore	-31	-7.2

Source: Radhakamal Mukherji, *The Changing Face of Bengal* (Calcutta, 1938), p. 90, based on *Agricultural Statistics of India* and *Census of India, 1931*, vol. 5, Bengal, Pt 2.

It was only in small pockets of old alluvium left by the shifting rivers in Faridpur, Dacca and Mymensingh, that malaria and agricultural decline made their appearance. In the coastal districts of Noakhali and Bakarganj, extensive fruit orchards and gardens of betelnuts helped sustain high densities. In north Bengal where the new river Jamuna and the Tista were building a new delta over the old, the Rajbansis found a productive region which lent itself to double cropping.[18] In 1931, when the mean density of population of the province was 646 to the square mile, in the populous districts of east and north Bengal, the mean densities were: Dacca 1265, Tippera 1197, Noakhali 1124, Faridpur 1003, Bakarganj 834, Mymensingh 823, Pabna 795, Bogra 785 and Rangpur 742. In the 50 years from 1881 to 1931, the population rose by 88% in Chittagong division, 60%

Report put it, 'almost entirely to a large surplus of births over deaths', *Dacca SR* (1910-17), p. 34. The Census reports of 1891, 1901, 1911 and 1921 bear this out. For the east Bengal region taken as a whole, immigration was not an important factor in demographic growth, but there was some internal movement from unhealthy to more salubrious areas and from over-populated to newly cleared jungle tracts.

18 Radhakamal Mukherji, *Changing Face of Bengal*, pp. 66-72.

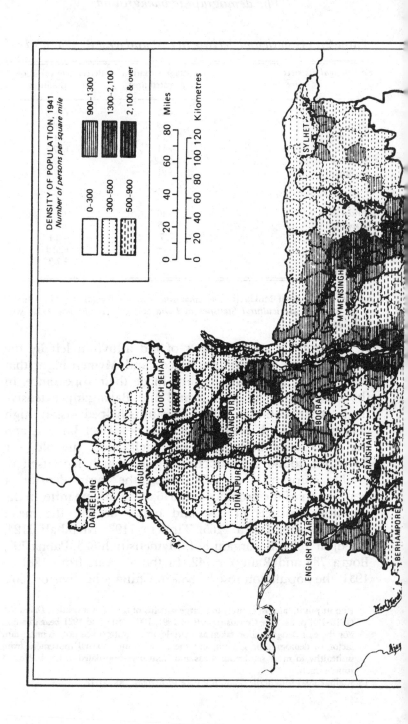

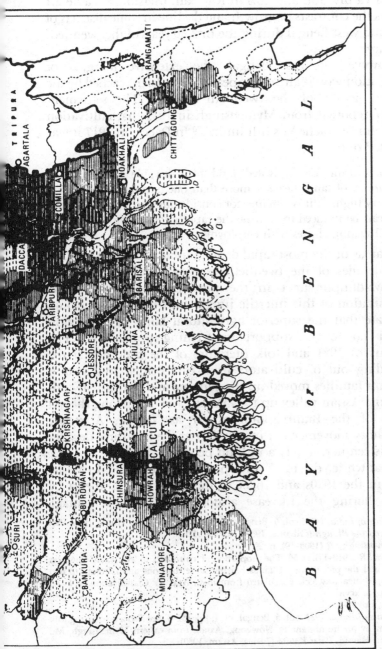

Map 4: Density of population, 1941

Source: S.P. Chatterji, *Bengal in Maps* (Calcutta, 1949)

in Dacca division and 26% in Rajshahi division.[19] Table 2.1 shows the contrasts of growth and decline in some districts of east and west Bengal during the first 30 years of the twentieth century.

However, in east Bengal, the extensive margins of cultivation would already appear to have been reached by the second decade of the twentieth century. The settlement officer reported from Mymensingh in 1919 that cultivation had 'almost reached its full limits'.[20] In Dacca, in 1917 it was pointed out:

the proportion of cultivated land to cultivable land and the proportion of lands bearing more than one annual crop is extra-ordinary high. . . it is a matter for consideration to what extent the land can be induced to provide the rapidly increasing numbers of the cultivating classes with employment.[21]

The areas of the most rapid demographic growth in the first two decades of the twentieth century were the thanas in the Madhupur tract in the north-east of Dacca.[22] The colonisation of this infertile jungly tract of stiff clay would indicate that the superior agricultural lands of the region could no longer support its teeming population. The Census of 1921 and folk literature of the time depict the crowding out of cultivators from east Bengal to Assam.[23] Peasant families moved up the Jamuna and north-eastwards into the Assam valley up to Gauhati, and then along the left bank of the Brahmaputra as far as Tejpur. A steady migratory movement, it involved, over the first three decades of this century, nearly a million people.[24]

Meanwhile, the total rural population of Bengal rose by 6.5% in the 1920s and 16.5% in the 1930s, west and east by now sharing the increase almost equally in percentage

19 *Census of India, 1931*, vol. 5, Bengal, pt 2, cited by M. Azizul Huque, *The Man Behind the Plough* (Calcutta, 1939), pp. 194, 125.
20 *Mymensingh SR* (1908-19), p. 29.
21 *Dacca SR* (1910-17), p. 50. The proportion of 'cultivated' to 'cultivable' land was 92% and the proportion of 'lands bearing more than one annual crop' to nett cropped area was 35%. Calculated from *ibid.*, App. J, 'Classification of Land Area', p. xcviii.
22 *Ibid.*, pp. 33-4.
23 *Census of India, 1921*, vol. 5, Bengal, pt. 1, pp. 132-3. See also a fascinating folk poem by an immigrant to Nowgong, Assam from eastern Mymensingh, Md Abdul Hamid, *Pater Kabita* (Juriya, Assam, 1930).
24 Radhakamal Mukherji, *Changing Face of Bengal*, p. 275.

terms, although the eastern districts still held an edge. Between 1941 and 1951, famine and forced migration following partition resulted in a 0.9% decrease in what became east Pakistan while there was an 8.5% increase in the rural population of the area that fell to west Bengal.[25]

As the pressure of population intensified after 1920, holdings subdivided and shrank in size. In the fertile regions of east Bengal, the number of uneconomic holdings multiplied as a function of demographic growth in the inter-war period. The process is more obscure in the infertile tracts of west Bengal: here a considerable fraction of the land in most holdings continued to lie fallow, but this may have been because the decline in the fertility of the soil made frequent fallowing necessary, and a large part was not, therefore, available for cultivation by an expanding population.

Estimates of the size of an economic holding varied between the extremes of 2½ acres for the most productive areas of the active delta and 10 acres for the single-cropped moribund delta. On a general view, 5 acres in east Bengal and 8 acres in west Bengal[26] were thought to be the minimum required to maintain a family of five. Against these estimates, the Director of Land Records and Surveys produced some chilling figures in 1938 for the Land Revenue Commission. On the basis of a survey, 41.9% of agricultural families were found to hold 2 acres or less, and 20.6% between 2 and 4 acres.[27] In 1940, there was slightly less than 1 acre of cultivated land per head of the agricultural population. The Commission concluded that the 'fundamental reason' for the difficulties of the rural population was that there was simply 'not enough land to go around'.[28] The process of diminution of landholdings was compounded by Hindu and Muslim laws of inheritance and from 1928 the right to transfer freely,

25 *Census of Pakistan, 1961,* vol. 2, East Pakistan; *Census of India, 1951,* vol. 6, West Bengal, pt 2.
26 A survey directed by P.C. Mahalanobis after the 1943 famine suggested a much lower minimum acreage figure. Two acres of paddy land was thought to be enough to ensure subsistence for an average family of five. See P.C. Mahalanobis, R. Mukherjee and A. Ghosh, 'A Sample Survey of the After-effects of the Bengal Famine of 1943,' *Sankhya',* 74, (1946).
27 *Report of the Land Revenue Commission, Bengal, 1938-40* (hereafter as *Land Rev. Coms. Report)* vol. 1, p. 86. (Alipur, 1940).
28 *Ibid.,* p. 74.

resulting in fragmentation of the diminishing holdings. The basic problem was not, however, the carving out of a number of holdings from the parent holding, but the increasing number of people that the original holding had to support. 'It is only the cultivation of jute,' observed a contemporary commentator, 'which partially compensates for the diminution of the size of the holding in the fertile districts. What is lost in area (in east and north Bengal) is gained, to some extent, by the produce in jute, and what is lost in fertility (in west and central Bengal) is partially made up by the increased size of the average holding.'[29] Concentration on the market aspect in arguments, either about rational peasant response to new opportunity[30] or of forced commercialisation of agriculture and imperialist exploitation through a 'mercantilist function',[31] has tended to leave the demographic background to the cultivation of jute in east Bengal out of account. In order to apprehend the nature of the commercialisation of Bengal agriculture, the analytic distinction between the social organisation of production and the wider economic system is indispensable. Plantation sowing of indigo on peasant fields in mid-nineteenth-century western Bengal was clearly a forced, unremunerative enterprise; opium advances also involved interference on the part of the trading and state machines in production decisions. In the post-indigo period in Bengal, however, capitalism in extracting the agricultural surplus did not follow the path of concentrating land and proletarianising the peasantry. In early twentieth-century Bengal, an agrarian system of scattered small peasant production was drawn into the capital's wider economic sphere of influence.[32]

29 Huque, *Man Behind the Plough*, pp. 124–5.
30 Dharm Narain, *The Impact of Price Movements on Selected Crops in India*, pp. 59–68; M.M. Islam, *Bengal Agriculture*, chapter 4.
31 Saugata Mukherji, 'Imperialism in Action through a Mercantilist Function' in Barun De (ed.), *Essays in Honour of Professor Susobhan Sarkar* (Calcutta, 1974), pp. 725–59.
32 The capitalist economic system had made much deeper inroads into the social organisation of production in the indigo economy and opium economy of the early and mid-nineteenth century than in the jute economy of the early twentieth. This apparent instance of retrogression might form an interesting problematic in a study of Marxian periodisation by economic stages. It has to be noted, however, that indigo was virtually confined to west Bengal and jute to the east.

The logic of the switch from the cultivation of a subsistence crop to a commercial crop for the world market on peasant smallholdings must be seen in the context of agrarian overpopulation.

To the smallholding east-Bengal peasant faced with a rapidly deteriorating land–man situation, jute held the attraction of not only a higher gross income,[33] but also a higher per-acre expenditure of labour energy. According to an estimate by the Director of Agriculture in 1930, labour input per acre in the normal cultivation season in the case of jute was 82 man-days, while it was only 39 man-days for aus rice and 33 man-days for aman rice (see table 2.2). The replacement of autumn rice by jute made it possible to use more than double the quantity of labour on the same area. But higher labour costs[34] and higher interest charges for jute[35] almost certainly cut into the higher gross returns it brought. The higher labour requirement for jute together with coinciding labour intensive periods of different crops

33 The Bengal Banking Enquiry Committee gave the following estimates of the gross value, cost of production and profit per acre of jute and rice:

	Average cost of production	Normal yield per acre	Harvest price per maund in 1928-9	Value of produce per acre	Profit
	Rs.	Maunds	Rs.	Rs.	Rs.
Rice (cleaned)	47	12.4	6.63	82.13	37
Jute	92	16.2	9.00	145.75	54

Source: *Report of the Bengal Provincial Banking Enquiry Committee 1929–30*, vol. 1, p. 27.

34 Estimated labour cost per acre of jute, aus paddy and aman paddy

	Jute	Aus	Aman
Estimated total labour cost 1929–30	Rs. 61.50	Rs. 29.25	Rs. 24.25
Estimated total labour cost 1936–37	Rs. 30.75	Rs. 14.63	Rs. 12.38
Estimated labour charges paid 1929–30	Rs. 20.50	Rs. 9.75	Rs. 8.08
Estimated labour charges paid 1936–37	Rs. 10.25	Rs. 4.88	Rs. 4.13

Source: Huque, *Man Behind the Plough*, p. 105.

35 See below, chapter 4.

Table 2.2.

Labour expenditure per acre of jute, aus paddy and aman paddy

	Jute Man-days per acre	Aus Man-days per acre	Aman Man-days per acre
Land preparation	14	14	14
Weeding	25	16	2
Harvesting	20	8	9
Carting	—	1	—
Extracting, etc.	23	—	—
Transplanting	—	—	8
Total	82	39	33

Source: Evidence of the Director of Agriculture, Bengal Provincial Banking Enquiry Committee 1929-30 cited by M. Azizul Huque, *The Man Behind the Plough* (Calcutta, 1939), p. 104.

in a double-cropped area[36] led peasant families to make some use of hired labour. Accepting on an impressionistic basis the family-hired components of labour on an average holding to be in the ratio of 2:1, labour charges paid per acre would have been about Rs. 20 for jute and Rs. 9 for paddy in 1929-30 and Rs. 10 for jute and Rs. 4 for paddy in 1936-7. It is likely that, as in the case of Russian smallholders growing flax, the net profits earned by jute cultivators of Bengal were low except in years of an extremely favourable market situation. The forcing up of labour intensity and the augmentation of gross income were probably most often achieved at the price of lower unit-labour payment. This transgression of the optimal limits of labour use is explicable in terms of Chayanov's theory that diminishing returns of the value of marginal labour do not impede the

36 The sowing, transplanting and harvesting dates for jute and paddy cultivation were approximately as follows:

	Sowing	Transplanting	Harvesting
Capsularis Jute	March		July-August
Oliturius jute	April		September
Aus rice	March-April		July-August
Aman rice	June	July-August	December-January

Jute had much the heavier labour need than paddy for weeding in the early stages and for stripping and washing after harvest. The stripping-washing operation would happen at the time of aman transplanting.

peasant family farm's self-exploitation until family needs are satisfied.[37]

As Bengal's single predominating 'money-crop', jute proved especially susceptible to severe fluctuations of price.[38] Jute and aus rice were direct and easy alternatives in the crop cycle and short-term switching between the two was possible. It is known that the responsiveness of the acreage of the two crops to relative price was positive though low, and peasants tended to grow one if the price of the other had been discouraging the previous year.[39] This option of falling back on aus rice would be closed when the jute and rice markets were both depressed, as happened over an extended period during the 1930s slump. The unavailability of any suitable alternative cash-crop that could replace jute greatly restricted the scope for substitution. Jute acreage which once and for all had taken an upward jump in 1907 stubbornly refused to contract significantly, even when its cultivation clearly became unremunerative.[40] Jute did not prove to be the panacea the hard-pressed peasant smallholders of east Bengal had hoped it would be.

Between 1907 and the 1940s, jute occupied 10-22% of the cropped area in the seven leading jute-growing districts of

37 For the peasant family without enough land and means of production for the complete use of all its labour, it is sometimes logical and advantageous to force up labour intensity, violating the optimal combination of production elements in its activity. This strategy, while losing on unit labour payment, increases gross income and effects a basic equilibrium between the drudgery of labour and consumption within the limits of agricultural activity at a level of well-being lower than would be the case of a farm optimal in size and proportions. The forcing up of labour intensity could be achieved by the intensification of work methods or by using more labour-intensive crops, e.g. the switch in late nineteenth and early twentieth-century Russia from oats to flax. The smaller unit labour payment derived from labour-intensive crops than from more extensive crops (except in years of highly favourable market situation) meant that peasant farms would resort to these only in a situation of an adverse land-man ratio where it was not possible to meet consumption needs with an optimal labour payment. See A.V. Chayanov, *The Theory of Peasant Economy*, (Homewood, Illinois, 1966), pp. 40, 113-16, 239-41 and *passim*.

38 A more detailed price-history is undertaken in chapter 3 below.

39 M.M. Islam, *Bengal Agriculture*, pp. 118, 124-5, 129.

40 The average cost of production of jute in the late 1920s was generally estimated at Rs. 5.50 per maund. See note by R.S. Finlow, Director of Agriculture, *Report of Royal Commission on Agriculture, 1926-28* (London, 1928), vol. 4, p. 81. The price per maund of jute fell below this level in 1929-30, reached its lowest point of Rs. 3 in 1933-4 and remained unremunerative until the end of the decade. The switch to autumn rice was not made as the rice market was equally

east Bengal.[41] How far did it displace food-crops and to what extent did peasants come to depend on it? Jack's enquiries in Faridpur, which relate to the jute boom period of 1907–13, give some insights into this question. 'It is probable,' Jack wrote, 'that no cultivator has ceased altogether to grow his own food.'[42] He pointed out that although nearly all the land in east Bengal was suitable for rice, only a portion was suitable for jute, and it was rare that the entire holding of any cultivator was fit to grow jute. The cultivator tended in that period to grow jute on all the land fit for the purpose and to grow rice and other food-crops only on the remainder, preferring to buy rice to meet any deficiency in family needs. While the jute market was buoyant, this strategy paid off on the whole, though in some years, dipping prices left very small margins. In every 100 families, about 35 grew all their food on their land, 25 needed to work as labourers to cover a deficit and 40 bought grain because they either preferred to grow jute or were unable to feed themselves, but 'certainly far more often' because they preferred to grow jute.[43] The outbreak of the First World War broke the jute cultivators' idyll:

At the beginning of the present war, the jute market collapsed completely, and as a result for the first time in many years, cultivators in Eastern Bengal were short of money to buy their food

depressed. There was some talk about growing more sugarcane, but it did not encroach upon any significant proportion of the jute acreage during the depression decade. A marketing infrastructure for sugarcane (a perishable crop) was non-existent, and there were few sugar-mills in the jute-growing east Bengal districts. The Second Jute Committee was led to conclude that 'in particular in *char* and *bil* areas and in low-lying areas jute must continue to be the principal crop without any substitute'. See *Report of the Bengal Jute Enquiry Committee, 1940* (Chairman L.R. Fawcus) cited by B.B. Chaudhuri, 'The Process of Depeasantization in Bengal and Bihar, 1885–1947', *Indian Historical Review* 2, 1 (1975), p. 118.

41 For the percentage of jute area to net cropped area in each of the Bengal districts in 1936–37, see Huque, *Man Behind the Plough*, p. 59. Also, *Agricultural Statistics of India* (annual).
42 Jack, *The Economic Life of a Bengal District*, p. 85.
43 *Ibid.*, p. 86. The Mymensingh settlement officer reported on the extension of area under jute: 'The ryots came to look upon their harvest as the source from which they would meet all cash expenditures including rent, new houses, interest on their debts, etc. They only grew enough aus paddy to provide fodder for their cattle and to feed their families for the few months for which the previous aman harvest fell short. In many thanas, the bulk of the ryots did not even do this, and preferred to buy imported paddy out of the proceeds of their jute. When the prices fell during the war, they naturally suffered'. *Mymensingh SR* (1908–19), p. 28.

and it is probable that it will be many years before they again become so trustful as to grow less food than the family needs for the consumption of the year.[44] Jack's prediction of a probable aversion to jute in the future was proved wrong. In the interwar period, as the size of holdings diminished under the pressure of population, growing for subsistence via the market became the only viable strategy for the mass of east Bengal peasants. The Land Revenue Administration Report for 1930–1 described the situation in which the next major collapse of the jute market intervened:

Distress was worst in the jute growing districts, which owing to half a century of prosperity are densely populated, and where about half the population live on holdings of an acre in area or less. The rice that can be produced on such petty holdings cannot support them for a year; and in the past they have relied on the jute which they grow on part of their lands providing them with the wherewithal to supplement their food and pay the rents. With the fall in the jute market and their jute remaining unsold, they have been very badly hit.[45]

Faced with the problem of ensuring subsistence from a diminishing holding, the Bengal peasant, especially in the east, laid himself open to the vagaries of the world market own which he had little control. The complex of credit relations, which critically affected the liquidity of the internal economy, transmitted external influences on to the internal market. A few weakly monetised sectors of the rice economy persisted in areas where produce-sharing and grain-lending intermediary rural elites shielded the primary producers from the direct impact of the market. More widespread was the incidence of an inelastic cash demand on the peasantry, which had made it imperative for rice producers to be at least partially involved in the grain market. In the nineteenth century, within a limited market, prices had responded to the internal supply situation determined by good or bad harvests. As the grain market expanded in close integration with commodity production

44 Jack, *ibid.*
45 *Report of the Land Revenue Administration in Bengal, 1930–31* (Calcutta, annual) p. 5.

for the industrial west, the price system became increasingly subject to international rather than internal conditions. Its sensitivity to crises in the world capitalist economy was complicated by the colonial government's financial manipulations.

The intensification of demographic pressure was one powerful force which propelled the commercialisation process in twentieth-century Bengal and significantly moulded its nature. The peasant world of Bengal was now oriented to a novel set of market opportunities and risks. The prices of the Bengal peasants' produce were determined by the conditions of demand in remote markets and the state of the Indian currency. The following section will briefly chart the external fluctuations that were transmitted to the internal economy and take stock of the pressures of an unstable world market and colonial political economy that came to bear on the Bengal countryside.

The context of the world market and the colonial political economy

From about 1870 onwards, an export–import sector of Bengal's rural economy, based on the export trade in rice, jute, tea, oil-seeds and hides and the import trade in cotton cloths, salt and sugar, grew rapidly under the aegis of European capital. In speaking of 'an export–import sector', however, it is necessary to steer clear of the analytic cul-de-sac of 'dualism' which views western capitalism as an alien enclave in a traditional economy.[46] The dualist perspective obscures the keen sensitivity of Bengal's regional economy to external fluctuations, and under-development, in any case, had less to do with 'sectoral distortions'[47] than with the fundamental aims and logic of metropolitan

---

46 The lack of any developmental impact of a growing export surplus on the internal economy has tempted at least one historian to discern 'a dualistic pattern of colonial economy' and to characterise the export–import sector as 'an island isolated from the rest of the economy'. Rajat Ray, 'The Crisis of Bengal Agriculture 1870–1927 – the Dynamics of Immobility', *IESHR*, 10, 3 (1973), pp. 252–3.
47 *Ibid.*

Table 2.3 Value of major exports of Bengal (in Rs. lakh) ·

Year	Total	Raw jute	Jute manufactures	Tea	Opium	Oilseeds	Grain & pulse	Hides & skins	Lac
1900-1	5400	1036	779	907	612	416	426	556	105
1905-6	6722	1561	1239	645	702	232	631	776	315
1910-11	7787	1361	1692	845	1061	608	695	685	211
1915-16	8788	1489	3789	1467	147	159	204	627	171
1920-1	10 830	1583	5285	734	253	361	93	277	758
1925-6	14 602	3599	5874	1771	193	433	384	485	688
1930-1	8114	1246	3185	1464	122	328	236	333	311
1935-6	6122	1317	2346	1095	—	123	113	246	158
1940-1	10 277	783	4510	2256	—	187	—	124	225
1945-6	13 157	1584	5926	2876	—	282	172	113	433

Note: The 1900-1 to 1935-6 figures relate to exports from Calcutta; those of 1940-1 and 1945-6 include the subordinate ports of Bengal as well. The total includes less important exports not listed individually.
· 1 crore = 10 million = 100 lakh.
Source: Annual Report on the Maritime Trade of Bengal.

Table 2.4 Distribution of the foreign trade of Bengal 1900–01 to 1940–41: percentage share of total trade

Year	Britain	Australasia	China-Hong Kong	Straits Settlements	Ceylon	Egypt	Mauritius	S. Africa	Canada	Germany	Belgium	France	Austria	Italy	Russia	U.S.A.	Japan	Java	Burma
1900-1	47.8	4.5			4.6		2.1			7.6						7.3			
1905-6	43.8	5.6	6.4	3.6	2.5	0.5	1.0			7.6	2.1	3.0	2.7	1.8	0.6	10.1	0.4	1.1	
1910-11	40.9	4.0	5.3	3.9	2.5	0.6	1.0			6.7	2.5	2.9	2.1	1.8	1.1	9.3	1.3	4.8	
1915-16	46.7	4.4	0.5	2.0	0.9	0.5	0.6			0.1	0.0	2.5	0.0	3.5	3.7	14.1	1.1	5.6	
1920-1	44.0	3.0	0.9	1.5	0.9	0.8	0.4	0.5	0.8	1.7	1.8	2.0	0.1	1.1	0.1	21.1	4.6	3.9	
1925-6	36.2	3.7	0.6	2.1	1.0	0.8	0.5	0.9	1.1	6.4	2.3	3.5	0.1	2.1	0.1	17.1	3.8	4.3	
1930-1	30.7	4.7	0.7	2.4	1.3	2.2	0.5	1.1	1.4	6.4	2.4	2.4	0.1	1.9	0.4	16.1	5.3	4.6	
1935-6	35.9	3.6	0.4	2.5	0.9	1.1	0.4	1.2	1.8	6.7	2.3	1.9	0.2	1.6	0.7	14.5	8.5	0.7	
1940-1	33.3	4.3	0.5	2.5	0.9	1.5	0.5	1.7	2.3	0.0	0.3	0.2	0.0	0.2	0.8	18.2	4.1	0.8	14.6

Note: Bengal's trade with Burma appears under the 'foreign' trade classification only after the separation of Burma from British India in 1936–7; but Burma was, of course, an important trading partner of Bengal even before. We can calculate from data under 'coasting' trade that the percentage of Bengal's trade with Burma to its total 'foreign' trade was in the earlier period 4.6% in 1900–1, 9.3% in 1915–6, 8.9% in 1920–1, 8.1% in 1925–6, 24.3% in 1930–1 and 21.0% in 1935–6.

Source: Annual Report on the Maritime Trade of Bengal.

capitalism. On the other hand, the case of external determination has been carried to extreme lengths by the votaries of a hold-all and explain-all 'colonial mode of production',[48] weakening the analysis of the rich detail and variety of the internal social organisation of production and the understanding of the set of linkages that transmitted disturbances in the world economy to even the relatively self-contained sectors of the internal economy. In the present discussion, the world capitalist system is kept analytically distinct from the inner workings of the regional economy, although its ultimate dominance is acknowledged.

A high proportion of Bengal's foreign trade in the period of 'high imperialism' conformed to the classic colonial pattern of exchanging raw agricultural produce for manufactured goods of the industrial economies of the West. Imperial Britain was the dominant trading partner, though this dominance was much more marked in imports than in exports. The value of Bengal's export trade stood at Rs. 54 crore at the turn of the century and nearly tripled in the next quarter of a century (see table 2.3). The value of raw jute exports rose from Rs. 10 crore in 1900 to Rs. 36 crore in 1925, but the export values of oil-seeds, grain and hides showed no significant upward trend. During this period, the trading ties with Britain slackened a little, and the industrial nations of Continental Europe, the USA and Japan stepped into the breach (see table 2.4). Trade of quite a different order developed with Burma which supplied paddy, mineral oil and teak and received jute manufactures, til-seed, tobacco and betelnuts, and to a lesser extent with Java which sent sugar and accepted jute manufactures.

The growth and spread of Bengal's foreign trade brought the region's economy increasingly under the influence of forces of economic change of an international character. As a proportion of total agricultural production, exports were probably not very large. The best estimate for the whole of India puts it between 9% and 17% in the late 1920s.[49] The

---

48 See, for instance, J. Banaji, 'Capitalist Domination and the Small Peasantry', *EPW* 12, 33 and 34 (1977), pp. 1375–404; Hamza Alavi, 'India and the Colonial Mode of Production', *EPW*, 10, 33, 34 and 35 (1975), pp. 1236–62.
49 *Central Banking Enquiry Committee*, vol. 1, pt 1, cited by B.R. Tomlinson, *The Political Economy of the Raj 1914–1947* (Cambridge, 1979), p. 10.

disproportionate impact of the external economy has recently been provided with a monetary explanation. The import of funds from abroad to pay for agricultural exports was 'qualitatively the most important way in which the money supply was augmented each year'.[50] This ensured that the world demand for Indian currency and movements in interest rates in financial centres outside India had a decisive influence on the state of the entire monetised economy. The linking of the internal and external financial systems by the government's monetary policy merely intensified this impact. Difficulties in obtaining remittances to meet obligations in London entailed regular government interference with the currency and the money market, reducing the domestic credit resources for exports and forcing foreigners to import currency. The close intermeshing of the export and local trading sectors, notably the fact that they depended to a great extent on the same money market meant that the effects of these monetary manipulations were felt in the region's economy as a whole.[51] By the early decades of the twentieth century, the fluctuations of demand in the world market and the foreign buying price of the rupee had become the key determinants of the price of Bengal's produce.

In the early years of the twentieth century, the tug of demand in the primary produce markets of the industrial West was strong, and the prices of Bengal's growing exports

According to K.M. Mukerji, *Levels of Economic Activity and Public Expenditure in India* (London, 1962), table 3, as much as 30% of the value of total agricultural production was exported in 1913. Tomlinson works out a proportion of 17% for 1913-14, p. 169.

50 Tomlinson, *The Political Economy of the Raj*, p. 24. This external monetary factor would, in theory, have a powerful impact in the absence of internal cash balance reserves. Tomlinson is reluctant to accept the Keynesian argument that after the closure of the mints the only way in which the money supply in India could be increased was the import of funds through the Council Bill system. (See J.M. Keynes, *Indian Currency and Finance* (London, 1913), pp. 57-8; K.N. Chaudhuri, 'India's International Economy in the Nineteenth Century: A Historical Survey', *MAS*, 2, 1, (1968), pp. 49-50. He acknowledges, however, that since the domestically supplied money market was inelastic and unresponsive (funds for agrarian trade often being held in bullion) the import of funds to pay for export crops came to play a critical role in the annual augmentation of the money supply. See Tomlinson, *The Political Economy of the Raj* pp. 24-9; 35-44 and *passim*.

51 *Ibid.;* C.J. Baker, *An Indian Rural Economy 1880-1955: The Tamilnad Countryside 1880-1955* (Delhi, 1984), chapter 2, gives an excellent account of

rose steeply.[52] Between 1906 and 1913, the market in raw jute enjoyed its greatest and probably only period of boom. During the First World War, however, the inflated aggregate export prices were not reflected in rising incomes for primary producers. The jute manufacturers and exporters were able to exercise their monopsony power as purchasers of raw jute to push their losses to the peasantry, and then, capitalising on the wartime demand for the manufactured rather than the raw article, reaped a windfall.[53]

The government meanwhile had decided to secure its war supplies by resorting to the printing of money against 'credit' building up in London. The note circulation in India increased from some Rs. 66 crore in 1914 to Rs. 153 crore in 1919.[54] The increased money supply chased fewer goods available in the economy as imports had fallen off. Shortages and high prices of essential commodities became the order of the day. In spite of a burgeoning export surplus,

'the connections between the external and internal economies'.

52   *Index numbers of export and import prices of Bengal*

Year	Import price	Export price	Year	Import price	Export price
	(10 major articles, unweighted)	(13 major articles, unweighted)		(10 major articles, unweighted)	(13 major articles unweighted)
1898–1901	100	100	1921–2	276	205
1907–8	117	125	1922–3	239	227
1908–9	112	119	1923–4	230	215
1909–10	109	110	1924–5	216	225
1910–11	113	128	1925–6	192	227
1911–12	116	124	1926–7	175	198
1912–13	117	133	1927–8	174	197
1913–14	117	134	1928–9	170	192
1914–15	122	135	1929–30	163	186
1915–16	141	138	1930–1	134	135
1916–17	199	162	1931–2	119	108
1917–18	263	165	1932–3	103	102
1918–19	308	190	1933–4	106	97
1919–20	312	247	1934–5	113	101
1920–1	344	229	1935–6	107	106

Source: Annual Report on the Maritime Trade of Bengal.

53 The profit ratios of the manufacturing and exporting firms are estimated in Saugata Mukherji, 'Imperialism in Action through a Mercantilist Function', p. 741. The 'huge income drain from the agriculture of east Bengal', during the war is also discussed in Rajat Ray, 'The Crisis of Bengal Agriculture', pp. 264–6.

54 Baker, *An Indian Rural Economy*, p. 111.

the government resisted pressures to increase the exchange
value of the rupee until 1917, thereby distorting the terms of
trade against Bengal's products. The worst effects of the
Government's inflationary policy were seen in the east-Bengal
countryside where grain prices rocketed in the early part of the
war and articles of daily use such as cloth, salt, kerosene and
medicines were scarce and dear at a time when raw jute prices
remained low.[55] A spate of agrarian violence swept the land.

After a short-lived postwar boom (1919–20), Bengal's
foreign trade was caught in the web of the worldwide
depression of 1920–2. The rupee exchange rate, which had
risen in 1917, fell drastically during the slump, and the
wartime 'credits' were never really recovered by the primary
producers of Bengal. However, as recovery in the postwar
industrial world got under way, demand for raw materials
picked up and reached record levels. Between 1923 and 1925,
the foreign demand and prices of Bengal's agricultural
produce looked in an exceptionally buoyant state. Yet the
period of high prices in the aftermath of the First World War
was not as prosperous as has sometimes been supposed. The
prices of Bengal's two most important crops, rice and jute,
lagged behind the all-commodities price indices, and the
terms of trade remained unfavourable for the agricultural
sector throughout.[56] It was only the devastating impact of the
1930s slump, which left the whole economic and social fabric
of rural Bengal in tatters, that made people look back with
some wistfulness on the halcyon days of the 1920s.

By 1926 there had been a slowing down in the rate of growth
in demand in the industrial West, and primary produce prices
started to weaken. Supply of agricultural produce was
outstripping demand in the world market, and a price crash
was postponed only by government efforts to protect its
internal economies through price-support schemes. In 1929,
there was a glut and prices tumbled.[57] This crisis in agrarian
production and prices coincided with a massive disorder in the
industrial economies of the West, to which the industrial
nations responded with the erection of protective tariffs,

55 Shah, Abdul Hamid, *Krishak Bilap* (Mymensingh, 1921), pp. 17–19.
56 See chapter 3 below.
57 W.A. Lewis, *Economic Survey 1919–1939* (London, 1949); V.P. Timoshenko,
　　World Agriculture and the Depression (Ann Arbor, Michigan, 1933).

policies of deflation and huge cutbacks in foreign lending.[58] These measures served to reinforce the trade slump and accentuate the fall in agricultural prices. Peasant production, however, proved to be much more inelastic than manufacturing production. The export of primary produce did not consequently fall as much in terms of volume as the trade in manufactures, but continued to be sold at drastically reduced prices. From 1933, the industrial economies began to recover, but long-term shifts in demand meant that much of the agrarian world did not emerge from the depression until the close of the decade.[59]

The trend of rising value and prices of Bengal's exports of the last half a century underwent a dramatic reversal during the slump. The total value of exports, which had risen to Rs. 146 crore in 1925-6, was down to Rs 61 crore in 1935-6, and export and internal prices over the same period more than halved. Bengal's internal economy could hardly have remained immune from the world crisis. A key factor in the annual augmentation of the money supply of the regional economy was, as we have seen, the flow of the foreign funds to pay for agricultural exports. Since export crops were usually cultivated on credit, the liquidity of the economy depended to a great extent on the rate of circulation of credit instruments.[60] The lower levels of the credit and marketing chain were staffed by men whose capital was small or who worked entirely on a commission basis, and these levels were characterised by a very rapid turnover of funds.[61] The overall flow of credit was determined by a gigantic financial superstructure consisting of the formal indigenous banking sector, the export–import firms and the exchange banks registered in London, and was influenced by government monetary policy. Over the period in which the demand for Indian produce was strong and the balance-of-payments on the whole showed a surplus, this flow was maintained. One rather rough index of the inflow of capital into rural Bengal is the import of gold in the early decades of this century (see table 2.5). As the depression struck

58 C.P. Kindleberger, *The World in Depression 1929–1939* (Stanford, Calfornia, 1973).
59 A. Maizels, *Industrial Growth and World Trade* (Cambridge, 1963), pp. 79–110.
60 For a more detailed analysis, see Baker, *An Indian Rural Economy*, pp. 121–7.
61 See chapter 3 below.

Table 2.5. *Flows of gold into and out of Bengal from 1896-7 to 1945-6*

Quinquennium	Average annual flows of gold in Rs. lakh		
	Import	Export	Balance
1896-7 to 1900-1	258.86	1.84	+ 257.02
1901-2 to 1905-6	581.00	11.21	+ 569.79
1906-7 to 1910-11	421.21	10.73	+ 410.48
1911-12 to 1915-16	264.84	18.43	+ 246.41
1916-17 to 1920-1	533.68	92.84	+ 440.84
1921-2 to 1925-6	35.76	7.00	+ 28.76
1926-7 to 1930-1	26.16	0.01	+ 26.15
1931-2 to 1935-6	0.41	79.69	- 79.28
1936-7 to 1940-1	0.11	4.22	- 4.11
1941-2 to 1945-6	4.76	0.04	+ 4.72

Note: the figures include both government and private trade in gold that had to pass through the Chief Controller of Customs at Calcutta port.
Source: Annual Report on the Maritime Trade of Bengal.

at the roots of Bengal's export trade and cast shadows on the future exchange rate of the rupee, the foreign investors and lenders and their banking agencies were scared away from holding surplus funds in rupees. The shrinking of commodity exports and capital imports upset the balance-of-payments position, and led government to meet its remittances to London by raiding the currency reserves. As a result, in each of the years 1929-30 and 1930-1, the money supply fell by some 6%.[62] The government was also compelled to borrow in India to meet a budget deficit, which briefly pushed up interest rates and reduced funds available for agrarian trade.[63] There was, of course, nothing new in the government's tinkering with currency and credit. In a healthier economic climate it had not deterred foreign firms from importing funds; but now, with Bengal's export prospects looking bleak, they withdrew operations. The local money market did not fail to feel the effects, and in the early part of the 1930s, the liquidity of Bengal's agrarian economy dried up.

In September 1931, the rupee was in effect devalued against gold, as it was tied to the pound sterling which had been taken off the gold standard. From this date, the

62 The figures relate only to circulating currency and deposits in foreign banks, K.M. Mukerji, *Levels of Economic Activity*, cited by Tomlinson, *The Political Economy of the Raj*, pp. 36, 171.
63 *Ibid.*

direction of Bengal's gold flow was decisively reversed.[64] A good part of the exports constituted a considerable dis-investment by the agrarian population of Bengal since gold had been offered as a firm security for loans. The proceeds from these gold sales must in part have gone to pay for the now expensive imports, and in part were probably channelled, as rural moneylending became quite unprofitable, into investments in the urban sector. Money credit in the rural areas became exceedingly scarce. We shall have occasion later to return to the material distress and psychological insecurity that the loss of gold symbolised in the Bengal countryside.[65]

The reduction in liquidity kept prices depressed. The prices of jute, rice and oil-seeds reached their nadir between 1932 and 1934, and remained quite low until 1937–8. The volume of the export trade, which had diminished by not more than 15–20% in the years between 1930 and 1933 on its 1929 level, revived and reached the 1920s level in the latter part of the decade.[66]

The outbreak of the Second World War closed off markets for Bengal's agricultural exports, notably raw jute, and witnessed an unprecedented inflation of prices. The market for raw jute was extremely weak, and even though the government moved at long last in 1940 to compulsorily regulate the jute acreage,[67] the relative price of this famous cash-crop of Bengal remained weak in a period of high inflation. The inflationary pressures, resulting largely from public expenditure expansion in a war economy, were of a magnitude several times greater than was the case at the time of the First World War. Nearly Rs. 3500 million were spent on defence purposes in India between 1939 and 1945.[68] Civil and military construction was carried on in Bengal on a far bigger scale than elsewhere, and the inflationary pressures in this region were consequently more acute. While some half

64 Madras displays a very similar pattern in flows of treasure. Cf. Baker, *An Indian Rural Economy*, chapter 2.
65 See chapter 4 below.
66 S.N. Sengupta, 'The Depression', in Radhakamal Mukherji (ed.), *Economic Problems of Modern India* (London, 1939), p. 334.
67 On the background to this measure, see chapter 3 below.
68 N.C. Sinha and P.N. Khera, *Indian War Economy* (Calcutta, 1962), cited by Baker, *An Indian Rural Economy*, p. 128.

of the total war expenditure was 'recoverable' as sterling
credits accumulated in London, for the present it had to be
financed to a very great extent by printing rupees in India.
The money supply rose from Rs. 317 crore in 1939 to Rs.
2190 crore in 1945.[69] Since the sterling balances were
regarded as assets against which the Reserve Bank of India
was 'entitled to print notes about two and a half times their
total value', the recoverable war expenditure had a vastly
disproportionate inflationary effect.[70] Meanwhile, imports
had dropped drastically and government purchases of war
material diverted some goods from home consumption.
Serious shortages developed in essential commodities like
cotton textiles, kerosene oil and, most important of all, food.
With so much money about, prices soared beyond the reach
of the vast majority of the rural population. It was in an
environment of a spectacular price boom that the great
Bengal famine of 1943 occurred.

In the long period of international instability that
stretched from the outbreak of the First World War to the end
of the Second, agrarian Bengal was subjected to a series of
external shocks of different kinds, characterised in particular
by a great volatility of price movements. During both the
price-fall of the late 1920s and the 1930s and the price-rise of
the 1940s, the external terms of trade moved against Bengal's
agricultural export products. Throughout the entire period
from the First World War until grain prices rocketed during
the Second, the internal terms of trade were against its
agrarian sector. The disruptions caused by world-market
fluctuations were merely exacerbated by the colonial
government's monetary policies in moments of crisis.

To complete the portrait of the unstable economic world
in which the Bengal peasant lived, it is now necessary to see
more closely how these various crises were brought home to
him. The slump, for instance, might be announced when the
village bepari would fail to turn up at his doorstep after
harvest, and walking to the market he would discover that no

---

69 R.N. Poduval, *Finance of the Government of India since 1935* (Delhi, 1951), pp.
    119-20, cited by Baker, *An Indian Rural Economy*, p. 129.
70 D.R. Gadgil and N.V. Sovani, *War and Indian Economic Policy* (Poona, 1943),
    cited by Amartya Sen, *Poverty and Famines: An Essay in Entitlement and
    Deprivation* (Oxford, 1981), p. 75.

one was prepared to pay a remunerative price for his produce. He would be unable to service his debt with the mahajan, and would consequently be refused a loan for the following year. He would be angry, and perhaps set alight the mahajan's haystack, but somehow be able to struggle through the depression at a much reduced standard of living. If he could not grow enough food for his family's yearly needs in a period of scarcity and rising prices, starvation would be staring him in the face.

We must next look at the peasant's involvement in the major produce markets in close connection with the subsistence question, and then turn to the question of the peasantry's debt and the working and rupture of systems of rural credit relations.

3

Subsistence and the market II: The peasants' produce

The Bengal peasant's encounter with the market economy was fraught with inequities and uncertainties. The inequities were imposed by a marketing structure, unwieldy in appearance, but highly efficient in short-changing the primary producer. The uncertainties stemmed from wildly fluctuating price levels, determined by the state of demand in remote markets and the exchange value of the Indian currency, which the peasant could neither control nor influence.

In rural Bengal, in a sense it was not so much a case of the peasant going to the market, as of agents of the market coming to his doorstep. It was reported from Rangpur, for instance, in 1926 that 'almost 75% of most of the important crops find their first market in the houses of the producers themselves'.[1] Small itinerant traders known as paikars in north Bengal and farias elsewhere, or even the slightly bigger men called beparis, travelled from door to door after the crops had been harvested, buying from individual peasant households in small quantities. The peasants did frequent the hats, periodic markets held usually twice a week, where together with small-scale retail trade, some collecting business was done by middlemen for export from the locality. These were scattered in profusion all over the countryside. In the mid-twenties, the average distance between one hat and another was only four miles, and there was one for every 1000 of the male population of 15 years and

1 SDO Nilphamari to collector Rangpur in *Marketing of Agricultural Produce in Bengal 1926* (Registrar of Cooperative Society, GB, Calcutta, 1928). The Central Jute Enquiry Committee confirmed that 75.1% of Bengal's jute crop found its first market in the village of the producer.

over.[2] It was a great social and economic institution of the rural interior, and the peasant would in fact visit more than one hat as they were of easy access and gathered on different days – either to buy or sell something, or sometimes simply to exchange gossip, a much-valued rural commodity. It was much more rare, but not altogether impossible in the event of geographical proximity, for peasants to sell part of their paddy directly to the milling centres, and jute to agencies of the baling firms in the bigger mofussil trading marts. There was one other kind of market – the melas or annual fairs – but these were mainly concerned with the cattle trade, even though a great variety of other articles were also bought and sold.

This chapter will focus on the marketing mechanism and the trends in the markets of jute and paddy, the two crops which were by far of the greatest commercial importance in Bengal.[3] It is difficult to say with accuracy how much of the total agricultural produce entered the market. Jute was grown almost entirely for the market. It was the dominating cash-crop of Bengal, although its cultivation was virtually confined to the eastern districts. The situation with regard to paddy was much more complicated. It was first of all the staple food for the great majority of the people of Bengal. The Paddy and Rice Enquiry Committee entrusted with the investigation of the slump in the rice market commented in 1940: 'paddy cultivation in this province belongs to an order of agricultural economy which is still predominantly of the subsistence variety'.[4] Paddy was at the same time the most important commercial crop in a few districts of north and

2 *Royal Commission on Agriculture in India, 1926-28, Appendix,* vol. 14, p. 70.
3 Some proportion of almost every other crop did, of course, come on to the market. Oil-seeds were quite important, the chief varieties being rape-seed, mustard, til and linseed. There was an organised market in tobacco, especially in Rangpur and Jalpaiguri, from where it was exported by Arakanese and Tamil merchants. Bankura and Murshidabad were noted for lac cultivation and export. The impact of the markets in all these other commodities was, however, slight in comparison with the markets in jute and paddy. 'Note on Marketing of Agricultural Produce in Bengal', GB, A and I Dept, Agr. Br., File 5A-6/27, A Sept. 1927, Progs. 10-16 (WBSA), pp. 7-8; *Report of the Bengal Provincial Banking Enquiry Committee 1929-30,* Vol. 1 (hereafter *Banking Cmt. Report),* 105; *Bulletin District Bankura,* Bengal Board of Economic Enquiry (1935), pp. 7-8.
4 *Report of the Bengal Paddy and Rice Enquiry Committee* vol. 1, 1940 (hereafter *Rice Cmt. Report),* p. 12.

central Bengal and in almost all the districts of west Bengal. In contrast to jute, however, the marketed portion of paddy generally formed a small percentage of the total harvest of most cultivators. Nevertheless, in 1941, a marketing report estimated that as much as 44% of the total rice production was sold in the market at some level.[5] The rice market, even if small, relative to what was produced and consumed on the farm, had a close bearing upon the peasantry's subsistence concerns.

We will first analyse the marketing mechanism which extracted the peasants' surplus. Our purpose is not to examine the marketing pattern and hierarchy as a whole but simply to see how the primary producers stood in relation to it. Next, we will turn to tracking the trends in the produce markets over time, and see how the peasantry fared under different price regimes.

The marketing mechanism

Jute

The dispersed nature of peasant production meant that the jute grower had little bargaining power over prices *vis-a-vis* the highly organised trading sector.[6] In the interwar period, slightly over 50% of the total jute crop was taken by the mills that had sprung up around Calcutta, while the rest was exported abroad.[7] A long chain of middlemen handled the

5 *Report on the Marketing of Rice in India and Burma* (Delhi, 1941), p. 35.
6 The manufacturers and exporters of jute at the helm of what was in appearance a somewhat unwieldy marketing structure were bound together by the 'quasi-homogeneous' nature of their interests, many of the firms involved being interested in shipping as well as in manufacturing raw jute. These purchasers of jute had well-organised trade associations, of which the most important was the Indian Jute Mills Association. In spite of some internal rivalry, they were able to take many joint decisions regarding purchasing policy, particularly through the mechanism of short-time working of the mills and they had the ready ear of government officials. The peasants, on the other hand, operated under conditions of 'atomistic' competition. See Amiya Bagchi, *Private Investment in India* (Cambridge, 1969), pp. 266, 268-9, 286.
　　Bagchi also points out the European dominance in the internal jute trade. Firms like Duffus, Steel, Landale and Clark, Ralli Brothers, Sarkies and Company, David and Company, and R. Sim and Company, all had agencies in the mofussil trading marts of Narayanganj, Serajganj and Dacca. These merchants were organised into trade associations, such as the Narayanganj Chamber of Commerce. *Ibid.*, pp. 264-5.
7 *Banking Cmt. Report*, vol. 1, 104-105; *Report of the Bengal Jute Enquiry (Finlow Committee) 1934*, vol. 1, (hereafter *First Jute Cmt. Report*), p. 157.

movement of the produce from the village to the manufacturers and exporters. The lowest grade of intermediary was the paikar of north Bengal or faria of east Bengal who bought small quantities of jute at the peasants' houses or local hat and sold to the bepari. The beparis were local dealers, sometimes, but not always, moneylenders, who either bought directly from the cultivators or from the faria or paikar. The bepari could sell to paid agents of balers at outstations or directly to the balers and merchants who were to be found at the important steamer stations in east Bengal, such as Narayanganj in Dacca, Serajganj in Pabna, Sarisabari in Mymensingh and Chandpur in Tippera, and at the important trading marts on the railway line in north Bengal. The aratdar or warehouseman was a very frequent intermediary between the bepari and the European, Marwari or Bengali merchant at one of the major mofussil trading centres. The aratdar charged a rent for storage and also collected interest from the bepari. Sometimes the dalal or broker of the purchasing company took the place of the aratdar as an intermediary between the bepari and the baler. The broker was responsible for disbursing all advances made by the baling firm to the lower levels of the marketing chain.[8]

Very often each trading intermediary was merely a commission agent of the one just above him in the chain. The faria sometimes traded on his own small account, but more often as an agent of the bepari. The bepari, as the collector of Faridpur reported in 1926, 'usually works on a commission, but sometimes uses his small capital which he is able to turn over quickly and profitably especially during the jute season'.[9] The report from Tippera made plain the importance of the systems of financing brokers from the top: 'Very large capital is required to finance the jute crop. Beparis, aratdars and brokers supply some but the bulk is provided by the purchasing companies who borrow from banks.'[10] The margins that went to the different middlemen

8 'Note on Marketing of Agricultural Produce', GB, A and I Dept, Agr. Br., File 5A-6/27, A. Sept. 1927, Progs. 10-16 (WBSA), pp.1-2, 6-7 14-15; Evidence of J.M. Mitra, Registrar of Cooperative Societies, Bengal, in *RCA Report* vol. 4, pp. 137-8; *Banking Cmt. Report*, vol. 1, pp. 104-5.

9 Collector Faridpur to Registrar of Cooperative Societies in *Report on the Marketing of Agricultural Produce in Bengal 1926* (Calcutta, 1928).

10 'There are two systems of financing brokers. One on estimation where Rs. 5000

varied, but a substantial chunk of the cultivators' due was taken away by the middlemen as commission. The slice was estimated by the Director of Agriculture in his evidence to the Royal Commission on Agriculture to be 20%[11] and in the Commission's report itself at 'not perhaps far short of 20 or 25% of the current value of the crop'.[12]

In addition to commission charges and margins of profit taken by intermediaries, various other factors kept down the price received by the peasants. If the produce was sold in a hat, various tolls would be charged by the zamindar who owned the hat or by his lessee.[13] Tolls would also be imposed

or so is advanced at the beginning of the season, and as jute is received by the Company, 75% of the estimated value is paid to the broker for further purchases. In the other system, advances of a lakh or so are made to brokers who buy jute and store it with the Company. After assortment, further advances are made.'

Brokers dealing directly with the purchasing companies received a commission of 9 pies or 1 anna in the rupee. Collector Tippera to Registrar of Cooperative Societies in *ibid.*

11 Evidence of R.S. Finlow and K. Mclean, Director and Asst. Director of Agriculture Bengal in Evidence, *RCA Report* vol. 4, p. 13.

12 *RCA Appendix*, vol. 14, p. 70.

13 *List of articles with rates of tolls at Gafargaon Hat, Mymensingh*

Names of articles	Rates
1. Jute	6p. per md from the purchasers
2. Eggs	6p. per hundred and 8 as. per thousand from the purchasers
3. Fowl	4 as. per basket
4. Condiments	
(a) Vegetables	Varying from 3p. to 6p. per shopkeeper selling the articles
(b) Green chillis	6p. per seller
(c) Brinjals	6p. per seller
5. Wooden articles	
(a) Plough sticks	6p. per stick from the purchasers
(b) Plough	6p. per piece from the purchasers
(c) Yoke	6p. per piece from the purchasers
(d) Other wooden articles	6p. per piece from the purchasers
6. Other articles	
(a) Mat, etc.	6p. per piece from the purchasers
(b) Fish	6p. per seller
(c) Paddy and rice	6p. per bag from the purchasers
(d) Pulses & mustard	6p. per maund
(e) Pan (betel-leaf)	6p. per seller
(f) Iron articles	6p. per seller
(g) Cloth	6p. per seller
(h) Tobacco leaves	6p. per seller

Note: The rates relate to the late 1930s. Agitations against the payment of hat tolls were very common in east Bengal from the early 1930s and in north Bengal from 1939–40.

on the producers by middlemen. For instance, dryage allowance known as dhalta would be deducted in calculating the weight of jute.[14] The baler's agent was also notorious for manipulating the scales and local weights through his koyal or weighman.[15] There were other methods to force down the prices of jute. The most pernicious of all was the manipulation of the grading of different qualities of jute at the behest of the trading interests in Calcutta.[16]

Much more significant than the middleman's profits was the peasant's lack of holding power which compelled him to dump his produce immediately after harvest when prices were at their lowest.[17] Not only did he not have facilities of storage, but the small and indebted peasant required cash at the time of harvest to pay exorbitant interest to the moneylender and rent to the landlord. Jute was an expensive crop to cultivate, partly because of its higher labour costs, and consequently enlarged the credit needs of the peasantry. Often the jute cultivator received an advance called dadan on the security of the crop from a trader-moneylender. The district agricultural officer of Mymensingh, which supplied more than one-fifth of Bengal's jute, wrote:

In case of jute, cultivators are given dadans by jute agency people for growing a certain quantity of jute. . . the cultivators never get the

Sources: 'Levy of duties at hats and markets, and tolls on the rivers of Bengal', File 4-I-51, GB Rev. A. July 1940 Progs. 13-14 (WBSA).

14 Various other charges were levied known as mutti kabari (staff allowance), mutti baset, birti or newaj.

15 'Note on Marketing of Agricultural Produce in Bengal', GB, A and I Dept, Agr. Br., File 5A-6/27, A. Sept. 1927, Progs. 10-16 (WBSA), p. 7.

16 Length, gloss, colour and strength were taken into account in grading raw jute. The grades – 1,2,3,4 and rejections – would be manipulated in order to depress the prices. Sometimes, as the season advanced a little,·purchases of the top grades would be suspended by concerted action, so that later the same jute would have to be tendered against lower grades. Witnesses before the Banking Committee claimed that the loss to jute-growers on account of manipulation of grades amounted to several crore of rupees each year, *Banking Cmt. Report*, vol. 1, pp. 106-7.

17 The (unweighted) average prices of loose jute in Calutta were higher than the (unweighted) average harvest prices of jute in Bengal by 32%, 31% and 33% for the decades 1911-2 to 1920-1, 1921-2 to 1930-1 and 1931-2 to 1940-1 respectively. Bagchi, *Private Investment in India*, p. 287. The data, especially on harvest prices, is far from perfect, but it would appear that this divergence between harvest prices and the annual average of Calcutta prices was somewhat greater than the slice taken away as middlemen's commission.

prevailing market rate. The cultivators are entirely at the mercy of these 'dadandars' and have to dispose of the produce as dictated by dadandars.[18]

The system of dadan was quite widespread in the jute districts, although its terms varied. Basically, it constituted the enforced sale of the produce to the lender at a preferential rate, and was resorted to by the jute traders to get an assured supply of the crop. The interest charged on the advance ranged from 24% to 75% and the rate at which the grower bound himself to sell was generally lower by 10% to 25% than the market rate prevailing at the time of making the advance.[19]

Even where there was no dadan, cultivators required credit for cultivation expenses and for subsistence until the harvest. In Tippera it was found:

Funds for this purpose are provided by moneylenders who are often farias and beparis. But the security isn't the standing crop but general personal security of the recipient or mortgage. When the crops come to be sold, the lender, if faria or bepari, naturally insists on sale to him in order to liquidate the debt. In most cases this results in some kind of preferential rate in favour of the purchaser.[20]

The creditor was not invariably connected with trade, but was often a talukdar-mahajan. In that case, too, the harvest was the time to service the debt, and the general conditions of credit precluded the possibility of holding on to the crop and exercising any real freedom in marketing it. It had to be disposed of quickly for whatever price it might fetch.[21]

This picture of the organisation of the jute market relates mainly to the 1920s. The onset of the depression disrupted the flow of credit and led to substantial cuts in the elaborate marketing pattern. In a situation where peasant production failed to adjust to the weakening of demand, dadan became

18 District agricultural officer Mymensingh to collector Mymensingh in *Report on the Marketing of Agricultural Produce in Bengal 1926.*
19 'Note on Marketing of Agricultural Produce', GB, A and I Dept, Agr. Br., File 5A-6/27, A Sept. 1927, Progs. 10-16 (WBSA), pp. 15-16.
20 Collector Tippera to registrar Cooperative Societies in *Report on the Marketing of Agricultural Produce in Bengal 1926.*
21 The linkages between the product and credit markets are analysed in chapter 4 below.

largely unnecessary. It was possible to secure the required raw material at rock-bottom prices.[22]

Rice

Although the rice acreage in Bengal was seven or eight times greater than the jute acreage, as a commercial crop it was less important than jute. The greater part of the produce was consumed locally. Only a few districts, *viz.* Dinajpur, Bakarganj, the 24-Parganas and the districts in the Burdwan division had a regular trade in rice, and only the first two would appear to have had a definite surplus of production over local consumption needs.[23] Some rice from Bengal was exported overseas from Calcutta and Chittagong ports, and some went across the western border over land to Bihar, Orissa and the United Provinces. It is probable that these exports were made possible in the interwar period by a steadily rising trend of imports from Burma, and there is some evidence to suggest that finer varieties shipped abroad were replaced by coarser grain from Burma.[24] The total exports of paddy and rice to foreign countries as well as other Indian provinces was, however, by no means very large, and in the years 1933-4 to 1937-8, they constituted no more than 4.5% to 7.5% of annual production.[25] Over the same years, imports from Burma varied between 1.6% and 10.7% of annual production in Bengal.[26] The trade in rice was overwhelmingly interdistrict in character. But unfortunately there are no statistics relating to the movement of paddy and rice from one district to another. We have merely a general idea of

22 On the squeezing out of the local trading intermediaries during the depression and the concentration of the surplus-extracting mechanism by the monopsonistically organised jute industry in its own hands, cf. Saugata Mukherji, 'Some Aspects of Commercialization of Agriculture in Eastern India, 1891-1938', in A. Sen *et al.*, *Perspectives in Social Sciences 2* pp. 225-84. Also, see chapter 4 below.

23 *Banking Cmt. Report*, vol. 1, p. 106.

24 *Ibid.*, p. 23; Saugata Mukherji, 'Imperialism in Action through a Mercantilist Function', pp. 748-9. During the first two decades of the twentieth century, for which statistics are available, the exports of rice from Calcutta to east and north Bengal rose sharply. There was also a fairly high correlation between imports from Burma and total exports from Calcutta.

25 *Rice Cmt. Report*, vol. 1, p. 21. Owing to the discontinuance of rail and river-borne trade statistics between 1922-3 and 1932-3, the figures for Bengal's trade with the inland provinces are not available prior to 1933-4.

26 *Ibid.*, p. 22.

the 'surplus' and 'deficit' districts and the principal directions of the rice trade. The bigger rice mills were mostly located in the 24-Parganas, the west Bengal districts of Burdwan, Bankura, Midnapur, Birbhum, Hooghly and Howrah, and Dinajpur in north Bengal.[27] The geographical position of these major centres of the milling industry largely set the direction of their trade. Bakarganj had developed a substantial export trade in dhenki-husked rice to other east Bengal districts and to Chittagong from where it was sent abroad.[28]

The marketing mechanism for rice was similar in pattern to that for jute. But the chain of middlemen was somewhat shorter; each intermediary usually worked with his own capital and in most cases was not a commission agent of another intermediary of a superior grade. There were the local faria or bepari and goladar or aratdar on the one hand and the importing aratdar and merchant in Calcutta on the other. Sometimes the rice producers sold directly to the brokers of mill-owners in the districts. The margins of profit on which the intermediaries worked varied with local conditions, but as in the case of jute, a fair bit was taken away.[29] The system of dadan to needy cultivators on the security of the standing crop was not as widely prevalent as in the case of jute. In Dinajpur and Jalpaiguri, the rice-exporting districts of north Bengal, the big jotedars were the principal grain-dealers and they obtained half the crop on a sharecropping basis. They also made grain loans to tide the adhiar over the lean period, and recovered these in kind at the time of harvest at derhi or 50% interest. Almost everywhere the primary producers came under heavy pressure to sell at the time of harvest when prices were much lower. As was reported from the 24-Parganas: 'Prices are governed by the aratdars who dictate the terms. Producers being poor cultivators who are mostly indebted to Mahajans and who've

27 *Ibid.*, p. 14.
28 Evidence of J.M. Mitra, Registrar of Cooperative Societies, in *RCA Report*, vol. 4, p. 137.
29 'Note on Marketing of Agricultural Produce in Bengal', GB, A and I Dept, Agr. Br., File 5A-6/27, A. Sept. 1927, Progs. 10-16 (WBSA), pp. 1-2; Evidence of J.M. Mitra, Registrar Cooperative Societies, *RCA Report* vol. 4, p. 137; *Banking Cmt. Report*, vol. 1, p. 106; *Rice Cmt. Report*, vol, 1. pp. 49-50.

to pay off their rent to landlords are always in a hurry to dispose of their produce'.[30]

In all the paddy-growing districts, prices rose steadily at the onset of the monsoons when the rice merchants gradually released their stocks. These had been collected between the autumn or winter harvest months and February when prices were at their lowest.[31] So the rice-grower was forced to settle for the low harvest price. But he was sometimes saved from buying in a rising product market. During the non-harvest season, he usually lived on credit, which was often made available in the form of grain loans.[32]

Trends in the produce markets

In the last chapter we saw that prices in Bengal's internal markets were subjected to violent external fluctuations. Here we make a more detailed examination of the vicissitudes in the jute and rice markets that the Bengal peasantry encountered from the early years of this century to the Second World War and the great famine.

Jute

In the first decade of the twentieth century, demand from Dundee for raw jute was strong and growing, and this was reflected in the prices in Bengal. A substantial rise in the price in 1906 resulted in a spurt in the jute acreage in 1907. Between 1907 and 1913, except for one or two bad years, the jute market enjoyed a boom period. With the outbreak of war in 1914, the price fell suddenly by nearly 40% on its 1913 level. The European buyers of jute successfully combined to transfer the losses on to the jute cultivators, while cashing in on the demand for sandbags in the war zones to make enormous profits themselves. Prices recovered at the end of

---

30 Addl collector 24-Parganas to Registrar of Cooperative Societies in *Report on the Marketing of Agricultural Produce in Bengal 1926*.

31 *Rice Cmt. Report*, vol. 1, pp. 57-8.

32 This is not to say that the higher price of grains at the time of lending was not reflected in the terms of credit, notably in the interest rates, but it is of critical importance that until the late 1920s, grain redistribution belonged largely to the domain of the credit market rather than the product market. During the slump, as we shall see in the next chapter, a qualitative change took place in many areas in the character of 'grain loans'.

the war in 1919, only to go down again in the 1920-2 slump. It was not until 1922 that prices really picked up to their prewar level. Another brief boom peaked in 1925, and then the prices graph began to taper downwards, plummeting with the onset of the depression until it reached an all-time low in 1933 and 1934. Jute prices in these two years were 75% below the 1925 level and over 60% below the 1928 level. Prices rose again slowly from 1935, but jute was not to recover from the depression until as late as 1939 (see table 3.1).

The euphoria that jute cultivation created in the east Bengal countryside in the 1907-13 period was never to be known again. The boom in the aftermath of the First World War was, as the Bengal Provincial Banking Enquiry Committee put it, 'more apparent than real'.[33] A study of relative price indices shows that the rise in the price of jute and cereals lagged behind the all-commodities index. It was certainly much less than the rise in the prices of cotton manufactures. The terms of trade were against Bengal agriculture, and it is probable that the Bengal peasant got less real value for jute throughout the postwar period, despite high jute prices, than in 1913.[34] In 1907 the rustic poet of east Bengal sang in praise of the wonderful qualities of jute, or nailya as the jute plant was locally called. 'Say brother', he cried, 'there is no crop like nailya. The one who deals in jute has seven huts in his homestead and instead of the traditional bamboo, his four-roofed house is built on posts of strong Joanshahi timber'.[35] In later years, the woes of the jute cultivator became the burden of his song. The foolish peasant had embraced the fickle jute and sent good old paddy away to rot in exile in Rangoon.[36] The

---

33 *Banking Cmt. Report*, vol. 1, p. 65.
34 Capital, 15 Aug. 1929, cited in *ibid.*
35   Balo bhai, nailyar shaman kirshi nai.
           Nailya bepari, satkhanda bari,
           Joanshaiya thuni diya banchhe choari.
                              From the memory of Charu C. Chowdhuri
36 One poem describes a meeting of all the various crops and plants other than the
   arriviste jute with paddy presiding:
           Dhanya bale duiti katha shuno mor kachhe
           Tomader katha shuni aphshos hoiachhe
           Chharilo tomader hoilo durgati
           Rangoon deshete jano amar bashati
           Gariber lagia ami eshechhi sada

inordinately high costs of jute cultivation, the inevitable descent into indebtedness, the profits of the wily Marwari trader and the bane of over-production were harped on – themes that are beginning to be taken seriously by the economic historian of today.[37] Apart from the conditions of demand in the world market and the monetary factors which reduced the general level of prices, the fall in the price of jute was made more acute by over-production and stockpiling than for other agricultural produce in India.[38] The unorganised peasantry could not and did not combine to cut production. But the manufacturing interests restricted production by getting the Indian Jute Mills Association (IJMA) to push for shorter working days, and once again succeeded in cutting their losses. Between 1927 and 1934, there was a wide disparity between prices of raw jute and jute manufactures, although the situation began to change in favour of the raw product from 1935 onwards.[39]

The plight of jute cultivators quickly became a political

Kinia khailo dekho oishab gadha
Nalita dekho kata jatan karilo
Amay hela kore chhariat dilo
Tomra amake dekho karilet raja
Hoitechhe krishaker kata jeno shaja. . .
Abdul Samed Mian, *Krishak Boka*
(Ahara, Mymensingh 1921)

37 Beshi pata karo bhaire beshi takar ashe
Jemon asha temon dasha dena pater chashe
Taka taka majur diya niran kulan kam
Marwarira ghare boshe panch taka dey dam

Again

Eto pat dili keno tui chasha
Ebar pater chashe desh dubali ore budhhinasha
Bujhhli na tui burar beta, Abeder katha noyko jhuta
Khete habe pater gora thik janish mor bhasha
Mone korechho nibo taka,
She asha tor jabe phanka,
Panchiser poya habe tor, hrine probi thasha
Nibi bate taka ghare,
Peter daye jabe phure
Hisheb kore dekhish khata, jato kharacher pasha.
Abed Ali Mian, *Desh Shanti*
(Gantipara, Rangpur 1925)

38 *First Jute Cmt. Report*, p. 158.
39 *Report of the Bengal Jute Enquiry Committee 1940*, (Chairman L.R. Fawcus). vol. 1 (hereafter *Second Jute Cmt. Report*), p. 97.

issue. In 1928, Subhas Chandra Bose, who was then president of the Bengal Congress, had already directed the Congress Committees in the jute-growing districts to launch a propaganda campaign to restrict the jute acreage.[40] In 1932, the government decided to adopt the same tone. The IJMA did not oppose the propaganda, but would have nothing to do with it.[41] However, a government proposal to prepare and widely publicise an official statement about excess stocks of jute at the mills in Bengal and outside India was strongly opposed by the Bengal Chamber of Commerce.[42] In 1931, Naresh Chandra Sen Gupta of Mymensingh, a bhadralok champion of peasant causes, wrote a bill to control and regulate the production of jute through a central jute board as well as union boards and village jute boards by means of a system of licensing. The government decided to oppose it on the grounds that it 'interferes with the existing rights and is impracticable'.[43] The first Bengal Jute Enquiry Committee in 1934 saw no justification for compulsory regulation by legislative action.[44] Consequently, Congress and government propaganda for voluntary restriction met with a very limited response. The slight fall in production in 1931 and 1932 had probably more to do with climatic factors than with the propaganda campaigns. There was no real substitute for jute other than aus, and the rice market was also depressed. Besides, as someone pointed out to the second Jute Enquiry Committee, there was a psychological factor in operation as 'most of the cultivators wanted to steal a march over... (others) by not restricting their own areas'.[45] In 1940, the second committee eventually recommended the adoption of compulsory restriction with suitable penal measures and a nominal fee for licenses.[46] The Jute Regulation Act of 1940

40 Subhas Chandra Bose, 'Jute Cultivation Must be Reduced ' (circular dated 19 March 1928), printed in *Arthik Unnati*, April 1928.
41 'Jute Situation in Bengal', GB, A and I Dept, Agr. Br., File 1-J-11/1932 (1-2), B. Jun. 1933, Progs. 24-25 (WBSA).
42 Secy Bengal Chamber of Commerce to Secy A and I Dept, 6 Nov. 1928, GB, A and I Dept, Agr. Br., May 1929, Progs. 1-4 (WBSA).
43 'The Bengal Jute Bill 1931 by Dr. Neresh C. Sen Gupta, MLC', GB, A and I Dept, Agr. Br., File 1-A-10/1931(1), Feb. 1932 Progs. 4-5 (WBSA).
44 *First Jute Cmt. Report*, p. 40.
45 *Second Jute Cmt. Report*, vol. 2, cited by B.B. Chaudhuri 'The Process of Depeasantization', p. 118.
46 *Second Jute Cmt. Report*, vol. 1, p. 99.

implemented this recommendation and a jute commissioner and his staff were appointed to regulate the cultivation of jute. But by then, the Second World War had broken out, and a dramatically different phase in the price movement had begun.[47] The pull of demand for raw jute, however, continued to be relatively weak.

Rice

From the beginning of this century to the outbreak of the First World War, the price of rice climbed slowly but surely. It shot up in the first two years of the war, fell in the next two, and in a postwar boom reached a record high of over Rs. 7 a maund in 1920. The price level fell slightly in 1921 but, from then on, an upward trend was maintained until the late 1920s. From 1929, the price curve for rice entered a deep and long trough. The bottom years were 1932 and 1933 when prices were 60% below their 1928 level. They remained sluggish for much of the remaining decade. The 1938 price was still more than 50% below the level ten years earlier[48] (see table 3.1).

We have earlier taken note of the monetary shock waves from which no part of the monetised economy could remain immune. A comparison of the different price indices, however, shows that the price of ballam, the more common variety of rice, was not only below the all-commodities price index, but was also consistently below the prices of other food-grains and agricultural commodities except raw jute.

---

47 Jute prices increased during the war, but the real income of jute cultivators did not rise because of the rocketing of grain prices. Ostensibly to check the inflationary spiral, the Bengal government fixed the minimum and maximum prices of jute in 1943. The price ceiling proved to be a convenient instrument for the purchasers of raw jute in the immediate postwar years. The demand of MLAs to decontrol jute prices in the autumn of 1946 met with stiff opposition from the manufacturing interest and officialdom. See *Millat*, 12 July 1946; Gov. to Gov. Gen., 6 Sept. 1946, 20 Oct. 1946. L/P and J/5/153 (IOR).

48 Amartya Sen has taken only a long-term view of the price-history of this period. He writes, 'Prices had been more or less stationary for decades (the 1941 rice price was comparable to that in 1914).' (Amartya Sen, *Poverty and Famines*, p. 78). The 1941 rice price was indeed roughly comparable to the 1914 price but the period in between saw major fluctuations, including the drastic slump in prices during the liquidity crisis of the depression. The depression had a momentous impact on social relations in rural Bengal and deeply influenced the evolution of government policy on questions of food availability and food prices, and cannot be ignored in any analysis of the Bengal famine of 1943.

Table 3.1. *Index numbers of prices in Bengal 1914 = 100*

Year	Rice	Cereals	Raw jute	All commodities
1917	n.a.	92	65	145
1918	n.a.	110	75	178
1919	n.a.	163	115	196
1920	166	154	104	201
1921	144	145	83	178
1922	125	137	110	176
1923	112	114	90	172
1924	104	123	102	173
1925	147	136	154	159
1926	133	140	120	148
1927	144	139	93	148
1928	141	133	100	145
1929	114	125	95	141
1930	105	120	63	116
1931	71	76	49	96
1932	58	68	45	91
1933	57	66	41	87
1934	63	69	39	89
1935	62	75	50	91
1936	71	79	50	91
1937	67	77	56	92
1938	69	72	48	95
1939	75	n.a.	51	96
1940	84	n.a.	95	n.a.
1941	106	n.a.	n.a.	n.a.
1942	131	157	77	185
1943 Jan.	n.a.	260	125	250
1943 Feb.	n.a.	266	110	253

Note: The index numbers are based on Calcutta prices. Statistics on 'harvest prices' exist, but are less reliable, being in truth unweighted annual averages of prices in the rural areas. Calcutta prices are used as the aim here is to bring out temporal trends. The spread between village prices and Calcutta prices are discussed in pp. 72-9 above.

Sources: Index Numbers of Indian Prices 1861-1931 (Delhi, 1933) and annual addenda to 1940; for 1917-28, Bengal Provincial Banking Enquiry Report, vol. 1, 65; for 1928-38, Report of the Bengal Paddy and Rice Enquiry Committee, vol. 1, 25; for 1942-3, GB, ACCRI Dept, RI Br., Conf. File 13 of 1943, B. Oct. 1945, Progs. 1 conf. to 10 conf. (WBSA). Also, *Indian Trade Journal* (1920-44).

What we have here is a curious phenomenon: an unusually great and irremediable downhill slide in the price of the major food-crop despite an undoubtedly strong internal demand for rice from a growing population. To make sense of this disproportionate fall, one has to look at the special features of the rice market.

During the depression years, internal demand did not slacken, and internal supply bore no significant correlation with price. Production and available net export figures for the years 1933-4 to 1937-8 show a small increase in domestic consumption, except in the year 1935-6 when crops failed all over western and central Bengal causing scarcity and much distress.[49] The calculations of the Paddy and Rice Enquiry Committee also made it clear that there was no close relation between the variations in prices and the supply changes caused by harvest fluctuations. Given the inelasticity of internal demand, this indicated that there were other factors which had a greater influence than vicissitudes of output.[50] Indeed, in addition to the wider causes which affected the general price level, two factors, one on the demand side and the other on the supply side, may be seen to have contributed to the depression in paddy prices. On the demand side, there was a decline in Bengal's export trade. More importantly, on the supply side, there were huge exportable surpluses in Burma. These accounted for almost all of Bengal's imports and brought down internal prices.

From the middle of the 1920s, exports of rice underwent a dramatic decline as Bengal lost its markets both inside and outside India to the three great paddy-exporting countries – Burma, Thailand and Indo-China. The quinquennial annual average volume of exports to foreign countries for the years 1929-30 to 1933-4 was 27% below that in the previous quinquennium, and the triennial annual average for 1934-5 to 1936-7 was a further 19% below the figure for the preceding five years. Coastwise trade statistics show that Bengal's exports to Madras, which amounted to more than 100 000 tons of rice and paddy in each of the years 1923-4 and 1924-5, collapsed after 1925-6, and in the post-depression quinquennium averaged only 11 000 tons a year. Between 1934-5 and 1936-7, the average fell to 4000 tons. During this period, the Madras market was invaded by rice imports from Burma, Thailand and Indo-China, with exports from Burma alone rising from 343 000 tons in 1929-30 to 956 000 tons in 1935-6. The absence of statistics of rail and river-borne exports to other inland provinces of India prior to 1933-4 does not allow a comparison, but imports from Burma are known to

49 *Rice Cmt. Report.* vol. 1, pp. 11, 19-21, 33.
50 *Ibid.,* pp. 35-9.

Table 3.2. *Trend of imports of rice into Bengal from Burma*

Annual Average (tons)		Annual Average (tons)	
		1931–2	
1923–4	45 514	1932–3	303 578
1924–5		1933–4	
1925–6		1934–5	
1926–7	271 302	1935–6	502 832
1927–8		1936–7	
1928–9		1937–8	
1929–30	294 783	1938–9	366 000
1930–1		1939–40	
		1940–1	411 000

Sources: Report of the Bengal Paddy and Rice Enquiry Committee, Vol. 1, p. 41 and File 5A-22, GB Agriculture and Industries Dept, Agr. Br., B. Jan. 1942, Progs. 269-50 (WBSA).

have dislodged Bengal rice in these areas as well.[51] In a general climate of depression, this decline in external demand is likely to have accentuated the fall in rice prices in Bengal.

In the meantime, from the mid-1920s onwards, Burma was sending increasing quantities of rice to Bengal itself. The volume of imports fluctuated from year to year, but the construction of three-yearly averages from 1925–6, when there was a substantial increase, up to 1939–40, brings out the underlying trend of a steady rise (see table 3.2). Not only Burma but also Thailand and Indo-China, were placing increasing surpluses on the world market, which had a depressing effect on the international price of rice. While its own production surpluses rose, Burma was losing out to its two competitors in the western and far eastern markets from the late 1920s, forcing it to turn its attention increasingly towards the markets in India and Ceylon.[52] The presence of a large exportable surplus just across the border, both ready and able to swamp its markets, had a critical influence on rice prices in Bengal.

There are a number of reasons why Burma was able to cast its shadow so easily on the Bengal rice market. Basically, the

51 *Ibid.,* pp. 35-9.
52 *Ibid.,* pp. 33-5.

old and tired production regimes of the Ganges delta were not able to compete in costs with the young and virile frontier economies of the Irrawady, Chao Phraya and Mekong deltas. The costs of transport across the Bay of Bengal were low, while railway and steamer freights within Bengal were inelastic and high.[53] The marketing network in the Bengal districts were also ruptured as a result of the liquidity crisis in the depression. When in the 1940s, Burmese supplies were cut off, the government discovered that the internal marketing system was in shambles, and had to intervene directly to procure rice from the countryside for the principal urban markets.

War and famine

The Bengal National Chamber of Commerce had put forward a calculation in a memorandum to the government that the total requirement of rice in Bengal was in the region of 10.4 million tons, which was nearly 1.6 million tons in excess of the average annual production during the quinquennium 1932-3 to 1936-7. The Paddy and Rice Enquiry Committee dismissed the contention of the Chamber on the grounds that:

The calculations are based entirely on hypothetical consumption standards which may or may not prevail in real life. What we are concerned with, in this context, is not the food requirements of this province, but the effective demand for the food-crop by its rice-eating population. The former is a problem of nutrition, which raises far-reaching issues of national well-being; the latter is a severely limited problem of economics, in which we are interested at the moment.[54]

Having made a fairly thorough diagnosis of this 'problem of economics', the Committee prescribed a few measures to raise the price of rice to cure the rice market of its malaise. These included a remission of the export duty on rice if budgetary

---

53 *Ibid.*, pp. 77-81. The Rice Cmt. noted, 'During the last ten years [the 1930s], not only did freight rates fail to come down in sympathy with the fall in the general level of prices or in the price level of paddy and rice, but since 1935, the average rate of freight actually registered a slight increase', p. 79.
54 *Ibid.*, p. 33.

conditions permitted, and a control over the Burmese imports in the form of a duty on imports in excess of a prescribed quota.[55] But these recommendations were made in 1940, by which time the winds of inflation were already blowing. Powerful inflationary pressures created by massive government expenditure in a war economy pushed up prices. The price of rice was up by 33% in September 1940 and by 69% in September 1941 on its August 1939 level, and in March 1942, the index stood at 159.[56] The next quarter witnessed a very sharp rise. The fall of Burma in March diverted the demand from its rice markets in Ceylon, western India, Travancore and Cochin to the major rice-producing areas in India which had themselves lost the Burmese supplies. In Bengal, a net import balance figure of 296 000 tons for the first seven months of 1941 was turned into a net export balance of 185 000 tons over the same period in 1942.[57] There was no relation in terms of magnitude between the scale of the external demand caused by the cutting off of Burma rice and the dramatic price-hike. What is important is that at this point, a whole set of uncertainties connected with the fall of Burma sparked off vigorous speculative tendencies that were to become such a disastrous feature of the rice market in Bengal in the following months. In June, the government of Bengal made an attempt to fix the maximum price of rice, which failed because officials had no control over supplies; in July the government banned exports from the province except on permits.[58] By September 1942, prices appeared to have stabilised somewhat. In October, a severe cyclone struck western Bengal, destroying large parts of the aman crop in Midnapur and the 24-Parganas, and causing considerable damage in Burdwan, Howrah and Hooghly. The expectation of a poor harvest aggravated the tendency to speculative buying and panic hoarding. In the winter of 1942–3, as Amartya Sen puts it, 'a moderate short-fall of *production*' was translated into 'an exceptional short-fall in *market release*'.[59] The wholesale price of rice jumped from

55 *Ibid.*, pp. 45-8.
56 *Famine Enquiry Commission Report on Bengal*, (Chairman J. Woodhead) (Delhi, 1945) p. 217.
57 *Ibid.*, p. 28.
58 *Famine Enquiry Cms. Report*, p. 29.
59 Amartya Sen, *Poverty and Famines*, p. 76.

between Rs. 9 and 10 per maund on 13 November 1942 to between Rs. 13 and 14 on 11 December, and then sky-rocketed to Rs. 21 by 12 March 1943 and to over Rs. 30 by 21 May. According to unofficial reports, rice sold at more than Rs. 100 per maund in some districts later in the year.[60]

In the early part of the war, both the central and provincial Governments welcomed the price rise, which they believed would benefit agriculturists who had suffered during the long period of unremunerative prices. By the end of 1941, there was some concern in Delhi about wheat prices. After April 1942, there was growing anxiety about conditions in the rice markets.[61] Yet, some strange notions about the effects of the rise in agricultural prices in the Bengal countryside persisted in government circles. The revenue secretary's circular to district collectors as late as 14 January 1943 is a perfect example of high-flying bureaucratic prose compounded by lowly errors of perception:

The rise in the price of agricultural produce has. . . placed greatly increased purchasing power in the hands of the agriculturists which unless drawn off would merely push up the cost of living. Government therefore consider that this year should afford a marvellous opportunity to enforce collection of as near as 100 p.c. of the outstanding demand of agricultural loans as possible with a view to reduce the inflationary pressure due to the increased purchasing power of the people as also to restore the Provincial finances by setting right the loans position which is causing considerable anxiety to Government. I am therefore to request you to take a personal interest in the progress of the collections in your district and to do all in your power to ensure that the fullest advantage is taken of the present opportunity of recovering the bulk of the very large outstandings in your district.[62]

60 *Ibid.*, pp. 54-5.
61 *Famine Enquiry Cms. Report*, pp. 18-21.
62 B.R. Sen, Secy, Rev. Dept. to district collectors, 14 Jan, 1943; much before this circular went out, there had been a resolution in the Assembly brought by Rajibuddin Tarafdar of Bogura that certificate procedure for realisation of debt settlement kists and cooperative society debts should be suspended for one year from October 1942 to September 1943 and various representations to government from the districts urging the same owing to the poor prospects of the paddy crop and the economic dislocation caused by the war. See 'Note dated 15 Mar. 1943 from Secy to H.E. the Governor', GB, ACC & RI Dept, RI Br, Conf. File 13 of 1943, B Oct. 1945, Progs. 1 conf.- 10 conf. (WBSA). The outstanding agricultural loans in question had gone up from Rs. 32 lakh in April 1937 to Rs. 137 lakh in 1942. Gov. Bengal to Gov. Gen. India, 22 Oct. 1942, L/P & J/5/149 (IOR).

This directive provoked a horrified response from men on the spot and their communications to Calcutta, sent mostly in March 1943, give some idea of what high prices at this time meant for the peasantry in Bengal. In Rajshahi division, jute did not fetch a high price and the paddy harvest was much below the average. At the same time, there had been an abnormal rise in the prices of other necessities, such as cloth, kerosene and salt. It was discovered that 'except a few substantial men who have little liabilities to meet, the indebted peasantry as a class have either no stock of agricultural produce to sell at the present high prices or spend to pay for their other needs what they earn by selling their own small stock. It is the shrewd middlemen who are profiting themselves [sic] enormously through straight business or speculation or black market.'[63] In the Presidency division most of the cultivators had neither the patience nor the means to hold out. They had sold their produce at harvest-time to middlemen. 'Being needy and ignorant they could not fully reap the profit of the present high prices.' They could never imagine that rice could be sold at an unprecedented Rs. 20 per maund and were quite content to dispose of their produce at Rs. 9 or 10 per maund. Consequently 'very little of the present prices, now prevailing in the market, have gone into the pockets of the cultivators'. The cultivators had also been hit by the rise in the prices of necessities, and 'if they have got more in one hand on account of the rise in the prices of agricultural produce, they had to give out equally more [sic] in another hand for the purchase of other commodities of daily consumption'.[64] It was pointed out that in Dacca division 'the great bulk of the cultivators concerned have small holdings' and could hardly benefit from the high prices. In any event, the cultivators were 'finding less scope of augmenting their income by labour (except, of course, in

63 Dy Director Debt Conciliation, Rajshahi Dn to Asst. Secy. ACC & RI Dept, 26 Mar. 1943, GB, ACC & RI Dept, RI Br., Conf. File 13 of 1943, B. Oct. 1945, Progs, 1 conf.- 10 conf. (WBSA).
64 Dy Director Debt. Conciliation, Presidency Dn. to Asst. Secy. ACC & RI Dept, 30 Mar. 1943 in *ibid.*
    Bibhuti Bhushan Bandyopdhyay's novel *Ashani Sanket* located in the *abadi* (reclaimed) area of the 24-Parganas gives a graphic account of the impact of the unprecedented price hike on small paddy cultivators who had sold early.

areas where constructions because of war conditions are in progress)'.[65] In Burdwan division, where there had been a diminished harvest, a large majority of cultivators were actually purchasing rather than selling paddy.[66]

The strongest warning to government came from H.S.M. Ishaque, who was then Director of Rural Reconstruction and Chief Controller of Jute Regulation. He reported that in east Bengal, the price of jute in the early part of the jute season had been low, and that the later improvement had gone more to the middlemen than to the primary producers. Recent tours of the districts of Faridpur, Pabna, Mymensingh, Dacca, Comilla and Noakhali had made clear to him that 'businessmen excluded, the condition of the generality of cultivators is none too good. More jute means less paddy and the price of paddy at the moment is about one and a half times that of jute. Principal jute-growing districts cannot, therefore, be considered well-off' (cf. jute and cereals price indices in table 3.1). In the principal paddy-growing districts of western Bengal, the crop had been poor, and would-be sellers were having to buy. That left the only two paddy-surplus districts – Bakarganj in the south-east and Dinajpur in the north-west. In spite of the rise in the prices of other essential commodities, Ishaque reckoned that

the balance of advantage in these two districts would appear to be in favour of the cultivator, though. . . not in favour of all the cultivators. Only the haoladars and talukdars in Bakarganj and dewaniyas in Dinajpur can generally be expected to be really well-off and perhaps they are. But they form only a small minority of the total number of cultivators. The average cultivator is a small person and a very large majority are adhyars and bargadars with no lands of their own.

So Ishaque advised the government:

to give the matter their most serious consideration before they launch on any general drive of collection of old dues, especially

65 Dy Director Debt Conciliation, 'E', Dacca to Asst Secy ACC & RI Dept, 23 Mar. 1943, GB, ACC & RI Dept, RI Br., Conf. File 13 of 1943, B. Oct. 1945, Progs. 1 conf.-10 conf. (WBSA).
66 Dy Director Debt Conciliation, Burdwan Dn to Asst Secy ACC & RI Dept, 5 Apr. 1943; the ACC & RI Dept noted about paddy-growers all over the province in a briefing to the Governor: 'A large percentage of the cultivators are themselves purchasing paddy for family consumption, instead of selling' in *ibid.*

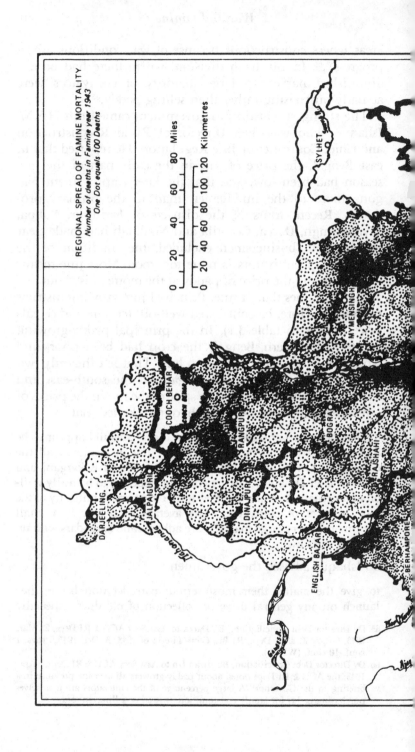

REGIONAL SPREAD OF FAMINE MORTALITY
Number of deaths in Famine year 1943
One Dot equals 100 Deaths

SYLHET

MYMENSINGH

COOCH BEHAR

RANGPUR

BOGRA

JALPAIGURI

DINAJPUR

RAJSHAHI

DARJEELING

ENGLISH BAZAR

BERHAMPORE

0   20   40   60   80   Miles

0   20 40 60 80 100 120 Kilometres

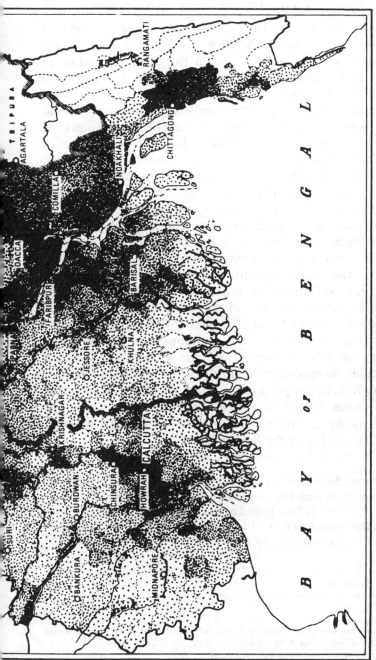

Map 5: Regional Spread of famine mortality
Source: S.P. Chatterji, *Bengal in Maps* (Calcutta, 1949)

during a period of such an acute food crisis as is prevailing today'.[67]

The near-landless and the totally landless were undoubtedly hardest hit by the unhealthy inflation of this period. Amartya Sen has recently shown the dramatic decline in price–wage exchange rates between 1939 and 1943 against labour.[68] The rates of mortality and destitution were predictably highest in the 'landless agricultural labour' occupational category.[69] The key feature of the agrarian class structure in most parts of Bengal, however, was a mass of smallholding peasantry tapering off into the landless strata. Sen does not undertake an analysis of the decline in the entitlement to rice of the smallholding peasantry – both jute-growers and rice-growers. Consequently, there is no explanation of the ways in which the famine affected the whole spectrum of the poor in the Bengal countryside.

Sen's study contains a discussion of the exchange rates between rice and commodities, such as wheat, mustard-oil, cloth, bamboo umbrellas, milk, fish and haircut.[70] But the more important question of the exchange rate of rice in relation to jute is left out of account. We have already noted the critical dependence of smallholding jute-growers of east Bengal on relative prices, and the vulnerability of that particular determinant of entitlement. During the Second World War, in a context of booming inflation and rocketing grain prices, the relative price of jute remained weak. The jute-growing, grain-deficit districts of east Bengal were the areas hardest hit by the famine.[71]

As for the rice-growers, Sen suggests:

One group that could not have suffered a deterioration of exchange entitlement *vis-a-vis* rice would have been the rice producers. This category would include large farmers as well as peasants. To some extent this would apply to share-croppers as well, since the share is fixed as a proportion of the output, which in this case is rice.[72]

67 'Note by Director of Rural Reconstruction and Chief Controller Jute Regulation' in *ibid.*
68 Amartya Sen, *Poverty and Famines*, pp. 63-7.
69 *Ibid.*,pp. 70-5.
70 *Ibid.*, pp. 67-70
71 *Famine Enquiry Cms. Report*, p. 1; P.C. Mahalanobis *et al.*, 'A Sample Survey of After-Effects of the Bengal Famine of 1943', pp. 337-400.
72 Amartya Sen, *Poverty and Famines*, p. 69.

This assertion is potentially misleading. In the late 1930s, the Paddy and Rice Enquiry Committee had attempted to make a quantitative estimate of the surplus and self-sufficient categories of rice-growers. Based on 'the testimony of mufassal witnesses' and 'the results of some special enquiries', they concluded:

the percentage of paddy-growers belonging to these two categories is extremely small. The great majority of the paddy-growers have neither a saleable surplus nor sufficient food to last them throughout the year. It is this third class that forms the bulk of the agriculturists of this province.[73]

So a large majority of rice-producers had to obtain grain either in the credit market or in the product market. In 1942–3 the diminished harvest reduced the direct entitlement of many rice-growers, especially in west Bengal, turning would-be net sellers into net buyers and would-be small buyers into large buyers. Moreover, many small peasants had sold immediately after the harvest and were taken unawares by the unprecedented rise in prices which took place later in the year.[74] As we have seen, the qualitative evidence of the decline in exchange entitlement to rice in 1943 of the small-holding peasantry, both jute-growers and rice-growers, is considerable.

73 *Rice Cmt. Report*, vol. 1, 27.
74 The government's policy of 'denial', which came into effect from April 1942, caused acute problems in the coastal paddy-growing districts of Midnapur, 24-Parganas, Khulna and Bakarganj. The policy was to deny transport and food-stuffs to the Japanese in the event of a landing by sea. The removal of boats 50 miles away from the coast involved considerable economic dislocation, especially in the sphere of marketing. Both the paddy trade and the trade in kerosene, mustard oil, etc, were affected; many fishermen lost their livelihood altogether; and it was impossible to ferry bargadars and cattle to carry on cultivation in the char areas. What government considered to be 'surplus stocks of paddy' were procured from the coastal districts and removed to storage depots in the north-west of the province. The Government of India placed Rs. 1½ crore at the disposal of the Bengal Government for the purpose, as the principal merchants refused to move the stocks unless it had the financial backing of the government. See Gov. to Gov. Gen., 8 Apr. 1942, 21 Apr. 1942, 6 Jun. 1942. 19 Jun. 1942, 7 Jul. 1942. 23 Jul. 1942 and 10 Aug. 1942, L/P & J/5/149 (IOR).
    A combination of natural calamity, government policy determined by strategic considerations and economic pressure to sell early had made a larger number of paddy-growers than usual dependent on a highly volatile food market. The lines of academic battle as at present drawn appear to subsume a variety of elements, not unconnected with one another, in any explanation of famine, under the rival categories of 'food availability decline' (see M. Alamgir, *Famine in South Asia* (Harvard, 1980)) or 'decline in exchange entitlements' (see.

The poor in the Bengal countryside appear to have been gripped by a feeling of helplessness as food disappeared beyond their reach. Between December 1942 and March 1943, there were some reports from the districts of sporadic 'crime' against property, paddy-looting and hunger marches.[75] As the year wore on and the crisis intensified, there were no further militant marches. In the autumn of 1943, rural Bengal bore the tragic spectacle of ragged, spiritless creatures trudging towards the urban centres in search of relief. Some 3 million died without a murmur during and as a consequence of the great Bengal famine.[76]

We have seen in this chapter how disturbances in the produce markets affected the peasantry. Yet, the historian cannot but be intrigued by the scale of the impact of the market-and-price mechanism on the livelihood of the rural population in the crisis of the 1940s, and the apparent absence of other forms of exchange. We saw that the bulk of the primary producers did not have a saleable surplus, nor sufficient food to last through a normal year. How did they survive? Although these small peasants would sell some proportion of their crop to meet cash obligations like rent and debt interest and cash payments for other necessaries, their involvement in the product market as buyers had, not so long ago, been limited or at least tempered by the operation of systems of rural credit. Even in the 1930s, the Paddy and Rice Enquiry Committee found on investigation into this question:

cash purchases of paddy by the growers of this crop in order to

Amartya Sen, *Poverty and Famines*, especially p. 63). The predicament of the small paddy cultivators in the Bengal famine would indicate that it is important to show how fluctuations in food-grain availability for peasant family economies (and this may happen without macro-level disasters) relate to their shifting exchange entitlements in the food market, and what bearing this has on the phenomenon of starvation.

75 Excerpts from reports of divisional commissioners and district officers in *Famine Enquiry Cms. Report*, App. 6, pp. 225-7. For a more detailed comment on the peasantry's response to the famine, see chapter.6 below.

76 The Famine Enquiry Commission's toll of 1.5 million deaths is a clear underestimate. For an excellent analysis of famine mortality, see Amartya Sen, *Poverty and Famines*, pp. 195-216. Also, Paul R. Greenough, *Prosperity and Misery in Modern Bengal: The Famine of 1943-1944* (New York, 1982).

meet the deficit of their annual requirements have become increasingly uncommon. Paddy loans rather than cash purchases are the method by which they adjust the gap between their actual consumption and their consumable surplus. Except in a few jute-growing areas, we were told that this was now the common practice in the countryside. It is a well-known feature of all loans in kind that their terms respond very little to changes in the price of the commodity in which loans are made or recovered. Consequently, the price of paddy does not directly influence the terms on which paddy loans are contracted. The evidence that we recorded in all parts of the province confirmed this finding.[77]

Before the slump, rural credit in cash and kind had played a critical role in the annual reproduction of the small peasant economy of Bengal. This sort of moneylending by different kinds of rural elites in different parts of Bengal did not amount to a benign village redistributive mechanism, and did not exclude exploitation in terms of surplus value being expropriated; but it included a reciprocal role of tiding the peasant over a time of need that recurred annually and of guaranteeing his subsistence in a year of scarcity.[78]

In the famine of 1943, charity was rare. Selfishness is understandable. But there were hardly any grain loans being made to dependent cultivators, and, of course, there was little money credit. The only way to get money to buy food was to sell any possessions one might have and to sell land. Whatever had happened to that ubiquitous figure on the rural scene of earlier times – the peasant's mahajan? To find out what happened, we now turn to the history of rural credit relations in the decades leading up to 1943.

77 *Rice Cmt. Report.* vol. 1, p. 28. A subtle but significant change was taking place, however, in the character of 'grain loans' during the 1930s, which the Rice Committee failed to notice. A relatively flexible system of 'grain lending' recoverable in kind was being replaced by a more rigid system of 'grain selling' on condition of deferred payment, often in cash, at the time of harvest. See chapter 4 below.

78 Cf. Scott, *The Moral Economy of the Peasant;* for a detailed analysis and assessment of these credit relationships, see chapter 4 below.

4

The peasantry in debt: The working and rupture of systems of rural credit relations

In early twentieth-century Bengal, the debt relation worked simultaneously as a mode of surplus-appropriation and as a vital factor in the reproduction of existing agrarian structures. Rent itself had by now become less important as a means of surplus-appropriation than the credit mechanism. At the same time, borrowing in cash and in grain for both cultivation and consumption purposes had come to play an integral role in sustaining production in the peasant economy and in its reproduction over time.

The reproductive function of the credit relation through the annual replenishment of working capital and a consumption fund of peasant families can be observed in relation to each of the types of agrarian social structure that predominated in the different regions.[1] The social composition and character of the creditor groups and consequently the nature of the creditor-debtor relationship varied, of course. As for the surplus-appropriating function, the relative importance of the rental and credit markets and the links between the two need further clarification. In the strongly market-oriented economy of east Bengal where raiyati rent was low and difficult to collect, the interlinked product and credit markets had developed into far more important channels of the drain on the peasantry. Some of the rentiers of old had learnt, however, to play the credit market. In west Bengal, rates of raiyati rent continued to be relatively high. The rent-collectors were involved to a much greater extent in the landholding and credit structures, and it was discovered in some districts in the 1930s that rental arrears formed a major portion of debts. In north Bengal, by contrast,

1 See chapter 1 above.

the revenue-collecting structure was indeed divorced from possessory dominion over the soil and the production process. In this domain of the rich farmer, debt interest was inextricably intermeshed with the crop share that was exacted as rent from the tiller.

No aspect of Indian economic history has been more written about and none left in a more confused state than the subject of rural moneylending. Lamentations that 'utter improvidence' and 'fondness for litigation' led to peasant indebtedness, which became part of British district officer culture, are not taken seriously any more. Yet, many issues relating to the social setting and social implications of borrowing and moneylending remain obscure. To this day, the mahajan of Bengal has eluded precise identification. There has been a recent tendency amongst historians to describe the interlacing of village landlordship, credit and trade in catastrophic terms. The 'jotedar' is variously defined as village landlord, big farmer or rich peasant, as well as the chief moneylender in the countryside.[2] This is not a valid generalisation. The point of departure in this respect still remains B.B. Chaudhuri's cautious and somewhat pessimistic remark. 'It is nearly impossible to ascertain which of the different groups dominated the rural credit scene. It is perhaps futile to look for a uniform pattern throughout eastern India.'[3] This does not mean that a generalisation based on an identification of the major patterns that prevailed in the different regions cannot be attempted.

The analysis of rural credit relations in this chapter seeks to consolidate further the typology of agrarian social structure and the links with the wider economic system that were formulated in chapter 1. The operation of systems of rural credit entailed an unequal symbiosis in social relations, which served to hold together the agrarian structure in Bengal. This chapter assesses the impact of the depression on credit in the different sectors of our agrarian typology, and examines how far and in what ways the symbiotic relationships were

2 R. and R. Ray, 'Zamindars and Jotedars', pp. 81-4; Abu Ahmed Abdullah, 'Landlord and Rich Peasant under the Permanent Settlement', *Calcutta Historical Journal*, 5, 1 (1980), pp.116-18.

3 B.B. Chaudhari, 'The Process of Depeasantization in Bengal and Bihar, 1885-1947', *Indian Historical Review*, 2, 1 (1975), p.129.

ruptured. The study of rural credit relations in the slump is in fact a study of the impact of the great depression on petty commodity producing peasantries in the colonial periphery of the world economy. The rupture that occurred in the 1930s is of critical importance in understanding the subsistence crisis of the 1940s as well as the nature of the social and political conflict that gripped agrarian Bengal (and much of agrarian Asia) in the final decades of colonial rule.[4]

Debt relations of peasant smallholders in east Bengal

Who were the moneylenders?

A Bengali tract, *Krishak Bilap*, published in Mymensingh in 1921, describes the genesis of two groups of moneylenders – sadharan mahajan (ordinary moneylenders) and bhuswami mahajan (landlords who were also moneylenders).[5] The writer, Shah Abdul Hamid, suggests that until the turn of the century, there was a separate class of 'professional moneylenders' or usurers who ran a profitable business by lending at high rates of interest. These mahajans lent out money on bonds (karjapatra). The great majority of their debtors would be peasants, who in most cases, were Muslims.

The debtor who regularly made his interest payment from the year's income from agriculture, the mahajan loved more than his eldest son. And since the principal lay with him, the mahajan blessed him saying, 'This time too the amount of my interest lies in your plot; may God provide a good crop, and may you live a hundred years' But be damned that debtor, the poor wretch who in three years would have been unable to pay a pice towards interest or principal. After three years, having impatiently waited through the period of limitation, he would eventually calculate the compound interest and put in a claim in the court for more than ten times the principal, and obtain a decree towards principal, interest and costs amounting to fifteen times the original outlay.[6]

4 On the social and political impact of the depression, cf. James C. Scott, *The Moral Economy of the Peasant*, pp. 114-56; Michael Adas, *The Burma Delta* pp. 185-208; Baker, *An Indian Rural Economy*, chapters 3 and 4; also, see chapter 6 and Conclusion below.
5 Abdul Hamid Shah, *Krishak Bilap* (Mymensingh, 1921), pp. 4-17.
6 *Ibid.*, pp. 4-5.

For a brief period in the later nineteenth century, the mahajan was able to siphon off the peasant's surplus simply through usury interest, while the landlord was unable either by law or the lathi, to collect the full rent. It was at this stage that the zamindars and talukdars of east Bengal decided to enter the credit market in a big way. According to *Krishak Bilap*, those who had liquid cash at hand were the first to take this step. The raiyat was tempted to enter into this new debt relationship with his rentier landlord in the hope of gaining temporary relief from the exactions of the 'professional moneylender', as the landlord's refusal to recognise a new purchaser could save him from being ultimately sold up for default.[7] The initial success of the pioneers in getting some return from this new business at harvest time encouraged others to follow their example, even if they themselves had to borrow to enter the field. Shah Abdul Hamid mentions a big zamindar in his locality who had Rs. 3 lakh invested in the money-lending business. He also notes with displeasure that even his neighbour, a Muslim talukdar, whose rental assets amounted to less than Rs. 75 per annum, had obtained a loan of Rs. 2000 from a Hindu mahajan by mortgaging the whole of his property and had distributed the sum in small amounts among his prajas at very high rates of interest.

This tract provides a plausible and intimate, albeit somewhat over-simplified, account of the emergence of an important section of the money-lending class in early twentieth-century east Bengal, *viz.* the talukdar-mahajans. The Bengal Tenancy Act of 1885 had given legal recognition to the shift in the political balance against rentier landlordism, and placed important curbs on enhancements. From the turn of the century, realisation of rent, especially by the smaller gentry, became increasingly difficult, and, if figures from Wards' and Attached Estates can be taken as an index, after 1907 there was scarcely a year when collection reached 50% of the total rental.[8] A section of the bhadralok, who had taken to service and the professions, were able to detach themselves from the land, and in the political arena

7 The right of free transfer of raiyati holdings was not legally recognised until 1928.
8 Annual Reports on the Wards' and Attached Estates, cited by Rajat Ray, 'Social Conflict and Political Unrest in Bengal, 1975–1908' (Cambridge Ph.D. dissertation, 1973), pp.113-15.

broke with the landed interests and led the radical stream of nationalist politics. Those who remained on the land tried to adapt to the changing means of surplus-appropriation. The rates of returns from alternative sources of investment, especially in urban areas, held little promise. It was, therefore, a question of playing the old game, but according to the new rules of the credit market. This adaptation was made possible in the context of a widening market for the peasants' produce.

Shah Abdul Hamid's use of the category 'ordinary moneylenders' or 'professional moneylenders', however, obscures the growth of the other important section of the moneylending class in this period – the trader-money-lenders. It had been common even for the traditional village mahajan to be involved in shopkeeping and in trade in agricultural produce. The expansion of the jute economy from 1906-7 enlarged the credit needs of the peasantry and increased manifold the importance of the form of credit known as dadan or advances on the security of the crop. As merchant capital flowed in to extract the valuable commercial crop, many country traders became commission agents of the purchasing companies in an elaborate marketing chain. Some also employed their own small capital. The vast annual flow of funds from the financial superstructure that was distributed in the form of dadan tied up with the smaller lagni or usury capital that circulated in the countryside.

Although the term 'professional moneylender' conveys little about the social background and precise economic function of the creditor, the only figures that we have on the number of moneylenders in the different districts come under this category. The number of moneylenders in proportion to the population was much greater in the principal jute-growing districts of east Bengal than in other parts of the province. Their number to every 100 000 of the population in the late 1920s was 280 in Dacca, 175 in Mymensingh, 150 in Faridpur and 134 in Tippera, as against the provincial average of 70.[9] Did the proliferation of the number of creditors and the existence of different elements within the moneylending class enable peasant debtors to play one off against the other and

9 *Banking Cmt. Report*, vol. 1, p. 194.

bargain over the terms of their credit? For a smallholding peasantry with heavy credit needs and little security to offer, this was not possible. As the settlement officer of Mymensingh reported, 'The mahajan has always as many demands on hand as his capital will sustain'.[10] Usurious rates of interest were commonly charged in all the districts, but the rates were even higher in east and north Bengal than in west and central Bengal.[11] Among the causes of usury, the Banking Committee mentioned 'low credit position of borrowers, absence of suitable financing agencies, limited resources of money-lenders, insufficiency of accommodation provided by co-operative societies and loan offices'.[12]

Although the debtor may initially have been tempted to switch to the landlord for credit as a bulwark against the demands of the non-landlord moneylender, it is clear that the talukdar-mahajan interested in reasonably regular interest payments and the trader-mahajan interested in the crop at a low price worked in effective, through not formal, collaboration. The talukdar-mahajan was usually not directly involved in the product market; but he could turn from declining rental income to usury only because of increased market penetration in east Bengal' agriculture. The bepari

10 *Mymensingh S R* (1908-19), p. 27.
11 This was the Banking Committee's general view, though it is not entirely clear from the figures it supplied. The rates of interest charged in the different districts in the late 1920s were of the following range:

West Bengal (%)		East Bengal (%)	
Burdwan	24-175 p.a.	Dacca	12-192 p.a.
Birbhum	15-37½ p.a.	Mymensingh	24-225 p.a.
Bankura	15-25 p.a.	Bakerganj	24-100 p.a.
Midnapur	12-75 p.a.	Faridpur	15-150 p.a.
Hooghly	12-37½ p.a.	Chittagong	15-75 p.a.
Howrah	12-175 p.a.	Noakhali	24-75 p.a.
		Tippera	24-75 p.a.
Central Bengal (%)		Rajshahi	18¾-75 p.a.
Nadia	37½-75 p.a.	Pabna	37½-300 p.a.
Jessore	18¾-75 p.a		
Khulna	25-37½ p.a.	North Bengal (%)	
Murshidabad	18-120 p.a.	Dinajpur	24-75 p.a.
Malda	10¾-75 p.a.	Rangpur	37½-66¼ p.a.
24-Parganas	15-150 p.a.	Jalpaiguri	10-50 p.a.
		Darjeeling	30-60 p.a.

Source: *Banking Cmt. Report*, vol. 1, p. 198.
12 *Ibid.*

involved in dadan karbar was on his part aided by the simple usurer, who made his interest demand at harvest time and deprived the primary producer of any freedom in marketing his crop.

It is sometimes wrongly suggested as part of the broad 'jotedar' thesis that the debt relation was mainly one between richer and poorer peasants.[13] There is no evidence that the predominently Muslim peasantry of east Bengal were involved in moneylending on a wide scale in the early part of this century. Registration Department reports showing that land transfers in the later nineteenth century took place mostly between 'raiyats' is no proof that the purchasers were the chief moneylenders. The Banking Committee's observation that there was 'not much loaning among agriculturists them-selves'[14] is substantially correct for east Bengal in the period prior to the great depression.[15]

The two major sections of the moneylending class in this period in east Bengal can be defined as trader-mahajans and talukdar-mahajans. In 1929-30 the Banking Committee's report on Bengal as a whole showed most mahajans were Bengalis, but a good many Marwaris had also taken to the business with conspicuous success.

Some of the mahajans are rich people and have acquired landed properties and rank among the territorial aristocracy, but the majority both in towns and villages are small people owning small capitals, on the income of which they manage to maintain themselves and their families. Mahajans are chiefly Hindus, but a very few Muhammadan money-lenders are also found in rural areas.'[16]

---

13 See R. and R. Ray, 'Zamindars and Jotedars', pp. 81-4, Abu Abdullah, 'Landlord and Rich Peasant under the Permanent Settlement', pp. 109-38.
14 *Banking Cmt. Report*, vol. 1, 65.
15 Some degree of differentiation and forms of exploitation within the peasantry had indeed emerged. The favoured means of surplus-appropriation, however, of those peasant families who possesed more land than could be brought under self-cultivation was under-raiyati rent and, in some cases, a share of the crop. By the early twentieth century, the intensification of population pressure in east Bengal meant that there was sufficient competition for the equivalent of a landlord's rent to emerge. Tenancy legislation having produced a category of occupancy tenants protected against rent increase, the competitive rent, often double the rate of raiyati rent, made its appearance only on that portion of raiyati land that was sublet to under-raiyats.
16 *Banking Cmt. Report*, vol. 1, p. 195.

A great majority of the talukdar-mahajans of east Bengal were high-caste Hindus while the small trader-mahajans were mainly drawn from the intermediate Nabashakh castes – Sahas, Telis and Baniks. These categorisations should not, however, be taken too rigidly. It was not unusual for a talukdar-mahajan to have bought some raiyati rights in land, or for a trader-mahajan to have acquired some talukdari as well as raiyati rights.

Debt in east Bengal in the early twentieth century
Evidence on the extent and burden of debt among the peasantry is somewhat scattered and the different sources are not easily comparable. Nevertheless, it is reasonably clear that indebtedness was widespread and that its volume steadily increased during the first three decades of this century. Annual interest payments were certainly a much heavier burden in this period than annual rent payments.

The first attempt at estimating the volume of indebtedness was made during settlement operations in Faridpur between 1904 and 1914. The average indebtedness per family of cultivators worked out at Rs. 55 per family, but as 55% of the families were said to be free from debt, the average per indebted family was Rs. 121.[17] According to a survey of a Faridpur village carried out on similar lines in 1927, the corresponding figures were Rs. 128 and Rs. 203, and 37% of all families were free from debt.[18] Another survey of 424 sample families of cultivators with permanent rights in land showed that in 1933 the family average of the total principal debt was Rs. 217; the average per indebted family was Rs. 262, and only 17% of the families were found to be free from debt.[19] The figures from these surveys[20] should not be taken too literally as

17 Jack, *Economic Life of a Bengal District*, pp. 77-8.
18 Note on Economic Survey of Talma Village by L.B. Burrows, Collector of Faridpur in *RCA Report*, vol. 4, p. 493.
19 Bengal Board of Economic Enquiry, *Bulletin District Faridpur* (Alipur, 1934), p. 4.
20 *Extent and volume of debt in Faridpur*

	1916	1927	1933
Percentage free from debt	55	37	17
Persons indebted			
(1) up to one year's income	43.5		
(2) up to two years' income		63	46
(3) more than two years' income	1.5		37
Average debt per family	Rs. 55	Rs. 128	Rs. 217
Average debt per indebted family	Rs. 121	Rs. 203	Rs. 262

the sample sizes and modes of enquiry varied widely, but they are a rough-and-ready indicator of the general trend in the volume and pervasiveness of indebtedness.

Surplus-appropriation through debt interest

The Dacca Settlement Report (1917) provides both an estimate of the amount of indebtedness as well as a comparison of debt interest and rent. The cultivator's 'payments to his landlord in rent, premiums and *abwabs* form [ed] but a small percentage of his gross earnings; the only danger, and that a vital one, [was] the result of his thriftlessness – his burden of debt and the consequent domination of the moneylender'.[21] The average indebtedness per family (or more accurately per homestead plot) was Rs. 121, which the settlement officer thought was an underestimate, and the figure per indebted family worked out at Rs. 256. An average rate of interest of 45% necessitated the annual payment of Rs. 21 420 000 to the moneylenders, which was approximately a fifth of the value of the total produce of the soil and five-and-a-half times the total amount paid as rent to the landlords. Every person supported by agriculture, while having to make an average rent payment of Rs. 2.50, was expected to make an annual interest payment of Rs. 12, or slightly less than a quarter of his average share in the produce.[22] The massive increase in indebtedness was believed to be a recent phenomenon:

Knowledge of past agricultural conditions is not sufficient to indicate the period when the tide of indebtedness commenced to flow, but it appears to date roughly from the passing of the Bengal Tenancy Act, the period when the value of the produce of the soil commenced to rise rapidly and the security afforded by the Act gave the cultivator a greater security for his thriftlessness.'[23]

The Mymensingh settlement officer in his report (1919) doubted whether the situation in his district was as bad as in Dacca, but acknowledged that 'interest is so high in this country that its payment constitutes a severe drain on the

21 *Dacca SR*, p. 50.
22 *Ibid.*, pp. 47-48.
23 *Ibid.*, p. 48. The 1885 Act ensured for the occupancy tenant moderation of rent and security of tenure.

resources of the agricultural population, especially as only a small fraction of the total indebtedness can be considered as capital employed productively. Apparently it has jumped from an insignificant sum to its present proportions in the last thirty years.'[24] The same observer believed 'the ryot's rent proper' to be 'the least important factor in his budget'.[25] During settlement operations in Pabna between 1921 and 1924, indebtedness was reported to be 'widespread and crushing'.[26] Two family budgets of the 'average typical cultivator' in the paddy-growing Sadar and the jute-growing Serajganj subdivisions gave the following figures:

	Number of family members	Cash income	Cash expenditure	Expenditure on account of debt
Sadar	4	Rs. 76.75	Rs. 84.25	Rs. 9
Serajganj	8	Rs. 166.50	Rs. 208.00	Rs. 45

The first estimate of the total agricultural debt in Bengal was made by the Provincial Banking Enquiry Committee, and it suggested a figure of Rs. 100 crore in 1929, and an average per agriculturist family of Rs. 160.[27] The report referred to 'the undoubted increase in the volume of indebtedness in recent years' but sought to dispel the notion that it could be ascribed to any genuine expansion of credit of the agriculturist consequent to high prices. It pointed out the adverse terms of trade for agriculture and that real value for jute obtained in the postwar period of high prices was probably lower than in 1913. It held that 'agricultural indebtedness is a mark of distress in most cases'.[28] This point is not difficult to grasp if we remember that the introduction of a high-value and labour-intensive cash-crop on peasant smallholdings was itself a mark of distress.[29] The high rate of interest was correctly recognised by the Committee as not merely the cause of indebtedness but also its effect. The Bengal Board of

24 *Mymensingh SR*, p. 27.
25 *Mymensingh DG*, p. 64.
26 *Pabna SR*, quoted in Bengal Board of Economic Enquiry, *Bulletin District Pabna* (Alipur, 1935), p. 6.
27 *Banking Cmt. Report*, vol. 1, pp. 69-70.
28 *Ibid.*, p. 65.
29 See chapter 2 above.

Economic Enquiry produced a figure of Rs. 97 crore as the total capital debt in 1933, and a family average of Rs. 187.[30] The samples from east Bengal districts showed family averages of capital debt in 1933 to be Rs. 286 in Dacca, Rs. 280 in Tippera, Rs. 265 in Chittagong, Rs. 156 in Pabna and Rs. 150 in Bogra.[31] By 1933, however, the system of debt interest as the principal mode of surplus-appropriation was already breaking down.

Between the waning of the landlords' rent offensive in the later nineteenth century and the dramatic acceleration in the velocity of the land market in 1938 lies the heyday of the creditor. The trader and moneylender (often the two roles were combined) were well in evidence in the nineteenth century, but it is in the period from about 1900 to 1930 that appropriations through the credit market in east Bengal completely over-shadowed those through the rental and land markets. Some of the creditors were, as we have seen, agents of the product market, and the operation of dadan or advances to secure the crop has been described in the previous chapter. Others operated within the context of the market, but were chiefly concerned with collecting usury interest. Mahajans advanced paddy as well as cash. The ordinary rate of interest on loans in kind was derhi or 50% per transaction but as the loans were given for periods of a few months between sowing and harvest, the annual interest rate was much higher. In Serajganj it was as high as 300%.[32] Most money loans were issued against bonds (karjapatra) without any security.

The Banking Committee found that in the province as a whole, 80% of the loans advanced by moneylenders were unsecured, but the value of secured loans to unsecured ones were in the ratio of 9:10.[33] Some loans were granted on promissory notes and on hand notes called hat-chita. Repayments towards the principal and the annual interest were entered by the moneylender on the back of the bond or in the hat-chita, and separate receipts were never given. Loans were also given on pledge of jewellery or other moveable

30 Bengal Board of Economic Enquiry, *Preliminary Report on Rural Indebtedness* (Calcutta, 1935), pp. 5-6.
31 *Ibid.*, p. 13.
32 *Banking Cmt. Report*, vol. 1, p.198.
33 *Ibid.*, p. 197.

property, such as brass utensils. Where land was offered as security, the usual form was simple mortgage with the mortgagor retaining possession, the period usually not exceeding one year. Other arrangements, such as kat kabala (conditional sale) and the so-called English mortgage (with an ostensible clause of reconveyance) were not unknown. But as the mahajan in most cases did not have cultivation of his own, the incidence of any form of usufructuary mortgage, most commonly known as khai khalasi, was not very widespread. The periods of limitation of these kinds of mortgages tended to be six years or more. The bulk of rural credit was, however, a year to year circulation and expropriation of funds. Most mahajans insisted on punctual and fairly regular payment of interest as this was their main source of liquid capital. In spite of the usurious rates of interest charged, the Mymensingh settlement officer found in 1919 that 'the ryot is not inclined to regard the mahajan as his enemy. As long as he can pay the interest, he is in no hurry to pay off the capital, and he has no fear of being sold up.'[34] Ten years later, the Banking Committee observed that 'although by reason of usury or harsh treatment, an individual moneylender may be disliked in the locality, there is seldom any expression of public opinion against his conduct'.[35]

The role of credit in the process of reproduction

Appropriating the surplus was only one aspect of the moneylender's role. The credit system was also closely integrated with the process of reproduction in the small peasant economy of east Bengal. It helped to keep the peasant family alive over the lean period in each production cycle and from one production cycle to the next, and replenished capital for cultivation expenses.

There was extensive borrowing in cash and in kind for subsistence needs between the end of the Bengali year in Chaitra (mid-April) and the autumn and winter harvests. In some areas, trader-mahajans exacted a maund of jute at harvest for a maund of paddy lent in the lean months, but this practice died out as the margins of profit from jute cultivation

---

34 *Mymensingh SR*, p. 27. For the politics of peasant-debtors, see chapter 6 below.
35 *Banking Cmt. Report*, vol. 1, p. 198.

diminished in the later 1920s. Another method was to undertake, on sattapatras, to deliver a fixed quantity of the produce in return for a subsistence loan granted during the difficult months before the harvest. The Banking Committee explained:

Apart from the necessity of food and seeds, which makes borrowing on such unfair terms possible, the agriculturist has frequently to borrow for hire of labourers during the cultivation season, specially for jute, which requires careful weeding and washing. In fact, the dadan or advance system is as much required by the necessity of the bepari to procure a sufficient quantity of jute as by the cultivator for weeding etc. Temporary loans lead to permanent debts.[36]

Litigation and social extravagance were certainly not major causes of indebtedness. In the village of Karimpur in Bogra, in 1929, 52 agriculturist families had a total debt of Rs. 9132 in cash and 159 maunds of paddy. The loans in kind had been necessary to meet annual food deficits. Of Rs. 2715 borrowed in cash in 1928-9, Rs. 1087 were taken for capital and permanent improvements including purchase of cattle, Rs. 573 for land-revenue and rent, Rs. 434 for cultivation, Rs. 389 for repayment of old debts, Rs. 150 for social and religious ceremonies, Rs. 15 for litigation and Rs. 66 for unspecified purposes.[37]

Impressionistic testimony of observers in other east Bengal districts also suggests that rural credit was a vital factor in the reproduction of the peasant smallholding structure. The Dacca settlement officer found it impossible in 1917 to determine the exact constituents of the mass of indebtedness, but he could discern a certain pattern:

After a successful harvest the average cultivator will spend the whole of his proceeds; he will doubtless add a weight of corrugated iron to his homestead; he will purchase the best cattle available and the remainder will quickly be spent on feasts or litigation. When the sowing season approaches, he is compelled to borrow; as the flood rises, he is compelled to sell his cattle owing to lack of fodder at a price that is seldom ¼ of the original cost; that is the only return of his harvest expenditure; to reap the crop he is ordinarily compelled to borrow again. There is little inclination to repay. This

36 *Ibid.*, p. 70.
37 *Ibid.*

indebtedness is practically of a permanent character and is treated by the cultivator as his capital.[38]

Feasts and litigation excepted, repairs to the homestead, purchase of cattle, cost of labour, must all be regarded as integral to the functioning of the peasant farm as an economic enterprise. The ecology of east Bengal and the intensification of pressure on the land made purchase of cattle a burdensome recurring expenditure. This particular item is stressed as one of the chief causes of indebtedness in a report from Tippera in 1926 which also highlights the connection between production and consumption needs.

cultivators require much money for cultivating expenses and for subsistence until the crop can be harvested and sold by them. The purchase of cattle is one of the heaviest items in the cost of cultivation. In some areas where cattle cannot be kept in the rains or when paddy crops are standing, cattle are purchased solely for ploughing and then sold to dealers who graze them in more suitable areas. In most areas there is heavy mortality from epidemics among cattle and replacements require capital. Many cultivators have exhausted their means of subsistence before the harvest.[39]

Borrowing connected with a reproductive process of a slightly different sort – marriage – was also of some importance. There was certainly a rush to take loans for this purpose just before the slump. This was to marry off minor daughters before the Sardah Act, which raised the age of consent, took effect in 1930.

By and large, the credit system served an important role in reproducing the peasant smallholding structure in east Bengal in the early twentieth century, while exploiting it ever anew.

The rupture in credit relations in east Bengal
During the 1930s, the system of rural credit relations that had evolved over the past decades came apart. The Land Revenue Commission declared in 1940: 'it would not be too much to say that at present rural credit is virtually non-existent'.[40]

38 Dacca SR, p. 47.
39 Collector, Tippera to registrar, Cooperative Society Bengal in *Report on Marketing of Agricultural Produce in Bengal 1926.*
40 *Report of the Land Revenue Commission Bengal,* Vol. 1, p. 76.

From 1926 the product market had begun to wobble; by 1930 it had collapsed. The credit pyramid that had been erected on it lost its foundation. With the cataclysmic drop in crop prices, the primary producers, especially the jute-growers, were extremely hard put to find the cash to meet their obligations and their necessities of life. A report from Tippera describes their predicament as well as that of their creditors:

> In normal times they would have tided over the crisis by resorting to the village mahajan, but on this occasion this source of supply was practically dried up. The village money-lenders scarcely have much accumulated balances; they deal in fluid cash, lending, realizing and lending again. In 1930 the arrangement was reversed; they realized little, their debtors could not pay and prospective borrowers could not get relief.'[41]

The talukdar-mahajans were sharply affected by their debtors' inability to pay. The better-off stopped lending – it was simply bad business to lend. The trader-mahajans occupied a somewhat different position in the causal circuit of the drying up of rural credit. Most of them operated as commission agents of the ultimate purchasers of the peasants' produce. The flow of funds from foreign firms and their banking agencies had formed a critical element in augmenting the annual money supply. Their withdrawal in the face of Bengal's gloomy export prospects resulted in a major liquidity crisis. Governments' policies in Delhi and London to deal with the international dimensions of the crisis further reduced funds available for agrarian trade and credit in the regional economy.[42] As the financial superstructure stopped disgorging vast amounts of liquid capital down the marketing and credit pyramids, the intermediaries were left high and dry. Not only did they lose their urban source of finance, but they also came under pressure from urban creditors who sought to recover what they could before getting out of the agrarian sector. The domestically supplied money market largely held its capital in bullion. From the autumn of 1931, following the delinking of the pound sterling from the gold standard, there began a massive outflow of gold from Bengal (as from other

41 D.M. Tippera to Under-Secy Poll Dept, 26 Dec. 1931, GB, Home Poll Dept Conf. File 849/31 (WBSA).
42 See chapter 2 above.

parts of India) together with an almost complete cessation of
the inflow that was characteristic of the earlier decades.[43]
Much of the gold and silver that came on to the market in this
period must have emanated from the hoards of bazaar-bankers
and trader-mahajans, and some was probably sold by
talukdars and the better-off among the cultivators. The move
away from the gold standard meant that profits were made on
sales of gold that had been acquired in recent years. However,
these were clearly not channelled into the unprofitable
business of rural moneylending, but went to pay for the now
more expensive imports and various forms of urban
investment. The loss of gold also implied a long-term loss of
credit for the rural sector as a whole. During the flight of
capital from the countryside, some initial attempts were made
to foreclose on mortgages. But these were effectively resisted.[44]
Unsecured loans were largely to be lost.

The impact of the liquidity crisis on the credit market in the
highly monetised economy of east Bengal is not difficult to
comprehend. The flow of money credit was reduced to a
trickle. But the impact on the smaller yet significant grain
sector of the credit market is more complex. The period of
expansion of the jute economy had seen a change in the
currency of lending from grain to an increased use of cash, but
the transition was far from complete. There were production
and consumption aspects of the credit needs of a smallholding
peasantry which had turned to cash-cropping in an
environment of shrinking resources, and the latter were in
part met by the issuing of grain loans in the months before the
harvest. During the depression the fairly elastic and informal
nature of 'grain-lending' was replaced by a much more rigid
system of 'selling grain on credit'. Indeed, the mechanism of
redistribution of grain which kept the peasant family alive
over the lean months and in bad years largely shifted from the
domain of the credit market to that of the product market.

In July 1930, the district magistrate of Bakarganj found
during his tour in the interior that two groups of people were
seeking paddy – the landless people living on labour or
charity for whom grain doles had to be arranged and

43 See chapter 2 above.
44 See chapter 5 below.

cultivators with land who had no money to purchase rice. The latter were anxious to buy rice and had approached the leading mahajans for credit. The mahajans were willing to advance rice, the present price of which was Rs. 4 per maund, at rates varying from Rs. 7 to Rs. 13 per maund to be paid in December. Local officers were trying to obtain rice from the merchants at a reasonable rate, around Rs. 5 to be paid in December. This they hoped to sell to people who wanted it on bonds, but the merchants were not ready to cooperate. The district magistrate wrote indignantly in his diary: 'the Mahajans while still holding out for their last pound of flesh are intimating to us that they are afraid of loot [ing]. We are doing what we can to reassure them but they are certainly provoking the danger themselves'.[45] In the principal jute-growing districts of east Bengal as well, together with the stoppage of money credit, there was an initial reluctance to hand out paddy loans. Over the decade, the character of grain redistribution, insofar as it continued, changed from lending to selling, on condition of deferred payment fixed for the next harvest at a much higher price.

There were two aspects of the immediate political response of the peasantry to the dislocation in the product and credit markets. On the one hand, the indebted peasants combined to refuse interest payments to the moneylenders. The commissioner of Chittagong division wrote of the situation in Tippera district in 1931:

In ordinary economic conditions I do not think propaganda against paying rents to landlords and interest to mahajans would be possible in this district because nearly every cultivator goes to a money-lender for a loan each year. This year the money-lenders recovered nothing and so have had no money to give out.[46]

The main purpose of the numerous instances of agrarian protest in this period was the destruction of debt bonds. At the same time, in the first two years of the depression there were cases where moneylenders, especially those who had stocks of paddy, were besieged by people who produced bonds and begged for loans. Refusal, which was the usual response,

45 Bakarganj Collector Donovan's Tour Diary, July 1930, Donovan Papers (SASC).
46 Cmsner Chittagong Dn to Ch. Secy, 28 May 1931, GB, Home Poll Dept, Conf. File 105/31 (WBSA).

provoked anger; moneylenders' property was often damaged and a number of moneylenders were murdered.[47]

After the initial spurt of anger, the economic response of the peasantry to the rupture in rural credit relations had to be one of adjustment to the new situation. This involved both readjustment of consumption patterns at a lower level and less rigour in the choice of inputs for carrying on agricultural operations. Given the small size of most holdings and the primitive technique of cultivation, there were not many instances of land going out of cultivation in east Bengal. There is considerable evidence, however, of the use of fewer and poorer cattle and the reluctance to resort to hired labour unless absolutely necessary.[48] Figures from six mauzas in Pabna showed that between 1928-9 and 1932-3 the average family income fell by 55%, while expenditure fell by 45%.[49] The reduction in expenditure on consumption items would partly be explained by the fall in the prices of the commodities bought, such as cotton clothes, but there was also a real drop in living standards. The degree of lowering of standards was much greater for the peasants who had turned to jute, as the figures in table 4.1 - from a paddy-growing village, Rangalia, in Sadar sub-division and a jute-growing village, Barabil, in Serajganj sub-division of Pabna - demonstrate.

Resort to the rural moneylender, which had been a fundamental fact of life for the majority of east Bengal peasants in the early part of the century, steadily became a thing of the past during the depression decade. A random survey of 14 959 'agriculturists' all over Bengal by the Registration Department indicated that during the years 1931-2, 1932-3 and 1933-4, there had been less and less borrowing

47 See chapter 6 below.
48 It was reported from Bogra: 'In spite of this dearth of agricultural credit, the agriculturists have been able to bring all their lands under cultivation partly by leasing out part of their lands, partly by exchange labour and to a small extent by pledging their still remaining ornaments and by sale of their lands'. Collector Bogra to Jt. Secy. CCRI Dept, 8 Oct. 1937, GB Rev. B. May 1940 Progs. 14-57 (BSRR). In Dacca, 'about 10 000 tenants went to the Subdivision Officer's bungalow and complained that they could not get any credit to carry on agriculture'. Evidence of Dacca Bar Association, *Land Rev. Cms. Report*, Vol. 1, p. 136. In Bakarganj, the collector found cattle in miserable condition being offered at low prices, but there were no buyers. Donovan's Tour Diary, May 1930, Donovan Papers (SASC).
49 Bengal Board of Economic Enquiry, *Bulletin District Pabna*, p. 7.

Table 4.1. *Family averages of income and expenditure in Pabna*

	1921-4	1928-9	1932-3
Sadar (non-jute) sub-division			
Income	76.75	88	51
Expenditure	84.25	72	54
Serajganj (jute-growing) sub-division			
Income	116.50	147	57
Expenditure	208	144	61

Source: Bengal Board of Economic Enquiry, *Bulletin District Pabna* (1935), p. 9.

Table 4.2. *Decline in the number and value of registered mortgages and bonds in Pabna*

Year	Mortgages		Bonds	
	Number	Value Rs.	Number	Value Rs.
1928	19 503	2 902 496	789	139 026
1929	18 692	3 059 964	595	103 616
1930	18 939	2 852 848	760	143 132
1931	16 164	1 806 382	282	60 473
1932	12 861	1 266 356	343	100 304
1933	9 900	1 007 362	237	70 461
1934 (to Oct)	8 203	566 398	126	35 690
1934[a]	9 844	679 678	151	42 828

[a] Adding on for November and December on the average of the first ten months.
Source: Bengal Board of Economic Enquiry, *Bulletin District Pabna* (1935), p. 15.

and a slow rise in repayments.[50] Figures on the number and value of registered deeds of mortgages and bonds from Pabna (table 4.2) show a marked decline from 1928 to 1934. The number of mortgages fell by 50% and the amount borrowed on registered mortgage by 77%, while the number of bonds registered fell by 81% and the amount borrowed on that count by 69%. The credit market continued to languish throughout the slump. Even towards the end of the decade when the depression began to lift and trade and prices picked up, government efforts to deal with the debt problem ensured that no positive response was felt in the realm of rural credit. It is therefore, important to study the impact of government intervention in the rural debt problem during the 1930s.

50 Bengal Board of Economic Enquiry, *Report on the Activities of the Board During the Years 1934-5 and 1935-6* (Alipur, 1936), p. 14.

Effects of legislative intervention in the debt problem

During the 1930s, government efforts consisted of a series of delayed debt legislation. These aimed principally at providing relief for the peasant debtor and dampening the anti-moneylender agitations. A few hopelessly inadequate executive measures to provide institutional credit were also attempted.

The first legislative move, the Bengal Moneylenders Act 1933, was not a response to the new crisis of the depression, but an attempt to implement the Banking Committee's recommendations to stop usurious interest rates that had been found to prevail in the 1920s. As the Usurious Loans Act 1918, modelled on the British Moneylenders Act of 1900, had proved to be inoperative, the Bengal Government in 1933 took inspiration from the (British) Moneylenders Act of 1927 and tried to limit compound interest, suggest maximum rates of interest recoverable in courts, and made registration compulsory for non-resident moneylenders.[51] In 1932, a bill had been brought before the Legislative Council by an individual member who intended to give relief to the agriculturist, not by interfering with the interest rate but by providing simple machinery to settle debts through Cooperative Credit Societies. This, the author believed, would also have the indirect effect of popularising these societies, but the governor had refused to sanction the bill.[52]

It was not until January 1935 that the Bengal Board of Economic Enquiry produced the draft of a bill that was put on the statute books 12 months later as the Bengal Agricultural Debtors Act.[53] It provided for the establishment of debt settlement boards to scale down debts according to the debtors' ability to pay. The express purpose of the legislation was to relieve the burden of the debtors. But it was felt that it would be of advantage to the creditors as well, since in recent years 'the moneylenders as a whole had failed to collect any interest,

51   'The Bengal Moneylenders Bill 1933', GB Rev. LR Br., June 1933, B. Progs. 116-18, File 2A-7, of 1933. (WBSA).
52   'The Bengal Agriculturists' Relief Bill by Maulavi Saiyid Jalaluddin Hashemy, MLC', GB Rev. LR Br., Apr. 1932, Progs. 11-13, File 2A-14 of 1932.
53   For the draft, see Bengal Board of Economic Enquiry, *Preliminary Report on Rural Indebtedness;* for the Act, GB, CCRI Dept, RI Br., Feb. 1942, B. Progs. 53-9, File 2A-0/37.

much less any part of the capital of their outstanding loans'.[54] If amicable conciliation between debtor and creditor could not be achieved, the boards were empowered to make an award payable in yearly instalments on the basis of a reasonable offer from either party. If after an award any instalment became overdue, it was recoverable by a compulsory certificate procedure. As a deterrent to future borrowing, debts incurred after the award could not be sued for until all the certificated debts had been realised. The civil court had no jurisdiction while proceedings were pending before a debt settlement board, nor could it interfere with an award. Arrears of rent were to be regarded as debts. There was some initial confusion whether a decree obtained for the money value of the share of the crop under any barga system was a debt within the meaning of the Act until it was clarified in October 1938 that it was not.[55]

Debt conciliation boards were tried out as a pilot measure in 1935-6 in the Chandpur subdivision of Tippera district with encouraging results. There were 1996 cases settled by 39 boards. The principal involved was Rs. 213 919, creditors' claims amounted to Rs. 506 234 and the boards awarded Rs. 244 795, effecting a reduction of 52%. It was claimed by local officers that the boards had '(1) killed the agrarian agitation; (2) improved relations between debtors and creditors; (3) led to a drastic reduction of debt; (4) facilitated recovery of dues which the agrarian agitation had made almost impossible; (5) led to a reduction of crime and litigation brought to the notice of the courts and (according to *matbars* and Union Board members) of petty crime which is not reported.'[56] The passing of the Agricultural Debtors Act caused some panic among the creditors. From Kishoreganj

---

54 Bengal Board of Economic Enquiry, *Preliminary Report on Rural Indebtedness*, p. 5.

55 B.B. Chaudhuri states, citing a letter from GB to the collector of Mymensingh of 19 May 1938, that a decree obtained for the money-value of the share of produce under any adhi, barga or bhag system was regarded as a debt within the meaning of the B.A.D. Act. B.B. Chaudhuri, 'The Process of Depeasantization', p. 121. Another letter of 25 Oct. 1938 contradicted the view put forward in the earlier letter, and declared such claims to be excluded from debt within the meaning of the Act. See Jt Secy, CCRI Dept to collectors of Bogra and Mymensingh, 25 Oct. 1938, CCRI Dept, RI Br., July 1947, B. Progs. 215-18, File 2I-6/38 (WBSA).

56 'Introduction of Agricultural Debtors' Act', GB, CCRI Dept, RI, Br., Feb. 1942, B. Progs. 53-9, File 2A-9/37 (WBSA).

subdivision in Mymensingh, Chandpur in Tippera and Sadar, Noakhali, there were reports of a rise in the number of execution cases brought by moneylenders early in 1936 in an attempt to obtain decrees before the Act came into force.[57] After Fazlul Huq's ministry took office in April 1937, debt settlement boards were set up district by district all over the province. The scale of their operations was, however, much greater in the east Bengal districts which provided the chief political impetus for debt reduction (see table 4.3). By December 1938, the boards had judged creditors' claims amounting to Rs. 367 lakh and scaled them down in their awards to Rs. 179 lakh.[58] Although a majority of the applications were filed by debtors, in a very large number of cases, creditors had taken the initiative with a view to salvaging what they could of their outlay. By March 1945, the debt settlement boards had received applications from 34 lakh (3.4 million) debtors and creditors, disposed of 29 lakh cases (mostly by the end of 1942) and out of these had made awards in 13 lakh cases. The creditors altogether claimed Rs. 52 crore, Rs. 32 crore were determined to be the debt (under Section 18 of the Act), and the boards made awards to the magnitude of Rs. 19 crore.[59] Table 4.3 gives a comprehensive picture of the amount of debt reviewed by the boards in each of the districts from 1937 to the end of September 1945, and the extent to which debtors and creditors respectively made use of the debt-settlement facilities.

In September 1937, the Cooperative Credit and Rural Indebtedness Department of the Government of Bengal asked district officers to investigate and report on the fears being expressed about the effects of debt settlement operations on the flow of credit. Mahajans had reportedly stopped lending and this past source of agricultural credit was expected to freeze at least for a few years. The government had also heard that agriculturists could now obtain cash only by pledging ornaments or by outright sale or lease of part-holdings, and they wished to know how far this was true. The replies received from the districts provide some of the best insights

---

57 *Ibid.*
58 Huque, *Man Behind the Plough*, pp. 169-70.
59 K.M. Mukerji, 'The Problems of Agricultural Indebtedness in Bengal', *Indian Journal of Economics*, 29 (1948-9), p. 382.

Table 4.3. *Operations of debt settlement boards: 1937 to September 1945*

District	Applications received		Total amount of debt shown in applications	For all cases disposed of:	
	Filed by creditor	Filed by debtor		Creditors claims	Debt determined
East Bengal					
Bakarganj	77 162	160 208	69 826 601	28 621 605	15 851 770
Bogra	66 607	57 491	26 178 747	26 178 747	17 051 078
Rajshahi	65 721	48 638	17 015 249	15 183 030	8 977 866
Tippera	108 430	131 532	70 968 748	50 264 354	28 895 457
Dacca	69 952	133 024	79 239 644	34 371 538	21 879 472
Chittagong	34 604	96 481	15 583 894	16 653 221	9 099 613
Mymensingh	193 800	229 596	150 864 334	136 498 147	108 250 676
Faridpur	61 972	110 349	20 785 010	58 927 664	15 786 378
Noakhali	49 912	119 559	36 993 746	27 043 958	14 418 085
Pabna	79 921	67 833	18 769 268	19 433 455	13 866 213
West and Central Bengal					
Birbhum	25 953	43 389	18 305 188	8 748 323	6 186 696
Hooghly	22 525	23 752	6 728 007	5 439 309	3 592 709
Bankura	16 907	35 849	9 772 814	8 184 716	5 403 189
Burdwan	19 300	31 113	14 661 277	10 435 877	8 048 849
Howrah	10 642	17 013	2 762 111	3 315 195	2 350 064
Murshidabad	58 741	42 158	7 366 570	8 887 198	6 013 122
Nadia	50 941	45 509	9 873 800	6 099 781	4 692 022
Malda	32 831	25 358	20 767 258	6 961 362	4 992 494
Khulna	45 030	108 628	27 888 027	12 373 455	6 239 761
Midnapur	80 484	90 479	14 423 855	18 545 906	11 515 548
Jessore	77 585	37 290	14 605 968	7 057 165	2 811 962
The 24-Parganas	30 945	79 073	31 976 543	13 425 761	8 102 320
North Bengal					
Jalpaiguri	8017	9800	6 134 726	4 300 732	3 626 287
Dinajpur	74 235	56 452	20 492 519	17 612 876	12 130 137
Rangpur	128 750	76 375	22 999 197	18 857 949	13 615 382

Source: C.C. and R. Dept Credit Br., April 1947 B. Progs. 557-658 File 1R-14/46 (WBSA).
Note: Districtwise figures of awards made by the Boards could not be traced.

into the state of rural credit at the time and the important changes that were occurring in credit relations in the countryside during the slump.[60]

District officers were unanimous that the flow of rural credit had stopped much earlier at the onset of the depression. Some believed that the Debtors' Act had aggravated the position; others felt that the situation was already so bad that the boards could hardly have made matters any worse.[61]

The district magistrate of Mymensingh wrote in November 1937:

Enquiries seem to show that throughout the district, the village mahajans are *less willing* and also *less able* to lend money to agriculturists since the commencement of the depression of 1930-31 than previously and further that the introduction of the Agricultural Debtors' Act has undoubtedly still further restricted their willingness to lend.[62]

Actual figures from a couple of villages showed that it was possible still for a few reliable borrowers to obtain short-term loans from mahajans. In one village of 59 householders, 18 had no debt, 19 had applied to the debt settlement board, 22

---

60 'Restriction of Rural Credit - Possible Effect of Debt Conciliation Board', GB Rev. Dept LR Br., May 1940, B. Progs. 14-57 (BSRR).

61 Dacca reported, '.... for the last few years the professional money-lenders have generally ceased to lend any new money to the agriculturists. This has been primarily due to the economic depression which set in in 1929, but in recent years is partly accounted for by the Bengal Agricultural Debtors Act'. Addl Collr Dacca to Cmsner Dacca Dn, 7 Oct. 1937, *loc. cit.* From Tippera came the opinion, 'There is no justification for the belief that the Debt Settlement Boards have caused a cessation of loans by money-lenders. Mahajans were prevented from advancing money in the usual way by the depression long before the boards were created, and there is no reason to believe that they would have been in a position to continue operations to any very great extent had the boards not been set up'. Collr Tippera to Jt Secy CCRI Dept, 29 Oct. 1937, *ibid.*

The report from Bakarganj went into more detail: 'Owing to adverse economic conditions, there has been contraction of rural credit before the introduction of the Agricultural Debtors' Act. The cultivators were finding it difficult to repay their loans owing to the low price of grain and their own improvidence, and the Mahajans were finding it increasingly difficult to realise their dues even with the aid of the Courts owing to the fall in the value of land. Money was therefore tight, and with the introduction of the Debtors' Act, and the ill-informed criticism it aroused, the Mahajans restricted credit still further. The debtors on their side took advantage of the introduction of the Act to suspend repayment even of short term loans, and in some cases seized land which had been given to Mahajans in usufructuary mortgage. The result was that this season there was almost a complete suspension of credit'. Collr Bakarganj to Cmsner Dacca Dn, 22 Oct, 1937, *ibid.*

62 Collr Mymensingh to Jt Secy CCRI Dept, 27 Nov. 1937, *ibid.* (emphasis added).

indebted families had not applied and 6 had been able to borrow from mahajans in the past four months. These loans were obtained by pledging ornaments or other similar moveable and valuable property. 'It is clear, however, from all reports,' the collector added, 'that far from encouraging people to borrow, as they did before the depression, mahajans are very careful to lend only to those who can give security which can be easily realised.' He had no definite information that mahajans were insisting on the sale of lands when people approached them to obtain money; but he made a very interesting observation on the nature of usufructuary mortgages: 'There seems to be little borrowing at present on the basis of usufructuary mortgage from *genuine mahajans* though I have found it going on between *simple cultivators who have never done any money-lending business before* and aboriginals.'[63] As the older creditor groups – the traders and talukdars distanced from effective possession and use of the land – withdrew from the lagni (moneylending) business, cultivators in a position to lend stepped into the breach. When in 1938, economic and legislative changes gave a spurt to land transactions, these better-off moneylending peasants were best placed to make the most of the transition from 'surplus-appropriation' in east-Bengal agriculture to actual seizure of the principal means of production.

Reports from other east-Bengal districts confirm the general trend found in Mymensingh with some interesting variations in detail. According to the collector of Tippera, while mahajans were unable to advance loans extensively, they could still provide small loans on short terms. There was also a 'certain amount of mutual assistance rendered amongst the cultivators without interest'. Moneylenders had generally demanded sale or lease of lands for the advance of immediate cash. Ornaments were 'now rare' since most of them had been already pledged and disposed of in the early years of the slump.[64] In Dacca, except for urgent and pressing necessities, borrowing was uncommon. Agricultural borrowers did not get any loans, however small, without pledging their ornaments or mortgaging or leasing their lands. 'It is not

63 *Ibid.* (emphasis added).
64 Collr Tippera to Jt Secy CCRI Dept, 29 Oct., 1937, *ibid.*

often,' the collector wrote, 'that agriculturists have to sell off small parcels of their land in order to raise money for the cultivation of the rest of their holdings. The most common practice now is to borrow money on the usufructuary mortgage of lands.'[65] Once the 1938 amendment to the Bengal Tenancy Act set a limit on the period of usufructuary mortgage, credit on the security of land would also no longer be available. The only way then to obtain ready money would be outright sale of moveable property and land.[66]

The contraction or even extinction of rural credit was reflected in the demand for the meagre institutional credit the government could provide. There were three main sources from which the Government could disburse credit – its own agricultural loans, the cooperative credit societies and the land mortgage banks that were set up in the 1930s. The yearly allocation of agricultural loans showed no appreciable increase until the ministry elected under the 1935 Act took office in 1937.[67] In 1938, Rs. 50 lakh were issued in the form of agricultural loans against a normal grant of Rs. 6 lakh.[68] The outstanding amount on agricultural loans increased from Rs. 32 lakh in April 1937 to Rs. 137 lakh in October 1942.[69]

65 Addl Collr Dacca to Cmsner Dacca Dn, 7 Oct. 1937, *ibid.*
66 On the political background to the 1938 amendment of the Bengal Tenancy Act, see chapter 6 below.
67 The amounts advanced as agriculturists' loans were as follows:

Year	Amount		Year	Amount	
1919-20	Rs.	2 163 661	1931-2	Rs.	1 289 085
1920-1	Rs.	114 433	1932-3	Rs.	320 821
1921-2	Rs.	125 842	1933-4	Rs.	368 889
1922-3	Rs.	852 644	1934-5	Rs.	751 924
1923-4	Rs.	155 935	1935-6	Rs.	811 052
1924-5	Rs.	141 971	1936-7	Rs.	?
1925-6	No great demand		1937-8	Rs.	352 319
1926-7	Rs.	392 420	1938-9	Rs.	5 648 619
1927-8	Rs.	340 697	1939-40	Rs.	3 378 315
1928-9	Rs.	1 444 206	1940-1	Rs.	872 489
1929-30	Rs.	572 099	1941-2	Rs.	10 311 514
1930-1	Rs.	875 943	1942-3	Rs.	8 529 242

Source: *Annual Reports on Land Revenue Administration of Bengal.*
68 The Revenue Minister cited these figures at a cabinet meeting in arguing his case that district officers should be more careful in issuing agricultural loans, else government would be called upon to make good the shortage of loans caused by the contraction of credit. Gov. to Gov.-Gen., 19 Apr. 1939, L/P & J/5/144 (IOR).
69 Gov. to Gov. Gen., 22 Oct. 1942, L/P & J/5/149 (IOR).

There were some 25 000 agricultural credit societies in Bengal covering 6% of the rural population. When the Depression struck, many of these went into liquidation.[70] Even after discounting reports in the nationalist press as tendentious, the governor and his cabinet conceded in April 1939 that 'ordinary sources of credit are clearly now inadequate and that borrowers are not finding facilities for the short-term loans they require to cover the sowing season in many Districts.'[71] The Cooperative Department now produced a scheme to inflate rural credit. It involved government guarantees to the Provincial Cooperative Bank to the extent of Rs. 35 lakh, which was to be rapidly distributed in short-term loans through revived or quickly organised societies. To provide the Bank with liquid assets, Rs. 25 lakh, the balance of a long-promised subsidy, was to be paid to it with a further cash credit loan of Rs. 7 lakh from the government. The plan came to nothing. It was decided that the government would give no guarantee whatever, but would provide a cash credit of Rs. 5 lakh. The governor wrote with relief: 'I think Government have escaped lightly from what might have been a very dangerous commitment'.[72] The five Land Mortgage Banks were an absolute fiasco. Up to 1940, they advanced altogether some Rs. 6 lakh. No loan could be granted which exceeded 50% of the security and the security had to be land in which the applicant held at least a raiyati right.[73] The neediest had obviously no substantial collateral to offer.

One last legislative effort to protect the debtor, the Bengal Moneylenders Act of 1940, further reduced the possibility of an upswing in the credit market with the changed economic conditions of wartime. The main objects of this Act, introduced by the government and passed without opposition from the Congress, were to register moneylenders and reduce interest rates. No debt could exceed twice the original principal and interest ceilings were fixed at 8% on secured loans and 10% on unsecured loans.[74]

70 *Land Rev. Cms. Report*, vol. 1, p. 157.
71 Gov. to Gov.-Gen., 19 Apr., 1939, L/P & J/5/144 (IOR).
72 Gov. to Gov.-Gen., 6 June 1939, *ibid.*
73 *Land Rev. Cms. Report*, vol. 1, p. 157. Land values in the 1930s were very low.
74 *Ibid.* pp. 156-7.

During the slump, both the talukdar-mahajans and trader-mahajans had disengaged themselves from the process of reproduction of the small peasant economy of east Bengal. When the depression lifted, the rupture in rural credit relations was not repaired. To some extent, a whole succession of legislative interference made prospective creditors extremely wary of venturing back into the uncertain sphere of rural moneylending even in the climate of the trade and price boom of the Second World War. A more fundamental reason is that the jute economy never really recovered its buoyancy. The relative price of jute remained weak during this boom.[75] Aggregate figures on indebtedness for Bengal suggest that, in marked contrast to the period of the First World War and its aftermath, in the 1940s the burden of debt was reduced in real terms. But before we consider the available statistical estimates of this later period, we must first turn to the systems of rural credit in the other sectors of the agrarian typology and find out how they fared in the great depression.

Debt relations in the demesne labour–peasant smallholding complex in west and central Bengal

Who were the moneylenders?

'. . . the indigo disturbances' writes Blair B. Kling, 'mark the transfer of power from planter to moneylender in Lower Bengal'.[76] In 1920, 60 years after the Blue Mutiny, the collector of a Lower Bengal district found:

The average cultivator is heavily in debt. He hands over the greater part of his harvest to his mahajan to meet existing obligations and, as he is usually unable to maintain himself with the balance till the next harvest, he has to borrow again a few months after. He pursues his career of borrowing and repaying from year's end to year's end, always adding to his burden and never making any advance towards release.[77]

Who, in these parts, was the mahajan? The Bankura settlement officer tells us on the basis of his observations between 1917 and 1924 that 'as a rule, the landlord is also the

---

75 See chapters 2 and 3 above, pp. 67–9, 84, 94–7.
76 Blair B. Kling, *The Blue Mutiny* (Philadelphia, 1966), p. 221.
77 Quoted in *Bankura SR*, p. 17.

money-lender'.[78] The mass of evidence furnished before the
Indigo Commission suggests that in west Bengal, the
zamindars and patnidars had developed extensive usurious
interests long before their counterparts in east Bengal, who
began to play a major role in the credit market from only
about the turn of this century.[79] Joykrishna Mukherjee of
Uttarpara, a big magnate paying Rs. 90 000 in yearly revenue.
told the Commission that he had nearly Rs. 100 000 'floating'
in the moneylending business at rates of interest from 12% to
24%. Srihari Rai of Chandipur, a medium-sized zamindar
holding revenue-collecting rights over seven villages, was also
deeply involved in mahajani. His custom was to charge the
raiyats interest at the rate of 24% on cash loans, 37.5% on mixed
cash and grain loans and up to 50% on grain loans. Then there
were the innumerable small owners of patni taluks for whom
usury was an important subsidiary source of income. The
Basu family of Swarapur, who are the focus of Dinabandhu
Mitra's famous play *Nil Darpan*, are an example of this type.
So far as these moneylending landowners were concerned, the
cultivation of indigo was a nuisance, as it interfered with the
paddy crop. It obstructed their realisation of rice debts at a
time when, after a long sluggish period, grain prices had
begun to rise. The collapse of the indigo plantations
represented, in terms of the different forms of rural credit, the
victory of the lagni form of moneylending over dadni, and left
the patnidar-mahajans the ruling element in the west Bengal
countryside.

The long, secular movement of rising grain prices that
stretched with minor hiccups from the middle of the
nineteenth century to the 1920s, offered some scope for a
process of internal differentiation among the peasantry and
the emergence of a peasant elite who, as junior partners of the
moneylending rural gentry, came to control a fair portion of
the village grain heap. Srihari Pal and Daulat Sheikh,
prosperous tenants of the Babus of Kankana, a Birbhum
locality, in Tarashankar Bandyopadhyay's novels set in the
early twentieth century, are examples of such thrusting, grain-

78 *Ibid.*
79 Report of Indigo Commission, cited by Ranajit Guha, 'Neel Darpan: The Image
of a Peasant Revolt in a Liberal Mirror', *Journal of Peasant Studies*, 2, 1 (1974),
pp. 36-7.

dealing, rich peasants.[80] Scattered comments in settlement reports about 'agriculturist moneylenders' have led some historians to believe that affluent peasants were the chief sources of credit.[81] In Jessore, it was reported in 1925, 'the larger number of mahajans are agriculturists themselves';[82] in Burdwan, in the 1930s, 'the bulk of the money-lending business is in the hands of the richer cultivators who employ their surplus funds in this manner'.[83] These comments would run counter to the general picture of rural credit relations that can be gleaned from a wide array of sources unless the category 'agriculturist' or even 'cultivator' is meant to include the small patnidars, who in most parts of west Bengal were more akin to their peers in north India and did not keep the same distance from actual cultivation processes as the upper-caste talukdars of east Bengal. The Jessore report certainly speaks of the existence of 'gentlemen-farmers'.[84] In the Bishnupur subdivision of Bankura, there were a large number of very small estates, 'many of the proprietors being themselves the actual cultivators of the soil'.[85] There can be little doubt that landlords – large, medium and small – owning golas (barns) of various sizes, together with a small segment of surplus peasants, were the chief rural creditors in the early twentieth century. Rice-mill owners were a recent competitor. In an economy where the subsistence crop was also the principal commercial crop, paddy as the currency of lending continued to be of considerable importance. It was appropriated by the grain-dealing mahajans at rates of interest usually ranging between 25% and 37.5% for a period of a few months between sowing and harvest.[86]

Debt relations in early twentieth-century west Bengal

The recipients of loans can be classified into two broad categories – peasant smallholders belonging mostly to the

80 Tarashankar Bandyopadhyay, *Dhatridebata, Ganadebata* and *Panchagram, Hansuli Banker Upakatha* (Calcutta, 1971).
81 See, for instance, B.B. Chaudhari, 'The Process of Depeasantization', pp. 129-31; Abdullah, 'Landlord and Rich Peasant', pp. 109-38.
82 *Jessore SR*, p. 72.
83 *Burdwan SR*, p. 17.
84 *Jessore SR*, p. 48.
85 *Bankura SR*, p. 66.
86 Usually expressed as 10 or 15 seers per maund. See GB CCRI Dept RIBr., B. Sept. 1941, Progs. 29, File 2A-0/38 (WBSA).

clean agricultural castes and low-caste agrarian dependants. A much larger proportion of cultivable land was held khas in direct possession by landlords and tenure-holders in west Bengal than in the east. In the western tribal fringe, the best rice lands had all passed into the hands of moneylending middlemen, the original possessors continuing to cultivate on sanja (fixed produce) or bhag (share) rent. They were left in possession of strips of inferior upland and their labour attached through effective debt bondage to the cultivation of the extensive demesne. In the paddy lands in the rest of west and central Bengal, landlords' khas was considerable, but peasant smallholding predominated. The decline in soil fertility and the paucity of working members of peasant families notwithstanding, in the climate of rising paddy prices of the early twentieth century, peasant smallholding was still a viable proposition, albeit with its inevitable concomitant of usury which annually siphoned off a sizeable surplus.

'The real cause of the general indebtedness,' wrote the Bankura settlement officer, 'is to be found in the narrow margin which is left to the cultivator from the produce of his land to set by in case of an emergency after feeding himself and his family.'[87] In west Bengal it was usual for a major crop failure to occur once every three or four years. Peasant smallholders had to borrow heavily to obtain food and seeds to survive these bad years and to pay off their rents which were pitched high. A survey in six Birbhum villages in the early 1930s attempted a breakdown of causes of indebtedness. 'The chief cause of indebtedness,' the investigator remarked, 'is of course the general poverty of the cultivating class.'[88] Of the total outstanding debt, 4.5% were said to be for cultivation expenses, 23.7% for capital improvement, 24.2% for payment of rent, 22.3% for social and religious purposes, 1.3% for litigation, 8.4% for repayment of old debts and 15.6% for purposes 'miscellaneous'.[89] West Bengal districts, notably Burdwan, Hooghly, Howrah and the Bishnupur subdivision of Bankura, had been rather highly assessed for revenue at the

87 *Bankura SR*, p. 20.
88 Santipriya Bose, 'A Survey of Rural Indebtedness in South-West Birbhum, Bengal in 1933-34', *Sankhya*, 3, 2, (1937), p. 158.
89 *Ibid.*, p.159.

time of the Permanent Settlement and levels 'or raiyati rent were correspondingly high in what was then a highly cultivated area. The waning of the rent offensive in the later nineteenth century was predominantly an east Bengal phenomenon. In west Bengal, in spite of a demographic and agricultural decline, landlords, by virtue of their more direct role in the landholding and credit structures, were able to maintain the original high rent rates. Consequently, rents were much higher in west Bengal than in east Bengal, even though the pressure of population was greater and hence the competition for land much keener in the east.[90] In the Birbhum villages surveyed, rental arrears formed as much as a fifth of the total outstanding debt.[91] Officers connected with debt-settlement work were to discover in the 1930s that in Hooghly, Howrah and Burdwan, rental arrears constituted the major portion of debts and could not easily be paid off even in instalments spread over many years. Social and religious purposes, which apparently accounted for a large percentage of debts, were not simply ceremonial expenditure, but often an investment in vital life processes and social alliances. Among the labouring classes of west Bengal, the institution of bridewealth was well established. In the early 1920s, the price of a bride among the Telis ranged from Rs. 50 to Rs. 200 and among the Bauris and Santals from Rs. 5 to Rs. 20.[92]

Credit, a principal mechanism of exploitation in early twentieth-century west Bengal, was, therefore, closely integrated with the functioning of both the peasant smallholding and khamar labour sectors of the agrarian economy. It attached labour to sustain agricultural production on the landlords' demesne and the rich peasants' surplus lands; it also fleeced and at the same time, perpetuated, the smallholding sector which could not reproduce itself without credit. The dwarf-holders in this sector also needed small parcels of land from

---

90 On higher rents in west Bengal compared to east Bengal, see Secy Bd of Rev. to Secy Rev. Dept., 1 May 1925, GB Rev. Dept LR Br., A. Sept. 1925, Progs. 14-24 (19), File 1-T-2. The average raiyati rent in Hooghly was Rs. 7 as 12 per acre against a rough average of all districts surveyed and settled up to the early 1930s of Rs. 3 annas 2 pice 3 per acre. The average raiyati rent recorded in Dacca, for instance, was Rs. 2 annas 13. The average value of the produce per acre was also higher in jute-growing east-Bengal districts than in west Bengal.
91 Santipriya Bose, 'A Survey of Rural Indebtedness', p. 151.
92 *Bankura SR*, p. 20.

the surplus sector. But it was equally common in malarial west Bengal to find a poor labour–land ratio on many peasant smallholdings. Credit would be needed by the small peasant families short of labour power to underpin an unequal interdependence with the agricultural labour sector.

The impact of the slump in west and central Bengal

The onset of the slump occasioned a crisis for peasant smallholding in west Bengal. As paddy prices more than halved between 1928 and 1933, the burden of rental demands and money debts more than doubled in real terms. This, as the Director of Debt Conciliation (West) pointed out, happened within the context of a 'system of cultivation by which lands have to be cultivated by hired labour or by bhagchasis':

Hired labour is engaged, almost invariably, working members of families being so rare. Bhagchas unlike Eastern Bengal is resorted to by even the poorer class of cultivators who have not the wherewithal to pay for cultivation cost and manure. The former adds to the cost of cultivation and the latter tends to diminish the agricultural wealth due to indifferent cultivation.[93]

While the prices of agricultural produce had fallen catastrophically, the cost of labour, at least in Hooghly, had not decreased in the same proportion, being kept up by the mills in the neighbourhood. The Director of Debt Conciliation of the region was at some pains to explain to Calcutta that the conditions of agriculturists in Hooghly, Howrah and Burdwan were quite different from those in east Bengal districts. 'We are being asked,' he wrote, 'to find a solution regarding the accumulated debts of cultivators, the main item of which in most cases is arrears of rent.'[94] At the same time, he showed, by means of a comparison of Hooghly and Bogra, districts of roughly similar size, the preponderance of bhagdars and agricultural labourers in Hooghly as against occupancy raiyats with their working dependants in Bogra and the consequent increase in the cost of cultivation and

---

93 Note by Director Debt Conciliation (West) in 'Settlement of debts in Burdwan, Hooghly and Howrah districts where rate of rent is very high and rent arrears form the major portion of the debt', GB CCRI Dept RI Br., B. May 1938, Progs. 226, File 5R-5/38 (WBSA).
94 *Ibid.*

deterioration in cultivation that this entailed.[95] It created 'a maladjustment in the systems of rent assessment and cultivation, the accumulated result of which has been indebtedness of cultivators without any ability for repayment except by instalments spread over a number of years'. An enquiry in a village in Memari thana of Burdwan in 1933 showed that the total expenditure in money of families of 'typical cultivators' had fallen by 32%. Their expenditure on food had fallen by 48%, on cultivation by 35%, while expenditure on rent and taxes had fallen by only 7.5% and in 1933 formed 18% of the whole. Some 72% of the families were in debt, only a handful of them were considered to be solvent.[96] The depression made it increasingly difficult for peasants to command resources, even credit on stringent terms, to continue smallholding cultivation. Lands, formerly within this sector, began to pass into the managerial control of more substantial men, small raiyats in many cases being reduced to the status of bhagchashi on their own lands.

The agrarian social structure in west Bengal, particularly the increasing importance of the khamar labour sector, meant that the impact of the slump on the system of rural credit

95 Comparative figures from the Census of 1931 of Bogra and Hooghly showed:

Area (sq. miles)	Rural Population	Cultivating owners			
		Earners		Subsidiary occupation	
		Male	Female	Male	Female
Hooghly 1188	910 622	80 808	3339	5093	170
Bogra 1384	1 667 321	143 958	2140	11 304	145

	Tenant Cultivators			Agricultural Labourers				
	Earners	Subsidiary occupation		Earners	Subsidiary occupation		Working dependants	
	M F	M	F	M F	M	F	M	F
Hooghly	30158 1881	1499	50	85816 26349	6450	266	3897	500
Bogra	15046 140	2635	36	41805 1330	7130	52	36787	351

'Cultivating owners' are those classified as tenure-holders and raiyats with a permanent right in land. 'Tenant cultivators' are without permanent right and generally sharecroppers, known as bargadars in east Bengal, and bhagchasis in the west. 'Agricultural labourers' are those without any right, title or interest in the land but cultivate merely for wages in cash or kind. But 'working dependants', listed rather ambiguously under agricultural labourers include members of families of 'cultivating owners' and 'tenant cultivators' who assisted in family cultivation and there were 1802 and 35774 of such people in Hooghly and Bogra respectively.

96 *Burdwan SR*, p. 17.

Table 4.4. *Decline in the number and value of registered mortgages and bonds in Bankura*

Year	Mortgages		Bonds	
	Number	Value Rs.	Number	Value Rs.
1928	12 126	2 363 063	520	76 625
1929	9456	2 035 751	460	77 026
1930	8343	1 637 136	352	48 483
1931	6083	1 217 030	240	53 978
1932	6121	1 106 695	252	36 164
1933	5768	1 042 493	235	36 156
1934	5907	987 927	286	60 010

Source: Bengal Board of Economic Enquiry, *Bulletin District Bankura* (1935), p. 23.

would be somewhat different from that in east Bengal. There was a marked contrast in the impact on the cash and kind sectors of the credit market in this weakly monetised economy. The liquidity crisis had a similar disrupting effect on the flow of money credit. Bankura reported that 'the money-lender who used to serve as a shock absorber in times of economic crisis is no longer in a position to function in this capacity because he has no ready money to lend'.[97] Figures collected in that district show a fall in the number and value of registered bonds and mortgages (table 4.4), though not to the extent as in Pabna. Informal, unregistered lending is likely to have been hit much harder. Burdwan also witnessed a sharp diminution of mortgage deeds. In reply to the enquiry made by the Rural Indebtedness Department in 1937, the collector of Burdwan wrote:

There has been for some years past, a growing reluctance on the part of Mahajans to grant loans to agriculturists on account of the over-growing indebtedness of the latter and also on account of the depleted purse of the former brought about by the economic depression of the last years, from the effects of which the Mahajans have not yet had an appreciable revival. The propaganda for establishment of Debt Settlement Boards in the district during the last few months has resulted in some contraction of credit making it difficult for agriculturists to get loans from Mahajans except on solid securities in the shape of lands and ornaments.[98]

97 Bengal Board of Economic Enquiry, *Bulletin District Bankura*, p.11.
98 Collr Burdwan to Cmsner Burdwan Dn, 1 Oct. 1937, GB Rev. Dept LR Br., B. May 1940, Progs. 14-57 (BSSR).

During the summer of 1937, however, the agriculturists in the district had not been faced with real difficulties in finding short-term grain loans, and for very good reasons:

a fairly large percentage of them who cultivate lands as mere bargadars, had no difficulty in getting loans from their landlords as hitherto. Another factor to ease the situation is the widely prevalent system of bari-loan in the district by which agriculturists get loans of paddy at high rates of interest, usually 25% and *there has not been any appreciable contraction of this kind of credit facilities for the reason that the lenders of paddy-loans feel that their borrowers are too much under their influence to seek relief* to be afforded by D.S. Boards when established.[99]

Although agriculturists could obtain cash mainly by pledging of ornaments or by lease or outright sale of part-holdings, instances of such loans were rare. Few agriculturists had 'any ornaments worth the name left to pledge' and there were not many mahajans ready to advance cash on the security of lands.

Reports from other west and central Bengal districts corroborate this picture of a contraction of money credit. But grain loans which substantiated dependency continued to be made. In Jessore, quite apart from the establishment of debt settlement boards, agricultural credit was 'at [a] low ebb' and mahajans were reluctant to grant long-term loans except on security of ornaments or on mortgage of land. Yet, it was reported, 'as regards short-term loans, paddy loan which is the chief kind of credit in rural areas. . . have not been seriously affected'.[100] In Murshidabad, there had been a tendency among local Mahajans 'to wind up their transactions', and this was due, according to the collector, to the economic distress of the past few years, not the result of the proposed establishment of debt boards. However, in the previous summer as well as in the current two or three months preceding the harvesting of the winter crop 'the poor cultivators got paddy loans and consequently they were put to no trouble for want of short-term money loans'.[101] It was only after the Bengal Moneylenders Act of 1940 was put on the statute book that creditors in west Bengal became a little wary of making grain

99 Collr Burdwan to Cmsner Burdwan Dn, 1 Oct. 1937, GB Rev. Dept LR Br., B. May 1940, Progs. 14-57 (BSRR) (Emphasis added).
100 Collr Jessore to Secy Rev. Dept, 3 Dec. 1937, *ibid.*
101 Collr Murshidabad to Cmsner Presidency Dn, 6 Oct, 1937, *ibid.*

The peasantry in debt

loans. In June 1941, large creditors with stocks of grain were refusing to lend paddy on the grounds that they might be liable to prosecution under the Moneylenders Act. The district magistrate gave assurances that no action would be taken if paddy loans were granted to one's own bargadars or to a small trusted clientele.[102] In July 1941, the Burdwan division reported that a number of merchants were refusing to sell stock and mahajans were refusing loans.[103] For some, the recent legislation may just have been a convenient excuse to hold up stocks until prices rocketed in a year of wartime scarcity.

The east-Bengal talukdar usually held feeble rent-collecting rights over small tracts of land and, although he often had his own bit of khas khamar, could hardly be said to have exercised actual possessory dominion over the soil. His instrument of control over the indebted peasant in a highly monetised economy was essentially through usury. Under the impact of the slump, the old bonds snapped. The greater degree of control exercised by the bigger patnidars and zamindars of west Bengal in the landholding structure meant that it still made sense to advance grain loans for labour service directed on to demesne land. It was all the more important to maintain and expand this sort of credit operations since there were gains to be made for the landlords' personal demesne at the expense of a steadily weakening peasant smallholding sector. While some of the very small patnidars were snuffed out of the business, the bigger operators were well able to ride out the crisis in money credit. In west Bengal during the slump, the influence of the moneylending groups over smallholding peasants was extended; the existing ties of dependence in the khamar sector were strengthened.[104]

Debt relations in the rich farmer–sharecropper arrangement in north Bengal and the Abadi areas of the south

The creditors and their clients
Buchanan-Hamilton's surveys of Dinajpur and Rangpur in

the early nineteenth century and the excellent settlement reports on these two districts in the 1930s have made the broad outlines of rural credit relations in north Bengal fairly familiar to the historian. As F.O. Bell wrote:

The conception of a village 'bania', foreign to the cultivator in caste and tradition, and sucking the blood of a depressed peasantry does not fit the conditions of Dinajpur. If there is any blood-sucking, it is done by the richer cultivators themselves. People of non-agricultural tradition are few in the Dinajpur countryside. The Muslim jotedars are all peasants and agriculturists, and if a non-agriculturist lends money, it is usually within 2 or 3 miles of his residence.[105]

In the paddy-exporting north Bengal districts of Dinajpur and Jalpaiguri, jotedars generally combined substantial land-holding of anything from 30 to several thousand acres with moneylending and grain-dealing on corresponding scales. In the abadi areas of the 24-Parganas and Khulna in the south, credit advances to dependent small tenants to clear the forest in the early twentieth century were mainly provided by the holders of sizeable 'lots'. It was in the jute-growing north-Bengal district of Rangpur that trade was principally in the hands of immigrant Marwaris and east-Bengal Sahas, who were involved to some extent in dadan karbar. Even here, however, with the onset of the slump, these 'foreign' elements would withdraw, leaving a monopoly in the field to the substantial jotedars.[106]

The most widespread form of borrowing was paddy loans at derhi (50%) interest by which the poorer cultivators, adhiars and labourers were tided over the pre-harvest months. These were taken primarily to provide subsistence for the borrower, who might otherwise go hungry. Although loans were meant to be repaid with interest at the next harvest, there traditionally had been an 'elasticity about repayment'.[107] All borrowing was by no means in kind, and before the slump and even in the early days of falling prices, there was considerable borrowing in hard cash. Many articles of daily consumption such as oil, pulses and clothes had to be paid for in cash.

105 *Dinajpur SR*, p. 25.
106 *Rangpur SR*, pp. 13-14.
107 *Dinajpur SR*, p. 25.

Before 1930, the bigger cultivators also borrowed large sums for marriage ceremonies, and it was usual for cultivators of all size groups to take loans for the purchase of cattle and other cultivation expenses. An enquiry into indebtedness in Rangpur in the mid-1930s showed that of the outstanding debts, the greater part had been borrowed in the three years 1928, 1929 and 1930. Since then, the amount of borrowing had slackened off. Officers were asked to discover the causes of the original loan. For loans totalling about one-eighth of the nominal value at the time of investigation, the reason given was 'to pay off old loans'. Of the rest, more than a third was incurred for purchase of food, clothing and household expenses and more than one-fifth for marriages. Purchase of land or payment of nazar and purchase of cattle were the next largest classes of debt and these four groups together accounted for four-fifths of the total debt.[108] In Dinajpur, too, most of the borrowing was done before the break in prices or at the beginning of the slump. Among the reasons for borrowing, the categories 'marriage', 'purchase of cattle' and 'food or domestic purposes' were at the top of the list. A major part of the borrowing under the last category was in kind, expressed in cash value.[109]

The impact of the slump in the frontier regions

From 1931, lending in money declined dramatically. In 1930, a jotedar-moneylender of Charkai in Dinajpur had about Rs. 40 000 or 50 000 out on loan, but after then, he had lent only another Rs. 3000 or 4000. He was not lending because there

108 'Notes on Economic Enquiry in the Rangpur District by the Settlement Department' in Bengal Board of Economic Enquiry, *Preliminary Report on Rural Indebtedness*, App. V. The enquiry covered 11 villages of 508 families with 3272 persons. The original principal of outstanding loans was Rs. 66 000.

109 *Dinajpur SR*, pp. 24, 27-8. The results of the enquiry into the causes of borrowing in respect of the sum originally borrowed of Rs. 15 618 in 'D' Block of the settlement operations were as follows:

	Transac- tions	Value (Rs.)		Transac- tions	Value (Rs.)
1. Marriage	73	8134	6. Pay old debts	8	451
2. Food & domestic	126	2562	7. Buy land	7	395
3. Buy plough and cattle	46	1868	8. Pay rent	6	284
4. Business	8	929	9. Agriculture & cultivation	6	144
5. Litigation	2	850			

was little chance of getting his money back; after 1931 he had realised almost nothing.[110] Another creditor, who held nearly 1000 acres in raiyati right, had improved on the technique of the usual jotedar-moneylender and together with others had produced a joint stock bank with a capital of Rs. 175 000. Times were bad for moneylenders and even this bank showed a loss after 1931.[111] Before the depression, the jotedar-moneylenders made loans of Rs. 50 or 100 or 200 to cultivators, according to their resources, for purposes of cultivation and subsistence. How did the cultivators survive, now that no money was being lent? The common explanation was that they had cut down expenditure in various directions and had been living on savings by selling ornaments. They had also stopped paying rent. In the early years of the slump, officers of the Settlement Department had, indeed, found large quantities of gold and silver being sold in Dinajpur.[112] Weddings were now austere affairs and people bought fewer commodities at the hat. To some extent it was a matter of a reduction in the sum spent, since prices had fallen, but there was also a real drop in living standards. This was expressed picturesquely in the comment: 'Many who used to buy good milk and ghi, now live on rice and salt'. A man who was really in need of grain would now often go and work for someone who had a stock of grain. If it was essential for someone without cash to buy cattle, he might perhaps be able to scrape together Rs. 5 or 10 in loans to get some sort of animals. The cultivators maintained that the number of cattle being worked had decreased from some years ago and the quality was generally inferior. This resulted in poorer cultivation and less manuring with a consequent fall in crop yields. Lands had not been going out of cultivation on a very big scale, but there would be the occasional individual who had not cultivated a plot for lack of bullocks.[113]

To investigate the claim that 'credit had dried up', special enquiries were made during 1937–8 in 15 villages distributed

110 F.O. Bell's Tour Diary, Dinajpur, Nov-Dec. 1939, Bell Papers, Mss Eur D 733 (2) (IOR), p. 79.
111 *Ibid.*, p. 2.
112 *Ibid*, p. 80.
113 F.O. Bell's Tour Diary, Dinajpur, Nov.-Dec. 1939, Bell Papers, Mss Eur D 733 (2) (IOR), pp. 20-2, 64-5.

over 5 thanas in the west of Dinajpur district. It was found that
grain loans had not stopped. Out of a total of 504, 156 families
had taken derhi loans in grain. Adhiars figured prominently
among the borrowers, 42% of the indebted families holding
more land in adhi than in raiyati right. These 156 families
borrowed about 825 maunds of paddy in 1937 stipulating to
repay 1280 maunds. When further enquiries were made in the
spring of 1938, 668 maunds had actually been repaid, but the
amount might have been rather more if enquiries in one thana
had not been made as early as January. June and July were the
months of greatest borrowing, and January and February
generally stipulated for repayment. The 156 families were
indebted to 99 different creditors of whom all except 3 were
described as jotedars or cultivators.[114]

It might be expected that in a land of big jotedars and
masses of adhiars, some amount of lending would continue
even during a credit squeeze, since returns could be taken in
labour service and by appropriating the bulk of the produce.
In September 1937, the Press Officer of the Bengal
Government described how debts were being 'settled' in
Rangpur:

What is a debtor to do when he has a large number of able-bodied
youths in his family but not sufficient land to keep them employed?
Of such a case we hear from Rangpur where the creditor has given
some of his own land to the debtor to cultivate and *the entire crop is
to be delivered to the creditor*; the half value of the crop liquidates
the adjusted debt (the other half is rent), while as an *additional
benefit* (sic) the debtor secures occupation for his own family.[115]

In cases such as these, the bonds of serfdom in north Bengal
were undoubtedly strengthened.

This was, however, only a fragment of the north Bengal
story. The enquiry into derhi loans in Dinajpur revealed that
only in 25% of the cases was the lender in fact the jotedar of his
adhiar debtor.[116] In the export-oriented paddy and jute
economies of Jalpaiguri, Dinajpur and Rangpur, the jotedars
had taken the full brunt of the collapse in the product

114 *Dinajpur SR*, p. 25.
115 Quoted in 'Memorandum by the Bengal Provincial Kisan Sabha', *Land Rev.
Cms. Report*, vol. 6, pp. 51-2. (emphasis added).
116 *Dinajpur SR*, p. 25.

market. Unlike the situation in west Bengal, there was hardly a significant peasant smallholding sector left to prey upon, and consequently only a limited scope for recouping losses within the rural sector. In the abadi areas of the Sunderbans, however, where small tenants were still involved in the process of reclamation, there was a massive dispossession of occupancy rights by the lotdars and resettlement on bhag.[117] In north Bengal, at this time, reinforcement of the adhiars' dependency was not the jotedars' chief concern. In Jalpaiguri, Dinajpur and Rangpur, many more debt settlement applications were put forward by creditors than by debtors.[118] This was partly a reflection of the jotedar's intention to recover whatever he could and forsake the countryside for the now more promising urban pastures.

A good part of the grain advances that apparently continued through the depression was quite different from the grain loans of old. As one jotedar of Dinajpur put it, although grain advances were made in the autumn of 1937 and 1938 at the instigation of the subdivisional officer, this was 'not lending, but selling'.[119] The grain given in autumn was paid for after the harvest in February, mostly in cash and at the price prevailing in autumn. This was obviously a very profitable form of sale, as the price of paddy was much higher in autumn than in the post-harvest period.

Unlike the old moneylending groups of east Bengal, the north-Bengal jotedars were not entirely pushed out of the agrarian economy. But their role as creditors had been seriously damaged. As landholders they could not detach themselves from their unhappy rural existence until the land market picked up towards the end of the decade. As in east Bengal, grain redistribution had largely shifted to the domain of the product market, but there was one difference. Parts of north Bengal were grain-surplus, relatively labour-scarce areas; east Bengal was a densely inhabited, grain-deficit region, where jute had failed to work its magic. This

---

117 See chapter 5 below.
118 See table 4.3; also F.O. Bell's Tour Diary, Dinajpur, Nov.-Dec. 1939, Bell Papers, Mss Eur D 733 (2) (IOR).
119 F.O. Bell's Tour Diary, Dinajpur, Nov.-Dec. 1939, Bell Papers, Mss Eur D 733 (2) (IOR).

difference had an important bearing on the relative intensity of the famine of 1943 in the different regions of Bengal.

The permanence of the rupture in rural credit

Between 1935 and 1947 both the extent and volume of debts were definitely smaller than between 1929 and 1935.[120]

Money credit which had dried up during the depression never really flowed again. In the early 1930s, news of unrest among the peasant debtors of east Bengal had prompted the government to intervene. Its prescription, the Bengal Agricultural Debtors' Act of 1936 and the setting up of debt settlement boards, helped an already ailing system of rural credit relations to its demise. The Bengal Moneylenders Act of 1940 which imposed limits on the interest and the amount of the principal recoverable on any loan put the last nail in the coffin. Agrarian Bengal emerged from the Depression to enter a period of wartime boom. However, the jute economy, which had previously rested on a massive inflow of finance capital, did not in relative terms regain its vitality.[121] With famine looming on the horizon, the government, worried about its finances, thought of calling in its agricultural loans. Mahajans, if any remained in the villages, had long shut their money-chests. The supply of grain had largely been taken out of the orbit of credit and subjected to the convulsions of a wartime product market.

A comparison of the available quantitative estimates of the rural debt in Bengal in the early 1940s with earlier estimates from the late 1920s and early 1930s shows the decline. These estimates all have wide margins of error because of the small sample sizes and the highly conjectural multipliers used to arrive at provincial estimates. They are also not strictly comparable. Some refer to the total rural debt of cultivators and non-cultivators, others only to cultivators including sharecroppers, and one only to occupancy raiyats. Yet, the figures set out in table 4.5 provide a plausible picture of the growth and decline of agricultural indebtedness during the first half of the twentieth century.

120 *Census of India, 1951*, vol. 6, Bengal 1A, 105.
121 On the relative weakness of jute prices, see above chapter 2, pp. 67–9 and chapter 3, pp. 84, 94–7.

Table 4.5 *Estimates of rural debt in Bengal*

Year	Provincial total	Family Average Debt		Field of enquiry	Source
		All families	Indebted only		
1908-16		55	121	Faridpur	Jack, *Economic Life*
1910-17		121	256	Dacca	Dacca, SR
1927		128	203	Talma, Faridpur	RCA, 4
1928		146		Faridpur	Bd Eco. Eng., *Report* 1935
1928		112		Bengal	*Ibid.*
1927-8		167		Bogra	*Banking Cmt.*
1929-30	100 crore	160		Bengal	*Ibid.*
1929-30	212 crore	240		Bengal	Sen, *Sankhya*
1933	97 crore	187		Bengal	Bd Eco. Eng., *Report* 1935
1933		217	262	Faridpur	Bd Eco. Eng., *Bull. Dt Faridpur*
1943	25 crore	25	85	Bengal	ISI, *Rehabilitation Survey*
1944		46	82	Bengal	*Ibid.*
1944-5	150 crore	134		Bengal	Ishaque Report
1944		48	290	5 villages Faridpur	K.M. Mukerji, *Ind. Jl. Eco.*
1946	80 crore	80	148	Bengal	ISI, *Rural Indebtedness Report*

Note: the 1940s estimates relate to 'all rural families' and the rest to 'agricultural families', except the Board of Economic Enquiry estimates which include agriculturists with permanent and transferable rights, mostly occupancy raiyats but also some cultivating tenureholders and under-raiyats.

The first estimate of the total agricultural debt in Bengal in 1929 by the Banking Enquiry Committee suggested a figure of Rs. 100 crore, including Rs. 6 crore worth of paddy loans.[122] This was based on the sample of debts of the members of cooperative societies. An investigator at the Statistical Laboratory in Calcutta questioned the representativeness of the sample, pointing out that cooperative debts had been found to be much lower than the overall rural debt in other provinces. Using the alternative method of deducing the total indebtedness from the total value of registered mortgages per year, he produced an estimate of Rs. 212 crore with a family average of Rs. 240 as against Rs. 160 suggested by the Banking

122 *Banking Cmt. Report*, vol. 1, p. 65.

Committee.[123] In 1933, the Bengal Board of Economic Enquiry found it difficult to ascertain the accumulation of interest. Since moneylenders in any case were prepared in the slump to sacrifice the greater part of their accrued interest, they decided to calculate only the total capital debt of agricultural families with a permanent and transferable interest in their lands. This, they believed, to be in the neighbourhood of Rs. 97 crore and the family average was Rs. 187.[124]

There are four estimates of the total rural debt for the 1940s. The Indian Statistical Institute (ISI) team made estimates of indebtedness in 1943 and 1944 as part of their famine rehabilitation survey. The Ishaque Report gave an estimate for 1944–5 based on sample surveys in 77 villages. Finally, the ISI made another survey, this time specifically into rural indebtedness, in 1946. Of these, the highest estimate was in the Ishaque Report which suggested a figure of Rs. 150 crore in 1945 and a family average of Rs. 134.[125] A contemporary student of the debt problem, who had experience of local field work in 14 districts, regarded this estimate as 'too high and prima facie unbelievable'.[126] Even by this high estimate, as Ishaque himself pointed out, 'in terms of actual purchasing power of money and in relation to the annual income of the province, the average indebtedness may be considered to have decreased rather than increased'.[127] According to the Rehabilitation Survey, the total rural debt in 1943 was only Rs. 25 crore with a family average of Rs. 25, which increased in 1944 to Rs. 46.[128] In 1946, the Rural Indebtedness Report estimated the total rural debt at nearly Rs. 80 crore, the average for all families working out at Rs. 80.[129] As to the extent of indebtedness, the Board of Economic Enquiry had estimated that 77% of all agriculturists were in debt in 1933.[130]

123 S.N. Sen, 'Statistical Notes: An Estimate of the Rural Indebtedness of Bengal', *Sankhya*, 1, 1-4 (1933-4), pp. 335-7.
124 Bengal Board of Economic Enquiry, Preliminary Report on Rural Indebtedness, pp. 4-6.
125 H.S.M. Ishaque, *Agricultural Statistics by Plot to Plot Enumeration* (Calcutta, 1945, vol. 1 p. 55.
126 K.M. Mukerji, 'The Problems of Agricultural Indebtedness in Bengal', p. 383.
127 H.S.M. Ishaque, *Agricultural Statistics*, vol. 1, p. 56.
128 Cited by K.M. Mukerjee, 'The Problems of Agricultural Indebtedness', pp. 375-84.
129 *Ibid.*
130 Bengal Board of Economic Enquiry *Preliminary Report on Rural Indebtedness*, p. 6.

The ISI's estimates as fractions of all rural families were a mere 30% in 1943, 57% in 1944, and 54% in 1946.[131] Between 1930 and 1943, the volume and extent of indebtedness clearly declined. Large amounts of existing debts were either written off or settled and few new debts were incurred. If the statistical estimates are to be believed, debts were again incurred from 1943 onwards, though on a moderate scale. Considering that prices quadrupled between 1930 and 1945, the value of rural debts in real terms had shrunk drastically.

The differential impact

The collapse of crop prices and the stoppage of the flow of rural credit had, as we have seen, markedly different results in terms of changes in social relations in the countryside in the three sectors of the agrarian typology.

The bond-snapping character of the depression was most clearly evident in the highly monetised, market-oriented economy of east Bengal. The erstwhile creditors, the talukdars as well as the traders, made themselves redundant to the process of reproduction of the small peasant economy of east Bengal. By severely disrupting the system of rural credit relations, the slump cut away from the Hindu talukdar-mahajan, distanced from effective possession of the land, the major source of his economic control and power. The old awe of the mahajan, the great man of the countryside, also vanished, for he no longer played the role of guarantor of the peasants' subsistence security. In fact, now the talukdar was merely a source of irritation as a petty rent-controller. Those trader-moneylenders who remained on the scene now played the role of grain-dealer in a food-deficit region. If this aspect of the grain trade and the ultimate dominance of the purchasers of raw jute who had simply cut away the host of intermediaries were over-looked, it might be tempting to describe a situation of reversion to a semi-natural economy. With the withdrawal of the old moneylending groups, a few better-off peasants now entered the field via the lease market. Once the process of land alienation gathered pace after 1938

131 Cited by K.M. Mukherji, 'The Problems of Agricultural Indebtedness', pp. 375-84.

and rocketed during the subsistence crisis of the 1940s, they were well-placed to launch an expedition of (primitive) accumulation.

In west Bengal, the crisis of the 1930s had almost the opposite result of strengthening the ties of debt bondage. Credit in cash no doubt declined. Small lenders fared badly and credit came to be concentrated in the hands of the more substantial creditors. The chief moneylenders, who already had a sizeable khamar sector under their direct control, were able to gain at the expense of the more widespread peasant smallholding sector, which the fall in prices and credit had thrown into the doldrums. Under these circumstances, grain loans to dependent cultivators were not only maintained, but were probably extended to cover the new territories brought under the moneylender-landlord's and grain-dealing rich peasant's sphere of influence. The different perceptions of their interests by peasant smallholders and the traditionally landless prevented the emergence of any alliance that might have threatened the bases of dependency. While the east-Bengal debtor made jacquerie his pastime, his west-Bengal counterpart remained quiescent.

In north Bengal, the land of the rich and powerful jotedar, the picture is more ambiguous. The fall in the product market and the liquidity crisis were grievous blows to the grain-dealing, moneylending jotedar. Money credit became scarce. In cases where tied adhiars cultivated the land, grain loans in return for labour service continued. Where there was a measure of decentralised sharecropping, the character of grain distribution changed, as in east Bengal, from 'lending' to 'selling'. Raiding a troubled smallholding sector was not a significant option, except in the reclamation areas in the south. The rise in the land market at the end of the decade would give at least some jotedars an opportunity to wash their hands of the rural mess. With adhi of some kind being the universal norm, and bhag the life and death issue, here was a situation where, when the cloud of the depression lifted, a class-based challenge could aim at chinks in the jotedars' armour.

It is time now for the allusions to the land market to be clarified and elaborated on. What impact did the tumultuous developments in the product and credit markets from the First World War to the end of the Second World War have on the market in land? What patterns of change can we draw on the morphology of agrarian social structure in Bengal that was sketched in chapter 1?

5

Peasants into proletarians? The market in land and the question of change in the social organisation of production

The issue of land transfers has been central to the debate about the extent to which the structure of South Asian agrarian society changed under colonial rule. There is the well-worn view that the imposition of a relatively inflexible revenue demand in cash led to a greater involvement in the market economy and a permanent cycle of indebtedness resulted in a process of proletarianisation of the peasantry through rapid land alienation.[1] Morris D. Morris argues against this view, pointing out that its adherents cited evidence about land transfers mainly from periods of famine, which may not be representative.[2] Another line of attack against the old view was launched by Dharma Kumar whose work on south India demonstrates that landlessness existed in pre-British times and did not increase significantly under colonial rule.[3] C.J. Baker suggests a rather static picture in the patterns of land ownership over the last century of colonial rule in three regions of the Tamilnad countryside, marked by differences of economic ecology and in social structure.[4] Recent work on eastern India has produced apparently contradictory viewpoints on the nature and extent of pauperisation of the peasantry. Rajat and Ratna Ray, proponents of an equilibrium model, conclude: 'Such a development leading

1 See, for instance, D. and A. Thorner, *Land and Labour in India* (Delhi 1965), pp. 55-60.
2 M.D. Morris, 'Economic Change and Agriculture in 19th Century India', *IESHR*, 3, 2 (1966), pp. 185-209.
3 Dharma Kumar, *Land and Caste in South India* (Cambridge, 1965).
4 Baker, *An Indian Rural Economy*, pp. 318-329.

eventually to the complete disintegration of the self-employed peasantry on their own farms hardly seems to have ever been a serious possibility'.[5] B.B. Chaudhuri, on the other hand, describes a stark 'process of depeasantization' in Bengal and Bihar between 1885 and 1947 – occupancy tenants in debt being reduced to sharecroppers and agricultural labourers without any rights on their own land. Most alienations, he asserts, can be traced not to the stresses and strains produced by occasional famines, but to the more permanent conditions of rural debt. He concludes rather tentatively that 'such sales did not lead to any basic structural change in the peasant economy', adding that 'changes could be significant without being structural in nature'.[6] Abu Abdullah, making a rough comparison between a stratification among raiyats given by Ilbert in 1883 and the distribution of holdings given by the Floud Commission in 1940, finds the figures 'remarkable more for the stability they exhibit, over a period of about fifty years, than for any marked signs of a process of differentiation'.[7] The correlation coefficients that he works out show the association between indebtedness and land transfer to be either negligible or negative.

The approach in this chapter to the study of the land market and its relevance to the question of change in the social organisation of production differs in important respects from these earlier works. Firstly, statistical evidence on the volume of land transfer of the sort adduced by Chaudhuri cannot be directly related to a proletarianisation process in peasant society. The dynamism of the land market is not a sufficient criterion of social differentiation. Nor can the heterogeneity of farm size areas of the sort referred to by Rajat and Ratna Ray be accepted as class differentiation, and change or continuity in the structure of farm sizes be treated as change or continuity in agrarian class structure. In any case, the sharply polarised agrarian social structure that Ray and Ray generalised for Bengal does not accord well with the reality in the different

5 R. and R. Ray, 'The Dynamics of Continuity in Rural Bengal under the British Imperium', *IESHR*, 10, 2 (1973), p. 107.
6 B.B. Chaudhuri, 'The Process of Depeasantization in Bengal and Bihar, 1885-1947', pp. 164-5.
7 Abdullah, 'Landlord and Rich Peasant under the Permanent Settlement', p. 128.

regions of the province.[8] It is important to preserve the analytic distinction between the internal social organisation of production and the wider economic system, the complex circuit of finance capital and credit providing the critical linkage. In assessing the direction and extent of change in the social organisation of production, trends in land transfer must be related to the different types of agrarian social structure that predominated in the different regions. Based on the available evidence, this chapter will explore how developments in the land market affected the variety of social formations – the peasant smallholding structure in east Bengal, the peasant smallholding-demesne labour complex in west Bengal and the rich farmer–sharecropper type in the frontier regions.

Secondly, in the historiography of agrarian Bengal the effect of indebtedness on land transfer has been the focus of investigation, even for those who have tried to prove a negligible or negative correlation between the two. But changes in rural credit relations alone can explain shifts in the agrarian social structure and its link with the economic system. Regardless of its impact on the land market, the rupture in credit relations, at least in east Bengal, led to the withdrawal of important social groups from the reproductive process and undermined the erstwhile principal mode of surplus appropriation. The analysis of credit relations in west Bengal and the frontier regions made it apparent that an understanding of changes in relations of dependency in these parts, especially during the slump, would not be complete without reference to developments in the land market.

Finally, it is necessary to clarify the meaning of a 'land market'. In much of the literature on eastern India, the expression 'land market' has been used to mean the market in the proprietary rights of revenue collection created by the 1793 Permanent Settlement.[9] The circulation of these revenue-collecting rights, often misinterpreted as 'a bourgeois revolution in land', is not our concern.[10] More significant is the market in the right to occupancy and use of the land. Much

---

8 See chapter 1 above.

9 For a thorough study of the market in revenue and rent-collecting rights, see B.B. Chaudhuri, 'The Land Market in Eastern India (1793–1940)' *IESHR*, 12, 1 and 2 (1975), pp. 1-42, 133-68.

10 See chapter 1 above, pp. 3-9.

of the published, statistical evidence on 'land transfers' will inevitably relate to the nearest legal approximation of this right – the occupancy raiyati right – in which a market steadily developed during the later nineteenth and early twentieth centuries. We will, however, probe the changing balance between *de facto* khas khamar, land held in direct possession by proprietors and tenure-holders, and *de facto* raiyati, land held by cultivating peasants. The extent of subletting to under-raiyats, the incidence of sharecropping without occupancy rights and the use of wage labour, especially the contexts in which these take place, will also be of relevance.

The aggregate temporal trend in land transfer

By the time of the Bengal Tenancy Act of 1885, the sale of peasants' holdings was a fairly well-established custom throughout the province. The authors of this legislation considered giving legal recognition to the free transfer of raiyati holdings. But they refrained from doing so under pressure from landlord interest groups, who wished to reserve the legal right of choosing their own tenants and viewed non-landlord moneylenders with some suspicion. So the legal position was kept vague; the courts were advised to recognise only those transfers which were accepted by local custom. The chronology of agrarian cycles in the nineteenth century varied with the divergent demographic movements in the different regions. There can be no neat periodisation of the land acquiring a scarcity value. Here it is sufficient to note that due to the intensification of population pressure and the growing commercialisation of agriculture in the nineteenth and early twentieth centuries, the right of occupancy and use of the land increasingly became a saleable commodity. The 1885 Act, which attached security against eviction and protection against rent increase to the occupancy raiyati right, strengthened this trend. The fragmentary evidence available for the period between the close of nineteenth century and the late 1920s (1885 to 1928 in particular) suggests the existence of a brisk market in the occupancy raiyati right[11]

---

11 In the period 1885-1928, the courts almost invariably recognised sales of the raiyati rights to part-holdings.

and a steady rise in land values.[12]

It is only after the 1928 amendment to the Tenancy Act finally legalised the right of free transfer that comprehensive statistics on land sales become available. These statistics were, however, very incompletely reported in the Land Revenue Administration Reports. Consequently, the aggregate figures drawn from these reports provide a rather distorted picture of temporal and spatial trends.[13] The statistics in the Registration Department Reports are fuller and more reliable in this respect. Annual figures on sales and mortgages from 1929 onwards are set out in table 5.1. The crisis in rural credit during the depression decade is reflected in the sharp decline in the total number of mortgages. The figures for the complete usufructuary mortgage in the same period, however, shows a gentle upward trend. This phenomenon suggests the need of firmer security for loans and the entry of new social groups, directly interested in land for agricultural purposes, into the business of moneylending through the lease market. There was no substantial increase in the number of sales of occupancy raiyati holdings during the slump. Quite the contrary, local officials who looked into the earlier unpublished registration records found that the annual volume of sales was larger in the 1920s than in the depression.[14] The 1928 amendment, while legalising free

The Jessore and 24-Parganas Settlement Reports provide some figures on the number of deeds of transfer of occupancy holdings, valued over Rs. 100.

Jessore		24-Parganas	
1887–8	773	1901	15 237
1889–90	847	1906	18 895
1919	2937	1911	18 801
1921	3767	1916	24 313
		1921	16 388
		1926	16 676
		1931	9 829

Sources: *Jessore SR*, p. 72; *24-Parganas SR*, p. 25.

12 B.B. Chaudhuri, 'The Process of Depeasantization', pp. 143-4.
13 Figures on the sales of occupancy holdings were reported for some districts, but not for others, and the totals were made up only of those figures that were reported in the Annual Land Revenue Administration Reports for 1929–30, 1938–9 and 1939–40.
14 GB CCRI Dept, RI Br., Progs. B. Feb. 1939, File 3T-12 of 1937 (WBSA).

Table 5.1 *Land sales and mortgages in Bengal 1929-1943*

Year	Number of sales	Aggregate value of sales Rs.	Number of complete usufructuary mortgages	Value of complete usufructuary mortgages Rs.	Total number of mortgages
1929	79 929	13 016 351			588 550
1930	129 184	20 092 584			510 974
1931	105 701	13 133 716	41 353	3 013 472	376 422
1932	114 619	12 445 879	41 752	2 920 060	338 945
1933	120 492	11 749 507	38 294	2 516 784	313 431
1934	147 619	13 988 950	51 066	3 230 561	349 400
1935	160 341	13 986 133	60 715	3 873 536	357 297
1936	172 956	15 136 829	79 729	4 931 051	352 469
1937	164 819	14 597 687	77 232	4 941 457	302 529
1938	242 583	26 731 027	53 374	3 254 495	164 895
1939	500 224	63 215 376	62 491	3 681 815	154 780
1940	502 357	71 042 013	74 200	4 837 479	160 152
1941	634 113				151 553
1942	749 495				106 088
1943	1 532 241				183 371

Source: Annual Registration Department Reports. Some of the above figures on the number of sales and mortgages have been cited by K.M. Mukerji, *The Problems of Land Transfer*, pp. 38, 43 and B.B. Chaudhuri, 'The Process of Depeasantization', p. 138.

transfer of occupancy raiyati holdings, provided for a 20% transfer fee payable to the landlord who was also given a pre-emptive right to purchase the holding. According to the Banking Committee, after this enactment the number of such sales had 'fallen off greatly' and it was widely asserted that this had led to a fall in the value of the raiyat's holding.[15] It is likely that the slump in the land market was a consequence of the general economic conditions of the depression, and that the 1928 legislative move, which took effect from April 1929, merely confirmed the trend.

The 1938 amendment of the Tenancy Act abolished the landlord's fee and gave the right of pre-emption to co-sharer tenants instead of the landlord. It also limited the maximum period of a usufructuary mortgage to 15 years. Once again it is impossible to test whether the quite dramatic acceleration in

15 *Banking Cmt. Report*, vol. 1, p. 163.

Table 5.2 *Land alienation in Bengal 1940-1 to 1944-5*[a]

Number of sales of occupancy holdings				
1940-1	1941-2	1942-3	1943-4	1944-5
141 000	711 000	938 000	1 491 000	1 230 000

[a] Financial years rather than calendar years
Source: GB L&LR Dept LR Br, B Apr/48 Progs. 39-42, File 6M-21/46

the velocity of the land market in 1938-9 had more to do with legislative enactment or with the onset of the trade and price boom. But it is plausible to give the broad economic factors primacy in any causal explanation. The number of registered outright sales of occupancy holdings shot up from 164 819 in 1937 to 242 583 in 1938 and to 500 224 in 1939.

The wartime subsistence crisis, especially the great famine of 1943, occasioned land alienation on an alarming scale. Figures from a Revenue Department source, presented in table 5.2, show, that during the years 1940-1 to 1944-5, 43.7 lakh of transfers took place out of a total of about 164 lakh of occupancy holdings in the province. The government was forced to take the unprecedented step of passing a Land Alienation Act in 1944 to enable small owners to repurchase their holdings. The alienees did not, however, find it difficult to circumvent the law, and little of the land lost during the famine was restored.[16]

Differentiation in the peasant smallholding system of east Bengal

In chapter 1 it was shown that the differentiation within the peasantry in east Bengal around 1919-20 was one of extremely subtle and delicate gradation, the scale of inequalities being relatively small. The differences in landholding sizes at that time did not allow the development of exploitative relations through the control of large amounts of surplus lands by a

16 The Land Alienation Act of 1944 provided for the repurchase of holdings alienated during the famine up to a maximum value of Rs. 250 through the civil courts. Half the price had to be paid immediately on obtaining the sanction of the court, and the balance spread over ten yearly instalments. Most dispossessed families were not in a position to pay the initial instalment. Besides, the high fictitious values recorded in most sale deeds put many alienations beyond the pale of the legislation.

rich peasant class. The zamindars and talukdars were as a rule distanced from effective possession of the land, and raiyati land predominated over small patches of khamar. There were, however, already disquieting reports from a few areas that *de facto* khamar was increasing at the expense of raiyati. By the late 1930s, a keen observer of agrarian problems in Mymensingh said in his evidence to the Floud Commission:

at the present moment a very large percentage of the raiyati right in lands is held by non-cultivating tenants. The cultivator is an under-raiyat, bargadar or a labourer in a vast number of cases. This has been the result of a double process. When raiyati rights became valuable on account of the effective curtailment of landlords' demands, mahajans, zamindars, talukdars and middlemen became active purchasers of raiyati rights... On the other hand, the improved position of the raiyats and the adventitious prosperity due to increases of prices of crops enabled the cultivators to grow richer and buy more land with the result that every well-to-do cultivator ceased to cultivate and became an employer of labour.[17]

Instances of landlords and moneylenders as well as better-off peasants buying up raiyati rights are an indubitable fact of rural Bengal, including its eastern region. What needs to be investigated is whether these processes brought about a significant alteration in the predominating peasant small-holding system in east Bengal. These peasant smallholders were, of course, never wholly 'independent' because of their need for externally supplied credit.

Quite apart from market forces, peasant smallholdings were in this period subject to the eroding influence of the rising tide of population. The division of inheritances provoked by the demographic advance in east Bengal after 1920 saw a process of atomisation producing smaller and smaller holdings.[18] The context of agrarian over-population can be seen as exerting an aggregate downward shift on the mobility of the peasant society as a whole. The influence of the demographic factor on the mobility patterns of individual peasant households, which Chayanov believed played 'the leading part' in such movements,[19] does not lend itself to empirical investigation in

17 Evidence of N.C. Sengupta, *Land Rev. Cms. Report*, Vol. 6, p. 475.
18 For the broad demographic trends, see chapter 2 above.
19 Chayanov, *The Theory of Peasant Economy*, p. 249.

the case of Bengal. Dynamic studies tracing the individual histories of peasant households, especially their intergenerational demographic composition, simply do not exist. It is important, however, to bear in mind the theoretical implications of the existence of demographic differentiation in peasant society, which would have interacted with differentiation processes brought about by market forces. Whatever may be the precise roles of demographic and economic factors as well as random oscillations in determining peasant mobility, its multidirectional (combining centripetal and centrifugal forces) and cyclical nature, so graphically demonstrated by Shanin from early twentieth-century Russian evidence, cannot be overlooked.[20] The cyclical mobility displayed by many peasant households does not imply the existence of any 'mystic equilibrium mechanism'. The relative autonomy of the factors involved leaves open the possibility of a qualitative change in the structure of peasant households as well as in the agrarian social structure. The following discussion using available evidence on the land market can at best be a partial treatment of the problem of differentiation. The fact of demographic pressure and the splintering of holdings and plots can be emphatically established as an important parameter. But any assessment of its impact on the mobility patterns of peasant households remains speculative.

The settlement reports on east-Bengal districts surveyed in the second decade of this century do not record any polarising tendency within the peasantry. Jack, for instance, found the Faridpur cultivators to be a 'homogeneous class'.[21] Sachse reported that the land in Mymensingh was rather more unevenly divided than in Jack's district, but nowhere except in a small pocket in Dewanganj had there emerged any substantial landholders who could be regarded as village-controllers.[22] The general impression obtained from east-Bengal settlement reports is one of a peasant smallholding structure in which differences in landholding and wealth were

20 T. Shanin, *The Awkward Class: Political Sociology of Peasantry in a Developing Society, Russia 1910-1921* (Oxford, 1972),
21 Jack, *The Economic Life of a Bengal District*, p. 81.
22 The Mymensingh settlement report sets out the following picture of stratification within 'agricultural families' in 1919:

fluid. A tendency that was already reported in the 1910s was the disposition of moneylender-landlords in a few areas to force up the rent by dispossessing the actual cultivators, often clearers of the soil, of the occupancy right. This system of lending money leading to the deprivation of occupancy tenants of their rights was practised in Dacca, particularly in the jungly north-east, 'by some of the leading zamindar families as well as by parvenus of the mahajan class'.[23] Where the moneylender already held the zamindari or talukdari right, it was a matter of taking the holding of the indebted raiyat into khas possession and resettling it at a high produce rent or, by a stroke of reverse commutation from kind to cash known as taka dhaki, charging an extraordinarily high, new cash-rent. A moneylender who did not hold the rent-collecting right entered the landholding structure 'in the guise of the raiyat',[24] and in this case the land was cultivated by sharecroppers below the level of the raiyat. Apart from north-eastern Dacca, the extension of the area under produce rents owed to moneylender-landlords was reported from the thanas of Pangsa and Baliakandi in Faridpur 'where the conditions of land tenure approximate to those of northern Bengal'[25] and Gournadi thana in Bakarganj, a stronghold of moneylending bhadralok landlords.[26] Yet, land-hungry moneylender-landlords were exceptions rather than the rule. The Dacca Settlement Report, which contains an impassioned diatribe against moneylender-cum-landlords, goes on to say:

In the large areas of the district, however, occupied by petty landlords or the remnants of decaying families, the position of the cultivator

	Average cultivated land per family	Gross income per family
Families with net profit of Rs. 800 or more: 30 000 or 4%	12 acres	Rs. 1,000
Families with net profit of Rs. 240 or more: 270 000 or 36%	5 acres	Rs. 166
Families with net profit nil or subsistence ryots 450 000 or 60%	2 acres	Rs. 166

Source: *Mymensingh SR*, p. 25.

23 *Dacca SR*, Appendix 00, p. 5. In Raipura than, 'where the moneylender and the landlord are one and the same person, the evil is at its worst', *ibid.*, p. 76.
24 *Ibid.*, Appendix XI, p. xxx.
25 *Faridpur SR*, p. 31.
26 *Bakarganj SR*, p. 73.

can be painted in far brighter colours, and it would be erroneous to estimate the general condition of the Dacca cultivator from that of the less fortunate minority.[27]

Most often the mahajan was not anxious to sell up his debtors and claim their lands. As the Mymensingh settlement officer informs us, 'as long as he (the debtor) can pay the interest he is in no hurry to pay off the capital, and he has no fear of being sold up'.[28] The Noakhali settlement officer referred to the reported extension of the area under produce rents in other districts which was 'an imposition by small landlords and moneylenders on the defenceless and unsophisticated cultivators', and commented:

Persons of their class are quite unable to make such an imposition on Noakhali cultivators. I know of only one instance in which a landlord and moneylender has at all succeeded in doing so and that is in the estate of the Dalalbazar Babus in Lakshmipur Thana. . . The absence of the barga system in Noakhali is accounted for by the strength of the cultivating classes as a body. . . [29]

The story was much the same in the neighbouring district of Tippera.[30]

Did the small inequalities in the landholding structure at a particular moment develop into class differences over a period of time? Periods of rising prices, it has often been assumed, enabled peasants with a saleable surplus to consolidate their position in the agrarian social structure. For a number of reasons it is doubtful whether a distinct and stable peasant elite could have emerged in the first three decades of the twentieth century. Social anthropological work on rural east Bengal has suggested that instead of a process of unilinear class differentiation, there is considerable multidirectional mobility (within the broader parameter of aggregate downward mobility) in peasant society - centripetal trends consisting of the descent of richer peasant households and the rise of relatively poorer ones effectively countering centrifugal forces.[31] Even during the phases of rising prices in the early

27 *Dacca SR*, p. 44.
28 *Mymensingh SR*, p. 27.
29 *Noakhali SR*, pp. 91-2.
30 *Tippera SR*, *passim.*
31 Ramkrishna Mukherjee's survey of six Bogra villages shows that between 1921 and 1941, zamindars (landlords) and jotedars (rich farmers) accounted for 18% of all

twentieth century, the terms of trade remained tilted against agriculture and the indices of jute and rice prices lagged behind the all-commodities price index.[32] Jute, the cash-crop of east Bengal, never really enjoyed a sustained boom period like cotton and wheat in western and northern India. While there was little scope for serious class differences to develop within peasant society, the different strata of the peasantry in east Bengal, in addition to their cultural identity which included religion, found themselves involved in similar sets of tenurial, credit and market relations. A common set of external economic relations contributed to the remarkable degree of cohesiveness that the peasantry of east Bengal displayed in social and political action.[33]

If the peasantry were not being put asunder by a process of social differentiation through the market in the 1920s, neither did the talukdar-mahajans and trader-mahajans in this period go on a spree of investing their fortunes in the lands of an indebted peasantry. The operation of the system of rural credit in east Bengal typically entailed the appropriation of the peasants' surplus through reasonably regular interest payments over an extended period of time. The credit needs of a smallholding peasantry ensured their dependence even when left in possession of the chief means of production, and usury over the long term brought secure and probably higher returns than the alternative of selling up debtors and claiming their lands. The history of early twentieth-century east Bengal confirms the view that the independent development of merchant's and usurer's capital retards the differentiation of the peasantry.[34] There were also numerous disincentives and

land sold and ryots (self-sufficient peasants) and raiyat bargadars accounted for 36% of all land purchases. Ramkrishna Mukherjee, *Six Villages of Bengal* (Bombay, 1971), p. 217; for an interpretation of Mukherjee's data, see R. and R. Ray, 'The Dynamics of Continuity', pp. 107-10.

32 See chapters 2 and 3 above.

33 This is not to say that micro-differences in landholding are of no relevance in determining local structures of power and influence. Subtle problems of consciousness and role-taking are also involved. It is simply that the contradiction between the interests of a range of peasant smallholders on the one hand and those of rentier, usurious and mercantile exploiters on the other was historically the more fundamental one in pre-partition Bengal. See chapter 6 below.

34 This is one of the keenest insights of classical Marxist texts on the agrarian question. Cf. Karl Kautsky on the German usurer: 'In the present conjuncture, . . . usurious capital shows less and less interest in expropriating the indebted

obstacles in the way of potential land engrossers, not least of which was the fragmented nature of peasant plots. The collector of Mymensingh explained to the Banking Committee in 1929:

Lands tend to pass into the hands of the mahajuns and other creditors: but owing to the scattered nature of the holdings these creditors usually find it expedient to resell, so that the lands pass back again to the cultivator. It is the cultivator who is willing to give the highest price for good agricultural land. It is therefore the scattered nature of the holdings which prevents the cultivator from becoming a serf. I would emphasise the point. It is of the highest importance.[35]

The dynamism of the land market in the 1920s is no proof of the emergence of a stable peasant elite or the rapid growth of the moneylender–landlords' demesne. In the 1920s many moneylenders seem to have invested more in the purchase of talukdari rights than in occupancy raiyati rights.[36] The probable explanation for this phenomenon is not the desire for enhancement of status, rather the possession of taluks was regarded as sound security for obtaining credit from the urban sector. Moneylenders preferred to do their business in liquid capital; their hoards of bullion provided security for borrowing, and their investment in landed rights made sense insofar as it satisfied the same motive.

As agricultural prices plummeted at the onset of the depression, defaults in the payment of interest on the part of peasant debtors became common. The rupture of the delicately balanced system of rural credit in east Bengal

peasantry; if the property is auctioned, it stands to lose not only its interest but a part of its capital too. Far from hastening the process, it is therefore attempting to postpone it by granting arrears in payment and even advancing new loans'. K. Kautsky, *Die Agrarfrage* (London, 1976). See also K. Marx, *Capital*, vol. 3, chapters 20 and 36 (London, 1981); V. I. Lenin, *Collected Works*, vol. 3 (Moscow, 1977).

35 Evidence of the collector of Mymensingh, *Banking Cmt. Report*, vol. 2, pp. 192-3.

36 A talukdar-mahajan family, exterminated by peasant-debtors in the Kishoreganj riots of 1930, had between 1918 and 1930 invested Rs. 11 117 in 10 different purchases of shares in shikmi taluks. During the same period, according to registration records, they dispossessed only five Muslim cultivators of whole or part of their raiyati holdings. Altogether they bought 4.51 acres of raiyati land for just over Rs. 1000. Registered Deeds of Land Sales and Mortgages (Mymensingh Dt Registration Office).

brought about a crisis in agrarian relations. But during the slump, land became less attractive, its value fell drastically, and there was no massive expropriation of peasants' holdings. The Bengal Board of Economic Enquiry reported in 1935 that 'some of them [creditors] might have sued their debtors in the civil courts, but owing to the absence of purchasers at a reasonable price execution proceedings dragged on indefinitely, and if the land was sold it was difficult to get possession or to find other cultivators to take settlement'. The board estimated that 'the number of cases in which the creditors sold up their debtors was say 5 per cent only and in 95 per cent of cases the debtors paid nothing and remained in possession of their land without any penalty'.[37] In the early 1930s, there were political combinations of raiyats designed specifically to prevent settlement of holdings that were being sold by decree. In November 1935, an enquiry was conducted in Pabna through subregistrars into the debts of 400 families. The average area held by a family was 4.08 acres. Of the 400 families for whom figures were obtained, there were only 53 families against whom execution proceedings had been instituted of which 21 were pending and 32 had been satisfied. The average area sold privately for repayment was 0.19 acres. Of 0.31 acres sold by the court, more than three-fourths were purchased by non-cultivators. The total area sold per family was 0.50 acres or one-eighth of the area held on average by a family.[38] A Pabna pleader wrote to the government in 1935: 'For the last three or four years it is very difficult to find purchasers in civil court execution cases owing to economic distress. The decree holders are the only purchasers.'[39]

Between 1938 and 1940 the Land Revenue Commission conducted an enquiry into the manner of cultivation in raiyati lands transferred during the previous 12 years. The samples were small and the figures on the areas transferred seem to be underestimates. But the different types of cultivation in the transferred area are revealing of possible changes in the social organisation of production. In east Bengal (see table 5.3), some

37 Bengal Board of Economic Enquiry, *Preliminary Report on Rural Indebtedness*, p. 5
38 Bengal Board of Economic Enquiry, *Bulletin District Pabna*, p. 8.
39 Govt. Pleader, Pabna Sadar, to Collector, Pabna 25 July, 1935, cited by B.B. Chaudhuri, 'The Process of Depeasantization', p. 138.

Table 5.3. *The manner of cultivation of Raiyati area transferred during 1928-40 in east Bengal*

District	Area enquired into (acres)	Transferred during 12 years		Transferred area cultivated			
		Area	Percentage	Purchaser's family	Bargadars	Labourers	Under-tenants
Bakarganj	1752.66	99.97	5.7	56.09	43.88	—	—
Bogra	1984.45	59.23	3.0	28.37	18.60	0.50	11.76
Chittagong	1693.95	164.90	9.7	79.97	20.50	5.42	59.01
Dacca	1082.27	53.46	4.9	23.31	22.86	5.99	01.30
Faridpur	1796.54	120.19	6.6	90.79	24.53	—	04.87
Mymensingh	3597.55	201.93	5.5	88.78	105.33	—	07.82
Noakhali	1208.43	65.74	5.5	63.42	02.06	0.26	—
Pabna	1673.28	65.76	3.8	51.23	14.53	—	—
Rajshahi	5617.84	196.78	3.5	68.62	37.85	—	90.31
Tippera	2112.91	99.39	4.2	59.65	10.41	13.61	15.72
East Bengal Total	22 519.88	1127.35	5.0	610.23 or 54.1% of transferred area	300.55 or 26.7% of transferred area	25.78 or 2.3% of transferred area	190.79 or 16.9% of transferred area

Source: Land Revenue Commission Report (1940) Vol. 2, pp. 120-1.

5% of the raiyati area examined was transferred. Of this, 54.1%
was cultivated by the purchasers' family, 26.7% by bargadars,
2.3% by labourers and 16.9% by under-raiyats. The increased
use of wage labour under the impact of the market in land was
negligible. The Land Revenue Commission noted that the
increase in sharecropping was 'one of the most disquieting
features of the present times.'[40] Yet even on the basis of its own
figures, if 5% of raiyati area was transferred and 27% of it was
cultivated by sharecroppers, the area under barga in east
Bengal would have increased by just over 1% in 12 years. But
the small *areal* increase in barga does not imply that the
numbers of bargadars were not rising more rapidly. The
evidence of the noted anthropologist Radhakamal Mukherji
before the Commission provides a useful perspective on the
growth of barga in east Bengal:

The area normally held by the bargadar is small and scattered.
Raiyats have been sold off and are often bargadars in slices of holdings
which formerly belonged to them. Where there is heavy population
pressure and great competition for land, small tenants and
agricultural labourers clamour for and obtain barga. . . In East
Bengal, the man who lets out his land on barga exacts salami varying
from Rs. 3 to 5 per bigha. He can do this because there is competition
for barga holdings.[41]

Barga in east Bengal was more often than not an adjunct of
smallholding peasant cultivation. The resentment of the
occupancy raiyat at being reduced to a bargadar has often been
identified as an ingredient of political anger in the
countryside. Yet remarkably as holdings became more
numerous and exiguous, the demand for small parcels of land
on barga became an important feature in krishak samiti
(peasant political associations) meetings held during the late
1930s and 1940s in the east-Bengal interior.[42]

The depression saw the talukdars and traders, whose hold
over the land was distant and weak, withdraw from the rural
credit scene. In the event, they lost such influence as they had
over the indebted smallholders. Some better-off peasants now

40 *Land Rev. Cms. Report*, vol. 1, pp. 38-9.
41 Evidence of Radhakamal Mukherji in *Land Rev. Cms. Report*, vol. 2, pp. 569,
575.
42 See, for instance, Cmsner Chittagong Dn to Ch Secy, 8 May 1941, Home Poll Con.
File 13/41 (WB Home Dept).

entered the field and the rise in usufructuary mortgages can be attributed to them.[43] From the late 1930s, when the land market picked up dramatically, they were the chief beneficiaries. But evidence suggests that during the grievous subsistence crisis of the peasantry in 1943 and its aftermath, at least some of the more substantial zamindars, talukdars and grain traders had the final fling in their long history of exploiting the smallholding peasantry.

In the massive land alienation that took place in Bengal in the 1940s, the east accounted for a disproportionately high share. The grain-deficit districts of east Bengal were the earliest and hardest hit by the famine of 1943. The exchange entitlement of jute *vis-a-vis* rice had declined drastically,[44] and the golden fibre, which had enabled smallholders to postpone a crisis of the microfundium in the early part of the century, betrayed them abysmally at this critical juncture. A survey by the Indian Statistical Institute identified two regions to have been 'very severely affected' by the famine – a few subdivisions in the coastal south-west and a great majority of subdivisions in Dacca, Faridpur, Noakhali and Tippera in the east. Most of the subdivisions in the category 'severely affected' were also in east Bengal. In the 'very severely affected' subdivisions, 12.5% of all families surveyed sold land between August 1943 and April 1944 and 3.9% sold off all their paddy lands.[45]

K.M. Mukerji's village studies in Faridpur during the famine, together with the ISI's wider survey, provide some insights into the impact of land alienation on the agrarian social structure in east Bengal. Mukerji states that 'in other years (preceding 1943), land did sometimes pass on from the

43 It was reported from Tippera that 'suspicion of the (Bengal Agricultural Debtors) Act is not confined to the professional money-lender, but is shared by the comparatively well-off or 'bourgeois' Krishaks, who are said to hold most of the usufructuary mortgages', Cmsner Chittagong Dn to Ch Secy, 15 Oct. 1937, Home Poll Con. File 10/73 (WB Home Dept); in Mymensingh, usufructuary mortgages were mostly in the hands of 'simple cultivators who have not done any money-lending business before', DM Mymensingh to Jt Secy CCRI Dept, 27 Nov. 1937, GB Rev. B. May 1940 Progs. 14-57 (BSRR).

44 See chapter 3 above.

45 Mahalanobis *et al.* 'After-effects of the Bengal Famine of 1943', pp. 337-400. The 'very severely affected' subdivisions were in the south-west – Tambuk and Contai in Midnapur and Diamond Harbour in the 24-Parganas and in the east – Narayanganj, Munshiganj and Manikganj in Dacca, Goalundo, Faridpur and Madaripur in Faridpur, Brahmanbaria, Comilla and Chandpur in Tippera and Noakhali and Feni in Noakhali.

well-to-do cultivators to their compeers or even to their less fortunate brethren'.[46] There were various reasons for land transfers. It was different in 1943; scarcity and hunger were the order of the day and the single predominating cause of land transfers was the need for ready cash to buy food. Most of the sales were consequently from the poor to the rich at giveaway prices. The prices recorded in the documents were in most cases fictitious.[47] The ISI survey, which used categories of less than 2 acres, 2–5 acres and over 5 acres, found that while sales of entire holdings were highest in the less than 2 acres group, sales of part-holdings showed higher percentage in the 2–5 acres group, and alienation by families holding over 5 acres, though considerable, was less than those with smaller holdings.[48] An analysis of transferees by occupational categories in a Faridpur village showed that 40.5% of the total transferred area went to 'cultivators' including co-villagers and outsiders, 17.9% to 'zamindars', 15% to 'office employees', 10.1% to 'traders', 7% to 'jotedars', 5.4% to 'moneylenders' and 4.1% to 'priests and petty employees'. At least four families who owned no land in 1943 became landowners in 1944. But they came from the moneylending and trading classes and were not landless labourers. Mukerji described the non-cultivator transferees in the following terms:

Their association with land, apart from its ownership, was mostly round-about and far-fetched, that is, sometimes through hired labourers but mainly through tenants and tillers who paid them cash-rent or produce-rent. In the case of khas lands belonging to the families in question, that is, lands in their direct possession... most of them let it [sic] out on barga or bhag or adhi arrangement and lived on produce rent tendered by sharecroppers who, again, overcrowded the village like too many fishes in a congested, stagnant pool.[49]

The ISI survey for the period August 1943 to April 1944, which used the occupational categories of non-cultivating owner,

46 K.M. Mukerji, *The Problems of Land Transfer* (Santiniketan, 1957), p. 64.·

47 An analysis of acreage groups of transferers in a Faridpur village showed that in the 0–1 acre group, 19% of the land possessed by that group was transferred during the year 1943, 51% in the 1–2 acres group, 49% in the 2–3 acres group, 43% in the 3–4 acres group, 65% in the 4–5 acres group, 52% in the 5–10 acres group and 48% in the over–10 acres group, *ibid.*, p. 50.

48 P.C. Mahalanobis *et al.*, 'After-effects of the Bengal Famine of 1943'.

49 K.M. Mukerji, *The Problems of Land Transfer*, pp. 62-3.

peasant proprietor, part-peasant/part-labourer and agricultural labourer, reported an 'improvement' of status for 2.3% of
all families, mostly peasant proprietor to non-cultivating
owner, a 'deterioration' for 6.8%, mostly from peasant
proprietor to part-peasant/part-labourer, and 'destitution' for
4.4%.[50] In east Bengal after 1920, the landless agricultural
labourer had made his appearance largely as a result of rapidly
rising population in a context where land was scarce. Under
the conditions of the 1940s, the pure agricultural labourers as a
class were, according to Ambika Ghosh 'not able to sustain
themselves. The tremendous competition they face from the
cultivator-labourer along with the extremely high prices of
food-grains since 1940 is making the existence of such a class,
with all the uncertainties of employment, precarious. Hence
this class is either reverting to sharecropping – sharecroppers
with no land, no cattle, or migrating to the cities, or simply
dying out.'[51]

In the sea of peasant smallholdings in east Bengal, the
cumulative effect of population growth, partible inheritance
and market forces produced an irresistible wave of land subdivision with a few mild ripples of land consolidation. After
1920, the peasantry, victims of their own birth rate and quirks
of the market, were undergoing a process of pauperisation.
The inverse process – the emergence of a peasant elite – was
weaker to begin with and did not become very effective until
the late 1930s. Moneylenders and landlords made sporadic
forays into peasants' territory. Their principal mode of social
control was, of course, the credit mechanism. But once they
became redundant on the credit scene, a political counter-
attack gathered momentum. The partition of 1947 drove the
majority of Hindu zamindars, talukdars and traders from their
lands in east Bengal. It is not clear how far the 'kulakisation'
process was strengthened after 1947. In the 1960s, Bertocci
discovered an intergenerational circulation of economic and
social status among households of different landowning
classes and advanced the notion of 'cyclical kulakism'.[52]

50 P.C. Mahalanobis *et al.*, 'After-effects of the Bengal Famine of 1943'.
51 A. Ghosh and K. Dutt, *Development of Capitalist Relations in Agriculture* (Delhi,
   1977), p. 129.
52 Peter J. Bertocci, 'Structural Fragmentation and Peasant Classes in Bangladesh',
   Journal of Social Studies, 5 (1979), pp. 43-60. For evidence on centripetal mobility

Abdullah, writing on the agrarian structure in Bangladesh in the mid-1970s, accepted Shanin's point about 'the barriers to polarization set up by the internal structure of peasant society' with the qualification that over-emphasising this aspect might obfuscate 'emergent' class conflicts and change processes in rural society.[53] Sharecropping and wage labour continue to exist and are probably on the increase. But these cannot be regarded as having brought about a transformation of the predominating peasant smallholding structure.

The demesne labour–peasant smallholding complex in west and central Bengal during the early twentieth century

In west and central Bengal, the peasant smallholding sector was predominant. But landlords' personal demesne was quite substantial. The prolonged period of rising grain prices from the later nineteenth century had also afforded scope for a process of internal differentiation within the peasantry. A few *coqs de village* of peasant origin together with moneylending and grain-lending landlords exercised considerable influence over the working of the agrarian economy. In the western tribal fringe, the best paddy lands had already passed into the hands of moneylending tenure-holders. Elsewhere, too, there were instances of grain-lending landlords and rich peasants seizing the lands of their debtors. A large pool of landless labour was readily available to be directed on to these khamar lands. Yet on the whole, until the late 1920s, the peasant

in Bangladesh peasant society in the 1970s, see Shapan Adnan and H. Zillur Rahman, 'Peasant Classes and Land Mobility: Structural Reproduction and Change in Rural Bangladesh', in Bangladesh Itihas Samiti, *Studies in Rural History*, pp. 61-115.

53 Abu Ahmed Abdullah *et al.*, 'Agrarian Structure and the IRDP: Preliminary Considerations', *Bangladesh Development Studies*, 4, 2 *(1976)*, p. 217. A recent study of peasant mobility in Bangladesh concludes: 'the Bangladesh peasantry is neither a static, undifferentiated mass nor has as yet a clearly defined class structure but is a population characterized by both enduring inequalities and remarkable mobility between positions of abject poverty and affluence. Increasingly, this mobility shows a net downward trend leading to pauperisation (not proletarianisation) and uprooting of the poorest, and subsequently to 'quiet' starvation and large-scale famine'. Willim Van Schendel, *Peasant Mobility* (Delhi, 1982).

It would appear that after a period of massive expropriation through the land market in the decade after 1938, moneylending and usury re-emerged as a dominant mode of surplus-appropriation, although the composition of the exploiting classes changed dramatically as a result of the partition of 1947.

smallholding, often using hired labour to supplement family labour, remained a viable proposition at the cost of having a sizeable surplus regularly siphoned off in the form of usury interest.

During the late 1920s and 1930s, efforts were made to collect data in western and northern Bengal on 'the expropriation of hereditary cultivating classes by non-agriculturists'.[54] But this data does not help probe the question of differentiation or indeed the balance between khamar and raiyati. According to the Burdwan–Howrah–Hooghly settlement officer:

Almost all the landlords and professional men who lend money are also cultivators and as such the transfers that take place either in execution of money decree or voluntarily for debts incurred by cultivators are strictly not cases to be included in the return contemplated in your letter. . . Further it has been observed that the majority of the transfers is between the cultivating class themselves, i.e. amongst .raiyats.[55]

The small acreage reported to have passed from cultivators to 'people who may be said to be non-agriculturists' touched only a fringe of the land transfers. In the 1920s, the Jessore settlement officer categorically stated that barga lands held by under-raiyats were on the increase 'due to raiyati holdings passing to mahajans and others by purchase and subletting to original tenants on produce rents'.[56] In the western upland area of Malda, about 35 square miles out of a total of 802 square miles in a settlement block had during the 1920s passed from Santal and Oraon cultivators to non-agriculturist moneylenders.[57]

The 1930s depression hit both the microproprietors and the peasant smallholders hard. While crop prices slumped, rental demands and the cost of labour remained relatively high and the flow of money credit stopped. Those who had aspired to smallholding cultivation in the earlier part of the century

54 *RCA Report*, vol. 1, p. 355. This was a non-issue and no definition of 'agriculturist' or 'non-agriculturist' existed on the lines of the Punjab.
55 Settlement officer, Burdwan–Howrah–Hooghly settlement to Director of Land Records, 9 Aug. 1930, GB Rev. Dept, LR Br., B. June 1931, Progs. 39-4, Files 11R/27/30, 11R/8/31 (WBSA).
56 *Jessore SR*, pp. 113-14.
57 Settlement officer, Malda to Director of Land Records, 19 July 1930, GB Rev. Dept, LR Br., B. June 1931, Progs. 39-4, Files 11R/27/30, 11R/8/31 (WBSA).

could no longer command the resources to do so. The smaller moneylending landlords were unable to pay patni rents since the law on default was even more rigorously enforced than the revenue sale law. During the economic stress of the depression, many smaller patni tenures were purchased in Burdwan, Howrah and Hooghly by the Maharaja of Burdwan and by the larger patnidars.[58] The more substantial moneylender-landlords and rich peasants maintained their tight grip on the khamar sector through the continuance of grain loans to tied dependants. As peasant smallholders defaulted in the repayment of debts, the greater part of which were formed of rental arrears, many of them were forced into the ranks of the rural proletariat. In the slump, landlords' khamar was pushing back the frontiers of peasant smallholding. The landholding structure in west and central Bengal tended to sag in the middle, and was reinforced at the extremities by the extension of khamar and a land-poor, if not wholly landless, rural work-force.[59] It was a process not dissimilar to a shift from a *Grundherrshaft* to a *Gutsherrshaft* manorial or hacienda system – a peasant economy yielding ground to a sort of manorial enterprise economy – a process described in the Latin American literature as a *latifundia–minifundia* complex.[60]

The predicament of the peasant smallholders in west Bengal can be illustrated by the case of a family at Hooghly, relatively well-off, which came before a debt settlement board in 1938. The family of four adult and five minor members held

58 Note by Director, Debt Conciliation (West), GB CCRI, Dept RI Br., B. May 1942, Prog. 226, File 5R-5/38 (WBSA). 'The zamindars are in heavy arrears, the petty landlords and cultivators are losing their lands', it was reported in 1933-4, *Land Revenue Administration Report 1933-34*, p. 1; for statistics on the increased transfer of tenures from Land Revenue Administration Reports, see Partha Chatterjee, 'Agrarian Structure in Pre-partition Bengal' in A. Sen *et al.*, *Perspectives in Social Sciences 2*, pp. 140-1.

59 On the increase of proportionally petty and large landholdings at the expense of the medium-sized in northern India, cf. Stokes, *The Peasant and the Raj*, pp. 205-27.

60 See Cristobal Kay, 'Comparative Development of the European Manorial System and the Latin American Hacienda System', *Journal of Peasant Studies*, 2, 1 (1974).

   If, in west Bengal, the dispossessed raiyat was not immediately replaced by agricultural labourers who were available locally, it nevertheless meant for a raiyat-turned bargadar a loss of security of tenure for the future and an appropriation of a much larger proportion of the surplus. Bargadars were in fact evicted in west Bengal in 1946-7, as soon as there was a prospect of legislation in favour of bargadars in response to the adhiars' agitation in north Bengal and the abadi areas of the south.

some 30 acres of land in raiyati right. The tenant and his brother had two ploughs, a pair of bullocks and a pair of buffaloes with which they cultivated about half their lands and the other half was given in barga. The family had accumulated debts of Rs. 1434, mostly owed to their moneylending zamindars. This, the board, dominated by moneylending landowners, scaled down to Rs. 1278 and calculated that the debtor could only repay from his surplus income in ten annual instalments. But the landlords insisted that one-fourth of the dues should be paid in cash and the balance paid in four annual instalments. Their representatives suggested that the only feasible way to do so was to sell a portion of the holding, about 30 bighas (roughly 10 acres). However, the tenant and the landlords' gomasta pointed out that there were no purchasers and the value would be barely Rs. 25 per bigha. The landlords' agent disclosed that 200 bighas of other tenants' holdings had already been brought into khas possession. Of this, about 75 bighas had been placed under cultivation at the initial cost of Rs. 150. But there were likely to be no returns that year because of drought. Nevertheless the landlords refused to relent. This then was the fate of a tenant who during the previous two years had paid Rs. 165 and Rs. 200 towards arrears of rent and could not be regarded as a non-paying tenant.[61]

The figures collected by the enquiry of the Land Revenue Commission on raiyati area transferred between 1928 and 1940 show that in west and central Bengal districts, some 8.5% of the area surveyed was sold. Of this, 36.2% was cultivated by the purchasers' family, 31.3% by bargadars, 7.4% by labourers and 25.2% by under-raiyats (see table 5.4). Compared to the east-Bengal districts, the proportion cultivated by the purchasers' family was generally much smaller and the proportions cultivated by bargadars, labourers and under-tenants significantly higher.

The retreat of the small peasant in the face of the advancing grain-lending landlord and rich peasant during the depression turned into a rout in the ensuing period of war and famine. Rocketing grain prices on the eve of the famine

61 Note by Director, Debt Conciliation (West), GB CCRI Dept, RI Br., B. May 1942 Prog. 226, File 5-R-5/38 (WBSA).

Table 5.4. *The manner of cultivation of Raiyati area transferred during 1928–40 in west and central Bengal*

District	Area enquired into (acres)	Transferred during 12 years		Transferred area cultivated			
		Area	Percentage	Purchaser's family	Bargadars	Labourers	Under-tenants
Bankura	5479.86	368.05	6.70	48.47	77.06	36.99	205.43
Birbhum	3375.58	226.34	6.70	46.32	92.82	87.20	—
Burdwan	4759.15	185.88	3.80	82.32	65.36	38.15	—
Hooghly	2228.09	60.83	2.70	29.93	25.72	5.18	—
Howrah	1186.30	24.29	2.02	7.29	16.80	0.20	179.24
Jessore	5133.74	431.05	8.30	102.14	136.35	13.32	—
Khulna	1701.68	72.63	4.20	31.56	41.07	—	—
Malda	1107.93	77.02	6.90	48.51	17.95	—	10.56
Midnapore	4693.64	349.64	7.40	120.03	175.81	39.14	14.66
Murshidabad	5070.62	638.74	12.50	127.95	152.65	1.00	357.14
Nadia	4008.57	877.50	21.80	570.24	172.00	27.60	107.66
24-Parganas	5083.42	412.68	8.10	133.15	190.41	25.05	64.07
West and central Bengal Total	43828.58	3724.60	8.5%	1347.91 or 36.2% of transferred area	1164.00 or 31.3% of transferred area	273.83 or 7.4% of transferred area	938.76 or 25.2% of transferred area

Source: Land Revenue Commission Report (1940) Vol. 2, pp. 120-1.

spelled disaster for the mass of smallholding paddy growers of west and central Bengal who were net buyers of rice. The process of expropriation was described in stark terms:

valuable land is being sold by the small agriculturist to the larger agriculturists and to moneylenders (the two professions are commonly combined) for a small quantity of rice or paddy and the consideration entered in the sale deed is often fictitious. . . The smaller agriculturist, who was forced by poverty to sell his produce before prices rose to their present heights, is now being forced by the same poverty to buy food from the more well-to-do at an exorbitant rate and, in so doing, is forced to give up, by outright sale, his only source of livelihood. The larger cultivator, who was able to hold up his produce and sell for high prices, has an unusual amount of loose cash, which he is ready to invest in land.[62]

By the end of the war, the landlords' khas khamar together with the lands to which they and the richer peasantry held the occupancy raiyati right had increased rapidly. The emaciated smallholding sector was now more dependent on the khamar sector for grain advances and surplus lands than ever before. The smallholders and the landless had become more subservient. When the sharecroppers in the frontier regions began to assert themselves in the late 1940s, it was the dependant in west Bengal who quickly felt the backlash.[63]

It is sometimes assumed that the abolition of zamindari following independence marked the transfer of power from an upper-caste gentry to a rich peasantry.[64] In east Bengal, of course, the partition of 1947 removed most of the Hindu landed gentry from the scene. In west Bengal, zamindari abolition in 1953 – which involved compensation – no doubt deprived the erstwhile proprietors and tenure-holders of their rent-collecting rights. In the preceding two decades, these groups had been accumulating khas and raiyati lands. These land engrossers together with a minority of rich peasants drawn from the middle agricultural castes continued to rule the countryside as big raiyats, successfully evading ceiling legislation, for at least 20 years after independence. It was not until 1967 that a communist-led electoral challenge by the middling peasantry dislodged them from power.

62 Cmsner Presidency Dn to Secy CCRI Dept, 16 Sept. 1943, GB CCRI Dept RI Br., B.
   June 1943 Progs. 6-17, Conf Files 24 of 1943 and 10 of 1944 (WBSA).
63 See chapters 7 and 8 below.
64 See, for instance, R. and R. Ray, 'Zamindars and Jotedars', pp. 101-2.

The rich farmer–sharecropper system in the frontier regions

In north Bengal there was a rigid and permanent class division between a handful of substantial jotedars on the one hand and a mass of adhiars on the other. A sprinkling of small jotedars and chukanidars existed, but the jotedar–adhiar system remained the dominant form.

It would be interesting to ascertain the mobility patterns of the large jotedars, the small jotedars and chukanidars, and the adhiars. Unfortunately the sources give at best an impressionistic view of the broad trends. The giant jotedars at the peak of the landholding pyramid display a remarkable resilience through the nineteenth and early twentieth centuries.[65] It is possible that the composition of this class changed, but this assumes a degree of upward mobility that is highly unlikely in such a sharply polarised structure. The solid blocks of jotes, armed with capital, appear to have offset the effects of partition through inheritance, which brought about a powerful process of subdivisons in the peasant smallholdings of east Bengal. The smaller jotes were probably not as immune to the diminution of inheritances, but were at least in a more favourable land–man situation than in east Bengal. The smaller jotes were also vulnerable to a process of concentration launched by the bigger jotes. The clearers of the waste, who received credit advances from the big jotedars to push back the jungle were, in the course of time, dispossessed and left to continue as adhi tenants with no security of tenure. Relatively free peasants in the initial stages of a land-surplus frontier situation, they were reduced to bonded dependants in a manner reminiscent of the second serfdom in eastern Europe.[66] For the tied adhiars living in permissive possession of dismal homesteads on the jotedars' land, upward mobility was an unattainable dream. In contexts of more decentralised

---

65 Cf. F. Buchanan-Hamilton, *A Geographical, Statistical and Historical Description (1808) of the District, A Zillah of Dinajpur in the Province, or Soubah of Bengal* (Calcutta, 1883), and F.O. Bell, *Dinajpur SR* (1934-40); also *Jalpaiguri DG* (1911), *Rangpur SR* (1931-8).

66 Cf. W. Kula, *An Economic Theory of the Feudal System* (London, 1971), pp. 44-75, 112-59.

sharecropping, it was still difficult for the adhiar to buy into jotes. But it was not impossible, if he had the labour power and some access to the market to expand his operational holding by taking in more land on adhi. In the 1930s, it was not unusual to come across a man who 'held 40 bighas of land as an adhiar. . . He held more adhi land than he could cultivate with his own resources and had to employ labourers in addition. His "girasthi" or landowner advanced him small sums to carry him over the cultivation season and these were repaid at harvest.'[67]

Enquiries about the land market in the interwar period were addressed in north Bengal as in west Bengal to the question of transfers from 'agriculturist' to 'non-agriculturist', leaving out the more important question of accumulation of lands by rich agriculturists. The Dinajpur settlement officer reported that the transfer of the raiyati right in land to 'non-agriculturists' 'is no new thing, but has not gone very far, and is confined to villages within easy distance of the purchaser's residence'. The greater part was transferred by private sale, probably made because the vendor was in debt and chose to sell amicably rather than be subjected to the legal process. Cultivation by adhi was 'the most popular method of dealing with these lands'. The officer pointed out that 'attention so far has been directed towards the transfer of land to non-agriculturists. Another equally fruitful subject of study would be the transfer of lands to other agriculturists, and the accumulation of lands by the big jotedars'.[68]

In the neighbouring jute-growing district of Rangpur, there were instances of alienation of land to 'non-agriculturists' in the vicinity of the towns and big hats, where resident Sahas and Marwaris carried on moneylending operations. The Sahas tended to favour the adhi system, while the Marwaris and other moneylenders preferred subletting. The amount of such transfers was predictably higher in the jute areas than elsewhere. Raiyat moneylenders were 'very numerous', but the alienation of lands to them was not investigated as they were regarded as.'agriculturists'. As for the temporal trend, it was reported that 'whilst there has been some increase in

67 F.O. Bell, Tour Diary, Dinajpur, Nov.-Dec. 1939, p. 30. Mss Eur D 733/11 (IOR).
68 *Dinajpur SR*, p. 26.

transfers during the slump period, the increase is not serious'. This was attributed to the reluctance of mahajans generally 'to put a holding to sale when an outside purchaser is unlikely to come forward and the only resort is to resettle the land with the same tenant'.[69] More importantly, the peasant small-holding sector in these parts was so small and dispersed that preying on its pasture was hardly a significant or attractive option to jotedar creditors who already had much of their capital tied up in large blocks of sharecropped land at a time when agriculture was unprofitable. According to figures collected by the Land Revenue Commission in Dinajpur, Rangpur and Jalpaiguri, 5.6% of the raiyati area enquired into was transferred in the 12 years prior to 1940. Of this, 27.4% was cultivated by the purchasers' family, 40% by bargadars, 4% by labourers and 29.7% by under-tenants (see table 5.5).

In much of the abadi area of the south, the process of dispossession of the clearers of the waste, which had been spread in north Bengal over a fairly extended period of time, was compressed into the short period of the massive crisis of the depression. In the Sunderbans, where there was strict government control, it was discovered in 1938 that in areas where only 20 years ago land had been let out in 15 bigha plots to large numbers of cultivators, there had emerged holdings of 500 bighas or more.[70] After touring east 24-Parganas and west Khulna in 1939, the Presidency Commissioner commented on the tendency of chakdars and lotdars 'to take advantage of bad years to get lands made khas and to resettle in bhag'. Some had been 'foolish and rapacious'. In the 24-Parganas district there were instances of 30–40% of entire lots being converted during the depression decade. The destruction of the occupancy right was deeply resented and had 'given an opportunity to the communist'. He concluded pessimistically: 'All officers are alive to the necessity of warning landlords as to the danger of this policy, but the law allows it and the civil courts give effect to it, so that there will of necessity be cases of hardship if not of oppression pure and simple'.[71]

The frontier regions shared with the rest of the province, the boom in the land market following 1938. During the war and

69 *Rangpur SR*, p. 22.
70 GB Rev. Dept, LR Br., A. Dec. 1940 Progs. 42-52, File 2A-84/ 38 (WBSA).
71 Note by Cmsner, Presidency Division, GB Home Poll Con File 333/39 (WBSA).

Table 5.5. *The manner of cultivation of Raiyati area transferred during 1928–40 in north Bengal*

District	Area enquired into (acres)	Transferred during 12 years		Transferred area cultivated by			
		Area	Percentage	Purchaser's family	Bargadars	Labourers	Under-tenants
Dinajpur	6512.22	250.84	3.80	147.31	87.23	16.13	0.17
Jalpaiguri	4645.06	489.96	9.40	66.06	185.59	14.93	173.38
Rangpur	7964.30	380.60	4.70	80.60	144.92	10.73	144.35
North Bengal Total	19121.58	1071.40	5.6	293.97 or 27.4% of transferred area	417.74 or 40% of transferred area	41.79 or 4% of transferred area	317.90 or 29.7% of transferred area

Souce: Land Revenue Commission Report (1940) Vol. 2, pp. 120-1.

especially the famine, there is evidence from north Bengal of small jotedars and chukanidars being turned into adhiars.[72] The process of expropriation was most ruthless in the Sunderbans area of the 24-Parganas and Khulna. In 1946, K.B. Ray, President of the Krishak Sabha, described the pitiable condition of bhagchashis and khetmajurs who had been dispossessed of their lands and were living as serfs in flimsy shacks on the jotedars' lands. Some 50 to 100 people were attached to each of the substantial landholders in this area.[73]

In north Bengal, many of the sellers of raiyati rights in the post-1938 period were the big jotedars themselves. Instead of the usual reasons cited in deeds of land sales, such as 'indebtedness' or 'urgent need of cash for household expenses', one begins to find fairly substantial men selling because 'for various reasons it is no longer profitable or safe to keep jotejama'.[74] These sales might be partly explained by the unrest among bargadars, but also by the desire of some jotedars to create a nucleus of capital for investment in the more profitable urban sectors. When the adhiars of north Bengal launched their offensive in 1946, some of the jotedars had at least partially disengaged themselves from their rural commitments.

The tebhaga movement, of course, did not challenge the jotedar-dominated landholding structure in north Bengal. It merely sought to improve the terms of exchange. In the post-independence era, there were notable changes: the decline of share tenancies and the rapid increase in the number of agricultural labourers.[75] Yet, as late as 1969, the agrarian revolt that erupted in Naxalbari in north Bengal, but refused to spread like a prairie fire, still had as its main slogan – 'annihilate the jotedar'.

A focus on the purely agrarian issue reveals some enduring

72 'Adhiars and Jotedars in the district of Jalpaiguri', GB Rev. Dept, LR Br., B. Nov. 1940 Progs. 84-91, File 41-32 of 1940 (BSRR); K.B. Ray, *Chashir Lorai* pp. 17-18, cited in Badruddin Umar, *Chirosthayee Bandobaste Bangladesher Krishak* (The Bengal Peasant under the Permanent Settlement; Dacca, 1974), p. 78.
73 K.B. Ray, *Chashir Lorai*, pp. 18-19 cited in *ibid.*, p. 79.
74 Registered Deeds of Land Sales, Balurghat Subdivisional Registration Records (W. Dinajpur Dt Registration Office).
75 N. Bandyopadhyay, 'Causes of Sharp Increase in Agricultural Labourers, 1961-71:

qualities of the different types of social structure. In the first half of the twentieth century, these structures were subjected to increasing demographic and market pressures.[76] The agrarian world of Bengal was an organic part of the wider economic system. Tremors in the centres of the capitalist world economy were transmitted to the regional economy, transforming major elements in the relations of production and surplus-appropriation of the primary producers of agricultural commodities. The circuit of agrarian capital and credit linked the export sector with the relatively self-contained sectors so that no part of the agrarian economy remained wholly immune from fluctuations in the world economy.

Yet the dominance of the world capitalist system did not translate itself into capitalist relations in agriculture involving large-scale undertakings based on hired wage labour. The existence of large landholdings cultivated by sharecroppers and tied labourers in some regions, such as north Bengal, had to do with local conditions of the economic ecology of a clearing agriculture. On the whole, capital followed a path of vertical rather than horizontal concentration. It extracted primary products for the market without bringing about any major changes in the units of production characteristic of the different types of agrarian social structure. In many cases, small peasant producers were left in possession of the basic means of production-land. But they were never wholly independent agents in the process of production and reproduction, particularly since they were involved in inequitable conditions of trade and credit. The jute-growers of east Bengal and the paddy cultivators of west Bengal had to operate in the product market under extreme pressures. The trading machine was aimed at securing the crop without directly interfering in the social organisation of production. At most, in the early part of the century, where moneylending, trade and a fair degree of control of the landholding structure went hand-in-hand, the establishment of a few agricultural processing industries – rice-milling (mainly in west Bengal), oil-pressing, cane-crushing – impinged on some of the

A Case Study of Social Existence Forms of Labour in North Bengal', *EPW*, Review of Agriculture (Dec. 1977), pp. A-111-A-126.'

76 On the connection between demography and the growth of market relations, see chapter 2 above.

operations carried out by the peasants. But none of these changes altered the mode of agricultural operations of small subsistence peasants.[77]

Credit relationships are of critical importance in apprehending the direction of change in the relations of production and surplus-appropriation in the Bengal countryside. In the first three decades of the twentieth century, as the rural economy expanded and became increasingly tied to the market, credit formed an integral part of the process of reproduction, and was, at the same time, the principal mode of surplus-appropriation. The depression had a scything effect on the elaborate trading chain and ruptured the flow of rural credit. The impact of these developments was felt most acutely in the highly monetised economy of east Bengal. The talukdar-mahajans and trader-mahajans withdrew from the credit scene and became redundant in the small peasant economy. The disruption in the system of rural credit relations robbed these groups of their social and political clout. In west Bengal, the price and credit debacle saw the earth shrink under the feet of those who had lived by smallholding cultivation. The dominance of the landlords, which was reinforced in the khamar sector through the continuance of grain loans to dependent sharecroppers and labourers, was now extended to new territories wrested from the peasant smallholding sector. In some of the frontier areas, a relatively free peasantry was dispossessed and turned into serfs. But the fall in the product market had also adversely affected some of the jotedars in north Bengal. When the land market revived towards the end of the 1930s, they sought to partially disengage themselves from their rural commitments.

The agrarian crisis of the 1930s, moulded in its impact by the types of agrarian social structure and links with the economic system in the different regions, spawned agrarian tension and conflict of different kinds. It is to the major strands of agrarian protest and the role of the peasantry in Bengal politics that we turn in the next part of this book.

---

77 A census of agricultural implements taken in 1940 shows the primitive level of technique that persisted in Bengal agriculture: 4 330 804 wooden ploughs, 6304 iron ploughs, 821 194 carts, 128 power-worked sugarcane crushers, 17 670 bullock-worked sugarcane crushers, 128 oil-engines, 55 electric pumps for tube-wells and 52 tractors. Census of Agricultural Implements in Bengal (GB 1940).

PART II
PEASANTS AND POLITICS

6

Agrarian class conflict, nationalism and communalism in east Bengal

Between 1900 and 1930, rural credit was the nub of an interlocking set of relations of production and surplus-appropriation underpinning the agrarian social structure in east Bengal. The peasant smallholding structure could not reproduce itself without being subject to the exploitation of mercantile and usury capital. This unequal, but necessary, symbiosis between smallholding peasants and their trader and talukdar creditors had ruled out the possibility of any sustained conflict. It was only during 1930–47 that conflict between a Muslim peasantry and a predominantly Hindu landed-gentry and small trading community became endemic. The aim of this chapter is to identify the locus of historical initiative behind the forces which led to the disintegration of the plural society in east Bengal.

Agrarian politics will be seen in the context of broad economic trends with particular emphasis on the impact of the 1930s slump on social relations in the countryside. Since the peasantry were not less political than the 'elite', a structural analysis and periodisation of their politics is no less important than for the politics of the 'elite'.[1] Changes in key elements of the agrarian social structure had a decisive influence on the complexion and articulation of peasant politics. With the rupture in rural credit relations in the 1930s, the unequal and symbiotic social networks in east Bengal were torn apart. The talukdar-mahajans and trader-mahajans did not suddenly become more oppressive. In fact, it was during this period that their chief mode of surplus-appropriation

---

1 It is little more than begging the question to say that in addition to 'organised' and 'elite' politics, there is a vast arena of 'unorganised' and 'subaltern' politics. See the recent manifesto by a group of radical historians, Ranajit Guha (ed.), *Sub-altern Studies* I (Delhi, 1982). It is essential to locate the dynamics which link the different arenas and levels of politics. One influential view gives primacy to the role of the government's constitutional initiatives in the politicisation of the countryside, Gallagher *et al.* (eds.), *Locality, Province and Nation.* The post-1930 conjuncture in agrarian Bengal suggests a groundswell from below triggered by by the massive economic crisis of the depression, which government was able to

through debt interest collapsed. They withdrew from playing a role in the reproductive process, and lost their main source of influence over the peasant-debtors. The erstwhile creditors, if they remained on the agrarian scene, were now either simply parasitic, though ineffectual, petty rent-collectors or grain-dealers in a volatile product market.

The breakdown of social symbiosis reached its dramatic climax during the Noakhali and Tippera riots of 1946. In the final days of the Raj, while the politicians pondered their moves on the political chessboard of 'nation' and 'province', these two remote districts in littoral east Bengal witnessed an unprecedented orgy of communal hatred and violence. The strong religious overtone to the Noakhali and Tippera riots is intriguing when seen in the light of a long tradition of militant protest by krishak samitis which tended to operate on 'class' lines. Since the early 1920s, Tippera had been in the forefront of nationalist mass agitations. As early as 1906–7, 'communal' riots in Mymensingh and Comilla had revealed what was to become the Achilles' heel of mass nationalism in east Bengal.[2] Yet, except for the localised and short-lived violence of the Swadeshi days, the east Bengal countryside on the whole had remained remarkably free from conflict along communal lines. It was only after 1929–30[3] that the old symbiosis began to be undermined irreversibly. Collective protest by Muslim peasants became a recurrent feature. Three major conflagrations took place in this period: in 1930 in the Kishoreganj subdivision of Mymensingh district, in 1941 in the Narsinghdi circle of Dacca district and finally in 1946 the better-known riots in Noakhali and Tippera. This chapter

channel only in part into the extended electoral arena created by the 1935 Act. For a general interpretation which suggests that economic periodisation set broad patterns on political periodisation, especially in the case of agrarian-based agitations, see Stokes, *The Peasant and the Raj*, pp. 271-80.

'Organised' politics in pre-independence Bengal has been well served by historians, J.H. Broomfield, *Elite Conflict in a Plural Society: Twentieth Century Bengal* (Berkeley, 1969); Leonard A. Gordon, *Bengal: The Nationalist Movement 1876-1940* (New York, 1974); Shila Sen, *Muslim Politics in Bengal 1937-47* (Delhi, 1974).

2 For a discussion of these riots, see Sumit Sarkar, *The Swadeshi Movement in Bengal 1903-1908* (Calcutta, 1974), pp. 444-64; also, Rajat Ray, 'Social Conflict and Political Unrest in Bengal, 1875-1908' (Cambridge, Ph.D. dissertation, 1973), p. 274.

3 A little earlier, 1926-7, in the mofussil towns and markets.

will analyse agrarian conflict in east Bengal by focusing on the history of krishak movements in Noakhali and Tippera and the major outbreaks of peasant protest in contiguous districts. A detailed anatomy of these outbreaks will lay bare the nature of the economic grievances and the agrarian conflict that fed the communal fire. An interpretative history of peasant politics in two selected districts over more than three decades, both before and after the depression, will illuminate important shifts in its composition and character.

Agrarian social structure in Noakhali and Tippera

Agrarian society in Noakhali and Tippera consisted of predominantly Muslim smallholding peasantry with a sprinkingly of mainly Hindu upper-caste rent-collecting and moneylending groups. Nearly 80% of the entire population in the two districts were either directly or indirectly dependent on the land.[4] Here, the Hindu high-caste landed-gentry had a relatively weaker presence than in their traditional habitats in Dacca, Faridpur and Bakarganj. In 1911, 1 man received rent for every 48 who paid in Tippera; the ratio in Noakhali was 1 to 34.[5] There were fewer landlords' agents than elsewhere in the province.[6] But by and large, the tenurial pattern conformed to that in other districts of east Bengal. With the expansion of the jute economy in the early twentieth century, landlords, big and small, became increasingly involved in moneylending. The traders, mostly belonging to the intermediate nabashakh castes, notably the Sahas 'engaged as shopkeepers and [in] moneylending', were only 'gradually becoming middlemen in the land system'.[7] The bulk of the peasantry had rights of occupancy raiyats and were not sharply differentiated. At the time of 1910s' survey and

---

4 *Noakhali' SR*, p. 25; *Tippera SR*, p. 23.
5 The corresponding ratios in the other districts were as follows: Chittagong - 1:12, Dacca - 1:21, Bakarganj - 1:23, Faridpur - 1:23, Mymensingh - 1:48, Rajshahi division - 1:58, Burdwan division - 1:16, Presidency division - 1:14. *Noakhali SR*, p. 25.
6 In Noakhali there was 1 landlord's agent to 289 rent-payers and in Tippera to every 287. The corresponding ratios in the other districts were: Chittagong - 1:201, Dacca - 1:84, Bakarganj - 1:99, Faridpur - 1:150, Mymensingh - 1:216, Burdwan division - 1:124, Presidency division - 1:88, Rajshahi division - 1:201. *Ibid.*
7 *Ibid.* p. 26

settlement, the proportion of the cultivated area sublet to under-raiyats was small and produce rentals were negligible.[8] The Noakhali settlement officer attributed the failure of landlord-moneylenders to impose high share rents to 'the strength of the cultivating classes as a body'.[9] A relatively undifferentiated peasantry was bound by similar sets of tenurial, credit and market relations to the talukdars and traders. Although security against rent increase was assured, the primary producers had still to operate in the insecure environs of highly inequitable product and credit markets.

Another factor bound the peasantry together. Religion was an important element in the psyche of the Muslim peasantry. Almost all Sunni Muslims of the Hanafi school, they had described themselves as Sheikhs in the 1911 census returns. As the settlement officer commented, anyone visiting Noakhali district could not 'fail to notice at once what a large part religion plays in the behaviour of the people'.[10] There were historical reasons for this. Both Noakhali and Tippera had been affected by the Faraizi movement.[11] Local religious leaders kept the banner of Islam flying in the lives and imaginations of the Muslim peasantry. Maktabs and madrassahs, religious debates and mahfils, all served to heighten the sense of an Islamic identity.[12] It was only late in the nineteenth century that an internally fragmented Bengali Muslim society for the first time shed its syncretist habits and customs. Bengali names were rejected and Arabic ones adopted. Yet, interestingly enough, there was a discontinuity

---

8 In Tippera, out of the total area of land held by settled raiyats, only 2% was held in sanja (fixed produce rent) and 0.45% in bhag (half share rent). In Noakhali raiyats, settled and occupancy, paying a fixed produce rent occupied only 220 acres, 0.03%, and those paying a share of the produce, 329 acres, 0.04%. Non-occupancy raiyats at produce rents held only 43 acres in the whole district. *Ibid.*, pp. 91-2.

9 *Ibid.*

10 *Ibid.*, pp. 27-9.

11 The Faraizi teaching had been brought to Noakhali and Tippera by Maulana Shariatullah. The second wave of religious enthusiasm was triggered by the Wahabi preacher, Maulana Imamuddin, a native of Noakhali and a close associate of Syed Ahmad himself. A prominent religious figure of the later nineteenth century was Maulana Keramatali of the reformed Hanafi school. In the early years of the twentieth century, his son, Maulana Abdul Awal, regularly visited the district, and the crowds flocked to hear him.

12 See Rafiuddin Ahmed, *Bengal Muslims: The Redefinition of Identity 1876-1906* (Delhi, 1982).

between the acceptance of Islamic rituals and the timing and character of political conflict.[13] The connections between the ideological movements of the later nineteenth century and the relations of production and exploitation in rural east Bengal remain to be closely investigated. But evidence suggests that so long as symbiotic economic relationships prevailed, peasant protest stopped short at cultural dissidence without spilling over into overt political conflict. Religion, of course, was readily available as a powerful legitimising ideology when a change in the balance of class power brought the rejection of the old order within the realm of possibility.

Peasant politics: the First World War and its aftermath

The wartime scarcity of articles of daily necessity and the dramatic decline in the price of raw jute in relation to spiralling grain prices stirred the east Bengal countryside out of the relative calm of the 1907-13 golden boom. In July and August of 1915, there were reports of a possible famine in Noakhali:

There was in reality no shortage of food whatsoever, but the price of jute had fallen suddenly the year before, mahajans who had made advances to cultivators on the crop had lost and were not prepared to make advances again. The famine was a money-famine.[14]

The disaffections caused by the strains of war found expression in the looting of markets and grain stores, with sporadic attacks on the property of rural traders and moneylenders.[15] It was in this period that efforts were made to give peasant demands some organised expression. Grass-roots peasant political associations sprang into existence. These praja or krishak samitis soon set about bargaining collectively with landlords and creditors. They began with modest but

13 As Ahmed himself notes, 'incidents of serious communal violence in Bengal proper were quite small' and 'the few incidents occurred in urban areas'. *Ibid.,* pp. 178-9 and *passim.*
14 *Noakhali SR,* p. 39.
15 'War had brought the usual economic strains. Prices soared and sagged and the Bengali cultivator, the primary producer and usually a Muslim, suffered. In Noakhali District it was the Hindu landlord and moneylender who applied the suffering and it was the Muslim cultivator who rose and rioted. Markets were looted throughout the District'. A.J. Dash, A Bengal Diary, vol. 3, The First District Jan. 1919 to Oct. 1919, Dash Papers (SASC).

significant economic and social demands – the remission or
rent and debt interest in lean years, the right to a seat in the
landlords' kachchari and the courtesy of being addressed with
the polite *apni* rather than the colloquial *tui*. Impressive mass
meetings of krishaks and prajas were held on the expansive
chars of the east-Bengal delta.[16]

Not a great deal is known about the activities of local
krishak samitis in Noakhali and Tippera during the war. In
April 1919, a district krishak samiti was established in
Tippera with headquarters in Comilla.[17] In its initial stages,
the samiti was concerned with the immediate grievances of the
peasants and agitated for the amendment of the tenancy law.
During 1920-2, it was drawn into the more widespread
agitation of the non-cooperation and khilafat movement. The
sluggishness of jute prices in 1920-1 gave the opportunity for a
jute boycott campaign. But this proved to be short-lived. In
further efforts to disrupt the government's economic resources,
law courts were boycotted and numerous arbitration courts set
up in the villages; in Noakhali, an appellate court was
established consisting of pleaders at the local bar. An
agitation was also launched against the newly set up union
boards. In some places, village unions were formed to control
the export of rice by selling to Europeans and outside traders
only at exorbitant rates. As the movement gathered
momentum, it was not possible to channel it purely against
European and government's economic interests. In Tippera,
the local landholding and moneylending upper-caste stratum
came under fire from the Muslim peasantry and 'the situation
quickly assumed the shape of a fierce class conflict'.[18]

16 The large praja congress at Kamariar Char in the Jamalpur subdivision of
Mymensingh in 1914 was addressed by prominent Muslim leaders including
Fazlul Huq of Bakarganj, Akram Khan from Calcutta, Rajibuddin Tarafdar of
Bogra, Khondkar Ahmed Akalubi of Mymensingh and Maniruzzaman
Islamabadi of Chittagong. Humayun Kabir, 'Krishak Praja Samiti o Praja
Swartha' (Krishak Praja Samiti and the Praja Interest), *Krishak* (1945 Id
number), pp. 6-8; Abul Mansur Ahmed, *Amar Dekha Rajnitir Panchas Bachhar*
(Fifty Years of Politics as I saw it, Dacca, 1968), pp. 13-14.
17 Syed Emdadul Huque, popularly known as Lal Mian, became president and
Asimuddin Ahmed was appointed organising secretary. Notes on Krishak
Samiti, Comilla by Cmsner Chittagong Dn in GB Home Poll Dept, Conf. File
245 (1-5) of 1931 (WBSA).
18 Rajat Ray, 'Masses in Politics: The Non-Cooperation Movement in Bengal 1920-
1922', *IESHR*, 4 (1974), pp. 399-400.

By the end of 1921, the chaukidars and daffadars had stopped work in many parts of Tippera, no taxes were being paid and no agricultural rents were being collected either by the government or by the landlords. Attempts to execute distress warrants and criminal processes were met with assaults on government officers. When armed police were sent out to make arrests, they arrived only to find deserted villages. Although 'the agitation was entirely Muhammadan', it was 'not religious'. The peasants were merely trying 'to assert themselves and save money'.[19] Between 13 February and 9 March 1922, there were five determined attacks by large crowds on the police. On 9 March the district authorities took matters in hand and sent out a search party to apprehend the trouble-makers. A frenzied crowd received them with clods of earth and lathis. In the police firing that ensued, three people were killed and many more were injured.[20] Peasant nationalism in Tippera had been given its first martyrs.

In the immediate postwar period, both the product and the labour markets were uncertain bets. After 1922 there was an increase in agricultural prices. The inflow of finance capital ensured that the system of rural credit relations would be kept well-oiled. This set the pace for a period of relative quiescence in the history of agrarian relations. The unequal symbiosis in social relations was reinforced without adding new strains. But in 1926–7, when the demand for jute began to weaken, the latent tension between peasant and creditor began to surface. There were the expected attacks on Hindu fairs and markets. But there was a new feature. For the first time, Hindu religious festivals, the symbol of landholding and trading power, became the targets. Since the peasantry was predominantly Muslim, it was easy to give their economic discontent a communal colouring. For the mobilisers of peasant discontent, Islam presented an array of symbols to challenge existing disparities. There were communal riots in Calcutta and Dacca, and some fracas in the mofussil towns of Dacca, Bakarganj and Pabna.[21] But the frictions in the market centres

---

19 'History of the Non-Cooperation Movement in Bengal', p. 14, GB Home Poll Dept, Conf. File 395/24 (WBSA).
20 *Ibid.*
21 See Partha Chatterjee, 'Agrarian Relations and Communalism in Bengal 1926-1935' in Guha (ed.), *Sub-altern Studies* I pp. 9-38.

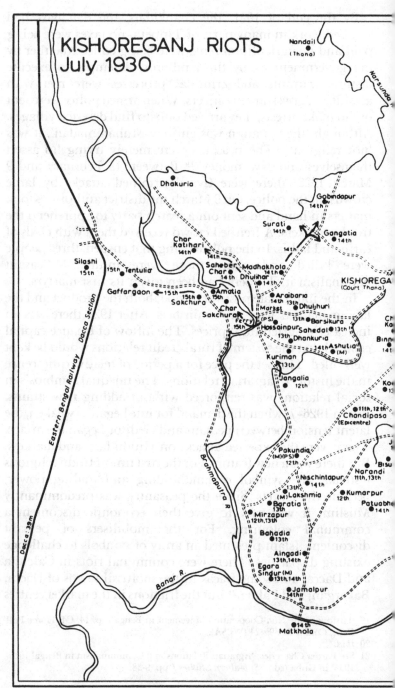

Map 6: The Kishoreganj disturbances
Source: Sugata Bose,

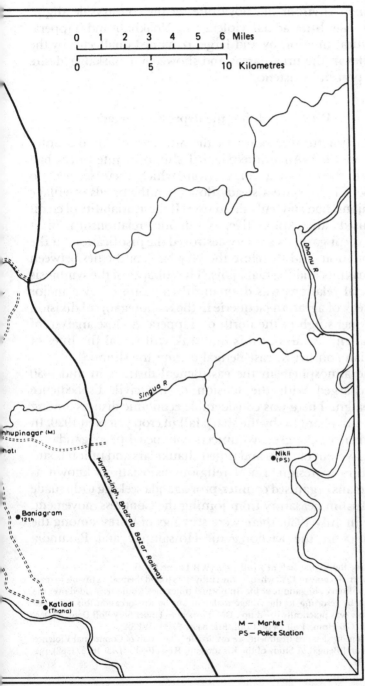

and their environs did not quite set the countryside alight. There was little actual violence in Noakhali and Tippera. The rural interior, by and large, remained unaffected by the troubles in the urban areas and showed a remarkable 'desire for a peaceful existence'.[22]

Peasant politics: the depression decade

The major turning-point in the attitudes of the peasantry came in 1930. An unprecedented slump in jute prices had pushed them into a corner from which there seemed no escape. Credit, once a steady flow from the hands of village mahajans, had suddenly dried up.[23] If the availability of credit disguised an exploitative, symbiotic relationship in a benevolent garb, its scarcity destroyed the justification for the exploitation, and therefore the very basis of the ties between the peasants and the mahajans. The collapse of the symbiosis in social relations was dramatically announced by a major outbreak of agrarian jacquerie in the Kishoreganj subdivision of Mymensingh to the north of Tippera. A close analysis of the salient features of this outbreak will reveal the lines of agrarian conflict in east Bengal during the slump.[24]

The atmosphere in the east-Bengal districts in mid-1930 was charged with the tension of the civil disobedience campaign. There was considerable economic distress among cultivators hard hit by the sharp fall in crop prices in 1929. In the interior, Congress volunteers conducted propaganda for non-payment of taxes and urged chaukidars and union board members to resign. Local religious associations known as Anjumans organised counter-propaganda seeking to dissuade the Muslim peasantry from joining the Congress movement. Early in July 1930, there were stirrings of unrest among the peasants in the Kishoreganj, Hossainpur and Pakundia

22 FR for the second half of April 1926 (WB Home Dept).
23 'The crisis came in 1930 when . . . the cultivators found themselves unable to meet the ordinary obligations of life. In normal times they would have tided over the crisis by resorting to the village mahajan but on this occasion this source of supply was practically dried up'. DM Tippera to Under-Secy Poll Dept, 26 Dec. 1931, GB Home Poll Dept, Conf. File 849(1-9)/31 (WBSA).
24 For a more detailed treatment, see my article 'The Roots of Communal Violence in Rural Bengal: A Study of the Kishoreganj Riots 1930', *MAS*, 16, 3 (1982), pp. 463-91.

thanas. Several peasant meetings were held. At one meeting on 7 July, the naib of the Atharabari zamindari kachhari at Hossainpur was castigated for interfering in a Muslim religious festival and oppressing his Muslim tenants. Resolutions were passed against the payment of interest to moneylenders.

On 11 July disturbances erupted in Pakundia thana. The houses of prominent Hindu moneylenders were attacked and looted. Within the next five days, the troubles had spread to Hossainpur and pockets of Katiadi, Nandail and Nikli thanas, and across the Brahmaputra to the Gaffargaon area. The primary objective of the rioters was to destroy the debt bonds held by the moneylenders. Usually a crowd of 100 to 1000 men would surround the house of a moneylender and demand the documents in his possession. If the documents were not produced, the house was looted and in some cases burnt. The most gruesome incident took place in the village of Jangalia where ten members of a moneylending family, who had fired upon the crowd, were hacked to death. Buildings were burnt and movable property was smashed. To quell the disturbances, reinforcements of military police had to be rushed from Dacca. A number of rioters were killed in several instances of police firing. By 18 July, the district magistrate could write with smug satisfaction: 'Captain Seagrim and the Eastern Frontier Rifles force have been as invaluable as usual. Johnny Gurkha commands the greatest respect in mofassil Bengal as a fighting man and the mere fact that he is present is a valuable asset to district authorities in troubled times.'[25]

Ironically enough, the rioters had been under the impression that the government would be on their side. Similar notions, real or imagined, of the support of a distant government against immediate oppressors have of course always played an important role in the translation of peasant grievances into peasant rebellion.[26] In Mymensingh,

25 DM Mymensingh to Chief Secy, 18 July 1930, GB Poll Conf. File 613/30 (WBSA).
26 DM Mymensingh to Chief Secy, 18 July 1930, GB Poll Conf. File 613/30 (WBSA). In the 1906-7 riots in Mymensingh also, the rioters had believed that the government had authorised the pillage of Hindu mahajans. *Mymensingh SR.*, p. 30; very similar notions appear to have been held by peasant rebels in the Deccan riots of 1875 (I.J. Catanach, 'Agrarian Disturbances in Nineteenth Century India', *IESHR*, 3, 1 (1966), pp. 70-2) and in the grain riots in Madras in 1918 (David Arnold, 'Looting, Grain Riots and Government Policy in South

maulavies from Dacca and Bhowal told the cultivators that the government was behind the Muslims. Muslims could demand or forcibly extort the debt bonds without fear of government reprisals. On 12 July, when the circle officer of Kishoreganj confronted the looters at Jaitra, he was politely told not to interfere since the authorities had done well to keep out of the troubles in Dacca. Some villagers believed they were acting on government orders in demanding their deeds back from the mahajans. The last words of one rioter, fatally wounded in the police shooting, were: 'ami British governmenter proja, dohai British government' (I am a subject of the British government, have mercy on me). The poor soul had not understood the inner logic of the law and order enforcing agencies.[27]

The disturbances had other interesting features. Personal violence was on the whole eschewed, except in Jangalia where the mob was fired upon. Significantly, no women were molested by the rioters. Looting usually took place before sunset in deference to the Shariat which considers it cowardly to steal at night. The wrath of the rioters was directed against property in general and loan bonds in particular. Altogether 90 villages had been attacked.[28] When the police investigations were completed, 142 cases were instituted.[29] Charge sheets were actually submitted in 129 cases against 631 people, who were considered to have been the 'principal culprits'.

Not surprisingly, there was considerable controversy over who was to be blamed for these riots, not to mention continuing uncertainties about their real nature. Some believed that the 'disobedience' campaigns had rebounded on the Congress. Others were certain that the disturbances were the result of a machiavellian colonial policy to divide Hindu and Muslim. There were those who attributed the troubles entirely to mischievous maulavies from the urban areas. The

India 1918', *Past and Present*, 84 (1979), p. 145; analogies can also be drawn in this respect with peasant behaviour in rural riots in eighteenth-century France and Russia. See George Rude, *The Crowd in History* (New York, 1964).

27 Superintendent of Police Mymensingh to DM Mymensingh, 2 Aug. 1930, GB Poll Conf. File 613/30 (WBSA).

28 One case being brought for all looting cases occurring in the same village on the same day and committed by the same gang.

29 Special Report Case No. 93/30 Report III by Additional Superintendent of Police Mymensingh, 30 Aug. 1930, GB Poll Conf. File 613/30 (WBSA).

more philosophical wondered whether Kishoreganj had witnessed a 'class battle' or simply a 'communal outbreak'.

According to the district magistrate, the Kishoreganj disturbances were, 'primarily economic with a necessary communal tinge because more than 90 per cent of the tenants and debtors in the affected area are Muhammadans, while the large majority of the moneylenders are Hindus. Muhammadan moneylenders have, however, been proportionately threatened and looted.'[30] At least nine Muslim moneylenders had lost their documents and several more had requested help from local authorities. The figures from first information reports showed that only a small proportion of the victims were unconnected with moneylending. According to these figures, 995 Hindu houses and shops and 6 Muslim houses were looted for loan documents, 33 Hindu shops were looted in which no demand for documents was made, and 21 Hindu and 3 Muslim houses lost documents under threat without any looting. Other reports indicate that the rioting, once it began, gathered its own momentum and the rioters were not always discriminating in their purpose.[31] Some poor low-caste Hindus were affected and there was a communal bias in the looting of shops. There is little doubt, however, that the principal target of the rioters was the moneylender, who in most cases in east Bengal happened to be Hindu.

According to the Hindu press, the Kishoreganj riots had been masterminded by those who had their own axes to grind. The urban-based Muslim politicians fighting with Hindus over jobs and council seats and their religious agents had used the poverty and misery of the Muslim peasantry as an asset to further their own ends. The *Charu Mihir* a local paper in Mymensingh complained that the maulavies had inflamed the peasants with stories about how the Congress campaign had caused the depression in the jute market.

'Too much violence and intimidation by Congress volunteers seems to have been allowed in Kishoreganj', the Commissioner of Dacca Division wrote angrily. This factor

30 DM Mymensingh to Chief Secy, 18 July 1930, GB Poll Conf. File 613/30 (WBSA).
31 Report about the looting and rioting in Kishoreganj subdivision by SDO Kishoreganj, 12 July 1930, GB Poll Conf. File 613/30 (WBSA); Notes on Kishoreganj Investigations by Superintendent of Police Mymensingh, 24 Aug. 1930, *ibid.*

alone had 'done much to undermine the respect for the authority of Government'.[32] But the available evidence suggests that the Muslim cultivators rose in revolt under the illusion of being encouraged and abetted by the government. As the local officials admitted, the mobs had been influenced by 'rumours' that the government had turned a blind eye when Muslims went on the rampage in Dacca. In Mymensingh, the district administration had goaded the local Anjumans into actively opposing the civil disobedience movement.[33] Widespread and uncontrolled violence was, however, a dangerous thing for the government to encourage and the Kishoreganj disturbances were put down firmly. Once order had been restored, there were convincing arguments against the imposition of punitive police. It might, for instance, be used by the nationalists 'to persuade the Mahommedans from their present opposition to the Civil Disobedience Movement'.[34]

Certainly in Tippera, the district Congress under Ashrafuddin Ahmed Chaudhuri was making efforts to mobilise the Muslim peasantry behind the civil disobedience movement. By May 1930, the commissioner of Chittagong division wanted to put an end to these activities since he 'could not afford to allow the Mussalmans to be decoyed'.[35] Until January 1931, he was satisfied that apart from 'Ashrafuddin's batch of vagabonds', the mass of the Muslim peasantry had not been affected by the movement.[36] By March 1931, however, there was 'a tendency for Muhammadans to side with congress', apparently because 'congress had gained in prestige and the Muhammadans were beginning to think that they would have done better if they had been with the congress all along'.[37] At a meeting held in Comilla on 19 and 20 January 1931, the district krishak samiti had been revived under the leadership of Mukleshwar Rahman, an associate of

32 Cmar Dacca Dn to Chief Secy, 31 July 1930, GB Poll Conf. File 613/30 (WBSA).
33 DM Mymensingh to Chief Secy, 1 July 1930, GB Poll Conf. File 511/30 (WBSA). See Bose, 'The Roots of Communal Violence'.
34 DM Mymensingh to Chief Secy, 18 July 1930, GB Poll Conf. File 613/30 (WBSA).
35 Cmsner Chittagong Dn to Chief Secy, 18 May 1930, GB Poll Conf. File 526(1-18) of 1930 (WBSA).
36 Cmsner Chittagong Dn to Chief Secy, 27 Jan. 1931, GB Poll Conf. File 105 (1-14)/31 (WBSA).
37 Extract from Confidential Fortnightly dated 27/3/31 from Cmsner Chittagong Dn, GB Poll Conf. File 105 (1-14)/31 (WBSA).

Ashrafuddin. The krishak samiti and Congress movements were now beginning to coalesce.[38]

After the local leaders, imprisoned for civil disobedience offences, were released following the Gandhi–Irwin Pact of March 1931, they consciously decided to assume direction of the economic grievances of the peasantry. Numerous krishak samiti meetings were held in Comilla and in the countryside. The principal organisers and propagandists were professionals, both Hindu and Muslim.[39] The samiti was closely interconnected with the local Congress organisation. The members of the executive committee of the district krishak samiti were all members of the Congress committee. Kamini Kumar Datta, a secret official report claimed, 'is the brain of the movement and also finances it. He is a well-known pleader at Comilla and has considerable social influence. But his professional engagements and obligations notwithstanding, he has not hesitated to go out into the interior and address meetings declaiming against landlords in general.'[40] The leadership of the krishak movement in Tippera consisting at least in part of professional Hindus is a useful corrective to a stereotype of 'bhadralok' antipathy to Muslim peasant interests.[41]

The propaganda against landlords and moneylenders fell on fertile soil. In April 1931, it was reported that in Nabinagar thana, 'the zamindar mahajans have become very unpopular because of their oppressive methods. There have been meetings in which it was resolved not to pay interest to money-lenders; the Zamindars and their families have removed themselves to Brahmanbaria for safety.'[42] On 1 May, a large procession of some 5000 peasants and labourers was brought out in Comilla and what the district magistrate

---

38 Cmsner Chittagong Dn to Chief Secy, 31 Mar. 1931, GB Poll Conf. File 245 (1-5) of 1931 (WBSA).
39 Most prominent were Kamini Kumar Datta, Mukleswar Rahman, Abdul Malek, Abdul Jalil, Abdul Wahed, Habibur Rahman, Abdul Latif, Krishna Sundar Bhowmick, Dhirendra Datta, Nibaran Ghosh and Basanta Majumdar.
40 DM Tippera to Under-Secy Poll Dept, 26 Dec. 1931, GB Poll Conf. File 849 (1-9)/31 (WBSA).
41 The Hindu 'bhadralok', who might be credited with some cultural identity, were a very diverse category in economic terms, and straddled a whole spectrum of politics from khadi beige to flaming scarlet.
42 Extract from Confidential Fortnightly dated 27/4/31 from Cmsner Chittagong Dn, GB Poll Conf. File 105 (1-14)/31 (WBSA).

described as 'a sort of Bolshie meeting' was held in the town hall maidan.[43] Resolutions were passed at the meeting, attended also by Congress leaders, urging an overwhelming representation of cultivators in the councils, the limitation of debt interest to 6%, the reduction of union board taxes, the release of Meerut conspiracy case prisoners, the provision of free education, the removal of untouchability and communal strife and free legal defence in rent suits. The political motive behind the timing of the event was to demonstrate Muslim support for the Congress on Subhas Bose's visit to Comilla the following day. According to the district magistrate, 'Congress was really behind the demonstration as they wished to make a good show to Subash [sic].'[44]

By the middle of May, reports on the economic and political situation in Tippera and Noakhali were sufficiently alarming to induce the Chittagong commissioner to conduct a personal investigation. He found that there was 'no famine in the ordinary sense of the word, but a pronounced shortage of money. The jute crop of the [Tippera] district of about 5 million maunds sold for Rs. 3 and 8 might have been expected, so the district is short by two and a half crores.' Mahajans and banks had 'dried up' and there was a great clamour for agricultural loans. There was 'much distress among landless labourers'; labour rates had gone down to two annas a day in some places and many were without work. Under the circumstances, the government had good reason to be anxious about the activities of the krishak samitis. The commissioner reckoned that in ordinary economic conditions the propaganda against payment of rents to landlords and interest to mahajans would not have been successful 'because nearly every cultivator goes to a money-lender for a loan each year'; but in 1931, the moneylenders recovered nothing and had no money to give out. People holding stocks of paddy were refusing to lend in expectation of selling at high prices

43 The procession was mainly composed of Muslim cultivators from the surrounding villages and from places up the railway line as far as Kasba with the Muslims of Mogultali Bazaar in some force and some Congress volunteers. The main organisers were Abdul Malek and Mukleshwar Rahman. The processionists carried ploughs, yokes, spades and brooms. Red streamers were floated at the end of long poles and it was proposed to form a red-cap association.
44 DM Tippera to Cmsner Chittagong Dn, 5 May 1931, in *ibid*.

the following year. The refusal of loans created a serious possibility of paddy looting and at least one granary was looted. There were fears in Noakhali that 'the unwillingness of Hindu money-lenders to give loans may give rise to riots like those in Kishoreganj'. Muslim peasants had threatened Hindu moneylenders that 'unless they gave loans freely, neither their lives nor their property would be safe'.[45]

Some detailed information is available on the extent of the krishak movement in Tippera in 1931 and the chief centres of krishak samiti activity.[46] In Brahmanbaria subdivision, the movement was particularly widespread in Nabinagar and parts of Kasba thanas:

Samitis have been started in almost every village with their own presidents and secretaries. Almost everybody in the village is a member of the samiti except the mahajans. As a rule, the debtors have eagerly joined the samitis as they have been told that by doing so they would not have to pay their dues. Those who have tried to remain neutral or loyal to the mahajans have been forced by social boycott and threatened violence, to join the samitis.[47]

The mahajans were placed under considerable pressure; their servants were asked to quit and vendors were persuaded not to sell to them. The demands of the samitis were unequivocal. The mahajans had to surrender their documents, leaving it to the samitis to decide how and when

45 Cmsner, Chittagong Dn to Chief Secy, 28 May 1931, GB Poll Conf. File 105(1-14)/31 (WBSA).
46 In the Sadar subdivision, the first symptoms of the movement came to light in the conflict between the management of the Lais estate at Barura in Chandina thana and the local tenants over the administration of the market there. There had been 'undoubted oppression on the part of the underlings of the zamindars', who were absentees in Calcutta. Under the leadership of Asimuddin Ahmed, the tenants banded together to boycott the market and set up one of their own, a quarter of a mile away. The new market had a moribund existence, but Barura continued to be a centre of turbulence and organised opposition to the local landlords. Charanal in Burichang thana was the base of Abdul Malek. The activities of the samiti here had to be restrained by bringing a case against Abdul Malek under section 107 of the criminal procedure code. From Burichang the movement spread under the leadership of Mukleshwar Rahman to several places in the Debidwar and Muradnagar thanas. In Laksam thana, Krishna Sundar Bhowmick was the chief organiser of krishak samitis with the support of 'cultivators and impoverished taluqdars'. A large krishak conference was held in December 1931 at Mudafarganj presided over by Lal Mian. DM Tippera to Under-Secy Poll Dept, 26 Dec. 1931, GB Poll. Conf. File 849(1-9)/31 (WBSA).
47 DM Tippera to Under-Secy Poll Dept, 26 Dec. 1931, GB Poll Conf. File 849(1-9)/31 (WBSA).

the debts should be repaid. Naturally, the mahajans were panicstricken. Some returned the documents and placed themselves at the mercy of the samiti leaders. Landlords were also prevented from cutting the paddy on their khas lands. Arbitration boards were established by the village samitis in many places. The krishak movement was also active across the border in Noakhali. A large krishak conference was held at Joyag on 3 and 4 January 1932 advocating non-payment of rents and debts.

Although the krishak movement had not yet taken to organised opposition of the government, the district administration believed that its leaders were anti-government in outlook. Many had taken part in the civil disobedience movement and the district krishak samiti was closely affiliated to the Congress organisation. The people had learnt the lesson of non-payment from the civil disobedience movement. 'The prevailing economic distress and real shrinkage of credit' as well as the 'extortionate acts of the village mahajans and the smaller landlords in the past' had prepared the ground for krishak samiti activities. Landlords and mahajans, the district officer lamented, were 'in a hopeless minority; they lack the strength and determination to fight the tenants and debtors. They have up till now, in spite of repeated advice, failed to form an organisation of their own to protect their own interests.'[48]

What role did communal feeling play in a situation where most of the debtors and tenants were Muslims and the landlords and moneylenders predominantly Hindu? Krishak samiti meetings were usually held on Fridays after the customary Jumma prayers. But, as an indignant official reported:

Occasionally a meeting is advertised as one for preaching the true spirit of Islam while in fact, only socialism of a wild nature is discussed and advocated. At the same time some of the leaders of the movement are Hindus while the Muhammadan mahajans though small in number have kept themselves aloof from it. The leaders have been at some pains to enlist the sympathy and cooperation of Hindus and Muslims alike.[49]

48 DM Tippera to Under-Secy Poll Dept, 26 Dec. 1931, GB Poll Conf. File 849(1-9)/31 (WBSA).
49 *Ibid.*

Despite the frequent use of mosques, the only real institutional facilities available, and the broad appeals to religion, the conflict in the east Bengal countryside did not, without external interference, flow easily into a communal mould.

Government's heavy-handed repression of the second phase of the civil disobedience campaign in 1932 drove the nationalist movement and much of the krishak movement underground. In February 1932, the police fired on crowds of peasants in the villages of Mahini and Hasnabad causing heavy casualties. Leading members of the krishak samitis were detained under the Emergency Powers Ordinance.[50] Peasant protest in Noakhali and Tippera was now restricted to small acts of defiance, such as burning haystacks and stealing or killing cattle. But there was the occasional large-scale organised dacoity. During the depression, agrarian violence contributed in large part to the rise in 'crime' statistics.[51] A study of the more dramatic dacoities is instructive. In May 1933, the house of a talukdar and mahajan in the village of Balshid on the Tippera–Noakhali border was attacked by a gang of about 100, consisting largely of his own tenants and debtors. One of the talukdar's sons was killed; valuable property and documents were also taken away.[52] Strained relations between debtors and creditors continued throughout 1933. By February 1934, the district magistrate of Tippera was sufficiently worried about the activities of the krishak samitis to want the Bengal Public Security Act to be put into force in the district.[53]

---

50 Cmsner Chittagong Dn to Special Officer, Chief Secy's Office, 2 Feb. 1932, GB Poll Conf. File 849(1-9)/31.
51 Province-wide statistics show a marked rise in the incidence of 'crime' in the early 1930s, especially a spurt of dacoities. The annual averages for the 1925–9 and the 1930–4 periods are as follows:

	Rioting	Murder	Culpable homicide	Dacoity	Robbery
1925–9 average	1338	509	252	705	394
1930–4 average	1628	612	322	1543	695

Source: 'Quinquennial Statement showing true cases of serious crime' in *Annual Report on Police Administration of Bengal.*
52 FR for the first half of May 1933 (WB Home Dept).
53 FR for the second half of Feb. 1934 (WB Home Dept).

On 30 August 1935, the Chhatarpaiya Bazaar dacoity in Noakhali created a stir not only among the local Hindu population but in the highest echelons of government as well.[54] Some 80 or 90 men armed with guns, spears and lathis attacked the bazaar and looted the premises of Hindu moneylenders and shopkeepers. They spent three to four hours ransacking the place in the presence of a large number of villagers. But after the incident, the police found it difficult to collect information. Members of the krishak samiti had apparently masterminded the incident. Various samitis in Noakhali and Tippera had sent men to participate in the attack.[55] The local jury who convicted the accused in the Chhatarpaiya Bazaar dacoity case were faced with social ostracism.[56] There were lavish celebrations when the Chhatarpaiya group was eventually acquitted by the high court.[57]

Once the Government of India Act of 1935 opened the prospect of provincial elections with a greatly extended franchise, a large part of the krishak movement was drawn into the arena of electoral politics. By October 1935, the krishak samitis of Noakhali and Tippera were 'efficiently organized on a widespread basis'. After the winter of 1935–6 large open meetings of krishak samitis once again became the order of the day. During November and December 1935, the Bengal Agricultural Debtors Bill was the 'favourite subject' and discussion of its provisions 'merged at times into an attack on landlords'. On 2 and 3 February 1936, the Tippera Krishak Samiti Assembly Election Party held a well-attended conference in the Sadar subdivision.[58] The president of the

54 The Governor expressed great concern at 'this disturbing affair in Noakhali' and warned district officers of the tendency of krishak samitis to develop 'on dangerous lines' at the Commissioners' Conference held at Darjeeling in September 1935. GB Poll Conf. File 986/35 (WBSA).
55 FRs for the first half to Sept. 1935, second half of Sept. 1935, first half of Oct. 1935, second half of Oct. 1935 (WB Home Dept). Similar dacoities took place during 1935 at Dattapara, Joyag and Sirajpur.
56 FR from Cmsner Chittagong Dn for the first half of Sept. 1936, GB Poll Conf. File 56/36 (WB Home Dept).
57 The news of the high court's decision was circulated by beat of drum. FR from Cmsner Chittagong Dn for the second half of Nov. 1936, GB Poll Conf. File 56/36 (WB Home Dept).
58 It might just as well have been a Congress jamboree. A group of Muslim volunteers, wearing khaddar lungis, punjabis and white khaddar Gandhi caps, and the two captains had haversacks and tricolour sashes. About 25 tea-stalls and

conference, Ashrafuddin Chaudhari, and Asimuddin Ahmed delivered impassioned speeches denouncing zamindari and mahajani, not to mention the members of the legislative council. There were seven resolutions passed calling for: (1) abolition of the zamindari system; (2) various amendments to the Bengal Tenancy Act in the krishaks' favour; (3) abolition of the mahajani system and creation of state agricultural banks; (4) immediate implementation of the Bengal Agricultural Debtors Act; (5) curtailment of the powers of the Court of Wards; (6) amendment of the Debtors Act so that amounts owed on 'kat' mortgages may be paid in 20 yearly instalments;[59] and (7) adoption of all legal and peaceful means to win independence.

In March and April 1936, krishak meetings became more frequent and more numerous. A popular demand at these meetings was the early establishment of debt settlement boards. There had been a notable increase in the number of execution cases filed by mahajans in the civil courts. This was a blatant attempt to forestall the provisions of the Debtors Act. The peasant debtors retaliated by combining to forcibly resist execution processes under civil court decrees. During March, a remarkable series of 12 dacoities took place in the Ramganj and Begumganj thanas of Noakhali, 'the victim in each case being a Hindu mahajan'. This was the area in which the krishak samitis were most closely organised. The mahajans identified the 'dacoits' as their own debtors and members of the local krishak samitis, who had been pressing for some time for the return of debt bonds and other documents. A

two eating-places were in attendance. The audience consisted of 'about 5000 Muslim cultivators with (a) sprinking of Hindus'. Lab Gazi of Comilla sang songs exhorting the krishaks to resist tyranny. Whenever a leading krishak samiti worker arrived, he was greeted with deafening shouts of *Bande-Mataram* and *Allah-o-Akbar*. 'Copy of proceedings of the Tippera Krishak Assembly' in FR from Cmsner Chittagong Dn for the first half of Feb. 1936, GB Poll Conf. File 56/36 (WB Home Dept).

59 A kat mortgage was a conditional sale of land which was delivered to the possession of the mortgagee in lieu of interest until the principal was repaid. In case the principal was not repaid within the period of limitation, the mortgaged land was sold to the mortgagee. The problem of kat mortgages was acute in some parts of Tippera. Out of an estimated total outstanding debt of Rs. 151.91 lakh in 1939 in 19 thanas of Tippera, debts on kat mortgages amounted to Rs. 40.34. The Bengal Agricultural Debtors Act had recommended five-year instalments for repayment of scaled down debts. DM Tippera to Cmsner Chittagong Dn, 6 May 1939. GB Rev. Dept LR Br., File 2-A-23(4) of 1939 (WBSA).

notable feature of the speeches at krishak meetings and conferences in Tippera was the inclusion of cooperative societies in the attack against creditors.[60] Government, as much as private moneylenders, was increasingly coming under attack in this district.

In other districts of east Bengal, similar peasant political associations had been mushrooming under the different names of praja (tenants') samiti or sometimes khatak (debtors') samiti. At a conference in Dacca in April 1936, over which Fazlul Huq presided, the krishak samitis of Tippera and Noakhali and the praja samitis of the other districts were brought under the banner of an all-Bengal Krishak Praja Samiti. This came to be known as the Krishak Praja Party (KPP) and was intended to give a semblance of unity to the activities of the samitis throughout the province.[61] The Muslim landlord interest in east Bengal reacted in May 1936 by forming a 'United Muslim Party' (UMP) under the presidentship of Nawab Habibullah of Dacca in alliance with the New Muslim Majlis, a Calcutta-based political group of Muslim business interests.[62] To seal the pact between the krishaks of Noakhali and Tippera and the prajas elsewhere, Fazlul Huq came to these two districts to address district krishak samiti conferences. The Noakhali conference was held on 2 and 3 June 1936 in Lakshmipur thana where krishak samiti organisation and propaganda had already made much progress, with samitis 'being formed in every village'.[63] At the Tippera conference at Comilla on 24 and 25 July organised by Ashrafuddin Chaudhuri, Huq gave his reasons for not joining the United Muslim Party. Any Muslim unity, he declared, had to be forged in the krishak's hut and not in the Nawab's ahsan manzil. He attacked the knights and

---

60 FRs from Cmsner Chittagong Dn for the first half of Mar. 1936, second half of Mar. 1936, first half of Apr. 1936, second half of Apr. 1936, GB Poll Conf. File 56/36 (WB Home Dept).

61 Abul Mansur Ahmed, *Amar Dekha Rajnitir Panchas Bachhar* (Fifty Years of Bengal Politics As I Saw It), pp. 98-9; Humayan Kabir, 'Krishak Praja Samiti o Praja Swartha' (The Krishak Praja Samiti and the Praja Interest), *Krishak* (1945, Id number), pp. 7-8.

62 See Shila Sen, *Muslim Politics in Bengal*, pp. 74-5; Humaira Momen, *Muslim Politics in Bengal: A Study of Krishak Praja Party and the Elections of 1937* (Dacca, 1972), pp. 46-7.

63 FR from Cmsner Chittagong Dn for the first half of June 1936, GB Poll Conf. File 56/36 (WB Home Dept).

nawabs, especially Khawaja Nazimuddin, a leading light of the UMP, and K.G.M. Faruqui, a sitting member of the legislative council from Tippera, for disregarding the interests of the Muslim masses.[64]

During the latter half of 1936, the election campaign of the krishak samitis gathered pace, interspersed with the occasional dacoity and efforts to dominate the membership of the debt settlement boards. The publication of local samiti newspapers – *Krishakbani* in Noakhali, *Janamat* in Tippera, *Chashi* in Mymensingh – gave a boost to the propaganda campaign.[65] The district krishak samitis of Tippera and Noakhali were, however, hardly models of camaraderie and unity. In Tippera, by mid-1936, there was a split between Ashrafuddin and Abdul Malek's group, which was close to the Congress and the Krishak Praja Samiti, and the group led by Asimuddin and Yakub Ali with pro-communist sympathies.[66] This division, however, was patched up before the elections, and all the prominent krishak leaders were returned on the panel of one faction or other to the Bengal Provincial Congress Committee.[67] In Noakhali, there were at least two factions – the so-called 'moderates' led by Rashid Ahmed and the 'extremists' led by Ghulam Sarwar and Mohammad Fazlullah. While Rashid Ahmed explained the value of debt settlement boards and the supply of stud bulls by the government, Ghulam Sarwar demanded complete remission of debts. He wanted the elimination of the mahajan element from the boards and urged the cultivators to give evidence collectively against the police in dacoity cases. A new paper *Krishak Hitaishi* was started by Rashid to counter Sarwar's propaganda through the *Krishakbani*. In an interview with the district magistrate in September 1936, Ghulam Sarwar expressed his distaste for Fazlul Huq's pro-Congress

---

64 Ashrafuddin Ahmed Chaudhuri, *Raj Birodhi* (Opponent of the Raj; Dacca, 1979), pp. 38-42; FRs from Cmsner Chittagong Dn for the second half of July 1936, first half of Aug. 1936, GB Poll Conf. File 56/36 (WB Home Dept).
65 FRs from Cmsner Chittagong Dn for the second half of May, first half of June, first half of July; FR from Cmsner Dacca Dn for the first half of July, GB Poll Conf. File 56/36 (WB Home Dept).
66 The Bengal Provincial Kisan Sabha (BPKS) set up in April 1936 by the Congress left was soon dominated by the communists. Asimuddin and Yakub owed first allegiance to the BPKS rather than the Congress or the KPP.
67 FRs from Cmsner Chittagong Dn for the first half of June, second half of June, first half of July, second half of July, GB Poll Conf. File 56/36 (WB Home Dept).

tendencies and his readiness to join the UMP for 'election purposes' provided he could 'keep his samities as a separate movement and avoid merging their work in any general programme'.[68] The extreme wing of the krishak movement was especially influential in the Ramganj, Raipur and Lakshmipur thanas,[69] where the krishaks were encouraged always to carry lathis. Part of their programme was the setting up of krishak samiti courts, which the government took quick legal steps to abolish. The activities of a group led by Mukleshwar Rahman and Syed Ahmad in Lakshmipur were curbed by having it listed as a 'criminal tribe'.[70]

On the eve of the elections to the legislative assembly, there was a krishak samiti candidate for every constituency in Tippera. In Noakhali, candidates of the 'left-wing krishak type' were contesting three of the six Muslim seats and there were 'right-wing krishak' candidates for the remaining three. In all the constituencies, the issues were complicated by candidates such as Ghulam Sarwar, belonging to krishak samitis, but describing themselves as members of the UMP.[71]

The Muslims of Bengal had gone into the 1937 elections deeply divided. Mohammed Ali Jinnah's attempt in August 1936 to bring them all under the umbrella of a Muslim League Parliamentary Board did not survive the first meeting of the Board on 8 September 1936. The Krishak Praja Party's manifesto included the abolition of zamindari without compensation, which the other Muslim political groups refused to accept. The Muslim seats were fiercely contested between (1) a conglomeration of the UMP and the New Muslim Majlis under the banner of a newly reconstituted Muslim League; (2) the Krishak Praja Party, which received moral and material support from the Congress; and (3) a host of 'independents'.[72] While Huq stressed the conflict between

68 FR from Cmsner Chittagong Dn for the first half of Sept. 1936, GB Poll Conf. File 56/36 (WB Home Dept).
69 These became the scenes of the Noakhali riots in 1946.
70 FRs from Cmsner Chittagong Dn for the first half of Oct. 1936, second half of Oct. 1936, first half of Nov. 1936, second half of Nov. 1936, GB Poll Conf. File 56/36 (WB Home Dept).
71 FR from Cmsner Chittagong Dn for the second half of Dec. 1936, GB Poll. Conf. File 56/36 (WB Home Dept).
72 Abdul Mansur Ahmed, *Amar Dekha Rajnitir Panchas Bachhar* pp. 103-11; Momen, *Muslim Politics in Bengal* pp. 48-54; Shila Sen, *Muslim Politics in Bengal,* pp. 75-8. During the campaign, Fazlul Huq was called Mir Jaffar

the peasants and their oppressors, both Hindu and Muslim, the League based its appeal on the need for Muslim solidarity as a prerequisite to ameliorating the condition of Muslim peasants.

The results of the 1937 elections showed that in the Muslim constituencies, the Muslim League had won 39 seats (33 of these were in the rural areas), the KPP had won 36 and another 36 had been bagged by 'independent' candidates. The Tippera Krishak Samiti, which had retained a degree of autonomy from the KPP, won 5 seats. Although the Muslim League won more seats, it polled fewer votes than the KPP. The League leader, Nazimuddin, was defeated by Huq in a straight contest in the Patuakhali rural constituency in Bakarganj. The Congress, meanwhile, had done as well as it could have hoped to do under the provisions of the Communal Award and the 1935 Act (which had reduced the Hindus in the province to a statutory minority), making a sweep of the general constituencies. It formed the largest group in the assembly with 54 seats.[73] Soon after the elections, negotiations were opened between the KPP and the Congress with a view to forming either a coalition ministry or a KPP ministry with Congress support. But the Congress High Command's dithering over office acceptance and the failure to agree on a common political and economic programme which might have enabled the Congress to support a KPP ministry, gave the League the opportunity to secure power in Bengal. On being offered the chief ministership, Fazlul Huq struck a deal with the League within 24 hours of the breakdown in his negotiations with the Congress.[74] He had to pay a heavy price. All the major promises made in the KPP election manifesto regarding abolition of zamindari, free primary education and

(traitor) for hobnobbing with the Hindu-dominated Congress; Huq retorted that Mir Jaffar had primarily conspired with Clive rather than the Hindus and denounced the League's unholy alliance with Clive Street. Clive Street in Calcutta was the centre of European business interests. *Chashi*, 2 Oct. 1936.

73 The KPP polled 31.78% of the total votes in the rural areas and the Muslim League 26.52%. The Tippera Krishak Samiti polled 3.83% of the rural votes. The rest were taken by independents. The percentage of the independents' share is inflated, because there was usually more than one independent candidate for each constituency. 'Return showing the results of elections in India', Command Paper No. 5589 cited by Momen, *Muslim Politics in Bengal*, pp. 62-8; Shila Sen, *Muslim Politics in Bengal*, pp. 88-9.

74 Sen, *ibid.*, pp. 89-93.

release of political prisoners had to be watered down. In an 11-member ministry, Huq had to accommodate 8 zamindars. Besides the chief minister, there was only one KPP representative, four Muslim Leaguers, three non-Congress caste Hindus and two non-Congress scheduled caste nominees.[75] It was now the turn of Huq's own followers in the Krishak Praja Party to bring charges of betrayal against him.[76] Between 1937 to 1941, there were always 20 to 30 rebel Krishak Prajas in the assembly who voted against the government.[77] As soon as Huq's League-dominated ministry took office, the Congress and the anti-ministerial wing of the KPP intensified their Muslim mass contact campaign. The agrarian crisis of the 1930s had unleashed a social wave on the crest of which the opposition planned to ride in their efforts to break the ministry. If the results of their efforts turned out to be somewhat different from what they would have liked, it was because even the zamindars in the ministry realised the futility of trying to play King Canute in the face of the rising tide.

The 1937 elections had recorded the strength of the krishak samitis of Tippera and Noakhali.[78] In the post-election phase, the different political parties fiercely competed for the allegiance of the krishak and praja movements in the east Bengal districts. The Congress mass contact campaign was most successful in Tippera, where it had a history of associating closely with peasant agitations, and, to some extent, in Mymensingh. At a meeting on 27 March, the executive committee of the Tippera district krishak samiti passed a resolution urging Huq to dissolve the present

75 Gov. to Gov.-Gen. 9 Mar. 1937, R/3/2/2 (IOR).
76 Many now abandoned Huq. In an editorial on 2 April 1937, the KPP newspaper *Chashi* published from Mymensingh warned him of the danger of his policy pointing to the fate of Ramsay MacDonald, the British Labour leader who had become Prime Minister on the sufferance of the Conservatives. Editorial entitled 'Atmasamarpan' (Surrender) in *Chashi*, 2 April 1937.
77 At one stage, in March 1938, 34 out of the original 36 Krishak Praja MLAs sat with the oppositon. The ministry survived in the assembly on several occasions during 1938 only with the support of the 23 European members. See Shila Sen, *Muslim Politics in Bengal*, pp. 118-20.
78 In Tippera, five out of the ten seats were won by the Tippera Krishak Samiti. The victorious candidates were Moqbul Hosaiṅ in Tippera North-East, Ramizuddin Ahmed in Tippera West, Asimuddin Ahmed in Tippera Central, Janab Ali Majumdar in Chandpur East and Shahedali in Matlab Bazaar. Nawabzada K. Nesirullah and Md Hasanuzzaman won Brahmanbaria South and Tippera South respectively for the Muslim League. Brahmanbaria North Tippera North

ministry and form a new one, consisting of people who genuinely sympathized with krishak interests.[79] In the following months, numerous krishak meetings were organised by Ashrafuddin and others, urging Muslim cultivators to join the Congress. By the middle of the year, the governor was reporting to Delhi that the krishak samitis were showing 'signs of definitely identifying themselves with Congress'.[80] Recommending the arrest of Abdul Malek, a local report held him and Ashrafuddin responsible for 'all the mischiefs and troubles concerning the peasants' and warned that 'a weak-kneed policy with regard to any of them would mean a slipping of the ground [sic] for the Administration'.[81]

The krishak movement in Tippera, like the district Congress, was divided into two broad factions, each of which competed for the support of the Muslim peasantry. There were attempts to set up local branches of the Muslim League, but the pro-Congress factions in this district were able to keep the upper hand. In October 1937, the Tippera Congress claimed as many as 39 000 members. Such claims might simply have been an effort by the two factions to outbid each other.[82] But to some extent, it indicated 'the attraction that the congress has for the general population of Tippera, including Muhammadans'.[83] Of the 69 delegates sent to the Provincial Congress Committee in December 1937, 22 were Muslims.[84] The non-communal nature of the krishak movement in Tippera ensured that the suspicion of the Debtors Act was 'not

and Chandpur West were taken by independent candidates. A number of Krishak Samiti leaders, including Ashrafuddin Chaudhuri and Mukleshwar Rahman, were disqualified as candidates because of their long prison records.

In Noakhali, according to the election returns, three out of the six seats were won by independents, two by the Praja Party and one by the Muslim League. These allegiances were quite fickle. It is of greater import that at least four of the winners – Md Ibrahim, Ghulam Sarwar, Syed Ahmad Khan and Abdur Rezzak were local krishak samiti activists.

79 FR from Cmsner Chittagong Dn to Chief Secy, 10 Apr. 1937, GB Poll Conf. File 10/37 (WB Home Dept).
80 Gov. to Gov.-Gen. 23 June 1937, L/P and J/5/141 (IOR).
81 Report by SDO Sadar Sub-dn, GB Poll Conf. File 95/37 (WBSA).
82 In mid-1936, the Tippera District Congress had reported 8958 members. See Bengal Provincial Congress Cmt. to Congress Mass Contact Cmt., 16 Aug. 1936, Rajendra Prased Papers IX/36/31 and Bengal PCC to AICC, 10 July 1936, File P6/707 of 1936, AICC Papers (Nehru Memorial Museum and Library).
83 FR from Cmsner Chittagong Dn to Chief Secy, 27 Oct.1937, GB Poll Conf. File 10/37 (WB Home Dept).
84 Including two MLAs, Janabali Majumdar and Maulavi Ramizuddin. FR from

confined to the professional moneylender' but 'shared by the comparatively well-off or "bourgeois" Krishaks', who held most of the usufructuary mortgages.[85] Towards the end of the year, there were reports from the Brahmanbaria and Sadar subdivisions of forcible dispossession of usufructuary mortgagees.[86]

In Noakhali during 1937 the tussle for the control of the krishak movement was even more intense. The krishak samitis in the Lakshmipur and Ramganj thanas were especially well-organised under two fiery leaders, Ghulam Sarwar and Syed Ahmad. Both had been elected to the assembly and their close connection with organised armed dacoity made them veritable culprits in the eyes of the district administration. These would-be local Robin Hoods encouraged their peasant constituents to seek debt cancellation rather than conciliation, to regard Civil Court processes as unjust and to withhold information from the police in the investigation of 'crime'.[87] Information about their own squabbles was more difficult to withhold. In May 1937, Syed Ahmad had fallen out with Ghulam Sarwar and 'along with Wasimuddin and Ashrafuddin of Tippera and a few local Hindu congressites', was trying to reform the krishak samitis on a non-communal basis.[88] Nazimuddin, the Home Minister, who saw this intelligence report noted:

This report supports my policy that we must get Gholam Sarwar on our side so that we can fight congressites like Wasimuddin and others who are trying to capture Noakhali Krishak Samitis. DM should try and bring about reconciliation between Gholam Sarwar and Maulavies Abdur Rashid, Ibrahim, Abdur Rezzak. If these four can work together there is no danger of Krishak Samitis going over to the Congress.[89]

Cmsner Chittagong Dn to Chief Secy, 24 Dec. 1937, GB Poll Conf. File 10/37 (WB Home Dept).

85 FR from Cmsner Chittagong Dn to Chief Secy, 15 Oct. 1937, GB Poll Conf. File 10/37 (WB Home Dept).

86 FR from Cmsner Chittagong Dn to Chief Secy, 24 Dec. 1937, GB Poll Conf. File 10/37 (WB Home Dept).

87 FR from Cmsner Chittagong Dn to Chief Sery, 10 July 1937, GB Poll Conf. File 10/37 (WB Home Dept). As the British District Magistrate lamented, 'the borderline between one type of agrarian leader and the dacoit' was virtually non-existent and he was convinced that at least some krishak samitis were no more than 'ordinary criminal gangs'.

88 DIB, CID Noakhali to IG of Police, 4 May 1937, GB Poll Conf. File 303/37 (WBSA).

89 Home Minister Nazimuddin's note in *ibid.*

Syed Ahmad, who had been dallying with Congress, was soon like his compatriot, Mukleshwar Rahman of Tippera, registered as a member of a 'criminal tribe'. Ghulam Sarwar, a political chameleon, wanted to retain his freedom of manoeuvre and was not won over easily by the Muslim League. His activities included the organisation of krishak samiti lathials to help debtors resist decree-holders and to picket zamindars' hats. Early in June, he told the district magistrate that local Congress leaders had been trying to get him to join them and that he would be ready to do so if the Congress took up the krishaks' cause and supported an amendment of the Bengal Tenancy Act. On 16 June 1937, he appeared as a speaker at a Deshabandhu Day meeting in memory of C.R. Das.[90] During July and August, the Congress pressed forward with their scheme to bring the Muslim peasantry into its fold and established some primary committees in the Ramganj and Begumganj areas. To counter this, efforts were made to set up Muslim League committees in important local centres. Ghulam Sarwar, meanwhile, continued to incite peasants against talukdars and mahajans. By the end of July, Sarwar had drifted closer to the Muslim League. Within a month he had become 'extremely anti-Congress'. But for good reasons. He was anxious that the 'Congress... [might] succeed in winning over his adherents' and their 'charges against him [might] get him into trouble with the Authorities'.[91] To stave off the threat to his following from the nationalists, Sarwar now decided to play the communal card. He warned his constituents that 'the real aim of congress was to oust the Muhammadan ministry so as to establish a Hindu Raj in its place'.[92] Two other MLAs from the district, Mohammad Ibrahim and Abdur Rezzak, also supported the ministry. But they threatened to join the Congress if the ministry made no attempt to redress the grievances of the

---

90 FRs from Cmsner Chittagong Dn to Chief Secy, 10 June 1937, 28 June 1937, GB Poll Conf. File 10/37 (WB Home Dept).
91 FR from Cmsner Chittagong Dn to Chief Secy, 27 July 1937, GB Poll Conf. File 10/37 (WB Home Dept).
92 This sort of propaganda had some effect. In one centre at least, local cultivators intervened to prevent a Muslim from presiding over a Congress meeting, leaving the Hindus to carry on the deliberations. FR from Cmsner Chittagong Dn to Chief Secy 10 Aug. 1937, GB Poll Conf. File 10/37 (WB Home Dept).

agriculturists.[93] The Chittagong Commissioner aptly summed up the situation:

> ...while the ministry has at present the support of the majority of the Krishak organizations in Noakhali, this is no blind allegiance, a considerable section of the cultivating populations is realising its new power and is on the watch to see how far the present Government will go to meet the demands formulated in numerous Krishak meetings.[94]

Here, it is necessary to digress briefly and take account of happenings at the provincial level, especially inside the legislature. In August 1937, Congress had moved a resolution in the assembly recommending the formation of a committee of experts 'to take immediate steps to acquire all landed interests in the agricultural lands of the province above those of the cultivating tenants'.[95] This was sharply opposed by the treasury benches. Instead, the government-sanctioned Bengal Tenancy Act Amendment Bill was passed in October 1937. It provided for the abolition of landlords' fees and the right of pre-emption upon the transfer of raiyati holdings as well as the suspension of enhancements of raiyati rents for the next ten years. The Congress leader, Sarat Bose, criticised the bill for not going far enough in protecting the actual cultivators who often held cultivating rights below raiyats, but did not oppose what was after all a pro-peasant legislation. The ministry had one narrow division on a Congress amendment which sought to suspend enhancements of rent in the case of under-raiyats. The Congress, the rebels of the Krishak Praja Party and several members of the ruling coalition voted against the government, which survived by 80 votes to 72.[96] The opposition's radical campaign inside and outside the legislature had left the ministry with 'no option but to introduce drastic tenancy legislation'.[97] To the Congress's policy of 'indefinitely whetting the appetite of the cultivator',[98] the

---

93 FR from Cmsner Chittagong Dn to Chief Secy, 10 Nov. 1937, GB Poll Conf. File 10/37 (WB Home Dept).
94 FR from Cmsner Chittagong Dn to Chief Secy, 27 Nov. 1937, GB Poll Conf. File 10/37 (WB Home Dept).
95 Sisir K. Bose (ed.), *The Voice of Sarat Chandra Bose* (Calcutta, 1978), p. 128.
96 Gov. to Gov. Gen., 6 Oct. 1937, L/P & J/5/141 (IOR).
97 Gov. to Gov. Gen., 7 Sept. 1937, L/P & J/5/141 (IOR).
98 *Ibid.*

ministry had retaliated by whetting communal passions. In October 1937, Fazlul Huq himself had joined the Muslim League.[99] While the Congress had in some areas, notably Tippera, gained a peasant base, the League's overtly communal counter-propaganda was begining to bite in many other areas. In Pabna, Hindu temples were desecrated. Summarising the position in that district, the Rajshahi Commissioner wrote:

it seems that in an area where owing to economic causes the small Hindu landlords, often Mahajans, for many years have not lived on very happy terms with the Muhammadan tenants and where expression of these strained feelings has been given vent to by acts of sacrilege on the part of the latter, unusual publicity by certain fortuitous circumstances...has been given to incidents of this nature. This has led not only to imitation of these sacrilegious acts by irresponsible people in various areas of the district, but acts of sacrilege and allegations of them have been utilised as convenient gambits in village politics quite apart from any economic or communal feeling.[100]

During 1938, the Congress–Krishak rural campaign continued apace in Tippera, in spite of some factional rivalry. The Muslim League, itself a house divided, strained itself further to win support for the ministry. Yet, as the Governor reported, the Congress continued to have 'really strong support among Moslems' in Tippera.[101] On 13 and 14 May 1938, the annual conference of the All-India Kisan Sabha presided over by Swami Sahajanand was held in Comilla.[102] The release of the detenus gave a fillip to krishak samiti organisation. During their detention, many of the former revolutionary terrorists had been influenced by socialist and communist doctrines and now began to take an active interest in the peasant movement.[103] In March and April 1939, as the

99 Shila Sen, *Muslim Politics in Bengal*, pp. 118-22.
100 Cmsner Rajshahi Dn to Home (Poll) Secy, 19 July 1937 GB Poll Conf. File 193/37 (WBSA).
101 Gov. to Gov. Gen., 8 Mar. 1938, L/P & J/5/142 (IOR).
102 Gov. to Gov. Gen., 3 June 1938, L/P & J/5/142 (IOR)
103 The large krishak conferences at Ibrahimpur in the Nabinagar thana on 27 December 1983 and at Sreebail in the Muradnagar thana on 31 December 1938 were reported to have been helped by 'terrorist' organisations, especially the Anushilan group. FR from Cmsner Chittagong Dn for the first half of Jan. 1939, GB Poll Conf. File 19/39 (WB Home Dept).

Congress split became imminent, there was a 'general intensification of left wing agrarian agitation... a process that may reasonably be connected with Subhas Bose's general programme'.[104] Subhas Bose's tour of Tippera in November 1939 was said to have 'intensified political activity and propaganda of [a] communist nature in the villages'.[105] Throughout 1940, there were continued efforts to establish krishak samitis and Congress committees in every union and to unite the factions of the district krishak samiti.[106]

In Noakhali during 1938 and 1939, the krishak movement continued to be vigorous, but here its promoters were 'on the whole, supporters of the Ministry'.[107] Debts were not paid and zamindars' hats were picketed. In February 1939, the whole of Limua Bazaar was burnt down by agitators demanding a reduction of tolls.[108] Ghulam Sarwar continued to fulminate against the Hindus. The Chittagong Commissioner wanted to prosecute him for a speech in which, while warning Muslims not to join the Congress, he referred to Hindu goddesses as prostitutes and told his audience that since the chief minister was a member of the Muslim League they need not be afraid of the police. The commissioner's tidings were prophetic: 'Golam Sarwar's talk is not merely hot air: he has a lot of goondas under his control and he is the son of a pir, so speeches of this nature are definitely dangerous to the public peace'. But the commissioner's instructions from Calcutta were categorical. The government did 'not wish to prosecute their own supporters', and the Muslim League would deal with Sarwar in the appropriate manner. So Sarwar's case was forwarded for 'suitable Party action', despite the commissioner's conviction that 'nothing but prosecution will really curb his tongue'.[109]

104 Gov. to Gov. Gen., 20 Mar. 1939, L/P & J/5/144 (IOR).
105 FR from Cmsner Chittagong Dn to Chief Secy, 27 Nov. 1939, GB Poll Conf. File 19/39 (WB Home Dept).
106 FR from Cmsner Chittagong Dn to Chief Secy, 10 Sept. 1940, GB Poll Conf. File 30/40 (WB Home Dept).
107 Review of events in Bengal in the second fortnight of Jan. 1938, L/P and J/5/142 (IOR).
108 The loss was estimated at Rs. 20,000 and the sufferers were both Hindu and Muslim. FR from Cmsner Chittagong Dn to Chief Secy for the second half of Feb. 1939, GB Poll Conf. File 19/39 (WB Home Dept).
109 Cmsner Chittagong Dn to Chief Secy, 4 May 1939, GB Poll Conf. File 242/39 (WBSA).

The pressure created by their own more extreme supporters and by the opposition prevented the ministry from reneging on the Tenancy Act amendment when it was presented in April 1938 to the legislative council.[110] The ministry had been prepared to tone down some of the more radical measures. But Nausher Ali, the sole KPP representative in the cabinet, was about to resign and join the Congress. Naturally, the ministry 'could not risk putting Mr Nausher Ali on such strong ground as he would have had if he could have resigned on that issue'.[111] After the bill had received the governor's assent in August 1938, both the ministry and the opposition parties claimed credit for it.[112]

The series of executive and legislative measures taken by Fazlul Huq's ministry to ameliorate the condition of the peasantry – the Tenancy Act amendment of 1938, the work of the debt settlement boards, the Bengal Moneylenders' Act of 1940 – were beginning to take the wind out of the sails of the Congress and Krishak Praja mass campaigns. In east Bengal, any effort to bring down the Huq ministry was widely interpreted as a betrayal not only of the Muslim cause, but also of the peasant cause. The left wing of the Congress continued to hold its ground in its Tippera stronghold and pockets of influence in other east-Bengal districts, but the psychological impact of Huq's measures had made it increasingly difficult for the opposition to gain any further support from the Muslim peasantry. The waves of arrests of nationalist leaders and workers between 1940 and 1942, especially the more militant who had been involved in the krishak movement, finally wrecked their organisation.[113] The outbreak of war had changed the nature of the economic problems faced by the peasantry of east Bengal and the government's wartime policy had a decisive impact on the political articulation of their grievances. The following section studies the nature of the

110 For terms of the Act, see above, pp. 123, 151–2.
111 Gov. to Gov. Gen., 5 Apr. 1938, L/P and J/5/142 (IOR).
112 The Nawab of Dacca told the governor that 'the whole political atmosphere throughout the country has altered as the result of the passing of this Bill!' Gov. to Gov. Gen., 19 Aug. 1938, L/P and J/5/143 (IOR).
113 The government was ready early in 1940 with a list of associations to be banned in the event of civil disobedience. It included almost all the district and subdivisional krishak samitis, GB Poll Conf. File 181/40 (WBSA). During 1941, there were large-scale arrests of those whose activities were considered prejudicial to the British war effort. In 1942, the ban on the listed associations took effect.

connection between agrarian crisis and conflict in a period of war and famine.

Peasant politics: The Second World War and its aftermath

At the end of the 1930s, the depression finally lifted and a new price conjuncture in the history of agrarian Bengal began. The wartime boom had, however, two striking features: first, the upswing in the product market did not elicit a commensurate response in the credit market;[114] second, in this period of high inflation, the price of jute continued to be weak in relation to grain and essential non-producibles.[115] Meanwhile, the jaws of the population–resources nut-cracker, which had begun to close from 1920 onwards, had further tightened its grip.[116] In Tippera, collection of dues was extremely poor in 1940-1 since the cultivators had 'not been able to dispose of the bulk of the jute crop at remunerative rates'.[117] In May 1941, Tippera's tenants forcibly cultivated the khas lands of the zamindars.[118] In June, the Chittagong commissioner anticipated that 'the economic distress and the high price of rice may lead to organized goondaism'. This danger was being felt most acutely in the Lakshmipur and Raipur areas of Noakhali. For once, Ghulam Sarwar was trying to help the authorities; the troublemakers for the government on this occasion were Fazlullah Mian and Mujibur Rahman, who together with some communist workers were encouraging people to demand relief collectively, not only from government officers but also from the local affluent class.[119]

As the price of rice continued to rise and demand for agricultural labour remained negligible, test relief works were started in the second half of June in many parts of Tippera and Noakhali. The basic rate offered for clearing water-

114 See chapter 4 above.
115 See chapters 2 and 3 above.
116 See chapter 2 above.
117 FR from Cmsner Chittagong Dn to Chief Secy, 23 Feb. 1941, GB Poll Conf. File 13/41 (WB Home Dept).
118 FR from Cmsner Chittagong Dn to Chief Secy, 8 May 1941, GB Poll Conf. File 13/41 (WB Home Dept).
119 FR from Cmsner Chittagong Dn to Chief Secy, 24 June 1941, GB Poll Conf. File 13/41 (WB Home Dept).

hyacinth from ditches and similar work was only 2½ annas for adults and 1½ for children. But 'a considerable number of people. . . [were still] willing to work at such a daily wage'. A cyclone and floods had damaged much of the jute and lowland paddy crops leaving little work to be done in the fields. By early July 1941, agrarian distress in Noakhali and Tippera, already 'very severe', was 'likely to get more acute'.[120] In Tippera, both the Forward Bloc, composed of left-wing Congressmen, and the Communist Party of India started relief samitis and organised hunger-marches of hundreds of people demanding work and food. The district officer of Noakhali complained: 'Designing persons are trying to utilise the distressed condition of this district in creating general discontent among the masses and inciting them to prejudicial acts by organized hooliganism.'[121] Later in the year, there was 'no agitation', except in the form of 'illegal paddy cuttings', but 'discontent' prevailed 'everywhere in the distressed area'. There were many reports of deaths from starvation, but these merely served to annoy the local officials who wanted to hear of more pleasant things.[122]

The year 1941 was generally a bad one for communal relations in Bengal. The death toll in communal killings in Dacca city and the mofussil towns in Bakarganj, Khulna and Chittagong ran into hundreds. Remarkably, the conflict in rural Noakhali and Tippera in a year of such distress did not take on an overtly communal complexion. Just across the river Meghna, in the Narsinghdi circle of Dacca district, 1941 is remembered as *popapurir bachhar* – the year of the great burning.[123] Between 1 and 5 April 1941, an area of about 215 square miles in the Raipura and Shibpur thanas of the Narayanganj subdivision were cleared of all Hindus, who fled for refuge to Tippera district and Tripura state. Mobs attacked

---

120 FR from Cmsner Chittagong Dn to Chief Secy, 7 July 1941, GB Poll Conf. File 13/41 (WB Home Dept).
120 FR from Cmsner Chittagong Dn to Chief Secy, 7 July 1941, GB Poll Conf. File 13/41 (WB Home Dept).
121 FR from Cmsner Chittagong Dn to Chief Secy, 21 July 1941, GB Poll Conf. File 13/41 (WB Home Dept).
122 FRs from Cmsner Chittagong Dn to Chief Secy for the second half of Oct. 1941, first half of Nov. 1941, first half of Dec. 1941, GB Poll Conf. File 13/41 (WB Home Dept).
123 Interview with residents of Hairmara, Narsinghdi in December 1980.

81 villages and 2519 households (joint families) including 15 724 persons were affected by looting or arson.[124] Nearly 7000 homesteads were completely burnt down.[125] The trouble began in Adiabad Bazaar, Rahimabad Bazaar and Hairmara in Raipura thana and quickly spread to most parts of the Raipura and Shibpur thanas and small pockets in the Narsinghdi, Keraniganj and Munshiganj thanas. The villages were attacked by mobs of anything between 200 and 2000 Muslims, mostly local people, but headed by leaders dressed in khaki or black shirts and shorts. Some of them carried swords. They set fire to property and, in some cases, demanded that the Hindus should accept Islam. Only one person was killed. The disturbances were put down by deploying the Eastern Frontier Rifles and a company of the Mahrattas.[126] Criminal charges were brought against 3935 persons in 120 separate cases.[127]

The Dacca Riots Enquiry Committee dealt with only the more proximate causes of the rural disturbances. The disorder in the rural areas was seen a direct consequence of the killings in Dacca city. As at the time of the Kishoreganj disturbances, maulavies told large gatherings of Muslims that they had been given immunity for seven days from any offences they might commit against the Hindus. In March, Fazlul Huq himself had urged the Muslims to establish a clear majority in the census enumeration that was taking place. According to Hindu witnesses, the slogans commonly used by the Muslim mobs were *Allah-o-akbar, Pakistan zindabad, Huq-saheb ki jai, Nawab-saheb ki jai* and *Salim-saheb* [the local MLA] *ki jai.*[128] It is important to note that Raipura and Shibpur were part of the Madhupur tract where, the Dacca settlement officer had observed, the evil of the aggressive moneylender-landlord was at its worst.[129] The village records of Hairmara and Adiabad and the sale deeds registered in favour of the local Pals, Sahas and the Murapara zamindars indicate that the land engrossers had continued to be active here, a marked

124 *Report of the Dacca Riots Enquiry Cmt.* (Alipur, 1942), p. 33.
125 'Communal Disturbances. Cases at Dacca and rural areas – their review', GB Poll Conf. File 396/42 (WBSA).
126 *Report of the Dacca Riots Enquiry Cmt.*, pp. 32-3.
127 73 in Raipura thana, 46 in Shibpur and 1 in Narsinghdi. DM Dacca to Cmsner Dacca Dn, 13 Jan. 1942, GB Poll Conf. File 396/42 (WBSA).
128 *Report of the Dacca Riots Enquiry Cmt.*, pp. 53-5.
129 See chapters 1 and 5 above, pp. 27-8, 155-6.

contrast to the general picture in east Bengal, throughout the 1930s.[130] The Muslim bargadars, who seized the lands made khas by moneylender-landlords in 1941, generally held on to them after the outbreak had been quelled.[131]

The Dacca disturbances inevitably had repercussions on the neighbouring districts. The communal situation in Noakhali, especially in the Feni subdivision, was reported to be 'very ticklish'. In Tippera, despite the huge influx of refugees from Dacca, the communal situation remained 'surprisingly good'. 'The really hopeful thing in Tippera', wrote the Chittagong commissioner, 'is that leaders of both communities are moderate minded people.'[132] Later in 1941, as Fazlul Huq began to distance himself from the All-India Muslim League, it was reported from the Chittagong division that 'the dissensions in the Muslim League have for the time being promoted more amicable relations between the two major communities'.[133] Even in Noakhali, at least two MLAs, Abdur Rezzak and Mohammad Ibrahim, who ranged themselves with Huq, were anxious now to promote a non-communal line on both economic and political issues. The troubles of 1941 had brought home to Huq the inherent danger for the unity of a Muslim majority province of identifying too closely with the communal stance of an all-India Muslim party. On 11 December 1941, he formed a new ministry as leader of an intercommunal Progressive Coalition Party.[134] This ministry 'placed in the forefront of their programme, the restoration of cordial relations between the two communities'.[135] As a first step, a general amnesty was granted to all those accused in

130 Records of rights in the land in mauzas Hairmara and Adiabad (Dacca District Collectorate Record Room); Registered deeds of sales of land in mauzas Hairmara and Adiabad from 1920-41 (Dacca District Registration Office).
131 GB Poll Conf. File 396/42 (WBSA).
132 FRs from Cmsner Chittagong Dn to Chief Secy, 23 Mar. 1941, 24 Apr. 1941, GB Poll Conf. File 13/41 (WB Home Dept).
133 FR from Cmsner Chittagong Dn to Chief Secy for the second half of Nov. 1941, GB Poll Conf. File 13/41 (WB Home Dept).
134 Fazlul Huq's second ministry had the support of the Progressive Assembly Party (those who broke with the Muslim League including some original Krishak Prajas who had remained with Huq since 1937) - 42, Krishak Praja Party - 19, Congress Bose Group - 28, Hindu Mahasabha - 14, Independent Scheduled Caste Group - 12, Anglo-Indians - 3, Labour - 1. The 25 members of the official Congress led by Kiran Shanker Roy promised responsive cooperation. Shila Sen, *Muslim Politics in Bengal*, p. 137.
135 Cabinet Note in GB Poll Conf. File 396/42 (WBSA).

communal incidents, including the ones in Raipura and Shibpur. While an immediate improvement was noticed in intercommunal feeling, there were problems for the future. Sarat Bose, who had been the prime-mover of the coalition effort, was imprisoned for the duration of the war on the day the new ministry was sworn in. Consequently, at a critical juncture, the Mahasabha leader, Shyama Prasad Mukherjee, became the most prominent Hindu voice in Bengal politics. The 'Shyama–Huq' ministry, as it came to be known, failed to win the trust of a large majority of Muslims, and was eventually replaced by a League ministry under Nazimuddin in April 1943.[136]

Between 1942 and 1945, the peasantry of east Bengal suffered privation on a scale unknown in recent history without showing much disposition to collective protest. The Quit-India Movement call of August 1942 met with a lukewarm response from the Muslim peasantry. Only sporadic attacks against government establishments occurred in Tippera.[137] In early 1943, the first symptoms of famine were detected in the eastern districts of the Chittagong division. Brahmanbaria, Sadar and Chandpur subdivisions in Tippera, and Sadar and Feni subdivisions in Noakhali were the regions most severely affected by the famine.[138] In these grain-deficit districts, while the mass of landless and land-poor peasants starved, the grain-dealers made a killing. Between December 1942 and March 1943, there were some instances of grain looting and hunger-marches by angry peasants. But from April 1943 they began to die in their millions without a murmur of protest. It has been suggested recently that Bengali 'fatalism' during the famine represented 'the continued acceptance in a crisis of the very values which hitherto had sustained the victims: that submission to authority is the essence of order, and that men and women, adults and children, patrons and clients, rulers and ruled stand in different relations of necessity to the establishment of prosperity'.[139] But peasant political protest

---

136 See Shila Sen, *Muslim Politics in Bengal*, pp. 158-63.
137 *District Officers' Chronicles of Events of Disturbances consequent upon the All-India Congress Committee's Resolution of 8th August 1942 and the Arrest of Congress Leaders Thereafter* (Secret Home Poll. Dept Report, 1943), pp. 159-61.
138 Mahalanobis *et al.*, 'After-effects of the Bengal Famine of 1943'.
139 Greenough, *Prosperity and Misery in Modern Bengal*, pp. 271-2. Greenough's point about the Bengali 'cultural ideal of prosperity' being used as an ideology of

during the 1930s and again after the end of the war clearly indicates that their decision to die quietly in 1943 and 1944 was not a matter of cultural choice. It is more plausible to explain the phenomenon partly by the sheer magnitude of the crisis, partly by the knowledge of the repressive capacity of the state and partly by problems of organisation and leadership. The colonial state had a stronger military presence in eastern India between 1942 and 1945 than ever before. The firm repression of the 1942 movement in some Bengal districts had hinted at the likely response of the government to any sort of disorder. Military construction works on evicted peasants' lands were a constant reminder of who was in charge. Political workers who might have provided the leadership in an anti-government movement had been locked away even before the Quit-India call was given. The two parties which had some freedom to operate – the Muslim League and the Communist Party – were collaborating with the British, and limited their activities to organising relief measures, such as running gruel kitchens. The Communist Party bent over backwards to avoid class conflict and even urged the krishaks to regard the zamindars as their friends.[140] It can hardly be a surprise that the peasants of east Bengal did not rally to an organisation which was asking them to regard the hoarders and profiteers in the famine of 1943 as their allies. At the same time, while the Muslim League ministry in the province remained cautious and conservative, the League party organisation, under a new radical leadership, from the winter of 1943 slowly began to adopt a clear anti-landlord stance. The memory of the famine

abandonment in a crisis by authoritative male patrons is much more acceptable. But it is stretching the point to claim that the same ideal constituted an 'active adaptation' to the crisis by dying victims.

140 The cadres of the Krishak Sabha, the Communist Party's peasant front organisation, were instructed in 1943 to propagate the government's Grow More Food Campaign and to build an alliance with the zamindars against the nationalists, who were described as 'the fifth column':

'Growing more food will not result in more profits and exploitation of the zamindar class at the expense of the krishak class – the country, the nation will profit. But if more food is not grown, it will help the fifth column, and dangers for the krishak class and the nation will increase. In this situation, *the zamindar class is not the enemy of the krishak class*, it is the fifth column which is the enemy of the krishak class and the enemy of the nation.

'The nation's common enemy, fascist Japan, is equally the enemy of the zamindars and krishaks. But the fifth column is not the enemy, but the friend of Japan.'

in no uncertain way contributed to the Muslim League's victory in the postwar elections. It was also to be a potent factor in the bitter reprisals by the Muslim peasantry during the Noakhali and Tippera riots of 1946.

While the famine swept the land, the politicians continued to try and elbow each other out of existence. In November 1943, an important *coup* took place within the provincial Muslim League organisation: the old zamindars' clique from east Bengal was ousted and a younger group led by Abul Hashim with socialistic ideas took charge. A major propaganda and organisational effort was launched in 1944 by the party wing of the provincial Muslim League focusing on the socio-economic demands of the Muslim peasantry. Major successes were claimed in recruiting primary members in the east Bengal districts.[141] Special attention was given to winning the allegiance of the erstwhile krishak prajas. Between the winter of 1943 and the 1945–6 elections, a majority of local leaders of the krishak praja samitis had trickled into the Bengal Muslim League.[142] In November 1945, Abul Mansur Ahmed, formerly a Krishak Praja Party leader and now propaganda secretary of the Bengal Muslim League, asserted in an article in *Millat* that the Muslim League had become the vanguard of the krishak praja movement. The Pakistan demand, an as yet undefined territorial expression of the Muslim claim to nationhood, encapsulated not only the Muslim right to self-determination but also the economic aspirations of the masses. The Muslim League was described as 'the revolutionary people's organization of Bengal': its primary membership was put at over ten lakh. While the

'If, as enemies of the fifth column, patriotic zamindars can be organized, it will be of benefit to the krishaks. *The krishaks must help the organization of zamindars.* By doing so, the unity of patriots will be enhanced, the fifth column will be cornered, and the patriots' organized unity will go forward in subduing bureaucracy'. *Krishak Karmir Shiksha Course* (1943) (Educational Course for Krishak Workers) quoted in Badruddin Umar, *Chirosthayee Bandobaste Bangladesher Krishak*, pp. 72-3.

141 Abul Hashim, *In Retrospection* (Dacca, 1974); Shila Sen, *Muslim Politics in Bengal*, pp. 181-6.

142 In 1945, prominent Krishak Praja Party leaders – Abul Mansur Ahmed, Abdulla-el Baqui, Shamsuddin Ahmed (erstwhile general secretary of the KPP), Hasan Ali, Nurul Islam Chaudhuri and Ghiasuddin Ahmed – had all joined the Muslim League. Abul Mansur Ahmed, *Amar Dekha Rajnitur Panchas Bachhar*, pp. 194-8; Sen, *Muslim Politics in Bengal*, p. 195.

League had established units in every union, the pro-Congress krishak praja samitis had become moribund.[143]

At the end of the war, the nationalist or, at any rate, the non-communal peasant leaders returned to a very changed economic and political environment. The scars of the famine had not healed. Grain prices ruled high and essential articles continued to be in short supply. Jute growers did not get a remunerative price, as a ridiculous price ceiling of Rs. 19 imposed in 1943, ostensibly to curb inflation, was maintained. With the return of the demobilised servicemen at the end of the war, the unemployment question again became particularly acute. During the wartime subsistence crisis communal relations had become more embittered, even though there had been little scope for violent protest. At a time of unprecedented material distress and psychological uncertainty for the peasant masses, the participants in the anti-imperialist struggle had been removed from the scene. In this political vacuum, the Muslim League was able to consolidate its position. Its propaganda was couched in religious terms and its vague but stirring goal of Pakistan was coming to assume a millennial appeal. The League branded all its opponents as 'kaumi gaddar' - national traitors - mere agents of the Hindus, who were not to be trusted.[144] Election meetings convened by the nationalist Muslims and the pro-Congress Krishak Prajas were systematically broken up.[145]

143 Abul Mansur Ahmed, 'The Background and Nature of Bengal Muslim Politics: It is the Muslim League which is today the vanguard of the Krishak Praja movement' (in Bengali), *Millat*, 23 Nov. 1945. Some of this was, of course, a propaganda secretary's rhetoric. There is no means of verifying the actual membership of the League at this time.

144 Ashrafuddin Chaudhuri of Tippera has described how on the day of his return home after a five-year spell in a distant prison, he was pelted with stones by Muslim League storm-troopers at his first public meeting. The non-League peasant leaders had little time to refurbish their organisations before the 1945-6 elections. Ashrafuddin Ahmed Chaudhuri, *Raj Birodhi* (Opponent of the Raj), pp. 102-5, 110-14.

145 During the central assembly elections, a prelude to the provincial elections of March 1946, 'the only excitements were provided in the Muslim constituencies from where a stream of complaints came that the Muslim League had adopted tactics of violence and intimidation against their "Nationalist" opponents - and that Government officers were assisting the Muslim League. There is no doubt that the Muslim League followers have been unduly rowdy - having, so I am told, possibly learnt the lesson from Congress habits in former days. The sense of the instructions that we have given to our local officers is that it is their

The elections of 1946 were fought in the Muslim constituencies between the Muslim League on the one hand and the KPP, the Nationalist Muslims and others who tried to form themselves into a Bengal/Nationalist Muslim Parliamentary Party with Congress support under Fazlul Huq, on the other.[146] In order to counter the communal propaganda of the League, the nationalists decided to call in the faction of the Jamiat, an all-India organisation of the Muslim ulema (theologians or learned men), under Maulana Husain Ahmed Madani which was opposed to Pakistan. On 9 February 1946, Madani addressed a large election meeting in Tippera organised by the nationalists.[147] But to no avail. In Noakhali and Tippera, those krishak samiti leaders who had not crossed over to the League lost their seats.[148] The constituencies were large, and even powerful local followings were not sufficient to carry them through against a wave in favour of the League. The results of the provincial elections in April 1946 showed that the League had won a massive victory in the Muslim constituencies. It won 115 of the 123 Muslim seats, most of them with overwhelming majorities. Of the 78 seats contested by the Nationalist Muslim Parliamentary Board, it was able to win only 5, 2 of them by Fazlul Huq himself.[149] The Congress

duty to "hold the ring" to the extent of maintaining public safety and order by all means at their disposal, but that it is not their duty to prevent heckling. shouting and so forth or, in short, to ensure that either party's meetings shall be a success.' Govt. to Gov. Gen., 7 Jan. 1946, L/P & J/5/152 (IOR).

146 Gov. to Gov. Gen., 5 Nov. 1945, L/P and J/5/152 (IOR); see also Shila Sen, *Muslim Politics in Bengal*, pp. 198-202.

147 The Nationalist Muslims staged a big conference in a district in East Bengal to which they had brought Maulana Husain Ahmed Madani from the U.P. The conference was organized by Asrafuddin Choudhury, a lieutenant of Subhas Bose; there was a clash with the Leaguers and Asrafuddin Choudhury mustered his forces and challenged the League to a free fight. The DM had to intervene by issuing an order under sec 144 Cr P C prohibiting the carrying of weapons and lathis in public meetings. The conference passed off with minor mishaps.' Secret Report on the Political Situation in Bengal for the first half of Feb. 1946, L/P and J/5/153 (IOR).

148 The Muslim League took all the seats in Tippera and Noakhali. Seven of the ten sitting members were defeated: Ramizuddin Ahmed (KPP), Janabali Majumdar (KPP), Asimuddin Ahmed (KPP), Shahedali (KPP), Syed Ahmad Khan (KPP), Abdur Razzak (Jamiat) and Ghulam Sarwar (Jamiat). Sarwar polled 4642 votes against the winning Muslim League candidate's 24 336 in the Ramganj-cum-Raipur constituency in Noakhali. Prominent krishak samiti personalities who also lost were Ashrafuddin Chaudhuri, Md Yakub Ali, Mukleshwar Rahman, Rashid Ahmed and Syed Abdul Wahed.

149 The Muslim League polled 2,013,000 votes; its opponents only 232,134 Muslim votes. Gov. to Gov. Gen., 11 Apr. 1946, L/P and J/5/153 (IOR).

won almost all the general seats and a good majority of the scheduled caste seats as well.

After the elections, the League leader Suhrawardy, despite his absolute majority, tried to form a coalition ministry with the Congress.[150] But the imperatives of the central high commands of both parties dictated against a broad-based intercommunal ministry in Bengal.[151] As a result, an almost purely Muslim ministry took office with an almost purely Hindu opposition. As the constitutional negotiations at the centre dragged on and coalition talks in Bengal continued to be shelved,[152] conflict in the localities began to get rapidly out of hand. The Great Calcutta Killing of August 1946 and the Noakhali and Tippera riots in October had a decisive influence on political attitudes and severely narrowed the options of politicians who at the provincial and national levels were seeking to preserve the unity of Bengal within a united India. The notion of a great communal divide over the Pakistan issue from the highest political level to the social base has fudged the analysis of disturbances, such as those in Noakhali and Tippera, which had dynamics of their own. The following section identifies the ingredients of the agrarian conflict in Noakhali and Tippera during the winter of 1946 and their connection with politics at the provincial and national levels.

The Noakhali and Tippera riots of 1946

The artificially depressed prices of jute at a time of scarcity and the high prices of grain had brought considerable hardship to the districts of east Bengal after the middle of 1946. The demobilised ex-servicemen who were unable to find any employment, formed a new and particularly volatile element in postwar rural society. The decision to decontrol jute prices was postponed until the end of September under intense pressure from the manufacturing interest and officialdom.[153]

150 Gov. to Gov. Gen., 25 Apr. 1946, L/P and J/5/152 (IOR).
151 See Ayesha Jalal, *The Sole Spokesman: Jinnah, the Muslim League and the Demand for Pakistan* (Cambridge, 1985), chapter 5.
152 Until 21 November 1946, a few seats in the Cabinet were kept vacant in the hope that an arrangement might be arrived at with the Congress. Gov. to Gov. Gen., 22 Nov. 1946, L/P and J/5/154 (IOR).
153 Gov. to Gov. Gen., 6 Sept. 1946, 20 Sept. 1946, L/P and J/5/154 (IOR).

The chief minister, Suhrawardy, while publicly declaring, 'we will not let the jute cultivators die',[154] tried to support the governor, who wanted the ceiling to continue, until a Congress MLA moved a cut motion in the Assembly, condemning the government for not fixing the minimum price of jute at Rs. 40 per maund.[155] At the time of the famine of 1943, the marketing network had collapsed, and the government had been forced to intervene directly in the food market. In early September 1946, the supply position of rice was causing 'extreme anxiety'.[156] In the second half of September, rationing had broken down in the Dacca division and local officers were 'embarrassed by the clamour for rice from Government stocks by people unable to buy in the ordinary market'. In Bakarganj, the stocks in the distribution godowns were dwindling and unless more was received, it was predicted, 'rocketting of prices in October cannot be prevented.' In Chittagong division, the supply situation was 'bad' and prices had risen sharply in Noakhali and Tippera. At the end of September, rice was selling at Rs. 28 per maund in Noakhali and Rs. 30 in parts of Tippera. These two districts with a population of about 5 million and a density of well over 1000 persons per square mile had even before the war been deficit in grain. Local production had to be supplemented by imports from Burma, Dinajpur, Bakarganj, Chittagong and Sylhet. Now they stood at the top of the list of food-deficit districts waiting to receive government-procured rice. The Supplies Department anticipated considerable difficulty in meeting the demands of these two districts which were estimated to be 200 000 and 120 000 maunds respectively for Noakhali and Tippera during October. Whether or not these requirements could be met depended entirely on the procurement of aus rice in north Bengal and on its efficient distribution. In the second fortnight in September, modified rationing had to be abandoned in Noakhali owing to shortage of supplies – the entire reserve stock had been depleted. Jute at this time was selling at between Rs. 17 and Rs. 19 per maund.[157] Early in October 1946, the 'rice supply position in

154 *Millat*, 18 Oct. 1946.
155 Gov. to Gov. Gen., 5 Oct. 1946, L/P and J/5/154 (IOR).
156 Gov. to Gov. Gen., 20 Sept. 1946, L/P and J/5/154 (IOR).
157 Secret Report on the Political Situation in Bengal for the second half of Sept. 1946, L/P and J/5/154 (IOR).

East Bengal' was described as 'critical'. The districts 'worst affected' were Noakhali and Tippera where rice prices had risen above Rs. 30 per maund.[158] This was considerably higher than the provincial average of Rs. 17 annas 11 on 9 October at the principal district marketing centres.[159]

Against such a background of economic crisis, the communal situation began to deteriorate rapidly in Noakhali. At mass meetings held at important centres, Muslim peasants were urged to enrol in a 'national guard' and incited to violence. The governor reported later that 'a strong movement of economic boycott of Hindus developed and Muslims found purchasing from Hindus were beaten up'.[160] The situation was particularly alarming in the Feni subdivision where in the first 10 days of October, 80 cases of incendiarism, often coupled with murder, were recorded.[161] On 9 October, a company of troops was moved there from Chittagong. Further trouble did not, however, develop in Feni, but instead erupted on 10 October in the Ramganj thana in the north-west of Noakhali district where Ghulam Sarwar, the former MLA who had been defeated by the League candidate at the last election, had been inciting the Muslims to rise in revolt against the local Hindu zamindars.[162] The conflagration began near the village of Panchgaon in the Ramganj thana where trouble had been brewing for some time at the local zamindar's hat.[163] Violence spread to the neighbouring villages and in about 36 hours, the rioters had extended their sway over the entire thana. The mob, about 4000-strong in the initial stages, were joined by local belligerents as they moved from village to village. Soon they split up into several groups and marched into the neighbouring thanas – Raipur,

158 Secret Report on the Political Situation in Bengal for the first half of Oct. 1946, L/P and J/5/154 (IOR).
159 *The Statesman*, 25 Oct. 1946.
160 Sir F. Burrows (Bengal) to Lord Pethick-Lawrence, 16 Oct. 1946, Telegram L/P and J/8/578 in N. Mansergh (ed.), *India: The Transfer of Power* (London, 1976-83), vol. 7, Document 472.
161 *The Statesman*, 26 Oct. 1946.
162 *The Statesman*, 21 Oct. 1946; Sir F. Burrows (Bengal) to Lord Pethick-Lawrence, 17 Oct. 1946, Telegram L/P and J/8/578 in Mansergh (ed.), *India: The Transfer of Power*, vol. 8, Document 475.
163 According to the Muslim League, there had been friction between the Sikh and Gurkha employees at the zamindar's hat and the Muslim peasants. *Millat*, 25 Oct. 1946.

Lakshmipur, Begumganj, Senbag and Sonaimuri. At the head of the groups were ex-servicemen who organised the raids on the villages in quasi-military fashion. The roving bands went about looting shops, burning houses, extorting money and booty under threats, abducting women, forcibly converting Hindus and committing brutal murders wherever there was the slightest resistance.[164]

The main centres of trouble in the Ramganj thana were Panchgaon, Karpara, Sahapur, Noagana Bazaar, Joyag and Dashgharia. In Panchgaon Bazaar, 28 shops were looted and in a neighbouring village, about 25 Hindu homesteads were burnt. On 10 October, in Sahapur, about 21 shops, in some of which Hindus and Muslims were in joint ownership, were burnt and another 8 shops were looted. At Noagana Bazaar, the rioters clashed with local Muslims and were able to loot only one or two shops. In Joyag, on 12 October, the houses of two Hindu zamindars were burnt down. In Dashgharia Bazaar, Muslim rioters looted 10 Hindu shops and 15 Muslim-owned shops.[165] These cases led the district magistrate of Noakhali to conclude: 'It is not exactly a communal trouble. It is mainly hooligans who have, of course, directed their activities primarily against the Hindus; in some instances attacks on Muslims have also been reported.'[166] In the neighbouring thanas, looting and burning took place on a massive scale. Prominent among those killed in the Begumganj thana were zamindar Surendra Kumar Bose, whose kachchari was destroyed, and Rajendra Lal Roy, president of the district Bar Association, together with 20 members of his family. An area of over 500 square miles in the Ramganj, Lakshmipur, Begumganj, Raipur, Senbag and Sonaimuri thanas with a population of about 100 000 was affected by the disturbances.[167]

On 15 October the mobs moved into the Fardiganj–Charhaim–Chandpur area in Tippera, leaving behind

---

164 *The Statesman*, 20 Oct. 1946; Sir F. Burrows (Bengal) to Lord Pethick-Lawrence, 16 Oct. 1946, 20 Oct. 1946, Telegram L/P and J/8/578 in Mansergh (ed.), *India: The Transfer of Power*, Vol. 8, Documents 472 and 482; Files G 53 and G 65 of 1946, AICC Papers (Nehru Memorial Museum and Library).

165 DM E.F. McInerney's Tour Diary published in *The Statesman*, 23 Oct. 1946.

166 *The Statesman*, 23 Oct. 1946.

167 *The Statesman*, 22 Oct. 1946; Mr Sarat Bose to Field Marshal Viscount Wavell, 14 Oct. 1946, in Mansergh (ed.), *India: The Transfer of Power*, vol. 8, Document

detachments to guard the 'occupied' areas in Noakhali. Nearly
70 villages in thanas Hajiganj, Faridganj and Chandpur with
a Hindu population of about 40 000 were besieged by the
rioters.[168] The major concentration of the insurgents' forces
was at Charhaim. The governor, who later toured this area,
wrote:

I also fitted in a brief visit to a village called Char Haim on the border
between Tippera and Noakhali districts which was very worth
while. . . . There is no doubt that the mobs, at least in Char Haim, did
their work most thoroughly and systematically. This village had a
prosperous bazaar which was the economic centre of the
neighbourhood. The bazaar stood on Government land and the
Government revenue office was untouched, as were a few Muslim-
owned shops; but the rest was a desolate ruin of charred timber and
twisted corrugated iron sheets. It is worth recording that many of the
shopkeepers had made fortunes in the 1943 famine, at the expense of
the Muslim peasantry.[169]

The peasants had clearly not forgotten or forgiven the callous
exploitation by the grain-dealers in 1943.

It is impossible to give a correct estimate of the total
casualties and losses in the Noakhali and Tippera riots of
October 1946. The government's suggestion that fatalities
were probably 'low in the three-figure category' was a clear
under-estimate, while the figure of 5000 quoted by the
Calcutta press was a gross exaggeration. Refugees who took
shelter in relief camps numbered at least 30 000.[170] There was
undoubtedly colossal damage to property. After a very slow
start, order was eventually restored by the end of the month but
only after some 400 armed police assisted by five companies of
troops and two reconnaissance planes were pressed into action
to locate the attacking gangs.[171]

The district magistrate of Noakhali attributed the riots to
'the political situation in the country, the economic
inequality between the two communities in certain areas, the

452; Mahendra Mohan Roy to DM, Noakhali in File G 65 of 1946. AICC Papers
(Nehru Memorial Museum and Library).
168 *The Statesman*, 20 Oct. 1946, 23 Oct. 1946.
169 Gov. to Gov. Gen., 6 Dec. 1946, L/P J/5/154 (IOR).
170 Sir F. Burrows (Bengal) to Lord Pethick-Lawrence, 20 Oct. 1946. Telegram L/P
    and J/8/578 in Mansergh (ed.), *India: The Transfer of Power*, vol. 8, Document
    482.
171 *Ibid.; The Statesman*, 22 Oct. 1946.

Map 7: Districts Tippera and Noakhali: chief centres of agrarian and communal
conflict, 1930s and 1940s

present rising against mahajans and landlords, and. . . mere hooliganism'.[172] At a time of great economic stress, the news of the killings in Calcutta and Dacca further embittered anti-Hindu feelings. The presence of a League ministry may also have encouraged the rioters, although there is no evidence to support the allegation that the League had deliberately engineered the disturbances. Indeed, communal trouble at this stage cut across the grain of the broader political strategy of preserving the unity of this Muslim-majority province.[173] The lower-caste Hindus were certainly not spared the rioters' mischief, but one newspaper report was probably quite accurate in saying: 'The well-to-do and educated people, many of whom had lost their lives, were the main targets of attack, while the rest were let off after conversion.'[174] The riots of 1946 were different from the 1930s risings of peasant-debtors in that the landless unemployed army roughs were at the forefront. In a marked departure from earlier rural disturbances, there were on this occasion cases of abductions of women and personal violence on a large scale.

During 1946, as the politicians in Delhi and Calcutta demonstrated their inability to negotiate a settlement, at the base social forces were being unleashed which they were even less able to control. The carnage in Noakhali and Tippera following in the wake of the Great Calcutta Killing frightened a large body of Hindu political opinion about their future in a Muslim-majority province. Those who had blazed the trail of Indian nationalism a generation ago by doggedly opposing the partition of 1905 were now beset by Curzon's ghost. In

172 'I consider it most important to emphasise,' he said, 'that the recent disturbances have not been an uprising of one community as a whole against the other.' *The Statesman*, 30 Oct. 1946.
173 See Jalal, *Sole Spokesman*, chapter 6. The overall political situation in the country lends credence to Suhrawardy's statement: 'The Government *could not afford* to see communal riots take place anywhere'. *The Statesman*, 17 Oct. 1946; in another statement to the Muslims, he said: 'even if you had grievances at one time that the Muslim League had been kept out of the Central Government, there is no justification for such feeling now – Hindus and Muslims must learn to live side by side and work in co-operation for the sake of a better Bengal'. *The Statesman*, 27 Oct. 1946.
    The government did, however, show itself to be totally inadequate to the task of maintaining order and protecting life and property. Ghulam Sarwar, the self-styled leader, was not apprehended until 23 October 1946. By the end of October, the army was able to bring the situation under control.
174 *The Stateman*, 21 Oct. 1946.

February 1947, the Hindu Mahasabha put forward the demand of partitioning Bengal. The idea was quickly taken up by the Congress High Command for reasons of its own. Some in the provincial Muslim League leadership and a handful of Bengali nationalists continued their efforts until the very end to secure a united Bengal. After such recent communal conflicts, the movement did not catch the Hindu imagination, nor was it enthusiastically supported by some east Bengal Muslims.[175] A set of far-sighted social and economic policies in favour of the predominantly Muslim smallholding peasantry might have lifted the crisis in social relations that had descended on east Bengal in 1930. But a plural society as prone to conflict, calamity and chaos as east Bengal was not offered a solution of that sort. By a cruel irony of fate, it was the legislators of west Bengal who cast the decisive vote to partition the province, suggesting that east Bengal's multiple problems called for a remedy rather different from the agonising political vivisection that took place.[176] But Bengal had long ceased to be the arbiter of her own political destiny. The critical decisions on the eve of independence were taken by men at the political centre who were anxious to quickly grab the centralised power of the Raj. The Congress president Kripalani dismissed a plea to save the unity of Bengal in unequivocal terms:

All that the Congress seeks to do today is to rescue as many areas as possible from the threatened domination of the League and Pakistan. It wants to save as much territory for a Free Indian Union as is possible under the circumstances. It therefore insists upon the

175 See Shila Sen, *Muslim Politics in Bengal*, pp. 223-45.
176 On 20 June 1947 the members of the Bengal Legislative Assembly met and decided on the partition of Bengal. At the preliminary joint meeting, it was decided by 126 votes to 90 that the Province, if it remained united, should join a new Constituent Assembly (i.e. Pakistan; the option of independence was not available under the terms of Mountbatten's 3 June Statement). At a separate meeting of the members of the West Bengal Legislative Assembly, it was decided by 58 votes to 21 that the Province should be partitioned and that West Bengal should join the existing Constituent Assembly. At a separate meeting of members of the East Bengal Legislative Assembly, it was decided by *106 votes to 35 that the Province should not be partitioned* and by 107 votes to 34 that East Bengal should join the new Constituent Assembly should partition eventuate. Mansergh (ed.), *India: The Transfer of Power 1942-47*, vol. 9, Documents 277-8, 369.

division of Bengal and Punjab into areas for Hindustan and Pakistan respectively.'[177]

The pleader, Ashrafuddin Chaudhuri, the veteran nationalist and peasant leader from Tippera, could only rue: 'The Congress high command has let us down.'[178]

During the first three decades of the twentieth century, so long as the Muslim peasant of east Bengal remained involved in a symbiotic economic relationship with the Hindu talukdar and mahajan, the possibility of a sustained conflict could be ruled out. The 1930s depression ruptured that relationship.[179] The momentous impact that the slump would have on the system of agrarian relations could hardly have been recognised at the time. Earlier, when lean years imposed strains on the system, the peasants did protest against unacceptable demands on their resources. But before long, the crisis would resolve itself and the system could revert to its homeostasis. The magnitude and the extended nature of the economic crisis of the 1930s were unprecedented. The old ties snapped once and for all. The period of war and famine that followed hardly afforded an opportunity for repair.

Ironically, the 1930s which brought untold hardship to the east-Bengal peasant also witnessed a decisive shift in the balance of class power in the countryside in his favour. The rupture in the system of rural credit relations deprived the Hindu talukdars and traders of their dominance. The talukdars remained a source of irritation as petty rent-collectors. The traders who took to grain-dealing were hated. As they no longer played the role of guaranteeing the peasant's subsistence as mahajans, the old deference disappeared. In the small peasant economy of east Bengal, they had ceased to perform any useful function. Once a political challenge came within the realm of possibility, the strength of a religious identity was exploited as a readily available and, for the privileged co-religionists, a safe ideology. To the vast mass of smallholding peasants living under similar, yet very splintered, conditions of economic existence in east Bengal,

---

177 J.B. Kripalani to Ashrafuddin Ahmed Chaudhuri, 13 May 1947, reproduced in
       Ashrafuddin Ahmed Chaudhuri, *Raj Birodhi*, pp. 119-20.
178 Ashrafuddin Ahmed Chaudhuri to Abul Hayat, 20 May 1947. in *ibid.*, p. 121.
179 See chapter 4 above.

religion, seemed to impart a sense of 'community'; so at a critical juncture in Bengal's history, religion provided the basis of a 'national bond', however stretched, and became the rallying cry of a 'political organisation' demanding the creation of a separate Muslim homeland.[180] Efforts by some Hindu and Muslim leaders to mobilise the Muslim peasantry under the banner of progressive nationalism and socialism proved abortive. Weighed under for decades by an economic, political and moral order they had long ago silently rejected, the Muslim peasantry responded to the appeals of religion and gave a powerful ideological legitimation to a breakdown in social relations that had already occurred, but which was only now being formally conceded.

Since 1930 the Hindu talukdars and traders were not merely hated but had increasingly become redundant on the east-Bengal agrarian scene. In August 1947 they were finally forced to begin their perilous trek towards the newly demarcated Indian border.

180 The phrases in quotes are those of Marx in *The Eighteenth Brumaire of Louis Bonaparte*, in K. Marx and F. Engels, *Selected Works I*, (Moscow 1962) p. 334.

7

Agrarian relations and mass nationalism in West Bengal

Peasant protest in west Bengal, especially during the depression decade, was much more muted than in east Bengal. It was also very different in character. Midnapur was an exception in some ways; nowhere else in west Bengal did the agitations reach the same degree of intensity. In 1942 there was a climax of a succession of agrarian-based nationalist agitations that had been launched in this coastal district of south-west Bengal since 1921. In west Bengal as a whole, major agrarian movements in this period invariably assumed an anti-government complexion and usually did not outlast the initial phase of a crisis. During these short outbursts, the countryside displayed remarkable solidarity – the conflict with the local arms of the colonial state over-shadowed the differences within the rural populace. In the periods of interregnum, the internal conflicts became apparent. In most parts of west Bengal, the grainlending landlords and rich peasants were able to reassert their dominance over the peasant smallholders and agricultural labourers during the 1930s depression. It was only in Contai and Tamluk in Midnapur, Arambag in Hooghly, and a few other small pockets, that the indebted small peasants and sharecroppers were able to achieve a measure of success in their collective bargaining with the rentiers and creditors. This chapter will provide a brief analytic survey of the connections between

1 DM Midnapur to Addl Secy GB, 30 Sept. 1942, Conf. File 23, Collection No. IB, 1942-3, Governor's Secretariat Bengal, R/3/2/36 (IOR). 'The agitators have been successful in inciting the peasantry to commit violent outrages and to interfere with the normal life of the countryside. The Congress have always exercised considerable influence on the masses...large crowds of peasantry are roaming all over the countryside ready to fall on and overpower any small Government agency'. This was the situation in Midnapur at the end of September 1942, after six police station headquarters in Contai and Tamluk subdivisions had been attacked by crowds of between 4000 and 12 000 men and women.

233

agrarian relations and mass nationalism in west Bengal. It will focus on the history of peasant politics in Midnapur, and point out the ways in which it was different from more typical west Bengal districts, like Burdwan.

Agrarian social structure in west Bengal: Midnapur's special features

The inequalities of the demesne labour–peasant smallholding complex in west Bengal were reinforced by patterns of differential mortality and morbidity among various social classes as a result of chronic malnutrition and recurring malaria epidemics. This was a region of demographic and agricultural decline where the smallholding caste peasants and the low-caste and tribal agricultural labourers were critically dependent on the landlords and rich peasants for credit and for small parcels of land from the extensive personal demesne. Landlords' dominance was realised in three ways: by relatively high rents extracted from the peasant smallholding sector, by their role – together with a section of rich peasantry – as the main creditors, and by their direct control of land and labour in the fairly substantial khamar sector. The caste peasantry were split by a process of differentiation into a minority of rich peasant patrons who had taken to grain-dealing and lending and a majority of indebted small peasants who carried on smallholding cultivation in the early part of the century at the cost of a large proportion of the surplus being taken away annually in the form of rent and loan interest. The low-caste agricultural labourers had their homesteads and scraps of inferior land, but they were severely dependent on the landlords and rich peasants whose lands they worked as bhagdars, krishans, munishes or mahindars.

Agricultural labour was not used on khamar lands only. In the period of the malaria epidemics, there were often few working members in peasant smallholding families and it was common to use sharecroppers and hired labourers even on fairly small holdings. This necessary but unequal collaboration between peasant smallholders and agricultural labour created conflicts of interest and prevented the emergence of any effective political alliance between them against landlord and rich peasant exploiters. In fact, bonds of dependence were strengthened in west Bengal during the depression, not ruptured as in east Bengal. Even when money credit dried up, the greater control of the moneylending groups in west Bengal over the landholding structure enabled them to continue grain loans in return for labour services. The crisis in credit placed the smallholding sector in enormous difficulties, leaving it no choice but to retreat in the face of an advancing khamar sector.[2]

In this general scenario, Contai and Tamluk subdivisions in Midnapur are in some ways an exception. These were areas to which Mahishya peasants fled to escape the ravages of malaria from 1860 onwards, and show a rising demographic trend in contrast to the decline all around. In these subdivisions there was no distinct reserve of low-caste agricultural labour. Although in some of the coastal areas there were big tenure-holders known as chakdars, the bhagchashis who performed the actual work of cultivation had definite chashi (peasant) status, and many were recorded in the survey and settlement of the 1910s as occupancy raiyats.[3] By the second decade of the twentieth century, however, the tightness of the land–man ratio was beginning to bite. The raiyat family on an average held less than four acres.[4] It was at a time when the Mahishya peasants' new frontier of opportunity was on the point of exhaustion that the economic and political dislocation of the First World War and its aftermath intervened.

The first wave of agitation: 1920-22

The non-cooperation movement in Midnapur in 1921 took the shape of a mass agitation against the colonial state on the issue of an increase in the chaukidari (village watch and ward) tax. Whether wittingly or unwittingly, the government had chosen a time of particular economic difficulty to introduce institutions of local self-government. The aim was to draw in a wider set of collaborators and to offset its own financial problems by extending local taxation. The introduction of the

2 See chapters 4 and 5 above.
3 *Midnapur SR*, p. 54.
4 *Ibid.*, p. 49.

Village Self-Government Act of 1919 in Midnapur in January 1921 and the setting up of union boards that followed entailed a 50% increase in the existing chaukidari tax.[5] The poorer peasants naturally resented this increase; 'they had not had good crops for years... [and] could hardly pay for their food and clothing'.[6] The landlords and richer peasants were faced with a choice of methods by which to translate their social and economic dominance into local political leadership. They could collaborate and work the institutions of local self-government as the reforms intended. Or they could mobilise the mass discontent in a society which had at least partially acquired a vertically segmented character in the wake of recent powerful caste movements.[7] Many opted for the latter course and threw their weight behind the anti-union-board movement.

Under the leadership of Birendra Nath Sasmal, a Contai lawyer, the whole countryside was pitched against the agents of the state. By October 1921, the 'refusal to pay any taxes had become general' and it was impossible to realise arrears by distraint since there were no bidders at the sales.[8] Not only chaukidars but also members of union boards resigned in large numbers. The strength of the agitation and the disaffection among the Santals in the western jungle areas compelled the government to retreat. On 17 December 1921, the Village Self-Government Act was withdrawn from Midnapur.[9] The tradition of the successful 1921 agitation was to become a great source of confidence for the Midnapur peasantry in subsequent campaigns.

In Midnapur and the other parts of west Bengal, the non-cooperation movement was at its peak only for a brief period during which the whole agrarian system reacted against what was viewed as outside interference in a time of stress. Subsequently, internal divisions came to the fore and, by March 1922, soon after the union board victory had been won,

5 Hitesranjan Sanyal, 'Congress Movements in the Villages of Eastern Midnapore, 1921-1931' in Gaborieau and Thorner (eds.), *Asie du Sud*, pp. 169, 172.
6 Report by Jt. Magistrate, Midnapur, dated 1 Nov. 1921, GB Local Self-Govt Dept, Progs. July 1922 Nos. 36-49, File L.2-U-5 S1 Nos. 1-7 (WBSA).
7 Sanyal, 'Congress Movements' pp. 170-2.
8 'History of Non-cooperation Movement in Bengal', p. 14, GB Poll Conf. File 395/24 (WBSA).
9 Notification No. 5025 L.6-G dated 17 Dec. 1921, GB Local Self-Govt Dept, Progs. July 1922 Nos. 36-49, File L.2-U-5 S1 Nos. 1-7 (WBSA).

the bhagchashis of Contai combined to demand from their landlords a reduction in the exactions above the customary half share of the produce. The landlords came to a meeting convened by the bhagchashis but made only small concessions. The bhagchashis remained disgruntled and complained that the landlords were not following the path of Mahatma Gandhi. But they had little bargaining power to force the issue.[10] Even as late as 1928, the legislators from Midnapur voted against an amendment to the Bengal Tenancy Act which would have strengthened the rights of tenants and sharecroppers. It was not until the aftermath of the civil disobedience movement in the early 1930s that the small peasants' and sharecroppers' agitations based on economic demands acquired a new intensity.

The depression decade

The agrarian dimension of the civil disobedience movement was strongest in its first phase when a wide range of agrarian social classes responded to the Congress call and pitted their strength against the government. Midnapur, as usual, showed greater political dynamism than other parts of West Bengal. The movement began in April 1930 with a defiance of the salt laws in the coastal areas, but in a month's time developed into a no-tax agitation.[11] Coercion by the local administration proved to be ineffective. 'People had begun to leave their houses and hide all around,' wrote a local officer, 'rather than pay their taxes.'[12] Satyagraha centres functioned in the villages with the full support of the local population. In the whole belt from Ghatal through Tamluk to Contai the government's intelligence-gathering machinery collapsed. Chaukidars, daffadars and panchayats were nowhere to be found. Government officers from the district magistrate downwards were 'jeered at wherever they went' and in most

10 *Nihar*, 7 Mar. 1922, cited in Sanyal, 'Congress Movements', p. 174.
11 'Programme of Work at Satyagraha Centres' dated 16 May 1930, English translation in GB Poll Conf. File 436 of 1930 (WBSA). The programme included 'stoppage of chaukidary tax and land revenue' which would 'make it impossible for the Government to function'.
12 General Note by the Addl DM Midnapur, 3 Nov. 1930, GB Poll Conf. File 249/30 (1-3) (WBSA).

places they were faced with an effective social and economic boycott.[13] At Dimari hat in Tamluk:

The ordinary cultivator, even when reasoned with, simply squatted on his haunches and laughing sarcastically said, 'We know how powerful the Sirkar is. Formerly even the zamindar of Narajole had to make an appointment with the District Magistrate and the Additional District Magistrate before he would find an opportunity to see them. Now we find the District Magistrate and the Additional District Magistrate coming round to us, villagers, begging us to pay our taxes'.[14]

In late May and early June 1930, five major clashes took place between huge crowds of peasants and the armed police at Gopinathpur, Pratapdighi and Balishai in Contai, Chechuahat in Ghatal and Khirai in Sadar subdivision.[15] There were many casualties from police shootings. On 12 June 1930, Peddie, the district magistrate wrote:

We have not got the force to deal with these mobs with lathis and the effect of lathis is insufficient. The best thing that could happen would be to have a few more shootings which would, I think, be more effective than anything else. I do not propose of course to encourage shooting, but when violent mobs refuse to disperse I think that the Police officers must not hesitate to use the arms they have. Unless this is done, collection of chaukidari taxes will I am certain be extremely difficult...[16]

This policy effectively drove the movement underground. A few more shootings did take place in Midnapur: Peddie himself and two of his successors were among those who were killed. It is sometimes suggested that individual terrorism impeded mass movements in Bengal. In Midnapur, at least, the two were closely interconnected and complemented each other in the face of government repression. As a report from the second of the ill-fated Midnapur district magistrates stated:

13 DM Midnapur to Chief Secy, 28 May 1930, GB Poll Conf. File 436 of 1930 (WBSA).
14 General Note by the Addl DM Midnapur, 3 Nov. 1930, GB Poll Conf. File 249/30 (1-3) (WBSA).
15 Recent Disturbances in Midnapur by DM Midnapur and Confidential Report by Addl DM Midnapur dated 7 June 1930, GB Poll Conf. File 434/1930; DM Midnapur to Chief Secy, 12 June 1930, GB Poll Conf. File 488/30; Superintendent of Police Midnapur to Chief Secy, 29 June 1930, GB Poll Conf. File 506 (1-36)/30 (WBSA).
16 DM Midnapur to Chief Secy, 12 June 1930, GB Poll Conf. File 434/1930 (WBSA).

in this district the distinction between the Congress volunteers and the terrorists is not very great. Few Congress volunteers are willing to indulge in serious political crime, but they undoubtedly sympathise with such crime and are willing to give every possible assistance to those who are willing to take the risks. I am afraid the same must be said of a very considerable portion of the general public.[17]

Behind the apparently solid phalanx of rural rebels there were internal conflicts of interest which the local Congress leaders balanced with considerable tact. Early in 1931 the bhagchashis in Contai combined to demand better terms from their landlords. As the local newspaper, *Nihar*, wrote, 'Mahatma Gandhi's movements have engendered new hopes and aspirations in the minds of the people. Inspired by the new ideas, the poor peasants and labourers have unified. Thus, this year the peasants of the region have combined and begun to protest against the oppression of zamindar mahajans.'[18] The bhagchashi agitation assumed serious proportions in Contai, Bhagawanpur and Khejuri thanas in Contai subdivision and Nandigram and Mahishadal thanas in Tamluk subdivision. The Congress leaders had to intervene to somehow preserve the united front against the government. In 1931, they were largely successful in this. For instance, in Contai subdivision, three of them – Pramatha Banerjee, Iswar Chandra Mal and Basanta Kumar Das – went to the major trouble centre in Khejuri and negotiated a five-point compromise between the bhagchashis and their landlords.[19] In this way, the Congress was able to secure both the material backing of the relatively privileged as well as the support of the small peasants and sharecroppers who provided the mass

17 DM Midnapur to Cmsner Burdwan Dn, 6 July 1931, GB Poll Conf. File 345 (1-17)/1931 (WBSA).
18 *Nihar*, 26 May 1931, quoted in Sanyal, 'Congress Movements', p. 176. The *Nihar* report in the Bengali original refers to the oppression of 'zamindar mahajans', but Sanyal in his rendering into English, equates the 'zamindar mahajans', with the 'jotdars'. The confusion in terminology especially over-use of the blanket-category 'jotedar', has confused the identification of social groups in rural Bengal. The term 'jotedar' took on a meaning in the 1960s and the 1970s that was quite different from its local connotations in the different regions of Bengal in the early twentieth century.
19 The five points were as follows: (1) all levies except the charges for preparing the threshing-floor should be abolished with effect from 1931-2; (2) the bhagchashis would pay towards the preparation of the threshing-floor only where it was the usual custom but the rates would be reduced; (3) straw should be shared equally

base with which to unsettle the district administration. During the Gandhi–Irwin truce of the latter half of 1931, government institutions in Midnapur continued to be boycotted and the countryside was honeycombed with arbitration courts run by the Congress.[20]

The second phase of the civil disobedience movement proved to be a damp squib in most parts of west Bengal. The broad united front that had briefly emerged during the initial difficulties of the depression had quickly disintegrated. Midnapur was the only district where collection of taxes and various punitive fines continued to be resisted during the 1932–4 period, while at the same time the small peasants and sharecroppers won concessions on their economic demands within the framework of the Congress-led coalition.[21] The turbulence of the Midnapur countryside was not curbed until 1934, when the governor, John Anderson, took matters in his iron hand. From the winter of 1934, an uneasy quiet descended on the district. The defiant wail of conch-shells died away in the wilderness as sounds of British drums and bugles reverberated in the region.[22]

Political activity revived in Midnapur on the eve of the 1937 elections to the provincial legislative assembly. Congress leaders Sarat Chandra Bose, Profulla Ghose and Amarendra Nath Chatterjee had toured the district and local Congress parliamentary boards had been set up in preparation for the elections. The administration was alarmed by these developments and tried to curb the parliamentary boards. The district magistrate complained, 'The congress campaign has... left a very bad impression throughout the district. It is only natural that when villagers find congress leaders saying what they like and virtually defy authority openly they should come to the conclusion that congress is once more on top.'[23]

between bhagchashi and landlord; (4) the bhagchashis would not refuse to cultivate the lands of their respective landlords; and (5) the landlords must not evict the bhagchashis unless there were definite charges against them. *Nihar*, 30 June 1931, cited by Sanyal, 'Congress Movements', p. 177.

20 Report of Superintendent of Police Midnapur, 11 June 1931, GB Poll Conf. File 335 (1-22)/1931 (WBSA).

21 Sanyal, 'Congress Movements' p. 177

22 Report on the Political Situation in the district of Midnapur from Oct. 1932 to April 1934 with special reference to the use of troops in anti-terrorist work by DM Midnapur, GB Poll Conf. File 277/1934 (WBSA).

23 DM Midnapur to Chief Secy, 23 Jan. 1937, GB Poll Conf. File 57/37.

The Congress reaped the fruits of civil disobedience by winning all the general seats from Midnapur to the legislative assembly. The official ban on the Congress organisation in Midnapur was finally lifted in April 1937. Soon after, in a remarkable change from its old tactics, it decided to capture the union boards in the local elections to be held in June 1937. By winning outright majorities on many of the boards, despite large nominated representations, the Congress in Midnapur gained considerable influence over the rural police.[24] The release of the detenus in 1938 gave a further impetus to the organisation. In May 1938, Subhas Bose as the Congress president, made an extensive tour of Midnapur. As the governor reported:

He [Bose] has succeeded in producing a great revival of Congress activities throughout the District; meetings are being held in many towns and villages and the local officers report considerable enthusiasm. One interesting feature has emerged, and that is that now that Subhas Bose has succeeded in getting the Congress leaders in the Midnapur District to waive their objection to the ex-detenus, the latter are making great efforts to capture the more important Congress Committees in the District and they have already succeeded in gaining a majority on several of them.[25]

As the left wing of the Congress gained strength, the agrarian agitation was intensified. There was a no-rent campaign in the khas mahal (government) estates and a stepping up of bhagchashi demands against the tenure-holders. Disputes arose over certain traditional demands of the landlords in the distribution of the produce after the harvest. Some Congress leaders in Contai realised 'the danger of indulging in activities which [were] likely to create trouble between small landlords on the one hand and the tenants and bhagchasis on the other'.[26] In February 1939, the district magistrate decided not to interfere in a dispute in the Khejuri thana in Contai because 'some small landlords concerned are

24 FRs from DM Midnapur to Cmsner Burdwan Dn, 22 Apr., 8 May, 23 May, 11 June, 23 June and 9 July 1937, GB Poll Conf. File 10/37 (WB Home Dept). In the union board elections held in June 1937, the Congress obtained absolute majorities in 20 out of 30 boards in Contai and 11 out of 22 boards in Tamluk.
25 Gov. to Gov. Gen., 3 June 1938, L/P & J/5/142 (IOR).
26 FR from Cmsner Burdwan Dn for the first half of Feb. 1939, GB Poll Conf. File 19/39 (WB Home Dept).

Congress supporters and...these may be given scope within certain limits to feel the effects of irresponsible agitation carried on by the Congress'.[27] In the Nandigram thana in Tamluk, on the other hand, the landlord concerned was a non-Congressman and the bhagchashis obtained the full support of the local Congress leaders. By April 1939, the Congress leaders had been able to settle the disputes through compromise. It was only in Lakhya union in Mahishadal thana that the krishak samiti broke with the local Congress and continued the agitation until May with the help of communist leaders from Calcutta.[28]

In the sowing season of 1939, 'the big mahajans' refused to settle their lands with bhagchashis who had joined the agitation during the previous harvest: 'where they have not found other bhagchasis, they have left some of their lands fallow – a course which they can easily afford to take in order to starve agitating bhagchasis into surrender'.[29] The bhagchashis tried to retaliate by destroying seedlings and injuring cattle. The bhagchashi–tenure-holder conflict continued intermittently. Terms were settled only to be followed by new demands.[30] As late as March 1942, the Contai subdivision reported 'tension between bhagchasis and tenureholders', but the trouble by now was 'endemic in these areas'.[31] Wartime strategic needs forced government to intervene increasingly in the agrarian economy of Midnapur. This provoked a remarkable resurgence of unity in the countryside leading to a massive rural revolt once the Quit-India movement was launched. But before studying the 1942 movement in Midnapur, it will be useful to contrast the connection between agrarian relations and the nature of rural protest in the neighbouring district of Burdwan in the 1930s.

27 FR from Cmsner Burdwan Dn for the second half of Feb. 1939, GB Poll Conf. File 19/39 (WB Home Dept).
28 FR from Cmsner Burdwan Dn for the first half of May 1939, GB Poll Conf. File 19/39 (WB Home Dept).
29 FR from Cmsner Burdwan Dn for the second half of July 1939, GB Poll Conf. File 19/39 (WB Home Dept).
30 FRs from Cmsner Burdwan Dn for the first half of Aug. 1939, second half of Aug. 1939, second half of Nov. 1939, second half of Dec. 1939, GB Poll Conf. File 19/39; FR for the first half of Aug. 1940, GB Poll Conf. File 30/40; FRs dated 11 Apr. 1941, 27 Apr. 1941 and 9 June 1941, GB Poll Conf. File 13/41 (WB Home Dept).
31 FR from Cmsnr Burdwan Dn for the first half of Mar. 1942, GB Poll Conf. File 31/42 (WB Home Dept).

The Damodar Canal Tax agitation in Burdwan: 1936–9

In Burdwan, as in most parts of west and central Bengal, the dominance of the grainlending landlords and rich peasants in both the peasant smallholding and the demesne labour sectors had been maintained, if not extended, during the crisis of the depression. Consequently, there was little protest by peasant debtors either of the east Bengal or of the Midnapur variety. The reason for the peasant movement in Burdwan between 1936 and 1939 was the imposition by the government of an 'improvement levy' of Rs. 5, annas 8 per acre per annum in the command area of the newly opened Damodar canal. The first to take up the matter were the pleaders and advocates of the Burdwan District Raiyats' Association who had landed interests in the canal area. The Association at first tried to 'keep aloof from the Congress for fear of government repression' which 'would scare away the peasants from uniting for a common cause'.[32] The Congress and its more radical peasant front organisation, the Krishak Samiti, entered the field after the 1937 election and quickly built up a united front of landowners, peasants and sharecroppers in a no-tax movement.[33] A Congress enquiry committee recommended in March 1938 that the levy be reduced to one maund of paddy and one pan of straw per acre, the price of which was then Re. 1, annas 8. Under extreme pressure the government had offered in December 1937 to reduce the tax to Rs. 3 per acre, and in May 1938, at the recommendation of an official enquiry committee, it now agreed to reduce it further to Rs. 2, annas 9. The Congress urged its followers to accept the offer. One observer has pointed out the reasons why the Congress took this course:

The Congress leaders who had been carrying on the agitation felt that, *with their present strength of organization*, it would be wise to strike a bargain at that point. The pressure of the Government for the realization of the water-rates was great, and there were also signs of *wavering and indecision among the peasants, for the latter did not belong to one class, but ranged from a fairly prosperous section to*

32 Buddhadeva Bhattacharyya, 'Damodar Canal Tax Movement', in A.R. Desai (ed.), *Peasant Struggles in India* (Bombay, 1979), p. 402.
33 'Grievances of the Assessees of the Damodar Canal Area', GB Poll Conf. File 415/37 (WBSA).

those who possessed no land. If a settlement could be arrived at this point, it would be at least lead to *a sense of success* among those who had tried to resist.[34]

However, the communist section in the Krishak Samiti refused to budge from the original demand of a reduction to Re. 1, annas, 8. So the government decided to exploit the heterogeneous nature of the interests in an unegalitarian agrarian social structure and the political divisions that had surfaced by slapping the draconian Bengal Criminal Law Amendment Act on Burdwan. The movement was repressed by the middle of 1939.[35] Both, in the initial success of the movement and in its ultimate disintegration, the structural constraints of the ties of dependency in a peasant smallholding–demesne labour complex had played a decisive role.

The 1942 movement in Midnapur

The year 1941 was one of scarcity and soaring prices in west Bengal. For the first time, grainlending landlords and rich peasants of this region showed a disposition to hoard stocks rather than provide credit for dependent cultivators. Numerous cases of paddy looting took place in all the districts. From April 1942, the government began to implement the denial policy in the coastal areas of Midnapur. This involved the removal of 'surplus' stocks of paddy to the north-west of the province and all means of transport including boats and bicycles to a distance of at least 50 miles from the coast.[36] A sudden cess revaluation and the pressure on the local population to purchase war bonds aggravated the situation. Throughout the year, the Congress urged a ban on food exports from the district, but the government paid little heed. So the Congress launched a propaganda campaign, exhorting the villagers to resist exports.[37] When the call for a

34 Nirmal Kumar Bose, *Lectures on Gandhism*, p. 27, quoted in Buddhadeva Bhattacharyya, 'Damodar Canal Tax Movement', p. 412 (emphasis added).
35 'Secret information regarding the attitude of the members of the Burdwan Krishak Samiti and that of the Burdwan Dist Congress Committee towards the Satyagraha movements dated 14 Feb. 1939', GB Poll Conf. File 71/40 (WBSA); Buddhadeva Bhattacharyya, 'Damodar Canal Tax Movement', pp. 405-7.
36 Gov. to Gov. Gen., 8 Apr. 1942, 6 June 1942, L/P & J/5/149 (IOR).
37 S.C. Samanta *et al.*, *August Revolution and Two Years' National Government in Midnapore* (Calcutta, 1946), pp. 6-10.

Quit-India movement was first heard on 8 August 1942, Midnapur was already a tinder-box, ready to be ignited.

Yet there were few outward symptoms of the gathering storm between 8 August and 28 September. This was because the Congress organisation was strong in the district and some time was spent in careful preparation and propaganda. The discipline and cohesion of the Congress organisation has been acknowledged in official sources:

Most of the Congress leaders belong to the Forward Bloc. A few owe allegiance to the orthodox Congress...The cultivators who form the backbone of the Congress movement mostly belong to one single community, namely, the Mahishya community. It is a well-knit community...Any order which goes out to the villages from the town leaders is obeyed without question. If, for example, the order be given that no food-stuff is to be exported from a village, everybody follows that rule, some through conviction and others through fear of social boycott.[38]

During August and the early part of September, training camps for volunteers were set up in remote villages. The Congress's influence over the union boards ensured that the district administration could collect little information and 'whenever any police party tried to approach these camps and centres, the volunteers were warned long before the party could reach [them]'.[39] In this initial phase, Congress picketers successfully prevented supplies from the village markets from reaching the towns. A major incident on 8 September gave an indication of the shape of things to come. A large crowd of villagers under Congress leadership converged on a rice mill at Danipur in Mahishadal thana of Tamluk subdivision and told the proprietor not to send a boat loaded with rice outside the district. The proprietor complied and was even willing to distribute a seer of rice to everyone present, but the police opened fire on the crowd killing at least four people. Attempts to arrest the leaders of the demonstration were frustrated by the proprietor of the rice mill who thought it more prudent to conciliate the Congress by paying Rs. 2000 to the bereaved families.[40] By the end of September, the Congress volunteer

38 *District Officers' Chronicles* (Secret, Home Dept), p. 16.
39 DM Midnapur to GB Addl Secy, 30 Sept. 1942, Conf. File 23, Collection No. IB 1942-3, Governor's Secretariat Bengal, R/3/2/36 (IOR).
40 *District Officers' Chronicles* (Secret Home Dept), p.18; Samanta *et al.*, *August Revolution*, pp. 10-12.

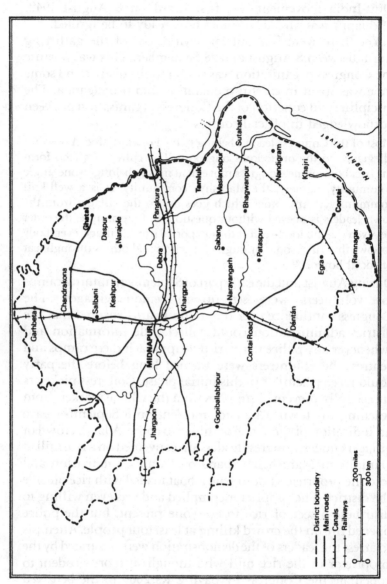

Map 8: District Midnapur: chief centres of 'Quit India' movement

District boundary
Main roads
Canals
Railways

200 miles
300 km

corps were ready for assaults on the major centres of government. Doctors and nurses had been mobilised to take care of the injured in case the police opened fire and an elaborate system of signals to coordinate the different groups had been worked out.[41]

On 29 September 1942, six police station headquarters in Contai and Tamluk were attacked simultaneously. The previous night, trees had been felled, culverts broken, telegraph wires cut and ferry boats sunk to prevent government forces from moving between thanas. Sutahata thana in Tamluk, and Potashpur and Khejuri in Contai 'fell' to the rebels, while the attacks on Tamluk and Mahishadal thanas in Tamluk and Bhagawanpur in Contai were repulsed with heavy casualties. On 30 September, Nandigram thana in Tamluk was attacked. The crowds also ransacked and destroyed several sub-registry offices, post offices, union board offices, as well as 13 kachharis of the Mahishadal Raj estate.[42] On 1 October, five companies of troops were pressed into operation in the district.[43] The arrival of the military prevented further attacks on police stations. But Congress volunteers retained the upper hand in the rural interior. They had 'a very well-organized system of spying' and were informed about the movement of troops well in advance.[44] The armed forces of the government were in most cases reduced to burning villages from which the chief rebels had already fled. On 13 October it was reported, 'The morale of the agitators and rebels still remains unbroken. The combined civil and military operation have been effective only in a partial manner.'[45]

41 Samanta *et al.*, *August Revolution*, pp. 16-20.
42 DM Midnapur to GB Addl Secy, 30 Sept. 1942; Addl DM to DM Midnapur, 20 Oct. 1942, Conf. File 23, Collection No. IB 1942-3, Governor's Secretariat Bengal, R/3/2/36 (IOR). *Biplabi*, No. 5, 6 Oct. 1942. I am indebted to Paul Greenough for letting me use his files of this fascinating underground newsletter.
43 The troops' deployment on 2 October 1942 was as follows: 1 platoon Lincolns at Mahishadal, 1 platoon Lincolns at Geonkhali, 1 platoon Lincolns at Basudebpur in Sutahata, 1 platoon Lincolns at Baleri in Sutahata, 1 company Lincolns at Hooghly Point on reserve, 1 company 6/2 Punjabis in the Tamluk-Narghat-Mahishadal area, 2 platoons 6/2 Punjabis at Tamluk, 2 platoons 18 Garhwalis in Contai, 1 company Eastern Frontier Rifles in Contai and 1 troop Hyderabad Lancers in Contai. Chief Secy to Governor's Secy, 2 Oct 1942, Conf. File 23, Collection No. IB, 1942-3, Governor's Secretariat Bengal, R/3/2/36 (IOR).
44 DM's Daily Report, 11 Oct. 1942 in *ibid.*
45 DM's Daily Report, 13 Oct. 1942 in *ibid.*

On 16 October 1942, a massive cyclone and tidal wave swept over Midnapur. An estimated 10 000 people died. Colossal damage was done to crops and homesteads. The district magistrate recommended that relief should be withheld from the disaffected villages until the stolen guns had been returned, the leaders handed over and undertakings given that they would take no further part in the political movement. The deputy inspector general of police in charge of military operations reckoned, however, that 'any delay in giving relief would encourage the people to seek help from Congress and give the latter grounds for the specious argument that they are more powerful than Government'. He wrote on 27 October:

Every attempt will be made to exploit the 'wrath of God' theory and to impress upon the villagers that it is only Government that can help them and nobody else... If we are to make any capital out of the cyclone, arrangements should, if possible, be made for the resources of all private associations to be put up at the disposal of Government so that distribution can be made under the guidance of local officers... It is significant that very few persons have come forward as yet to ask for help, though there must be thousands who are homeless and without food or good water.[46]

Consequently, relief by day and raid by night became the government policy in Midnapur. The Congress set up its own parallel government, matching in every detail the structure of the official district administration. An official report acknowledged, 'Government forces were located in selected spots but the rest of the countryside remained right up to the end of October under the domination of the rebels.'[47]

In order to sustain morale, it was of considerable importance for the Congress to show itself to be more resourceful and more powerful than the government. Although 'national governments' at the subdivisional level were not formally proclaimed until 14 December 1942, swaraj panchayats were effectively administering village affairs during October and November. The main propaganda plank of the Congress was that the British were losing the war against the Japanese. The Japanese bombings in Calcutta,

46　DIG Police Burdwan Range to IG Police, 27 Oct. 1942, in *ibid.*
47　*District Officers' Chronicles* (Secret, Home Dept), p. 20; Samanta *et at., August Revolution*, pp. 33-40.

late in December, were a great morale-booster for the rebels. They announced to the villagers that the British government would soon be overthrown and a new regime with Subhas Chandra Bose as the 'Raja' of Free India would be installed in its place.[48] Leaflets in Hindustani and Gurmukhi were left near the military camps, urging the Indian troops to join the nationalist movement as they had done in 1857.[49] The 'national governments' under subdivisional Congress 'dictators' set up their own police, their own courts of justice and their own prisons.[50]

The parallel government's attempt at economic administration was even more interesting. Early in November, the Congress workers told the villagers not to allow any export of paddy and warned them not to accept currency notes and to check the circulation of coins. Later in the month, influential landholders of Contai subdivision were served with manuscript notices bearing seals of different Congress offices demanding fixed amounts of paddy for relief work and for running Congress camps.[51] In December, cyclostyled Bengali handbills from the Nandigram centre of the 'national government' directed merchants not to export paddy and rice from their respective centres of trade, or to sell any at local hats and bazaars. In Khejuri thana in Contai, local Congress workers forced stockists to sell paddy to distressed people at cheap rates fixed by the Congress usually on credit without interest.[52] After the harvest in January 1943, the Paddy Control Subcommittee of the Contai Subdivisional Committee directed landowners in a leaflet entitled *Bhag Dhan Sammandhe Congresser Nirdesh* (Congress's Directive in Respect of Share Paddy) to take half the product and remit all arrears due from the bhagchashis. Tenants refused to hand over paddy to the employees of landlords unless they could produce the

48 DM's Daily Report, 25 Dec. 1942; Addl SP's Daily Reports, 30 Dec. 1942, 5 Jan. 1943, Conf. File 23, Collection No. IB 1942-3, Governor's Secretariat Bengal, R/3/2/36 (IOR); Conf. Report on the Political Situation in Bengal for the first half of Jan. 1943, GB Poll Conf. File W-102/42 (WBSA).
49 Addl SP's Daily Reports, especially of 7 Jan. 1943, Conf. File 23, Collection No. IB 1942-3, Governor's Secretariat Bengal, R/3/2/36 (IOR).
50 DM's Daily Reports in *ibid.*; Samanta *et al.*, *August Revolution*, pp. 33-40.
51 Addl SP's Daily Report, 2 Nov. 1942; DM's Daily Report, 30 Nov. 1942, Conf. File 23, Collection No. IB 1942-43, Governor's Secretariat Bengal, R/3/2/36 (IOR).
52 DMs Daily Reports, 11 Dec. 1942, in *ibid.*

Congress permission ticket. Ferry boatmen were under Congress orders not to carry anyone with more than 10 seers of paddy. In some cases, the Congress actively encouraged paddy looting in which 'poor and middle-class people with their females and children of all ages took part'.[53]

The unrelenting harassment of the military, however, gradually took its toll in the different parts of district. Faced with all manner of persecution,[54] people became less willing to risk sheltering Congress volunteers. By the end of January 1943, in Contai subdivision, the government felt confident enough to withdraw the bulk of the military forces.[55] From Tamluk, however, 'the first real capture' was not reported until early in March.[56] The government obtained some help from the communists in the krishak samiti in Lakhya union of Mahishadal thana in combing out the Congress rebels.[57] It was the onset of the devastating famine in mid-1943 which finally broke the back of the resistance movement. But some of the principal leaders were not apprehended until their surrender in August 1944.[58]

The agrarian scene in west Bengal on the eve of Independence

A fairly long period of relative quiescence in the west Bengal countryside followed the suppression of the 1942 movement. The tebhaga movement of the sharecroppers in the winter of 1946–7 was limited in Midnapur to only six unions in the Nandigram and Panskura thanas of Tamluk.[59] The movement was soon 'losing strength everywhere in west Bengal, especially in the Tamluk subdivision in Midnapur which was its stronghold'.[60] The backlash against the

53 Addl SP's Daily Reports, 2 Jan. 1943, 5 Jan. 1943, 21 Jan. 1943, 22 Jan. 1943, in *ibid.*
54 The most distressing was rape. The women did try to organise armed resistance groups. See Paul R. Greenough, 'Political Mobilization and the Underground Literature of the Quit India Movement, 1942-4', *MAS*, 17, 3 (1982), pp. 353-6.
55 DM's Daily Report, 31 Jan. 1943, in Conf. File 23, Collection No. IB 1942-3, Governor's Secretariat Bengal, R/3/2/36 (IOR).
56 DM's Daily Report, 7 Mar. 1943, in *ibid.*
57 Addl SP's Daily Report, 4 Feb. 1943, in *ibid.*.
58 Samanta *et al.*, *August Revolution*, p. 36.
59 SDO Tamluk Midnapur to Addl Secy Bd of Rev., 6 Mar. 1947, Rev. Dept LR Br., Progs. B., Dec. 1948, Nos. 15-107, File 6M-38/47 (WBSA).
60 Secret Report on the Political Situation in Bengal for the first half of Feb. 1947, L/P & J/5/154 (IOR).

bargadars of west Bengal in the wake of the powerful adhiar agitation in north Bengal and the publication of the Bargadars Bill[61] is testimony to the continued strength of the ties of dependence in the demesne-labour–peasant-small-holding complex in this region. There was no bargadar agitation, but 'a movement amongst the landlords, jotdars and big cultivators against the proposed Tebhaga Bill'. The bargadars were prepared to continue the existing custom of sharing the produce equally with their landlords. As a report from Burdwan pointed out:

The proposed Legislation of so-called Tebhaga Act has made the landholders panicky and they are taking various steps to ensure that the Legislation even if enacted would not affect their share of the produce. As for example in some cases they have given notice to the bhagdars that they would not allow them to cultivate their lands in the coming year and would cultivate themselves by means of hired labour. In some cases the bargadars have been induced to give written statements to the landlords that their plough and cattle belong to the landlord. Then again the landlords have threatened the bhagdars that they would not come to their rescue by advancing paddy at the time of their need if the bhagdars try to enforce their rights when the proposed Act comes into force. And for six months at least of the year the bargadar is practically dependent upon the landlord for their [sic] living.[62]

Independence and the abolition of zamindari in west Bengal initiated the era of the big raiyat. But this was not a straightforward victory of the rich peasant over the landlord. The big raiyat was often the zamindar and the patnidar of old who had held on to his substantial khas khamar. It was not until the communist-led land-grab movements of the late 1960s that an effective challenge to their dominance was mounted. Today, the smallholding peasants and share-croppers are asserting themselves, but the cause of the mahindar and the munish still goes unrepresented.

61 On the agitation in north Bengal and the background to the Bargadars' Bill, see chapter 8 below.
62 SDO Sadar Burdwan to Addl Secy Bd of Rev., 7 Mar. 1947, Rev. Dept LR Br., Progs., B., Dec. 1948, Nos. 15-107, File 6M-38/47 (WBSA).

8

Sharecroppers' agitations in the frontier regions

The crisis in agrarian relations in the rich-farmer–sharecropper system of north Bengal unfolded on a slower moving time-scale than in east Bengal. The climactic date here is 1939 rather than 1930. 'There are no signs of discontent, and one hears of no revolts of adhiars, or adhiar class consciousness,' says the Dinajpur Settlement Report. But it had to be added in a footnote, 'In the last two months (January and February 1940) this statement has been falsified, for there has been trouble between adhiars and jotedars in Atwari and Thakurgaon, as well as in the adjacent parts of Jalpaiguri.'[1]

The force of the world depression did not immediately rupture jotedar–adhiar relations as it did the ties between peasant-debtors and the various moneylending groups in the highly monetised small peasant economy of east Bengal. Nor did it result in a clear strengthening of ties of dependence as in west Bengal where moneylending landlords maintained their position in the khamar sector and made important gains at the expense of a more widespread, but weakening, peasant smallholding sector. Substantial landholders of north Bengal, who cultivated large blocks of jotes through tied adhiars, continued grain loans in return for labour services. In instances of more decentralised sharecropping, jotedars became wary of making grain advances and preferred to sell grain in the lean months on a definite understanding of deferred payment in cash.

By maintaining pre-capitalist forms of appropriation and acting as a buffer between the actual tillers and the market economy, the grain-dealing jotedars had successfully monopolised profits from agriculture in the early decades of the twentieth century. When the depression struck, they had to

1 *Dinajpur SR*, p. 22.

252

take the brunt of the collapse in the product market. There was little opportunity during the slump to recoup their losses within the rural sector. Small jotedars' holdings in north Bengal were generally too small and too scattered for a foray into the smallholding sector to be an attractive proposition. It was only in the abadi areas of the south that the substantial lotdars launched an offensive to convert cash-paying small tenancies into new settlements on much higher share rents. In north Bengal, ties with dependent adhiars paying a virtual labour rent were continued, but the strengthening of these ties of dependency was hardly the jotedars' primary concern. At a time when agriculture was unprofitable and the urban sector held alluring prospects, the big jotedars found much of their capital locked up in vast tracts of sharecropped land. The stickiness of the land market during the slump precluded the possibility of a complete disengagement from the rural sector until a revival took place from 1938 onwards. By the time this upturn in trade and prices occurred, the jotedars had at least put some of their eggs in the urban basket. Their stranglehold on the agrarian economy had loosened.

The first class-based challenge to the jotedars' power in north Bengal in 1939–40 was consequently led by the small jotedars-cum-adhiars and adhiars who sharecropped fairly large operational holdings in the grain-exporting districts of Dinajpur and Jalpaiguri. They aimed principally at gaining a more direct access to and better terms in the rising product market. The main centres of disturbances were the hats, and tolls collected by the ijaradars at these hats, the main issue. The inclusion of demands for the lowering of interest rates and the abolition of exactions above the customary half of the product, which promised a larger share of the harvest grain heap to adhiars in general, served to draw some of the poorer adhiars into the agitation. In the second round of the conflict in 1946–7, the demands of the adhiars were stepped up and two-thirds rather than the customary half was claimed as their rightful share. The tebhaga movement was sought to be orchestrated all over Bengal by the Krishak Sabha, the Communist Party's peasant front organisation. The share-cropping arrangement was to be found in all parts of Bengal to a greater or lesser degree, but in a variety of structural contexts. The tebhaga movement of the sharecroppers remained virtually confined to those districts in north Bengal (and the Sunderban lots in the south) which displayed a fairly clear, longstanding class dichotomy between jotedars and adhiars. Using evidence mainly from three contiguous north Bengal districts of Dinajpur, Rangpur and Jalpaiguri, this chapter will examine the articulation of the conflict between sharecroppers and rich farmers in the frontier regions of Bengal from 1939 to 1947. It will also contrast the very different implications of the tebhaga demand for share-croppers in the peasant smallholding system in east Bengal and the demesne labour–peasant smallholding complex in west Bengal.

The customary sharecropping relation in north Bengal

The identical crop-sharing terms with their jotedars lent a large measure of unity to a broad spectrum of adhiars in north Bengal. Generally, the adhiars paid half of the produce as rent. The jotedar made subsistence loans to the adhiars according to their needs which were recovered with derhi (50%) interest. The threshing floor was usually provided by the jotedar at a place convenient to the adhiar.[2] The degree of dependence of the adhiars for subsistence loans, implements of cultivation and decision-making varied according to their particular circumstance. A report from Jalpaiguri at the time of the tebhaga movement pointed out, 'As there are Jotedars of various types there are also adhiars of various kinds.' Some were in the wretched position of bonded serfs who lived on jotedars' lands and were left little of their half share after paying interest on advances and sundry charges. But there were some adhiars who 'do not much depend on their

2 A Revenue Department Enquiry in 1940 elicited detailed reports on the customary relations between bargadars and their landlords from each district. The following are summaries of information obtained from Dinajpur, Rangpur and Jalpaiguri.
  Dinajpur: 'Generally ½ of produce is paid by bargadars. Landlord does not supply seeds etc. Very often seeds are advanced by landlords and recovered with 50% interest from bargadar's share of produce. Threshing ground is supplied by landlord at a place convenient to bargadar. Commonly landlord advances grains to bargadars for maintenance and recovers with 50% interest.'
  Rangpur: 'Bargadars pay ½ share of produce. The seeds are provided by landlords. In cases, special advances of paddy are made by the landlord (known

Jotedars'. They had their own plough and cattle, perhaps also a bit of land in jote right, and 'their own land being not sufficient for their ploughs they take a few bighas of land from some other neighbouring jotedars'.[3] In the late 1930s, the Dinajpur settlement officer also found some men who 'have a few acres' and 'add to their produce by working as an adhiar'.[4]

The jotedars, apart from being substantial landholders from the thirty-acres to the several thousand-acres category, had been the chief creditors and grain-dealers of the region. During the slump, the credit relationship between the jotedars and the relatively less dependent of the adhiars weakened. From 1938 onwards, the jotedars' role as grain-dealer also began to come under attack from adhiars who had a surplus to sell and wanted to make the most of the high level of agricultural prices. Some of the adhiars of Dinajpur and Rangpur, although they might be described as 'poor peasants' in a Leninist categorisation of rich, middle and poor peasantry, were placed in a better land–man situation and tended to be better-off in terms of economic well-being than most peasant smallholders (middle peasants) of east Bengal. Rangpur, especially Nilphamari subdivision, whose ecology closely resembled that of the east Bengal districts, had a much heavier density of population,[5] and here jute was often grown on adhi lands. After the Jute Regulation Act of 1940 reduced the jute acreage by nearly two-thirds, the conflict of interests between the adhiars and jotedars came to centre on the grain

as 'lagni') and realised with 50% interest. In Kurigram advances are repaid in coins without any interest or in kind at the market rate of the produce prevailing.'

Jalpaiguri: 'Half of the produce is paid by bargadars. Landlord supplies seeds and equal quantity recovered after threshing. Implements are supplied by landlord either free or on payment in cash or kind. If bargadars supply manure they are allowed straw free. If it is supplied by the landlord, he charges ½ of cost in cash or kind, and sometimes nothing. Threshing ground is supplied by landlords. Paddy advance is made by landlords for bargadar's consumption and recovered with 50%–75% interest. In Alipur Duars, no interest is charged. Landlord supplies one bullock free for cultivation. If two bullocks are supplied, he receives 1½ mds of paddy per annum.'

Dt Officer Dinajpur to Secy Rev. Dept, 19 May 1940; Collr Rangpur to Secy Rev. Dept. 23 May 1940; Dy Cmsner Jalpaiguri to Secy Rev. Dept, 18 May 1940; GB Rev. Dept, B. Progs. 109, Nov. 1940 (BSRR).

3 Dy Cmsner Jalpaiguri to Secy Bd of Rev., 11 Mar. 1947, GB Rev. Dept LR Br., B. Progs. 15-107, Dec. 1948, File 6M-38/47 (WBSA).

4 *Dinajpur SR*, p.17.

5 See chapter 2 above, pp.38-9.

market. If economic conditions opened the possibility of an adhiar challenge to jotedar dominance after 1938, the release of the detenus that year and the need of the Congress, especially its left wing, to muster mass support in its opposition to Huq's League-dominated ministry provided the political catalyst. The detenus returned from their long spells in prison imbued with communist and socialist doctrines. It was in the jotedar–adhiar system of north Bengal (and not the other regions where sharecropping as an adjunct to other dominant forms had registered some recent increase through processes of demographic and market differentiation) that their demands closely fitted the social reality.

Adhiars versus jotedars: The first round 1939–40

The sharecroppers' movement originated in the Boda, Debiganj and Pachagarh thanas of Jalpaiguri and the Thakurgaon subdivision of Dinajpur in July 1939. In the autumn of 1939, adhiar volunteers organised by urban middle-class leaders of the krishak samitis picketed the hats and melas; they demanded a reduction in the exorbitant tolls collected from peasants who disposed of small quantities of agricultural produce. Lathis in hands, wearing Gandhi caps and waving flags bearing the insignia of hammer and sickle, they paraded the markets – both the small hats in the rural interior as well as the bigger fairs like the Aloakhoar Mela and Kalir Mela in the Thakurgaon subdivison of Dinajpur. In most cases, the jotedar-proprietors of the hats and melas conceded large reductions in the tolls. The initial success of the hat-toll agitation encouraged the adhiars to attempt to secure a larger portion of the grain heap in the winter harvest season of 1939–40.[6]

Over and above the half share of the product that was the customary rent, the jotedars commonly recovered grain loans with 50% interest and seed loans with 100% interest at the time of harvest. In addition, they arbitrarily levied a wide variety of

---

6 FRs from Cmsner Rajshahi Dn for the first and second half of Dec. 1939, GB Poll Conf. File 19/39 (WB Home Dept); Sunil Sen, *Agrarian Struggle in Bengal*, pp. 23-4; M. Abdullah Rasul, *Krishaksabhar Itihas* (History of the Krishak Sabha; Calcutta, 1969), pp. 85-7.

imposts.[7] In 1939, the adhiars demanded interest-free seed loans, a ceiling of 25% on grain loans and the abolition of all extras.[8] In many cases, the adhiars refused to thresh the paddy in the jotedars' kholians or yards, and demanded that the crop should be divided at a neutral venue. Some were bolder and carried away the entire harvest to their own houses.[9] The sheer strength of the agitation in Thakurgaon forced the subdivisional officer to hold a mass gathering of jotedars and adhiars in January 1940 and arbitrate an 11-point compromise.[10] This was simply grist to the adhiars' mill. Many of them now set about to recover what they regarded as their legitimate share from paddy stacked in the jotedars' kholians. The jotedars retaliated by lodging complaints of theft and dacoity with the police. The agitation took a violent turn in Jalpaiguri where patrols of armed police were sent into Boda, Debiganj and Pachagarh thanas to restore order. After 182 of the main propagandists were arrested, the agitation in those parts appeared to fizzle out.[11] In Dinajpur, it continued even after the harvest season in the form of refusal

7 Dy Cmsner Jalpaiguri to Secy Rev. Dept, 18 May 1940, GB Rev. Dept, B. Progs. 109, Nov. 1940 (BSRR).
8 M. Abdullah Rasul, *Krishaksabhar Itihas*, p. 88.
9 FR from Cmsner Rajshahi Dn for the second half of Dec. 1939, GB Poll Conf. File 19/39 (WB Home Dept); Sunil Sen, *Agrarian Struggle in Bengal*, pp. 24-5.
10 The 11 points were: '(1) Threshing floor will be fixed by the adhiars and jotedars jointly; (2) Paddy will not be taken to the jotedar's house if the adhiar objects; (3) No abwab like preparing threshing floor or the like shall be realised; (4) No interest for seed advance. Seed will be supplied 50:50 by each party and, if need be, jotedar will be prepared to advance the whole amount of seed to be recovered from the paddy produced; (5) Jotedar will get interest on paddy loan at 3 kathas for every 20 kathas; (6) For outstanding paddy loans jotedars will not take more than 1/3rd of the share of adhiars' paddy without adhiars' consent and will fully repay future loans every year. Outstanding loan will be paid in the way stated above (by taking 1/3rd of the adhiars' share at the maximum) until fully repaid; (7)' Of this year's paddy taken to adhiars' house, half will be given to jotedar after taking them to an agreed place in the hamlet of the adhiar, and jotedar will give half share to adhiar of the paddy taken to his house; (8) Jotedar shall grant receipt for adhi paddy and adhiars' unregistered kabuliyats for adhi settlement; (9) There will be no victimization by any jotedar on any adhiar for joining this movement; (10) When jotedars and adhiars have acted upon the terms, the cases bought by both sides shall be withdrawn; (11) There will be established a board with three representatives of either side and the SDO to carry out the terms and settle any disputes between jotedars and adhiars as such.' FR from Cmsner Rajshahi Dn for the first half of Jan. 1940, GB Poll Conf. File 30/40 (WB Home Dept).
11 'Appreciation of Jotedar–Adhiar situation in Jalpaiguri District', by Dy Cmsner Jalpaiguri, 7 June 1940, GB Rev. Dept, B. Progs. 109, Nov. 1940 (BSRR).

to pay hat-tolls and union-board rates, and fishing in large groups in jotedars' private tanks. Police action curbed some of the more overt illegal acts by April 1940, but jotedar–adhiar tension continued to simmer throughout that year.[12]

The winter of 1939–40 in north Bengal provides a remarkable instance of a sharecroppers' agitation in a dichotomous rich farmer–sharecropper class situation based on fairly clear-cut economistic demands. No doubt in Jalpaiguri 'Congress and Krishak Samitis fanned the discontent';[13] in Dinajpur, the outside leaders described in the official sources as 'communist workers of the ex-detenu stamp' operated through 'local sub-leaders of the Dewaniya class'.[14] Yet the adhiars required only the slightest provocation to stake their claim for a higher proportion of the grain harvest. The better-off among them were eager to play the market; the less fortunate were ready to agitate for their own subsistence concerns.[15] Allegiances of caste and community were of little relevance. The Rajbansi Kshatriya caste movement of yesteryear proved of no avail in preventing a conflict between Rajbansi adhiars and Rajbansi jotedars. At least one Muslim League MLA from the region sought to taint the agrarian agitation by imputing motives of communal vendetta against Muslim jotedars. This line of propaganda was insidious in view of the increasing crystallisation of communal categories in politics at the provincial and national levels. It was, however, effectively countered by the principal leader of the agitation in Thakurgaon, Haji Mohammad Danesh, who was a lawyer at Thakurgaon town and held the post of secretary of the subdivisional Congress

12 DM Dinajpur to Cmsner Rajshahi Dn, 5 June 1940, in *ibid.*
13 'Appreciation of Jotedar-Adhiar situation in Jalpaiguri District' by Dy Cmsner Jalpaiguri, 7 June 1940 in *ibid.*
14 DM Dinajpur to Cmsner Rajshahi Dn, 6 June 1940, in *ibid.* The Dinajpur settlement officer wrote of the dewaniya: 'There is no special qualification for a dewania, except brains and personality above the average. The "dewania" or tout, as he is sometimes dubbed is the adviser on all legal matters. He is a sort of "poor man's lawyer", and fills a place in rural society. If he becomes the agent of some unscrupulous town pleader, he can lead families into ruin, but left to himself is a means of lightening the darkness of rural life.' *Dinajpur SR*, p. 16.
15 Sunil Sen in his account of the agitation in Dinajpur says 'middle peasants' and even 'rich peasants' took the initial lead. He uses these terms not in a Leninist structural sense but in reference to different grades of adhiars according to levels of economic well-being. See Sunil Sen, *Agrarian Struggle in Bengal*, pp. 23-4.

committee. The district magistrate of Dinajpur, who was instrumental in putting down the agitation acknowledged:

There is no communal question involved in the movement. Although most of the Krishak volunteers are Kshatriyas still there are some Muslims who have also joined the movement. One Hazi Muhammad Danesh Mian, a pleader of Thakurgaon is one of the principal ring leaders of the communist group. This fellow has been prosecuted under rule 56 and restrained under rule 26 of the Defence of India Rules. It is only because most of the volunteers are Kshatriyas and most of the Jotedars are Muslims that any act of aggression or retaliation committed or threatened by the volunteers is liable to be interpreted as having been planned with a communal motive for harassing the Muslims although evidently *the clash is really between the Adhiars and Jotedars.*[16]

The adhiar agitation of 1939–40 had a great impact on official re-thinking about the whole barga question. Indeed, the impact was greater than its leaders recognised at the time or has been generally known so far. In May 1940 the government seriously considered passing a law on the share of the produce payable by sharecroppers. 'The object underlying the proposed legislation', the Revenue Department told all district officers, 'is to fix the maximum limit of the landlord's claim in regard to the share of produce of barga lands as also to the advances made by them for cultivation of those lands, so that there may be no ground for discontent among the bargadars owing to exorbitant demands of their landlords.'[17] Specific proposals were formulated for legislation which included limiting interest on subsistence loans to bargadars to 10% and treating arbitrary exactions above the half share as abwabs punishable under the Bengal Tenancy Act.[18] In Jalpaiguri, where the writ of the Permanent Settlement did not run, the Deputy Commissioner sought special powers

16 DM Dinajpur to Cmsner Rajshahi Dn, 5 June 1940, GB Rev. Dept, B. Progs. 109, Nov. 1940 (BSRR).
17 Secy Rev. Dept to All Dt Offrs, 12 May 1940 in *ibid.*
18 The proposals of the Revenue Department for legislation with regard to bargadars were as follows:
'(a) (i) A landlord is not to get more than ½ of the produce (including bye-products) of barga lands and is not to charge bargadars with more than ½ the cost of manure and/or seeds if advanced by him.
        (ii) If a bargadar is refused advanced of seed or manure by the landlord, the former is to be entitled to a minimum share of 55% of the produce.

through an ordinance to protect adhiars from eviction and illegal levies.[19] But as the adhiar agitation gradually died away after the harvest season, none of these proposals was actually implemented. The Krishak Sabha showed no disposition to bid up adhiar demands. Bhowani Sen, the chief communist theoretician of the adhiar agitation, has himself acknowledged the very limited goals of the movement:

In this movement the jotedar's share of fifty–fifty was not challenged. Only illegal exactions were challenged; and by their successful struggle they put an end to them. A big victory. That happened in 1939, against the background of the War and a spontaneous rumour that the Government was going to collapse, which gave confidence to the peasants. Prices had also begun to rise. The movement was very big but did not develop further; it subsided after winning some concessions. Things were then quiet until 1943.[20]

1941–5

The adhiar agitation was not entirely quiescent in the early 1940s. It was just that the provincial Krishak Sabha and the national Kisan Sabha were not interested in it. In mid-1940, a powerful no-toll agitation developed in the markets in Rangpur which forced the ijaradars of hats to reduce their levies. In August 1940 the district magistrate of Dinajpur estimated that 17 000 volunteers had been mobilised for a new

     (iii) Apportionment of produce is to be made by actual measurement of produce after harvest.
     (b) Bargadars must move the crop at their own expense from the place on which it has been grown to the recognised threshing floor and if he moves it therefrom to any other place before apportionment he should be made punishable with a fine to be inflicted under the procedure indicated in Section 58 of the B.T. Act.
     (c) If a landlord grants special advances in cash or in kind (not being advances of seed and/or manure) for the maintenance of the bargadars, he must not recover the same with interest exceeding 10%.
     (d) Recovery of any amount or part of the produce such as *sali, kharmar, khararu,* etc, from the bargadar other than the special advances mentioned above will be treated as abwabs and landlords making such recovery will be liable to penalty u.s. 58 of the B.T. Act.' Memorandum by the Revenue Department in *ibid.*
19 Dy Cmsner Jalpaiguri to Cmsner Rajshahi Dn, 17 June 1940, in *ibid.*
20 Bhowani Sen, 'The Tebhaga Movement in Bengal', *Communist,* Sept. 1947, cited by Hamza Alavi, 'Peasants and Revolution' in Kathleen Gough and Hari P. Sharma (eds.), *Imperialism and Revolution in South Asia* (New York, 1973), p. 321.

adhiar agitation during the coming harvest season.[21] In the winter of 1940–1, the cultivators of Dinajpur put forward four main demands: (1) the adhiars be allowed to take the produce to their own houses instead of the jotedars' houses; (2) the price of jute to be raised to Rs. 10; (3) no interest on paddy loans; and (4) government intervention to remit rents and stay decrees.[22]

The implementation of the Jute Regulation Act of 1940 in the early months of 1941 led to trouble in the heavily populated jute-growing district of Rangpur. Subsistence via the market had been the strategy of numerous poor peasants who grew jute on small plots of adhi lands. Jute restriction in February 1941 resulted in 'adhiars being allotted no jute lands'. Two-thirds of the area formerly under jute was to be sown with aus. But there was a shortage of seed, the price of which had soared above Rs. 5 per maund. After adhiars in the Nilphamari subdivision became violent, jotedars were advised by local officers to give some jute lands to them.[23] The hopes that jotedars and adhiars alike pinned on jute proved, however, to be totally misplaced. From 1941 onwards, the price of jute and tobacco, the other cash crop of Rangpur, remained weak in relation to the steep rise in grain prices. In the autumn of 1941, densely inhabited, food-deficit Rangpur turned into a major exporter of rice. Representations were received to stop this export, but the collector opposed a ban on the grounds that the 'sale price of rice and paddy will fall and although the middle-class will benefit, the large majority of cultivators would be adversely affected'.[24] This was palpably false since the large mass of small adhiars had no part of the rising profits in grain, which almost exclusively were seized by the bigger jotedars. The winter of 1941 was an unheeded portent of the devastation that was to strike Rangpur adhiars in the great famine of 1943. There was unrest, too, in Jalpaiguri and Dinajpur. Adhiars and landless labourers raided and looted paddy from jotedars' houses in Jalpaiguri in

21 FR from Cmsner Rajshahi Dn for the first half of Aug. 1940, GB Poll Conf. File 30/40 (WB Home Dept).
22 FR from Cmsner Rajshahi Dn for the first half of Jan. 1940, GB Poll Conf. File 13/41 (WB Home Dept).
23 FRs from Cmsner Rajshahi Dn for the first half and second half of Feb. 1941, GB Poll Conf. File 13/41 (WB Home Dept).
24 FR from Cmsner Rajshahi Dn for the second half of Aug. 1941, GB Poll Conf. File 13/41 (WB Home Dept).

October 1941. The reasons for the unrest were 'inability to get credit and dissatisfaction over profiteering',[25] During the same month, large numbers of adhiars demanded paddy from the jotedars in Dinajpur.[26]

In 1942, the leadership of the local krishak samitis in north Bengal was in a state of confusion following the decision of the Communist Party to collaborate with the British government during the war. As one participant-historian of the tebhaga movement has commented, 'The slogan of "resist Japan" hardly made any sense to the peasants.'[27] Consequently, adhiar economic grievances now found only sporadic expression in Congress-led mass actions in the course of the Quit-India movement. The most striking example comes from Balurghat in Dinajpur. On 14 September 1942, Saroj Ranjan Chatterji, a local Congress leader, led 8000 to 10 000 people armed with lathis and bows and arrows and attacked almost all the government buildings at the subdivisional headquarters. The crowd also looted paddy from hoards in the surrounding countryside.[28] In Jalpaiguri, a large crowd was poised to attack Kumargaon thana on 29 September 1942 but refrained from violence on being promised immediate redress of their grievances. As 'the chief grievance of the mob appeared to be scarcity of paddy in the locality', the khas mahal officer arranged for the immediate release of paddy in all khas mahal hats in the locality by requisitioning it from big jotedars and stockists.[29]

During the famine of 1943, the worst affected area in north Bengal was the Nilphamari subdivision of Rangpur which formerly bought rice in exchange for jute. In the early part of the year, the jotedars hoarded stocks and waited for prices to rise even further. Later, government decided on its policy to procure rice from north Bengal jotedars to feed Calcutta and the urban areas, paying little heed to the needs of the mass of hapless adhiars. In the immediate post-famine period, the Krishak Sabha instructed its cadres to concentrate on relief

25 FR from Cmsner Rajshahi Dn for the second half of Nov. 1941, GB Poll Conf. File 13/41 (WB Home Dept).
26 FR from Cmsner Rajshahi Dn for the first half of Nov. 1941, GB Poll Conf. File 13/41 (WB Home Dept).
27 Sunil Sen, *Agrarian Struggle in Bengal*, p. 30.
28 *District Officers' Chronicles* (Secret Home Dept). pp. 102-3.
29 *Ibid.*, pp. 104-5.

work allowing the class struggle to recede 'imperceptibly into the background'.[30] After the winter harvest of 1944-5, jotedars of Jalpaiguri again tried their hand at hoarding in the expectation that prices would rise and that government would not be procuring to feed Calcutta as in the previous year. Rangpur, of all districts, reported 'considerable export trade' towards Mymensingh, Dacca and Pabná. On this occasion, the government issued a notification prohibiting export and thana officers were ordered to see that it was enforced.[31] During 1945, several instances of jotedar-adhiar tension came to light.[32] But it was not until the autumn of 1946 that the battle over the sharing of the harvest once again began in earnest.

Adhiars versus jotedars: *Tebhaga Chai* 1946-7

Tebhaga propaganda was launched in the autumn of 1946 when the paddy fields of north Bengal promised a bumper crop. As in 1939, the initiative was taken by the bigger adhiars who were eager to benefit from the high postwar level of agricultural prices. Some of them who had more land in adhi than in jote right conceded tebhaga to their adhiars in respect of their jote lands. The two-thirds formula in dividing the crop instead of the customary half naturally proved attractive to adhiars in general, especially in such a good year as 1946. There had already been stirrings from below before the Bengal Provincial Krishak Sabha executive formally gave the call in September 1946 for a tebhaga agitation.[33] The origins of the movement were described in a report from Thakurgaon subdivision:

30 Sunil Sen, *Agrarian Struggle in Bengal*, p. 32.
31 FR from Cmsner Rajshahi Dn for the first half of Feb. 1945, GB Poll Conf. File 37/45 (WB Home Dept).
32 See, for instance, FR from Cmsner Rajshahi Dn for the second half of Mar. 1945, GB Poll Conf. File 37/45 (WB Home Dept).
33 The Land Revenue Commission had recommended two-thirds share of the crop for bargadars in 1940. The same year, the Krishak Sabha accepted 'tebhaga' as a matter of policy at its annual session at Panjia; but at subsequent sessions no further progress was made on the issue. No agitation on the basis of this demand was contemplated at the provincial conference at Moubhog in May 1946. The decision of the Communist Party to align itself with the tebhaga agitation stemmed from its national and international concerns wholly extraneous to agrarian questions in Bengal. It was an attempt by the party to rehabilitate itself having alienated Indian public opinion because of its wartime collaboration

Past history of landlords' behaviour towards Bargadars is not a happy one. It is full of illegal exactions, exorbitant rates of interest and deceptions by use of fraudulent weights and measures. [The] Field was ready and it was the communist agitators from outside who sowed the seed.[34]

During November, numerous baithaks (group discussions) and propaganda meetings were held in the rural interior. The chief slogans were *tebhaga chai* – a demand for two-thirds share – and *nij kholane dhan tolo* – urging the adhiars to take the paddy to their own houses instead of the jotedars' yards.[35] Removal of paddy from the fields by the adhiars and other communist volunteers began in the first week of December 1946. Their method was to arrive 200–300 strong at an adhiar's plot, reap the crop in 30–40 minutes, remove it to the adhiar's house and then repeat the process in other plots. The first incidents took place in the Atwari and Baliadangi thanas of Thakurgaon subdivision in Dinajpur and spread rapidly to the Ranisankail, Birganj, Thakurgaon, Bochaganj and Pirganj thanas.[36] The movement was particularly strong in 5 of the 12 thanas in the Dinajpur Sadar subdivision – Parbatipur, Chirirbandar, Kotwali, Kusumundi and Itahar, and Phulbari and Balurghat thanas in the Balurghat subdivision.[37] In Rangpur, the movement was powerful in Nilphamari subdivision and in Jalpaiguri it spread to seven thanas in the Sadar subdivision with Debiganj, Boda and Pachagarh leading the way.[38]

In some cases, the adhiars offered the jotedars a one-third share of the crop they had taken away on being granted tebhaga receipts; in others, no such offer was made. Some jotedars tried to retaliate, while others sought compromises on

with the British and having met with a recent rebuff from the CPSU. See Jnanabrata Bhattacharya, 'An Examination of Leadership Entry in Bengal Peasant Revolts, 1937-1947', in *Journal of Asian Studies*, 37, 4 (1978), pp. 617-19; M. Abdullah Rasul, *Krishaksabhar Itihas*, pp. 147-50.

34 SDO Thakurgaon Dinajpur to Addl Secy Bd of Rev., 10 Mar. 1947, GB Rev. Dept LR Br., B. Progs. 15-107, Dec. 1948, File 6M-38/47 (WBSA).

35 Sunil Sen, *Agrarian Struggle in Bengal*, pp. 36-7.

36 SDO Thakurgaon Dinajpur to Addl Secy Bd of Rev., 10 Mar. 1947, GB Rev. Dept LR Br., B. Progs. 15-107, Dec. 1948, File 6M-38/47 (WBSA).

37 SDO Sadar Dinajpur to Addl Secy Bd of Rev., 8 Mar. 1947; SDO Balurghat Dinajpur to Addl Secy Bd of Rev., 6 Mar. 1947, in *ibid*.

38 SDO Nilphamari Rangpur to Addl Secy Bd of Rev., 9 Mar. 1947; SDO Sadar Jalpaiguri to Addl Secy Bd of Rev., 11 Mar. 1947, in *ibid*.

the basis of a 9:7 share. At village Khagakharibari in Dimla thana in the Nilphamari subdivision, a number of jotedars raided the house of an adhiar to recover the crop, shot 1 man dead and injured 13 others.[39] As the jotedars happened to be Muslims, the communist leaders pursuaded the adhiars not to attack them. Instead, a large protest demonstration was held in Nilphamari town.[40] In the tense communal situation prevailing in Bengal in the aftermath of the Great Calcutta Killing and the Noakhali and Tippera riots, the peasant leaders were anxious to avoid doing anything which might spark off a communal riot. On the whole, in north Bengal, at least in the early phase of the movement, Rajbansi and Muslim adhiars fought against Rajbansi and Muslim jotedars. Some jotedars decided to call in the police to coerce the adhiars by lodging cases of 'paddy looting'. There was a clash at Talpukur village in Chirirbandar thana on 4 January 1947 when the police went to execute arrest warrants, and in the police shooting, two peasants, a Santal and a Muslim, were killed.[41] But most of the jotedars, although they 'viewed the movement with disfavour', 'felt the spirit of the times and were agreeable to meet the adhiar's demand half way'.[42] Local officers in Dinajpur made two attempts to mediate, first in the middle of December and again on 6 January; but these came to nothing as the spokesmen of the adhiars refused to negotiate.[43]

In Calcutta, a few members of the ruling Muslim League, including the Revenue Minister, had come round to the view that the tebhaga demand ought to be conceded. In the first week of January 1947, Fazlur Rahman, the revenue minister, confronted the governor with a draft ordinance proposing to reduce the share paid by the bargadar from half to one-third

39 SDO Nilphamari Rangpur to Addl Secy Bd of Rev., 9 Mar. 1947, in *ibid.*
40 Sunil Sen, *Agrarian Struggle in Bengal*, pp. 40-1. Badruddin Umar, *Chirosthayee Bandobaste Bangladesher Krishak*, pp. 109-10.
41 Sunil Sen, *Agrarian Struggle in Bengal*, pp. 44-5,
42 SDO Sadar Dinajpur to Addl Secy Bd of Rev., 8 Mar. 1947, GB Rev. Dept LR Br., B. Progs. 15-107, Dec. 1948, File 6M-38/47 (WBSA).
43 In the middle of December 1946 the district magistrate suggested the following terms for a compromise: paddy would be divided equally in the field, threshed there or near about and respective shares would be carried away by the two parties. This was turned down by the communist leaders. The second attempt was made in the first week of January. The terms suggested were: the entire harvest would be taken to the landlords' khamar and threshed there, and adhiars would receive half of the produce and 13 seers of paddy per bigha from the

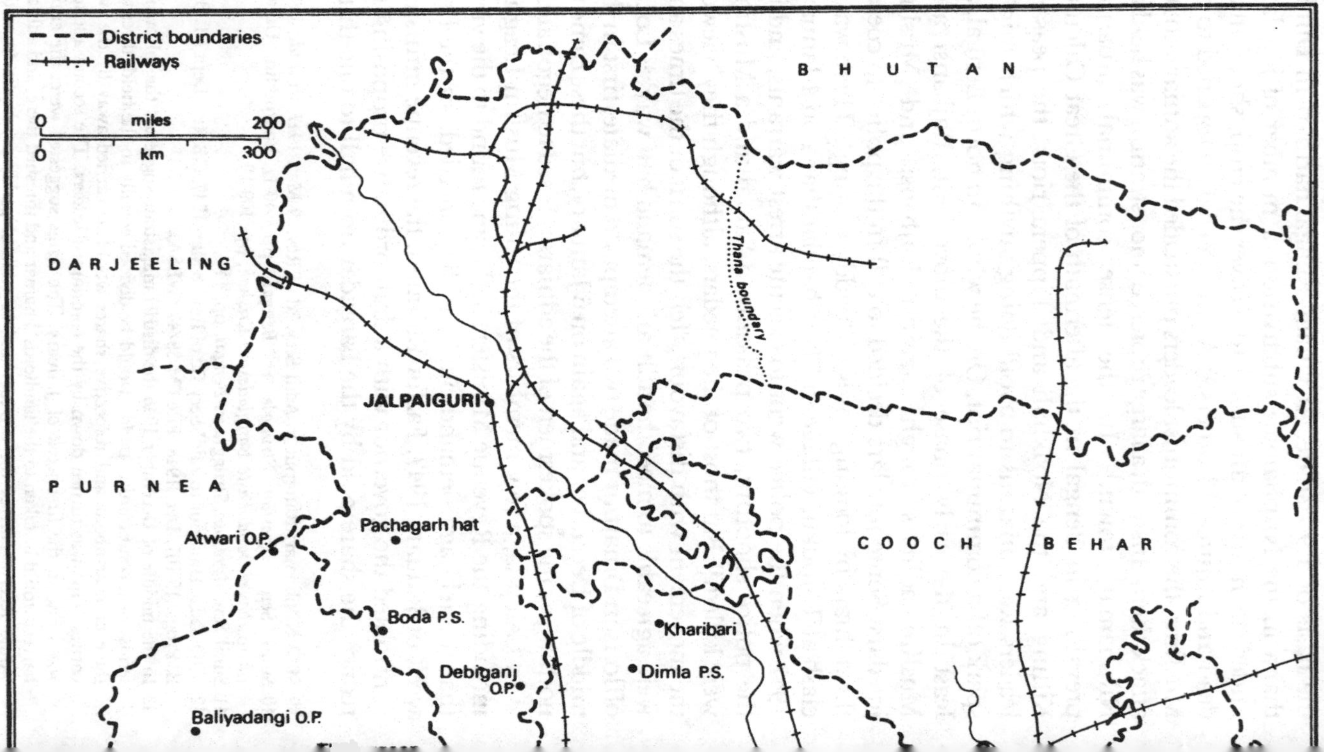

District boundaries
Railways
0 miles 200
0 km 300
B H U T A N
D A R J E E L I N G
Thana boundary
JALPAIGURI
P U R N E A
C O O C H B E H A R
Pachagarh hat
Atwari O.P.
Boda P.S.
Kharibari
Dimla P.S.
Debiganj O.P.
Baliyadangi O.P.

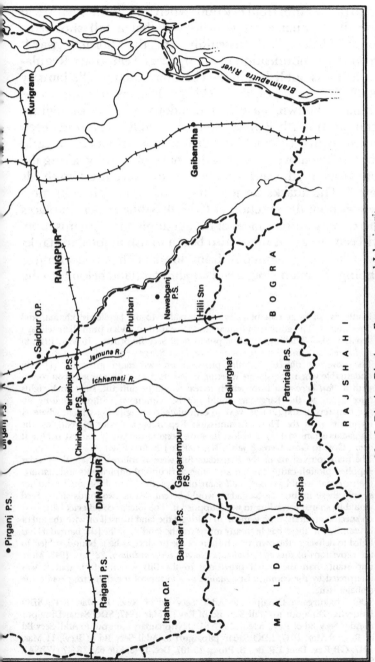

Map 9: Districts Dinajpur, Rangpur and Jalpaiguri: chief centres of sharecroppers' agitation, 1939-40, 1946-7

Labels on map:

Brahmaputra River

Kurigram

Gaibendha

RANGPUR

Saidpur O.P.

Phulbari

Nawabganj P.S.

Hilli Stn

BOGRA

Pirganj P.S.

Parbatipur P.S.

Jamuna R.

Ichhamati R.

Chiribandar P.S.

Balurghat

Patnitala P.S.

DINAJPUR

RAJSHAHI

Gangarampur P.S.

Banshari P.S.

Raiganj P.S.

Porsha

Itahar O.P.

MALDA

and to protect him from eviction. When the governor refused to issue the ordinance, it was decided that a bill should be brought before the assembly in the normal way.[44] Accordingly, notification of a Bargadars Temporary Regulation Bill was published in the Calcutta Gazette on 22 January 1947.[45] The news of the Tebhaga Bill, as it came to be popularly known, gave a tremendous fillip to the adhiar agitation in north Bengal. Since the paddy had already been stacked in the jotedars' kholians in some instances, in early February the movement took the shape of forcibly taking the crop away to the adhiars' houses to exact the two-thirds share.[46] The attacks on jotedars' houses took place in most cases without the sanction of Krishak Sabha leaders in places where, in the initial stages of the agitation, their organisation had been weak.[47] Adhiars also began to fish in jotedars' tanks and take away bamboos from jotedars' bamboo clumps. Echoing the main slogan *hal jar jami tar* (land belongs to the

landlords' share as cost of carrying the paddy to the landlords' khamar and threshing it. The adhiars and their leaders refused to budge from their tebhaga demand. SDO Thakurgaon Dinajpur to Addl Secy Bd of Rev., 10 Mar. 1947, in *ibid.;* see also Sunil Sen, *Agrarian Struggle in Bengal*, pp. 45-6.

44 The governor objected to the proposal on two main grounds: '(1) very undesirable when Legislature meeting in less than a month's time to confront it with a *fait accompli* from which retreat would be difficult, since such rights once given to the Bargadars could not be withdrawn without inviting an agrarian revolt; and (2) was weak to capitulate to an agitation which, whatever its merits (and the Floud Commission Report is in favour of reducing the Bargadars share to 1/3), had lost its sting because the paddy harvest is almost over'. Gov. to Gov. Gen., 8 Jan. 1947, L/P & J/5/154 (IOR).

45 The main provisions of the Bargadars Bill were as follows: where the jotedar supplied plough-cattle, plough and other agricultural implements and manure, the bargadar would get only half share of the produce; but if the jotedar did not supply these inputs, the bargadars would be entitled to two-thirds share. Seed would be shared according to who supplied it. The jotedar could evict bargadars on specific grounds: if he wanted 'to cultivate the land himself or with the aid of his family', if 'there has been any misuse of the land' or if 'he [the bargadar] has failed to deliver to the owner such share of the produce as he is bound, subject to the provisions of this Act'. *Calcutta Gazette Extraordinary*, 22 Jan. 1947. More important than the actual provisions in the Bill was the fact that it was interpreted by the communist agitators as a victory of the sharecroppers on the tebhaga issue.

46 SDO Thakurgaon Dinajpur to Addl. Secy Bd of Rev., 10 Mar. 1947; SDO Balurghat Dinajpur to Addl Secy Bd of Rev., 6 Mar. 1947; SDO Sadar Dinajpur to Addl Secy Bd of Rev., 8 Mar. 1947; SDO Nilphamari Rangpur to Addl Secy Bd of Rev., 9 Mar. 1947; SDO Sadar Jalpaiguri to Addl Secy Bd of Rev., 11 Mar. 1947. GB Rev. Dept LR Br., B. Progs. 15-107, Dec. 1948, File 6M-38/47 (WBSA).

47 Sunil Sen, *Agrarian Struggle in Bengal*, pp. 48-9.

man who drives the plough), the new slogans adopted were
beshal jar bansh tar, pal jar machh tar.[48]

The communist agitators from outside had at first tried to
channel the tebhaga agitation against only the bigger jotedars.
After the publication of the Bargadars Bill, the adhiars refused
to make any distinction between large and small landowners,
arguing that small jotedars should also concede tebhaga as it
had received legal sanction. Sunil Sen, a leading participant in
the Dinajpur agitation, has written: 'Inevitably new social
tension was created, and with it new complications. In the
earlier period, social tension was primarily confined to large
landowners and the bulk of poor peasants; now its area
extended to small landowners and rural middle class'.[49] The
tebhaga agitation with its limited regional and class base in the
north Bengal wilderness could hardly afford to widen its orbit
of opposition.

The implacable hostility of about 40 Muslim League
MLAs who were rich jotedars ensured that the government
was never able to introduce the Bargadars Bill in the
legislature.[50] The jotedars of north Bengal reacted to the
looting of paddy from their kholians by lodging charges of
'dacoity'. The police were sent into the villages to make arrests
in connection with these paddy-looting cases, and a number of
armed clashes between the police and the adhiars occurred.
On 20 February 1947, the villagers of Khanpur in Balurghat
thana fought the police with bows and arrows. The police
fired 121 rounds and killed 20 people. The following day there
was another clash at Thumnia in Baliadanga thana in which
four people were killed in the police shooting.[51] On 25
February 1947, the Krishak Sabha decided to organise a protest
demonstration against these firings in Thakurgaon town.
This demonstration was also fired upon, causing at least
another four deaths. The communist leaders now discovered
that they had not given serious thought to the 'forms of

48 'Bamboo belongs to the man who has the implements to cut it, fish belongs to
   him who has the fishing net.' SDO Thakurgaon Dinajpur to Addl Secy Bd of
   Rev., 10 Mar. 1947. GB Rev. Dept LR Br., B. Progs. 15-107, Dec. 1948, File 6M-
   38/47 (WBSA).
49 Sunil Sen, *Agrarian Struggle in Bengal*, pp. 49-50.
50 Gov. to Gov. Gen., 7 Mar. 1947, L/P & J/5/154 (IOR).
51 Secret Report on the Political Situation in Bengal for the second half of Feb.
   1947, L/P & J/5/154 (IOR).

struggle' that might be feasible in the face of police repression. The peasant cadres and volunteers were in total disarray. Sunil Sen has described their predicament:

How could they fight with lathis the police armed with guns. What should they do now? The leaders racked their brains but could not give any answer. There was no question of resisting police attacks with lathis. It was now clear that the police would shoot the peasants if there was any resistance. Retreat was the only course left. The morale of the peasants slumped, and the movement which reached new heights in Thakurgaon rapidly disintegrated.[52]

Tebhaga had taken the form of a fairly spontaneous and general movement in the winter of 1946-7 only in the north Bengal districts of Dinajpur, Rangpur and Jalpaiguri and the reclaimed areas of the 24-Parganas in the south. There was a contemporaneous but separate tribal rising of the Hajongs in the Garo foothills in the north-east of Mymensingh demanding commutation of tanka (the local fixed produce rent) to a low money rent. Wide regions of east Bengal and west and central Bengal remained virtually unaffected by any sort of bargadar disaffection. A combination of structural constraints and the exigencies of the political situation explain the absence of any tebhaga movement in these regions. In east Bengal, the barga system was largely an adjunct to the predominant peasant smallholding system of cultivation, and the competition for small plots of barga lands in a tight land–man situation gave bargadars little bargaining power over the terms of their tenancy. It was reported from Mymensingh on the tebhaga movement: 'the Bargadars, as it appears, do not want it because they find it difficult to get lands for barga cultivation'.[53] The subdivisional officer of Feni in Noakhali wrote:

there are not many big landlords and jotedars who have granted extensive barga settlement. Only the middle class people and some small jotedars have kept the system prevailing. The prospect of Tebhaga movement or Tebhaga legislation has made this [sic] middle class people and the small jotedars somewhat panicky and

52 Sunil Sen, *Agrarian Struggle in Bengal*, pp. 65-6.
53 SDO Sadar South Mymensingh to Addl Secy Bd of Rev., 12 Mar. 1947, GB Rev. Dept LR Br., B. Progs. 15-107, Dec. 1948, File 6M-38/47 (WBSA).

the landlords here have not taken kindly to this Tebhaga movement. The prospect of such a movement has adversely affected the interest of the Bargadars as in some cases landlords are refusing to let out land on barga to the Bargadars who used to enjoy the lands on annual settlement and these landlords are bringing the lands under their own khas cultivation. This attitude will change the position of some bargadars to mere day labourers.[54]

A report from Bogra highlights the difficulties caused by the communal question following the troubles of 1946: 'The movement has failed to evoke sufficient response. The main reason appears to be the communal cleavage. The Muslim bargadars have not so far joined the movement and the Communist leaders seem somewhat nervous in directing their operation against Muslim landlords who are numerous. . .'[55]

In west and central Bengal, tebhaga agitation flared in small pockets in the Narail subdivision of Jessore and briefly in Nandigram thana in Tamluk subdivision of Midnapur.[56] Soon, however, in west Bengal, there was 'a general reaction against the movement'.[57] The landlords' agitation against the proposed Tebhaga Bill was much more potent in west Bengal than any bargadars' movement. The dependent bargadars were cowed into submission by threats of eviction and stoppage of paddy loans for subsistence during the lean months. The very different perceptions of their interests by peasant smallholders and the traditionally landless precluded the possibility of any unity of political action against the landlords who operated large khamar lands and a section of rich peasants who controlled surplus lands and grain.[58]

Although the 1946-7 sharecroppers' movement was limited in its spread and intensity and never assumed the massive proportions that current tebhaga mythology would have us believe, it has had the most powerful lines of continuity to radical agrarian campaigns in post-independence west Bengal. In the summer of 1947, the Krishak Sabha formally called off the tebhaga agitation and resolved to give the new

54 SDO Feni Noakhali to Addl Secy Bd of Rev., 10 Mar. 1947, in *ibid.*
55 SDO Bogra to Addl Secy Bd of Rev., 10 Mar. 1947, in *ibid.*
56 SDO Narail Jessore to Addl Secy Bd of Rev., 7 Mar. 1947; SDO Tamluk Midnapur to Addl Secy Bd of Rev., Mar. 1947, in *ibid.*
57 Secret Report on the Political Situation in Bengal for the second half of Feb. 1947, L/P & J/5/154 (IOR).
58 See chapter 7 above.

governments in India and Pakistan a year of grace in which to fulfil their promises to the people. The Communist Party sought to revive the movement in the harvest season of 1948–9, but apart from a spectacular local action in the Kakdwip area of the 24-Parganas, it was unable to repeat the performance of 1946–7.[59] The Congress government responded with a legislative enactment – the West Bengal Bargadars Act of 1950 – which provided for the protection of sharecroppers against eviction and a 60:40 sharing of the crop between the bargadar and his landlord.[60]

Important changes have occurred in the agrarian social structure in the frontier regions in the decades following 1950, notably the decline in barga tenancies and the dramatic growth of agricultural wage labour. Yet, it is perhaps a measure of the enduring qualities of certain elements of *longue duree* social structures that the anti-jotedar agrarian explosions of the late 1960s invariably occurred in the frontier regions of north Bengal, western Midnapur and the abadi areas of the 24-Parganas. The place which put itself on the history map as the epicentre of the Maoist communist-led agrarian rebellion was Naxalbari in the Siliguri subdivision of Darjeeling district.[61] Historians writing under the shadow of the Naxalite movement tended to base their analyses of the modern social and political history of rural Bengal on a sort of double antithesis between zamindar and jotedar and jotedar and bargadar. Such a facile jotedar thesis is clearly untenable. It is perhaps no accident that Charu Majumdar, the author of

59 'Communist–Kisan disturbances at Kakdwip, Sunderban area (Diamond Harbour) 24-Parganas'; 'A brief review of the tebhaga movement sponsored by the CPI in 1948-49'. (Intelligence Branch Records, Calcutta, file numbers cannot be quoted.)

60 The main provisions of the Bargadars Act were incorporated in chapter 3 of the Land Reforms Act of 1955. By a major amendment to the Land Reforms Act in August 1970 the crop-sharing ratio has been changed to 75:25 and the bargadars' right to cultivate made hereditary. The current Operation Barga of the CPI (M)-led government in West Bengal is a drive to record the names of the bargadars and to give them certificates so that they may be able to claim some of the benefits that are provided for them in the statute books. The older communist leaders bred in the tebhagá tradition are to some extent living in the past in their obsession with the barga problem, since sharecropping tenancies have declined and landless agricultural labour has emerged as the major social class in rural West Bengal.

61 The main centre of the CPI (M)'s radical agrarian campaign in the late 1960s was the Sonarpur area of the 24-Parganas south of Calcutta.

the policy of annihilating the class enemy – the jotedar – had his baptism in agrarian agitation in the Pachagarh area of Jalpaiguri during the tebhaga movement of 1946-7. The policy was based on an incorrect and inadequate appreciation of the agrarian class structure in Bengal as a whole. The debacle of the students and youth who went out to preach the annihilation policy in the countryside clearly holds lessons for the future. Myth, of course, can become a more powerful social force than reality and no doubt the mythology of the jotedar and bargadar has already enshrined itself as an important part of Bengal's history. Yet at this stage, a reappraisal of the reality of the agrarian social structure and the extent to which the early twentieth century subregional structural types persisted may not be only of academic interest. In a province which has since the beginning of the century lost successive young generations in waves of political agitation and repression, it may help avoid adding to the heavy cost in human lives in fighting an imaginary enemy.

CONCLUSION

This book has challenged some of the ruling orthodoxies in the modern social and political history of rural Bengal. It has shown the limitations of the 'jotedar' thesis by developing a typology which is more representative of the agrarian social structure in Bengal. This broader typology and the new periodisation of peasant politics in the province can provide a useful basis for comparisons with other agrarian societies. But most importantly, the study has exposed the bankruptcy of the colonial revenue administration as the framework in which to examine Bengal's agrarian economy and society. Rural Bengal has to be seen inside a context which takes account of the twin strands of subsistence and market uncertainties, the consequence of demographic constraints and the unenviable position of an agricultural exporting economy on a colonial periphery of the world economy. The focus has been on the impact of the global crisis of the 1930s on the agrarian economy and society of the region – especially the differential impact on the types of social structure that predominated in the different areas – and the implications it had for the nature of peasant politics in the climactic decades of British rule in India.

The chain of credit relationships provided the transmission belt along which fluctuations in the world market, compounded by the colonial government's financial policies, were mediated to the regional economy. At the same time, credit relations formed the key thread in the texture of agrarian relations within the region. From the later nineteenth century and more emphatically from the first decade of the twentieth, the import of foreign funds to finance agricultural exports was the crucial determinant of the liquidity of the regional economy. The jute-growing peasant smallholding system of east Bengal was tied most firmly to the international economy. Some weakly monetised sectors persisted, as in the rich farmer–sharecropper system in north Bengal and the demesne labour section of the peasant smallholding–demesne labour complex in west Bengal. Grainlending and grain-dealing rural elites shielded the primary producers from the direct effect of market forces. But even here the impact of external forces on the elites had an important bearing on the ordering of their relations with the actual workers on the soil. The switch by peasant smallholders of east Bengal to petty commodity production cannot be explained simply in terms of a profit-motivated response to market opportunity or the forced cultivation implicit in a colonialism operating on mercantilist methods. Faced with rapidly diminishing holdings as a consequence of demographic growth, peasant smallholders could not maintain families with subsistence crops, so they opted for a strategy of supporting subsistence through the market by turning to a high-value and labour-intensive cash-crop. It was this fundamental constraint which, apart from the vested interests in manufacture, trade and state, prevented a return to the pre-1900 situation when, after 1930, jute failed to work its magic. The abject failure of the cash-crop economy in a situation where the subsistence foundation had already been eroded by demographic change was the crux of the long-run contradiction in Bengal's peasant economy. This is what culminated in the famine of 1943 – a crisis precipitated by more proximate factors of endogenous and exogenous origin.

Once the peasantry had become enmeshed in the domain of the market, they laid themselves open to all the disadvantages of highly inequitable and uncertain product markets, not to mention the interlinked credit markets. The marketing structures were specially geared to benefit the purchasers of agricultural products and the primary producers had no control over volatile price movements. Amartya Sen's analysis of the decline in wage-price exchange rates provides a partial explanation of the great Bengal famine.[1] The decline in paddy-growers' direct entitlement to rice placed them at the

1 Amartya Sen, *Poverty and Famines.*

mercy of the wartime food market. The relative price of jute never really recovered its buoyancy after the catastrophic fall in the 1930s. This was devastating for the peasant smallholders of east Bengal when grain prices rocketed during the war. The wage–price mechanism in the 1940s was merely the final link in a chain of causation. The antecedent links were located in the crisis of the depression decade, especially the massive disruption of rural credit relations in that period.

When at the onset of the depression Bengal's export prospects looked bleak, the flow of foreign funds was suddenly withdrawn resulting in a major liquidity crisis in the regional economy. This was exacerbated by the colonial government's financial manipulations. Prices, including that of rice, fell drastically. As the financial superstructure stopped pouring vast amounts of liquid capital down the trading and credit networks, small trader–moneylenders in the rural areas could no longer operate. The small landlord-usurers, unable to recover any money from their tenant-debtors, had nothing to lend. Government's legislative interference in the debt problem during the 1930s was the *coup de grace*, ensuring that even when trade and prices picked up at the end of the decade no commensurate response was felt in the credit market. The rupture in the flow of money credit in the rural areas had very different implications for the history of agrarian relations and peasant politics in the different parts of Bengal.

The impact of the credit crisis was most severe in the highly monetised economy of east Bengal. Here zamindars and talukdars held feeble rent-collecting rights over peasant smallholders. Although the talukdar-mahajan vaunted his position as rentier-landlord, his role as creditor had clearly assumed crucial importance in the twentieth century. It was the nub of an interlocking set of relations of production and surplus-appropriation which underpinned an uneasy symbiosis in social relations between them and the mass of indebted peasant smallholders. In 1930 the old bonds snapped. The trader-mahajans were suddenly snuffed out and the talukdar-mahajans made themselves redundant to the process of agricultural reproduction in east Bengal. In spite of the hardship that it brought, the slump witnessed a decisive shift in the balance of class power in the peasants' favour. It robbed the predominantly Hindu talukdar-mahajans and trader-mahajans of their chief source of economic control and power. From 1930 onwards, the east Bengal countryside increasingly became the scene of a violent conflict between a predominantly Muslim peasantry and a mostly Hindu rural elite. This conflict was interpreted and used by self-serving politicians for their own ends. Operating in higher-level political arenas with communal constituencies, the gift of government's successive constitutional reforms, these politicians unflinchingly used religion to mask an essentially economic conflict.

In the demesne labour–peasant smallholding complex of west Bengal, the crisis of the 1930s aided the landlords to the detriment of the smallholding peasants. With the fall in prices and the absence of credit, many peasant smallholders were in the doldrums, and the khamar sector took long strides at their expense. Landlords and rich peasants continued grain loans to dependent sharecroppers and labourers in the khamar sector. The strengthening of the ties of dependency in this particular form of agrarian organisation precluded the possibility of any sustained or widespread challenge to landlords' and rich peasants' power. Moreover, there was little scope for unified political action between the peasant smallholders and the traditionally landless, whose labour was required not only on demesne lands but also on smallholdings. Political agitations involving the peasantry occurred only where the bulk of the countryside could be unified against outsiders, especially the local arms of the colonial state. This happened on specific issues, such as local tax enhancements in times of economic stress and political turmoil, and became a recurrent feature in one district – Midnapur – where anti-government movements subsumed local internal divisions.

The rupture in interclass bonds of dependence in the rich farmer–sharecropper system that predominated in the frontier regions did not become apparent until 1939–40. The rich jotedars, who were also the chief creditors and grain exporters, took the brunt of the collapse in the product market in 1930. Their method of grain redistribution, especially in the context of relatively decentralised sharecropping, shifted from the domain of the credit market to the product market. The fall in land values during the slump meant that they could not disengage themselves from the land completely even if they were anxious to invest in the now more profitable urban sector. The first adhiar challenge to jotedar dominance in the frontier regions was launched at a time when land and crop prices had begun to recover. The better-off among the adhiars, demanding more direct access to the grain market and a larger share of the product, led the way against the jotedars whose stranglehold on the agrarian economy as creditors had been shaken by the shock of the depression. A distinct class line between jotedars and adhiars ensured that the agitations of 1939–40 and 1946–7 were conducted on the basis of clear-cut economic demands.

The classification of the world's peasantry into rich, middle and poor is clearly inadequate even as a heuristic device. The debate about the relative militance or proneness to rebellion of the middle or poor peasantry makes little sense unless directly related to a specific historical context. Some broad comparisons can, however, be made about the connection between types of agrarian social structure and the complexion and articulation of peasant protest. The ties of dependency in the peasant smallholding–demesne labour complex of west Bengal, which was perhaps the most widespread form of agrarian organisation in India, showed a strong tendency towards muting any expression of protest by the diverse dependent social groups. Here it was the dominant land-controllers who led the whole countryside in brief bursts of agitation against outside threats. The peasant smallholders in this sort of social structure provided some momentum in such agitations only in pockets, where the demense-labour sector was not very substantial and upwardly mobile peasant groups had built up a tradition of unified resistance to the colonial state. The Mahishya peasantry of Midnapur had their counterparts in pockets of other parts of India, notably in the Patidar peasantry of some Gujarat districts and the Kamma peasantry of the Andhra delta.[2]

2 See David Hardiman, *Peasant Nationalists of Gujarat Kheda District 1917-1934* (Delhi, 1981); C.J. Baker, *The Politics of South India 1920-1937* (Cambridge, 1976).

By comparison, it has been in situations of a clear-cut class dichotomy between rich farmers or village landlords and sharecroppers, as in the rich farmer–sharecropper system of the frontier regions in Bengal, that the weakening of landlord repression has provided the best field for class-based agitation and political radicalism. The tebhaga movement is comparable in this respect to the Telengana insurrection of 1946-51, but also has close parallels (despite some major differences of context) with the rising of tenant-cultivators against village landlords in the Mappilla region in Kerala in 1921 and with the sharecroppers' agitation in some of the valley districts of Tamil Nadu in 1946-7, and also with more recent agrarian movements in those areas.[3] In South-East Asia, the sharply polarised agrarian class structures in newly settled regions initially provided the bases of agrarian revolt and revolution after the onset of the depression. Studies on Vietnam, for instance, have made plain the contrast between the economic individualism and the socio-political conservatism of the peasant smallholders of Tonkin and Annam in northern Vietnam and the group solidarity based on economic class status and the collective political action of sharecroppers against village landlords in Cochinchina in the south. The newly opened-up tracts of the Mekong delta of Indo-China and the Irrawady delta in Lower Burma, with polarised village landlord forms, were also the principal agricultural exporting sectors. This provided the mix for the agrarian explosions of the 1930s and 1940s.[4] In Bengal it was the peasant smallholding system in the east which was most strongly oriented to the world market having gone through a process analogous to the Indonesian experience of 'agricultural involution'.[5] The politics of the smallholding peasant-

---

3 See D.N. Dhanagare, 'Social Origins of the Peasant Insurrection in Telengana (1946-51), *Contributions to Indian Sociology*, 8, (1974); R.L. Hardgrave, 'Peasant Mobilization in Malabar: the Mappilla Rebellion, 1921', in R.L. Crane (ed.), *Aspects of Political Mobilization in South Asia* (Syracuse, 1976); Stephen F. Dale, *Islamic Society on a South Asian Frontier* (Oxford, 1982); Baker, *An Indian Rural Economy*, chapter 3.
4 See Jeffrey M. Paige, *Agrarian Revolution: Social Movements and Export Agriculture in the Underdeveloped World* (New York, 1975), pp. 278-333; Scott, *The Moral Economy of the Peasant*, pp. 56-90. 114-56; M. Adas, *The Burma Delta*.
5 Clifford Geertz, *Agricultural Involution* (Berkeley, 1971).

debtors of east Bengal in the post-1930 period left the most profound impact on the politics of the province.

The strong individualism and isolated settlement patterns of these smallholders have been obscured by over-played theories of a pre-existing peasant communal consciousness and the notion that all rights, including the right to land, flowed from being members of the 'community'.[6] The basic right to land in Bengal, and for that matter, in most parts of India, was essentially an individual right. The perception of individual interest as collective interest was not easy to achieve. The peasant smallholders of east Bengal lived under identical yet very fragmented conditions of economic existence. The collapse of symbiotic bonds with the rural elite did not mean the rupture of relations between a peasant community and non-peasants. It meant the breakdown of many single-stranded ties of a multitude of smallholding peasants with the moneylenders and landlords. Religion, described as a crucial component of 'communal consciousness', to some extent imparted a sense of collectivity and an ideological legitimation in a specific historical conjuncture when the balance of class power in the countryside had already changed.

6 Partha Chatterjee, 'Agrarian Relations and Communalism in Bengal 1928–1935' in Ranajit Guha (ed.), *Sub-altern Studies* I, pp. 9-38.

GLOSSARY

abadi	newly reclaimed
abwab	traditional, arbitrary, exaction above the formal rent
adhiar	sharecropper (term in use in north Bengal)
adhi	half share
ahsan manzil	lord's palace or mansion
aman	winter rice
aratdar	warehouseman
aus	autumn rice
bahas	religious debate
baithak	meeting
ballam	common variety of rice
bania	trader
bansh	bamboo
barga	sharecropping
bargadar	sharecropper
bari	paddy loan (in west and central Bengal)
barind	rocky, infertile uplands in the western fringe of Bengal
bepari	small trader
bhadralok	gentleman
bhag	share
bhagdar	sharecropper
bhagchashi	sharecropper
bhuswami	landlord
bigha	measure of land (approximately one third of an acre)
boro	summer rice
chak	block of land
chakdar	tenure-holder in newly reclaimed tracts in the Sunderbans of coastal Bengal
char	alluvial land
chaukidar	village police
chukanidar	tenure-holder below jotedar in north Bengal
dadan	advance
dadni	moneylending
daffadar	rural police
dalal	broker
darchukanidar	tenureholder below chukanidar in north Bengal
darpatnidar	tenureholder below patnidar (in west and central Bengal)
derhi	50% interest on paddy loan
dewaniya	village leader (in north Bengal)
dhalta	type of fee or commission

281

dhan	paddy
dhankarari	fixed produce rent
dikku	foreigner or stranger (Santal)
dhenki	threshing implement
duno	100% interest on paddy or seed loan
faria	small trader
ganthi	a type of tenure (mainly found in Khulna)
ganthidar	holder of ganthi tenure
giri	landlord, usually jotedar in north Bengal
gnata	labour exchange
godown	warehouse
gola	granary
goladar	owner of granary
gomasta	landlord's employee
goonda	hooligan
grihasthi	householder
hal	plough
haola	a type of tenure (mainly found in Bakarganj)
haoladar	holder of haola tenure
hat	village market usually held once or twice a week
hat-chita	hand note
hauli	unpaid labour
hawaladar	type of tenureholder
ijaradar	lease-holder (of market)
jalpai	tracts reserved for salt manufacture
jami	land
jehad	holy war
jote	cultivable land
jotedar	holder of cutivable land; in north Bengal, often a substantial landholder
kabala	sale (of land)
kabuliyat	tenancy document
kachhari	landlord's office
karbar	business
karja	loan, interest
karjapatra	loan bond
kat kabala	conditional sale
katha	measure of land (20 bighas); measuring-pot for paddy (in north Bengal)
khai khalasi	usufructuary mortgage
khamar	personal demesne; threshing yard
khas khamar	personal demesne
khas mahal	government estate
khatak	debtor
khatiyan	settlement document
khetmajur	farm-labourer
kholian	threshing yard (in north Bengal)
korfa	under-tenant
koyal	weighman
krishak	peasant

krishan	agricultural labourer (in west Bengal) paid with a third of the produce
krishani	the system of cultivation by krishans
kulak	rich peasant
lagni	moneylending or investing
lathi	wooden stick
lotdar	leaseholder of government owned lots in the Sunderbans
lungi	lower garment worn by Muslim peasants in east Bengal
machh	fish
madrassah	Islamic educational institution
mahajan	creditor; literally, great man
mahajani	moneylending
mahal	estate
mahfil	debate
mahindar	farm-servant (in west Bengal)
maidan	open space
majur	labourer
maktab	Islamic educational institution
mandal	village head (especially in tribal area)
mathbar	village leader
maulavi	learned Muslim
maund	weight measure
mauza	village (revenue unit)
mela	fair
mofussil	district, countryside
munish	day labourer (in west Bengal)
nabashakh	nine intermediary castes in Hindu social hierarchy
naib	landlord's employee
nailya	jute
nazar	traditional fee to landlord on purchase of land, on obtaining tenancy or on ceremonial occasions
paikar	small trader
pan	betel leaf; measure of straw
panchayat	village government
pat	jute
patni	a type of tenure (mainly found in west and central Bengal)
patnidar	tenure-holder, usually intermediary between zamindar and raiyat in west Bengal
pir	Muslim saint
praja	tenant
pramanik	village elder
punjabi	shirt worn in Bengal
raiyat	peasant; tenant under meaning of the Bengal Tenancy Act of 1885
ryot	same as raiyat
sabha	organisation; meeting
safkabala	outright sale

salami	traditional fee to landlord on purchase of land or on obtaining tenancy
samiti	association
sanja	fixed produce rent
sattapatra	loan bond
satyagraha	non-violent non-cooperation; literally, quest for truth
seer	weight measure
se-patnidar	tenure-holder below dar-patnidar (in west and central Bengal)
shariat	Islamic law and code of behaviour
sir	demesne land (north India)
sirdar	holder of demesne land
swaraj	self-rule
taka dhaki	commutation of cash and kind rents
taluk	a type of tenure; usually the rent collecting right below the level of zamindar (in east Bengal)
talukdar	landlord or tenure-holder; usually collector of rent from raiyats
tanka	fixed rent in kind in Mymensingh
tebhaga	division in three
tejarati	moneylending
thana	police station
til	a type of oil seed
utbandi	a type of tenure in alluvial lands (in Nadia and Murshidabad)
wazmahfil	religious debate
zamindar	landlord; revenue-payer to the government under the Permanent Settlement of 1793

SELECT BIBLIOGRAPHY

I. MANUSCRIPT SOURCES

(a) India Office Records and Library

 (i) Bengal Governor's Fortnightly Reports 1937-47 L/P & J/5.
 (ii) Provincial Government Records transferred to London in 1947.
      Papers of the Bengal Governor's Secretarist R/3.
(iii) F.O. Bell Papers Mss Eur D 733.

(b) West Bengal State Archives and Bangladesh Secretariat Record Room. Records of the Government of Bengal

 (i) Proceedings of the Revenue Department.
 (ii) Proceedings of the Agriculture and Industries Department.
(iii) Proceedings of the Co-operative Credit and Rural Indebtedness Department.
 (iv) Proceedings of the Home Political Department.
 (v) Proceedings of the Commerce Department.
 (vi) Proceedings of the Local Self-Government Department.

(c) West Bengal Home Department

Political Confidential Files including Fortnight Reports from district magistrates and divisional commissioners.

(d) District Collectorate Record Rooms and District Registration Offices: Dacca, Mymensingh, West Dinajpur, Midnapur

Cadastral survey and settlement records and deeds of land sales and mortgages of selected villages.

(e) South Asian Studies Centre Archives, Cambridge

 (i) F.J. Donovan Papers.
 (ii) A.J. Dash Papers.

(f) Nehru Memorial Museum and Library, New Delhi

 (i) All-India Congress Committee Papers relating to Bengal.
 (ii) Rajendra Prasad Papers.

(g) Netaji Research Bureau, Calcutta

Subhas Chandra Bose and Sarat Chandra Bose Papers.

285

II. PRINTED SOURCES

(a) Official Publications

(i) Settlement Reports

Final reports on survey and settlement operations in the districts of:

J.C. Jack, Bakarganj (1900-8), 1915
F.W. Robertson, Bankura (1917-24), 1936
K.A.L. Hill, Burdwan (1927-34), 1940
F.D. Ascoli, Dacca (1910-17), 1917
F.O. Bell, Dinajpur (1934-40), 1941
J.C. Jack, Faridpur (1904-14), 1916
M.N. Gupta, Hooghly (1904-13), 1914
M.A. Momen, Jessore (1920-4), 1925
F.A. Sachse, Mymensingh (1908-19), 1919
A.K. Jameson, Midnapur (1910-18), 1919
W.H. Thompson, Noakhali (1915-19), 1919
D. Macpherson, Pabna and Bogra (1920-29), 1930
A.C. Hartley, Rangpur (1931-8), 1941
W.H. Thompson, Tippera (1915-19), 1919
A.C. Lahiri, 24-Parganas (1924-33), 1934

(ii) District Gazetters

Bankura, 1908
Bakarganj, 1918
Darjeeling, 1907
Jalpaiguri, 1911
Mymensingh, 1919
The 24-Parganas, 1914.

(iii) Other Official Reports

Agricultural Statistics of India, Delhi, annual.
Report on the Administration of Bengal, Calcutta, annual.
Report on the Land Revenue Administration Bengal, Calcutta, annual.
Report on Police Administration of Bengal, Calcutta, annual.
Report on the Wards' and Attached Estates, Calcutta, annual.
Census of India, 1911, 1921, 1931, 1941, 1951. Volumes on Bengal.
Census of Pakistan, 1951, 1961. Volumes on East Pakistan.
Report of the Royal Commission on Agriculture 1926-28, (Chairman Marquess of Linlithgow), 14 Vols, London, 1928.
Report on the Marketing of Agricultural Produce in Bengal 1926, Calcutta, 1928.
Report of the Bengal Provincial Banking Enquiry Committee 1929-30, 2 Vols, Delhi, 1931.
Bengal Board of Economic Enquiry, *Bulletin District Faridpur,* Alipur, 1934.
Bengal Board of Economic Enquiry, *Bulletin District Bankura,* Alipur, 1935.
Bengal Board of Economic Enquiry, *Bulletin District Pabna,* Alipur, 1935.
Bengal Board of Economic Enquiry, *Preliminary Report on Rural Indebtedness,* Calcutta, 1935.

Bengal Board of Economic Enquiry, *Report on the Activities of the Board During the Years 1934-35 and 1935-36*, Alipur, 1936.
Report of the Bengal Jute Enquiry Committee (Chairman R.S. Finlow), Alipur, 1934.
Return Showing the Results of Elections in India 1937, 1937-38 Cmd No. 5589.
Report of the Land Revenue Commission, Bengal 1938-40, (Chairman Sir Francis Floud), 6 Vols., Alipur, 1940.
Report of the Bengal Jute Enquiry Committee (Chairman L.R. Fawcus), Alipur, 1940.
Report of the Bengal Paddy and Rice Enquiry Committee, 2 Vols., Alipur, 1940.
Census of Agricultural Implements in Bengal, Alipur, 1940.
Report on the Marketing of Rice in India and Burma, Delhi, 1941.
Report of the Dacca Riots Enquiry Committee, Alipur, 1942.
District Officers' Chronicles of Events of Disturbances Consequent upon the All-India Congress Committee's Resolution of 8th August 1942 and the Arrest of Congress Leaders Thereafter, Secret Home Poll Dept Report, 1943.
Famine Enquiry Commission Report on Bengal (Chairman J. Woodhead), Delhi, 1945.
Ishaque, H.S.M. *Agricultural Statistics by Plot to Plot Enumeration*, 3 Vols., Calcutta, 1945.
Return showing the Results of Elections in India in 1945-46 to the Central Assembly and the Provincial Legislature Assemblies, Delhi, 1948.

(b) Newspapers and Periodicals

Amrita Bazaar Patrika
Arthik Unnati
Atmashakti
Biplabi
Chashi
Krishak
Millat
Nihar
The Statesman

III. PUBLISHED BOOKS AND PAMPHLETS AND UNPUBLISHED DISSERTATIONS

Abdullah, Abu Ahmed, 'Agrarian Structure and the IRDP: Preliminary Considerations', *Bangladesh Development Studies*, 4, 2 (1976), 209-66.
—— 'Landlord and Rich Peasant under the Permanent Settlement', *Calcutta Historical Journal*, 4, 2 (1980), 1-27 and 5, 1 (1980), 89-154.
Adas, Michael, *The Burma Delta*, Madison, Wisconsin, 1974.
Adnan, S. and Rahman, H. Zillur, 'Peasant Classes and Land Mobility: Structural Reproduction and Change in Rural Bangladesh', in Bangladesh Itihas Samiti, *Studies in Rural History*, pp. 61-115.
Ahmed, Abul Mansur, *Amar Dekha Rajnitur Panchas Bachhar* (Fifty Years of Politics As I Saw It), Dacca, 1968.
Ahmed, Rafiuddin, *Bengal Muslims: The Redefinition of Identity 1876-1906*, Delhi, 1982.

Alamgir, M., *Famine in South Asia*, Harvard, 1980.

Alavi, Hamza, 'Peasants and Revolution' in K. Gough, and Hari, P. Sharma, eds., *Imperialism and Revolution in South Asia*, New York, 1973.

——— 'India and the Colonial Mode of Production', *Economic and Political Weekly*, 10 (1975), 1236-62.

———'India: Transition from Feudalism to Colonial Capitalism', *Journal of Comtemporary Asia*, 10, 4 (1980), 359-98.

Ali, Mian Abed, *Desh Shanti*, Gántipara, Rangpur, 1925.

Arnold, David, 'Looting, Grain Riots and Government Policy in South India 1918', *Past and Present*, 84 (1979), 111-450

Ayyar, S.V. and Khan, A.K.A., 'The Economics of a Bengal Village', *Indian Jounal of Economics*, 6 (January 1926), 200-15.

Bagchi, Amiya, *Private Investment in India*, Cambridge, 1969.

Baker, C.J., *The Politics of South India 1920-1937*, Cambridge, 1976.

——— *An Indian Rural Economy: The Tamilnad Countryside 1880-1955*, Delhi, 1984.

Banaji, J., 'Capitalist Domination and the Small Peasantry', *Economic and Political Weekly*, 12, 33 and 34 (1977), 1375-404.

Bandyopadhyay, Bibhuti Bhushan, *Ashani Sanket* (Distant Thunder), Calcutta, 1953.

Bandyopadhyay, N., 'Causes of Sharp Increase in Agricultural Labourers, 1961-71: A Case Study of Social Existence Forms of Labour in North Bengal', *Economic and Political Weekly*, Review of Agriculture (Dec. 1977), A-11-A-126.

Bandyopadhyay, Tarashankar, *Dhatridebata, Ganadebata and Panhagram, Hansuli Banker Upakatha*, Calcutta, 1971.

Bertocci, Peter J., 'Structural Fragmentation, and Peasant Classes in Bangladesh, *Journal of Social Studies*, 5 (1979), 34-60.

Beteille, Andre, *Studies in Agrarian Social Structure*, Delhi, 1974.

Bhaduri, Amit, 'A Study in Agricultural Backwardness under Semi-feudalism', *Economic Journal*, 83 (1973), 120-37.

Bhattacharya Jnanabrata, 'An Examination of Leadership Entry in Bengal Peasant Revolts, 1937-1947,' *Journal of Asian Studies*, XXXVII, 4 (1978).

Bhattacharyya, Buddhadeva, 'Damodar Canal Tax Movement', in A.R. Desai, ed., *Peasant Struggles in India*, Bombay, 1979.

Blyn, George, *Agricultural Trends in India*, 1890-1947, Philadelphia, 1966.

Bois, Guy, 'Against the Neo-Malthusian Orthodoxy', *Past and Present*, 79 (1978), 60-9.

Bose, Santipriya, 'A Survey of Rural Indebtedness in South-West Birbhum, Bengal in 1933-34', *Sankhya*, 3, 2 (1937).

Bose, Sisir K., ed., *The Voice of Sarat Chandra Bose*, Calcutta, 1978.

Bose, Sugata, 'The Roots of Communal Violence in Rural Bengal: A Study of the Kishoreganj Riots 1930', *Modern Asian Studies*, 16, 3 (1982), 463-91.

Braudel, F., 'History and the Social Sciences' in P. Burke, ed., *Economy and Society in Early Modern Europe: Essays from Annales*, London, 1972.

Brenner, Robert, 'Agrarian Class Structure and Economic Development in Pre-Industrial Europe', *Past and Present*, 70 (1976), 30-75.

Broomfield, J.H., *Elite Conflict in a Plural Society: Twentieth Century Bengal*, Berkeley, 1969.

Buchanan-Hamilton, Francis, *A Geographical, Statistical and Historical Description (1908) of the District, A Zillah of Dinajpur in the Province, or Soubah of Bengal*, Calcutta, 1883.

Catanach, I.J., 'Agrarian Disturbances in Nineteenth Century India', *Indian Economic and Social History Review*, 3, 1 (1966), 65-84.

Chatterjee, Partha, 'Agrarian Relations and Communalism in Bengal 1926-1935' in Ranajit, Guha, ed., *Sub-Altern Studies I*, Delhi, 1982.

—— 'Agrarian Structure in Pre-Partition Bengal' in A. Sen, P. Chatterjee, S. Mukherjee, *Perspectives in Social Sciences 2, Three Studies on the Agrarian Structure in Bengal before Independence*, Delhi, 1982.

Chaudhuri, Ashrafuddin Ahmed, *Raj Birodhi* (Opponent of the Raj), Dacca, 1979.

Chaudhuri, B.B., 'Agrarian Economy and Agrarian Relations in Bengal 1859-1885', Oxford, D. Phil. dissertation, 1968.

—— 'The Process of Depeasantization in Bengal and Bihar, 1885-1947', *Indian Historical Review*, 3, 1 (1975), 105-65.

—— 'The Land Market in Eastern India (1793-1940)', *Indian Economic and Social History.Review*, 12, 1 and 2 (1975), 1-42, 133-68.

Chaudhuri, K.N., 'India's International Economy in the Nineteenth Century: A Historical Survey', *Modern Asian Studies*, 2, 1 (1968), 31-50.

Chayanov, A.V., *The Theory of Peasant Economy*, Homewood, Illinois, 1966.

Dale, Stephen F., *Islamic Society on a South Asian Frontier: The Mappillas of Malabar*, Oxford, 1982.

Danda, A.K. and D.G. *Development and Change in Basudha: A Study of a West Bengal Village*, Hyderabad, 1971.

Desai, A.R., ed., *Peasant Struggles in India*, Bombay, 1979.

Dhanagare, D.N., 'Social Origins of the Peasant Insurrection in Telengana (1946-51)', *Contributions to Indian Sociology*, 8 (1974), 109-34.

Frykenberg, R.E., ed., *Land Control and Social Structure in Indian History*, Madison, Wisconsin, 1969.

Gadgil, D.R. and Sovani, N.V., *War and Indian Economic Policy*, Poona, 1943.

Gallagher, John, 'Congress in Decline: Bengal 1930 to 1939' in J. Gallagher, G. Johnson, and A. Seal, eds., *Locality, Province and Nation*, Cambridge, 1973.

Ganguli, Birendranath, *Trends of Agriculture and Population in the Ganges Valley*, London, 1938.

Geertz, Clifford, *Agricultural Involution*, Berkeley, 1971.

Ghosh, A. and Dutt, K. *Development of Capitalist Relations in Agriculture*, Delhi, 1977.

Gordon, Leonard A., *Bengal: The Nationalist Movement 1876-1940*, New York, 1974.

—— 'Brothers against the Raj: Subhas and Sarat Chandra Bose 1937-47', *The Oracle*, I, 3 (1979).

Greenough, Paul R., *Prosperity and Misery in Modern Bengal: The Famine of 1943-1944*, New York, 1982.

—— 'Political Mobilization and the Underground Literature of the Quit India Movement 1942-4', *MAS*, 17,3 (1982) 353-6.

Guha, Ranajit, 'Neel Darpan: The Image of a Peasant Revolt in a Liberal Mirror', *Journal of Peasant Studies*, 2, 1 (1974), 1-46.

—— *A Rule of Property for Bengal*, Paris, 1963.

—— ed. *Sub-altern Studies, I*, Delhi, 1982.

Hamid, Md Abdul, *Pater Kabita*, Juriya, Assam, 1930.

Hardgrave, R.L., 'Peasant Mobilization in Malabar: the Mappilla Rebellion, 1921' in R.L. Crane, ed., *Aspects of Political Mobilization in South Asia*, Syracuse, 1976.

Hardiman, David, *Peasant Nationalists of Gujarat Kheda District 1917-1934*, Delhi, 1981.

Hashim, Abul, *In Retrospection*, Dacca, 1974,·
Hunter, W.W., *A Statistical Account of Bengal*, London, 1875-7.
Huque, M. Azizul, *The Man Behind the Plough*, Calcutta, 1939.
Islam, M.M., *Bengal Agriculture 1920-1946: A Quantitative Study*, Cambridge, 1979.
Islam, Sirajul, *The Permanent Settlement in Bengal: A Study of Its Operation 1790-1819*, Dacca, 1979.
Jack, J.C., *Economic Life of a Bengal District*, Oxford, 1916.
Jalal, Ayesha, *The Sole Spokesman: Jinnah, The Muslim League and the Demand for Pakistan*, Cambridge, 1985.
Jalal, Ayesha, and Seal, Anil, 'Alternative to Partition' in C.J. Baker, G. Johnson, A. Seal, eds., *Power Profit and Politics*, Cambridge, 1981.
Kautsky, K., *Die Agrarfrage*, London, 1976.
Kay, Cristobal, ' Comparative Development of the European Manorial System and the Latin American Hacienda System', *Journal of Peasant Studies*, 2, 1 (1974), 69-98.
Kessinger, Tom, *Vilyatpur 1848-1968*, Berkeley, 1974.
Keynes, J.M., *Indian Currency and Finance*, London, 1913.
Kindleberger, C.P., *The World in Depression 1929-1939*, Stanford, California, 1973.
Klein, Ira, 'Malaria and Mortality in Bengal 1840-1921', *Indian Economic and Social History Review*, 9, 2 (1972), 132-60.
Kling, Blair B., *The Blue Mutiny*, Philadelphia, 1966.
Kula, W., *An Economic Theory of the Feudal System*, London 1971.
Kumar, Dharma, *Land and Caste in South India*, Cambridge, 1965.
Lenin, V.I., *Collected Works*, Vol. 3, Moscow, 1977.
Le Roy Ladurie, E., *The Peasants of Languedoc*, Urbana, Illinois, 1974.
_____ 'A Reply to Professor Brenner', *Past and Present*, 79 (1978), 55-9.
Lewis, W.A., *Economic Survey, 1919-1939*, London, 1949.
Low, D.A., ed., *Congress and the Raj: Facets of the Indian Struggle*, London, 1977.
Mahalanobis, P.C., Mukherjee, R., Ghosh, A., 'A Sample Survey of the After-effects of the Bengal Famine'. *Sankhya*, 7, 4 (1946), 337-400.
Maizels, A., *Industrial Growth and World Trade*, Cambridge, 1963.
Mansergh, N., ed., *India: The Transfer of Power*, 12 Vols., London, 1976-83.
Marx, K., 'The Eighteenth Brumaire of Louis Bonaparte' in K. Marx and F. Engels, *Selected Works I*, Moscow, 1962.
Metcalf, Thomas R., *Land, Landlords and the British Raj: Northern India in the Nineteenth Century*, Berkeley, California, 1970.
Momen, Humaira, *Muslim Politics in Bengal: A Study of Krishak Praja Party and the Elections of 1937*, Dacca, 1972.
Morris, M.D., 'Economic Change and Agriculture in 19th Century India', *Indian Economic and Social History Review*, 3, 2 (1966), 185-209.
Mukerji, K.M., 'The Problems of Agricultural Indebtedness in Bengal', *Indian Journal of Economics*, 29, (1948-9).
_____ *The Problems of Land Transfer*, Santiniketan, 1957.
_____ *Levels of Economic Activity and Public Expenditure in India*, London, 1962.
Mukherjee, Ramkrishna, *Six Villages of Bengal*, Bombay, 1971.
Mukherji, Radhakamal, *The Changing Face of Bengal: A Study in Riverine Economy*, Calcutta, 1938.
Mukherji, Saugata, 'Imperialism in Action through a Mercantilist Function', in Barun, De, ed., *Essays in Honour of Professor Susobhan Sarkar*, Calcutta, 1974.
_____ 'Some Aspects of Commercialization of Agriculture in Eastern India, 1891-1938'

in A. Sen, P. Chatterjee and S. Mukherji, *Perspectives in Social Sciences 2: Three Studies on the Agrarian Structure of Bengal before Independence*, Delhi, 1982.

Narain, Dharm, *The Impact of Price Movements on Selected Crops in India 1900-1939*, London, 1965.

O'Malley, L.S.S., *Bengal, Bihar and Orissa, Sikkim*, Provincial Geographies of India, Cambridge, 1917.

Paige, Jeffrey, M., *Agrarian Revolution: Social Movements and Export Agriculture in the Underdeveloped World*, New York, 1975.

Palit Chittabrata, *Tension in Bengali Rural Society 1830-1860*, Calcutta, 1977.

Poduval, R.N., *Finance of the Government of India since 1935*, Delhi, 1951.

Popkin, Samuel, L., *The Rational Peasant: The Political Economy of Rural Society in Vietnam*, Berkeley, 1979.

Postan, M.M. and Hatcher, John, 'Population and Class Relations in Feudal Society', *Past and Present*, 78 (1978), 23-37.

Rasul, M. Abdullah, *Krishaksabhar Itihas* (History of the Krishak Sabha), Calcutta, 1969.

Ray, Rajat, 'Social Conflict and Political Unrest in Bengal 1875-1908', Cambridge, Ph. D. dissertation, 1973.

——— 'The Crisis of Bengal Agriculture 1870-1927 — Dynamics of Immobility', *Indian Economic and Social History Review*, 10, 3 (1973), 244-79.

———'Masses in Politics: The Non-Cooperation Movement in Bengal 1920-1922', *Indian Economic and Social History Review*, 11, 4 (1974) 343-410.

Ray, Rajat and Ratna, 'The Dynamics of Continuity in Rural Bengal under the British Imperium', *Indian Economic and Social History Review*, 101, 2 (1973), 103-28.

———'Zamindars and Jotedars: A Study of Rural Politics in Bengal', *Modern Asian Studies*, 9, 1 (1975), 81-102.

Ray, Ratnalekha, *Change in Bengal Agrarian Society 1760-1850*, Delhi, 1980.

Raychaudhuri, Tapan, 'Permanent Settlement in Operation: Bakarganj District, East Bengal , Frykenburg, R.E., ed., *Land Control and Social Structure in Indian History*, Madison, Wisconsin, 1969.

Rude, George, *The Crowd in History*, New York, 1964.

Samanta, S.C., Bhattacharryya, S., Das, A.M., Pramanik, P.K., *August Revolution and Two Years' National Government in Midnapore*, Calcutta, 1946.

Samed, Abdul Mian, *Krishak Boka* (The Foolish Peasant), Ahara, Mymensingh, 1921.

Sanyal, Hitesranjan, 'Congress Movements in the Villages of Eastern Midnapore, 1921-1931', in Marc Gaborieau and Alice Thorner, eds., *Asie du Sud: Traditions et Changements*, Paris, 1979.

Sarkar, Sumit, *The Swadeshi Movement in Bengal 1903-1908*, Calcutta, 1974.

Scott, James C., *The Moral Economy of the Peasant*, Yale, 1976

Seal, Anil, 'Imperialism and Nationalism in India' in J. Gallagher, G. Johnson, and A. Seal, eds., *Locality, Province and Nation*, Cambridge, 1973.

Sen, Amartya, *Poverty and Famines: An Essay in Entitlement and Deprivation*, Oxford, 1981.

Sen, Asok, 'Agrarian Structure and Tenancy Laws in Bengal 1850-1900' in A. Sen, P. Chatterjee, S. Mukherjee, *Perspectives in Social Sciences 2: Three Studies on the Agrarian Structure in Bengal Before Independence*, Delhi, 1982.

Sen, Shila, *Muslim Politics in Bengal 1937-47*, Delhi, 1947.

Sen, Sunil, *Agrarian Struggle in Bengal 1946-47*, Calcutta, 1972.

Sen, S.N., 'Statistical Notes: An Estimate of the Rural Indebtedness of Bengal', *Sankhya*, I, 1-4 (1933-4), 335-7.

Sengupta, S.N., 'The Depression' in Radhakamal Mukerjee, ed., *Economic Problems of Modern India*, London, 1939.

Shah, Abdul Hamid, *Krishak Bilap* (The Woes of the Peasant), Mymensingh, 1921.

Shanin, T., *The Awkward Class: Political Sociology of Peasantry in a Developing Society, Russia 1910-1921*, Oxford, 1972.

Sinha, N.C., and Khera, P.N., *Indian War Economy*, Calcutta, 1962.

Stokes, Eric, *The Peasants and the Raj*, Cambridge, 1978.

Thorner, D. and A., *Land and Labour in India*, Delhi, 1965.

Timoshenko, V.P., *World Agriculture and the Depression*, Michigan, 1933.

Tomlinson, B.R., *The Political Economy of the Raj 1914-1947*, Cambridge, 1979.

Umar, Badruddin, *Chirosthayee Bandobaste Bangladesher Krishak* (The Bengal Peasant under the Permanent Settlement), Dacca, 1974.

Van Schendel, William, *Peasant Mobility: The Odds of Life in Rural Bangladesh*, New Delhi, 1982.

INDEX

Printed in the United States
By Bookmasters